The
LOST CONTINENT
of
PAN

"Not since I read Charles Hapgood's *Maps of the Ancient Sea Kings* have I encountered such an exciting, mind-opening narrative about mankind's mysterious lost past. But *The Lost Continent of Pan* goes far beyond Hapgood in its exploration of the meaning of ruins, linguistic entanglements, and genetic markers to make a startlingly convincing case that our species experienced a vast catastrophe in the distant past, which we are just now beginning to recognize—and have not yet recovered from. An explosive, tremendously exciting book!"

WHITLEY STRIEBER, AUTHOR OF *COMMUNION* AND
THE SUPER NATURAL: A NEW VISION OF THE UNEXPLAINED

"*The Lost Continent of Pan* by Susan B. Martinez is an excellent book for anyone interested in archaeology, lost continents, and the true origin of man. The information in this book far surpasses anything taught in schools about the history of our planet Earth. I highly recommend this book."

MERRELL FANKHAUSER, MUSICIAN,
AUTHOR, AND MU AFICIONADO

"A scholarly work of great detail, *The Lost Continent of Pan* sheds light on a multicultural Pacific and Central America and presents compelling evidence for a mass migration across the world. I now have a better understanding of Lemuria (Mu) and the ancient past."

The
LOST CONTINENT
of
PAN

The Oceanic Civilization at the Origin of World Culture

Susan B. Martinez, Ph.D.

Bear & Company
Rochester, Vermont • Toronto, Canada

Bear & Company
One Park Street
Rochester, Vermont 05767
www.BearandCompanyBooks.com

Bear & Company is a division of Inner Traditions International

Library of Congress Cataloging-in-Publication Data

Names: Martinez, Susan B., author.
Title: The lost continent of Pan : the oceanic civilization at the origin of
    world culture / Susan B. Martinez, Ph.D.
Description: Rochester, Vermont : Bear & Company, 2016. |
    Includes bibliographical references and index.
Identifiers: LCCN 2016013274 (print) | LCCN 2016024872 (e-book) |
    ISBN 9781591432678 (paperback) | ISBN 9781591432685 (e-book)
Subjects: LCSH: Lemuria. | Civilization, Ancient. | BISAC: BODY,
    MIND & SPIRIT / Mythical Civilizations. | SOCIAL SCIENCE /
    Archaeology. | HISTORY / Ancient / General.
Classification: LCC GN751 .M338 2016 (print) | LCC GN751 (e-book) |
    DDC 930—dc23
LC record available at https://lccn.loc.gov/2016013274

Printed and bound in the United States by P. A. Hutchison Company

10 9 8 7 6 5 4 3 2 1

Text design by Priscilla Baker and layout by Debbie Glogover
This book was typeset in Garamond Premier Pro with Gill Sans MT Pro, Bernard
Modern Std, Helvetica Neue LT Std, ITC Legacy Sans Std, Kepler Std, and
Papyrus ICG

To send correspondence to the author of this book, mail a first-class letter to the
author c/o Inner Traditions • Bear & Company, One Park Street, Rochester, VT
05767, and we will forward the communication, or contact the author directly at
poosh8@gmail.com.

To Rose, Irv, and Bert

Contents

ACKNOWLEDGMENTS

I want to extend a special thanks to Mindy Branstetter for editorial support of the most welcome kind.

The flesh of the fruit hath perished; the seed still liveth. My seed is in languages, in words, in rocks and ruined walls; in fallen temples and buried cities. These remnants shall speak their parting words. ... Hear ye these, my sons and daughters; O ye that search for the light of ages past, but find not. I am the book of the past, of things that are past.

UNPUBLISHED PASSAGE FROM OAHSPE'S BOOK OF SAPHAH
(BEING AMONG THE PROOF PAGES OF JOHN LANT'S 1881
PRE-PUBLICATION COPY)

PANOLOGY

First Things First

The above quotation is about solving a (murder) mystery. This book is about a murdered continent (justifiable homicide?). The scene of the crime is twenty-four thousand years ago. Definitely a cold case, but still an open one. Open. Unsolved. No, there was no CCTV in those days, when the continent of Pan went down in the Pacific Ocean. Nevertheless, the science of crime detection wisely posits the theory of transference and exchange: the scene of the crime could actually be crawling with snippets of evidence. It is the same for history—if we read it right. Forensics in this case means bits and pieces, anatomical morphology, DNA. But no smoking gun. Or is there? Oral history and tribal legend, race, and language, geography, geology, and artifact— these are our clues, our smoking gun. We will start with the knowns and work our way back to the unknowns.

Pan said: I am beneath the water . . . [yet] in all nations I am found.

OAHSPE, BOOK OF SAPHAH: PAN 1.1, 1.4

The English language still contains words indicating the "all" of Pan—panoply (complete covering, full armor); pandemic (prevailing in all places); panacea (cure all); pantheism (god-in-all); pantheon (all gods); panegyric (speech before all); panorama (view of all). *Pan,* of course, meant "all" in Latin (Pandora = "all gifts"), as well as in Algonquian and Greek; *Pan*athenaea, for example, was the all-Greek festival. Pan, the name of the first great civilization on Earth, the engine of global culture, also clung to the *name* of the Greek god of all Nature: Pan.

And the whole earth was of one language and of one speech.

GENESIS 11: 1

They had a single language.

POPOL VUH

Once the whole world, in one tongue gave voice.

SUMERIAN *EPIC OF ENMERKAR*

The same is said in Oahspe (The Lords' First Book 1.74) that twenty-four thousand years ago "the world was of one language and one speech; in all the places of [the chosen] people, they spoke alike, person to person." Thus even today many different languages share not only common words but also common motifs and similar deluge accounts. "The chosen shall manifest many signs and words common to one another in these different divisions of the earth [and] they shall remember the flood" (The Lords' First Book 1.61–62). "I cannot doubt," said Godfrey Higgins, perhaps the foremost scholar of comparative religion in the nineteenth century, "that there has been . . . one Universal, one Pandaean religion with one language, which has extended over the whole of the world" (Higgins 1991, vol. 1). Thus did this oneness, this all-ness of Mother Pan come to be enshrined in our language in the prefix denoting "all-inclusive;" for example, Pan-American, Pangaea, and so forth.

Pan said: I am the "ah," signifying Earth.

OAHSPE, BOOK OF SAPHAH: PAN 1:3

In Oceania itself, in the Banks Islands, *pan*oi is the word for ancestral home, "land of the dead," or crossroads where the underworld and upper regions meet, perhaps expressive of the Great Submergence itself. In some cases *pan* became a generic word for land, earth, place.

Pan	land, in the Auca Indian language (Chile)
Teotlal-pan	land of the gods (Mexico)
Olel-pan-ti	lost lands (Mexico)
Totonaca-pan	land of the Totonacs (Mexico)
Tzom-pan-co	place of a skull (Mexico)
Pan-anu te tai	sea flows to the land (Polynesia)
Pan-u-pei	land of holy stones, original name of Panape (Micronesia)
Kadalaya-pan	location of the earliest people, according to legend (Philippines)
Pan-tiya	a land swept away by the flood (Tamil Nadu, India)

Pan place-names abound in Oceania and along the Pacific Rim.

- At *Pan*ape, the monarch (Saudeleur dynasty) of *Pan*apeol made his home on *Pan*kadira Islet.
- *Pan*-katara was the name of the king of Metalanim's palace.
- Sai*pan* is the largest island of the North Mariana chain (western Pacific).
- *Pan*gai Motu is a Tongan island.
- *Pan*go *Pan*go is a Samoan island.
- *Pan*akiwuk Island is in the Southwest Pacific.
- Kala-*Pan*a is on Hawaii's southern coast.
- Filipino Negrito places include *Pan*ay, Pam*pan*ga, *Pan*glao, *Pan*gasinan, *Pan*yibutan, and *Pan*tar.
- Malaysia contained a prehistoric kingdom called *Pan Pan,* along

with *Pan*gyans (Malacca), *Pan*yan, and Kota Tam*pan* (earliest known human site in Malaysia).
- Balikpa*pan* is in Indonesia.
- Ja*pan* (originally Zha'*Pan*).

The Exalted Pan

Because the sons of Noah brought the seeds of human culture with them to their several landing places, the highest honor was afforded these men of Pan, as seen especially in Peruvian terms of exaltation.*

- *Pan*aca designates royal lineage, inner circle; landholding kinship groups were called *pan*acas. The actual name of all the Inca kings was Panaca, from the first Panaca Chima to the twelfth Panaca Huaycac.
- Yu*pan*qui, fifth Incan king, considered direct descendant of the ancestor of Emergence, Manco Capac. (Emergence, we will see, is a metaphor for flood survival.)
- *Pan*ache, royal plumes (headwear).
- The largest pyramid at Tiahuanaco is called the Aca*pan*a (temple), set on a 56-foot-high mound, commemorating the beginning of all things.
- Za*pan*a is the legendary ruler of Tititcaca.
- Si*pan* is a major ceremonial center in the Moche culture on the northern Peruvian coast, in the Lambayeque valley.

The exalted Pan is also evident in Central America, as seen in tec-*pan*, meaning "chief's house." Sa*pan*i is a legendary Toltec chief, while Tlacahue*pan* is a Nahua deity and Tlauizcal*pan* tecutli is Lord of Dawn (represented with a white body, which is the standard complexion of the culture-bearing ancestor). Zi*pan*ca is a legendary hero of the Quiché

---

*Rather than rehash material that appears in the literature or even in my own previous books, I have chosen throughout this work to digest such matter by presenting it in charts or listed form.

Maya. Among the Massachusetts Indians the aristocracy of priests was called *Pan*eses.

No less conspicuous on the other side of the ocean are pan names for exalted ones.

- Polish *Pans*, eighteenth-century upper crust, the landed nobility
- *Pan*thus, the Trojan priest of Apollo; *Pan*kus, the Hittite council of nobles
- *Pan*ese, royal family of Sumer
- *P'an*-Fei, semimythical royal maiden of China, loved by Emperor Ho-Ti
- *Pan*du and his five sons, who are India's *Pan*davas in the Mahabharata heroic epic; *Pan*chala, a princess in the Sanskrit epics; also the *Pan*dya kingdom of first millennium BCE, at the southern tip of India (Madurai region)
- *Pan*opolis, sacred city of the god Pan on the Upper Nile
- *Pan*drasus, king of Greece after the Trojan War; *Pan*dion, head of the House of Atreus; and *Pan*tikapaion, capital of the Greek Bosporan kingdom
- Olo-*pan*a, honorary title of Hawaiian chiefs

Zha'Pan

The fleet of two ships carried to the north was named Yista, which in the Whaga [Pan-ic] tongue, was Zha'Pan . . . the same country that to this day is called Japan, signifying, Relic of the continent of Pan. Thus was settled Japan. . . . And of all people ye shall be reckoned the oldest in the world.

OAHSPE, BOOK OF APH 1:55–56

According to the Ama people of Japan the better part of their island kingdom vanished in a great flood. Japan (Ja-Pan), once the northwest corner of that great continent that extended from Japan to the Banks Islands and included the Philippines, betrays its Oceanian heritage in several ways, including the following:

1. More than 40 percent of their vocabulary is Malayo-Polynesian; and where did the Japanese people get their name for Mount *Fiji* San?
2. Yonaguni (Japan) and Nan Madol (in the Caroline Islands) share the same petroglyphs and frieze designs.
3. Stone towers in Japan and Easter Island are almost identical.
4. The Ainu people of Hokkaido, Japan, share cranial features with Polynesians; the Japanese themselves have the same long, smooth hair as their Polynesian cousins.
5. A study of Japanese mythology reveals many Polynesian elements.
6. Japanese bronze artifacts have been found deep in the coral beds of the Mariana Islands.
7. People of Japan and Oceania are world-class pearl divers.
8. The classic topknot in Japan is a variant of the Polynesian pukao.
9. Firewalking is practiced in Japan and Fiji, Raiatea, New Zealand, Tonga, and Hawaii.

Fig. 1.1. Easter Island topknot

10. Japanese and Tahitians practiced the unusual sport of hang-gliding (Childress 1988, 251–52, 264) on their man-lifting kites. Immense kites are still flown in Polynesia's Society Islands, requiring four men to hold them; in New Zealand as well, the Maori hero Tawhaki made a kite from tree bark and floated upward on a favoring wind.

Japanese puppeteering, which relates back to ceremonial traditions, is quite similar to Hawaii's. Wooden marionettes were formerly made on Easter Island and New Zealand as well, though the craft persists today only in Hawaii. The Maoris said they were taught how to make the marionettes, which "are peculiar for their dwarfness," by a blond forest people; the agile movements are in imitation of a sacred dance (Brown 1924, 142–43, 138). We'll hear a lot more about these tiny blonds in chapter 2.

EXAMPLES OF MAORI (NEW ZEALAND)/AINU (JAPAN) WORD CORRESPONDENCES*

Maori word	meaning	Ainu word	meaning
taku taku	recite	itak	speak
toko	spring out	tok	project
po	the underworld	pok	beneath
tohi	to cut	tui	to cut
toma	burial place	toma	burial mat

*"These have been taken at random out of scores of examples I have marked down in my Maori dictionary" (Brown 1920, 26).

Though language and customs can point the way to shared culture, there is nothing like demographics to pinpoint the arrival of Japan's first culture bearers: Archaeologists have discovered that the population of Japan swelled and blossomed at least *twenty-thousand* years ago. Around that time all their arts improved, as seen in their excellent microblade tools and the elaborate and sophisticated wares of the acclaimed Jomon potters. These Jomon people, ancestors of the present-day Ainu, then became the dominant race in the Japanese islands during the "reign of the gods"; in fact, they *were* (or rather, became) the deified ancestors. In sculptures they are seen with European features. Yes, a white race—the "Yista" Noahs. Their fine carvings, done in relief, are considered the *oldest* in all the world, yet not unique, for Jomon ware (with groove patterns, cross-hatching, braid impressions, and incised lines) has been compared to the work of other Pacific Rim people, including the Alaskan Ipiutak (pre-Inuit) and tribes along the Upper Amazon and Ecuadorian coast, the latter judged to be the oldest pottery in South America.

"Words cannot express adequately the degree of similarity between early Valdivia [Ecuadorian] and Jomon pottery," marveled archaeologist Clifford Evans. "Many fragments of both are so similar that they might almost have come from the same vessel" (Stuart 1973, 191).

Yet this early cord-marked Japanese pottery is also found in Melanesia and Micronesia—these Pacific lands standing as a kind of connecting link between the Japanese isles and the Americas. We also notice that the features of an Easter Island stone head with beard and faceted eyes (and similar to figurines found in Mexico) are seen on the Japanese *dogus,* clay statuettes with the look of Caucasian dignitaries.

Indeed, the earliest people, according to the Japanese themselves, were the white-skinned Yamato (which later became the name of a Japanese dynasty; the name also means "dwarf"): "Many thousand years ago, the islands of Japan formed a distant colony of Lemuria. . . . The Yamato enjoyed a sophisticated culture" (Chouinard 2012, 38). In the prehistoric tombs of Japan are found images of these Yamato, called *haniwa;* these curious clay figures of little people have noble Europoid faces. It is said that these people brought with them from the motherland an already developed civilization.

Apparently these Jomon or Yamato folk, whose descendants built megalithic stone circles, were diminutive (*tsuchigumo*): 4½-foot-tall remains have been found in association with their wares. Some of their genes survive today in the short, Caucasoid, Ainu people. Archaeologists know that this "undersized" Ainu stock once occupied much of Asia. Although there have been eons of intermarriage, the Ainu are still different from their Mongoloid neighbors. They have wavy hair and

European faces. Neither were their ancestors, the ancient Jomon, of typical Asian descent; they were proto-Caucasoids, fair skinned with prominent noses and full, light-colored beards.

The ruins at Japan's controversial Yonaguni site (which we will look at in greater detail in chapter 11) feature ancient pillars that Professor Masaaki Kimura noted as "pu-ru" holes, the sockets for pillars. We will witness those great pillars again—in Panama.

Panama

Crossing the pond, the next "Pan" on the Pacific Rim for us to consider is *Pan*ama. Mayan civilization, we realize, is bounded on the north by *Pan*uco, while its southern boundary is *Pan*ama. Linguistic coincidence? Maybe. Maybe not. I think not. There is a marvelous treasure locked up in language; let us find its hidden clues. The Arawaks of this region remember Ca-Mu, their tall, white, bearded progenitor who arrived on the shores of Panama after a cataclysm. Indeed, Panama, particularly Darien, is famous for its un-Indian-looking white tribes, many of the natives possessing authentic flood myths.

The San Blas people along the Caribbean coast of Darien have among them some individuals with almost white hair (a subject to be probed in the next chapter). Explorer Richard O. Marsh, who was the United States charge d'affaires in the early twentieth century, had traveled all over the Andes and Amazon; in Panama he was astounded when he first sighted three maidens of the Chukunaque:* "Their almost bare bodies were as white as any Scandinavian's. Their long hair, falling loosely over their shoulders, was bright gold!" (1934, 26). Also, among Panama's Guaymi agriculturalists are seen many pale and hazel-eyed people.

---

*Introducing *ku* names from Pan, we note the *ku* in Chu-kuna-que, which name actually embeds the name of Panama's Kuna Indians and the Jari-kuna people, Arawaks of the northern Amazon. Ku-bita is a *ku*-named village in Panama, while Chi-kuna is the name of Creator in native Panama. As we go on, we will find that the sign of Creator (wheel cross) in ancient Panama—as well as their script and densely packed houses—score a match with far-flung cousins from Pan in very different parts of the world.

Fig. 1.2. Photo of San Blas Indians taken in the 1920s

These San Blas folk, we learn from anthropologist A. H. Verrill's firsthand observations, are industrious, peaceful, clean; the gentler sex are "the most emancipated of emancipated women" (1927, 406). To Richard Marsh, who also stayed with them in the 1920s, relating his experiences in *White Indians of Darien,* "they were dignified, friendly, hospitable and cheerful . . . intelligent and quick-witted . . . skillful seamen and artistic hand-workers. Their social organization was highly developed and stable . . . [their] culture kept unchanged from time immemorial" (1934).

Other whites inhabit the coastal Panamanian town of Atlan, just as the Pucro River region in Darien has its White Indians—and little people. The tiny A-ku-rias (note the *ku*), unknown to the outer world until visited by Verrill in the 1920s, are described as like little Caucasians, the women about 4 feet tall. Their noses are thin and well bridged, chins well developed, foreheads broad.

At San Blas and the islands east of Panama we find the Tupi-Tawalis, another pint-size folk regarded as "extremely intelligent." Sedate and agricultural, their lifeways echo those of other little people, hinting at some common ancestry. Their namesakes in Brazil, according to Daniel Brinton, the esteemed American folklorist and linguist, "the Tupis . . .

Fig. 1.3. Lovely San Blas girl sitting on the ground

were named after the first man, Tupa, he who alone survived the flood . . . an old man of fair complexion, *un vieillard blanc . . .*" (1976, 200). The Tupi had an alphabetic script associated with similar ones in the Pacific islands.

Some of Panama's Kuna tribe have gray eyes and reddish hair, early writers calling them "albino-like moon children." These people, now concentrated in the San Blas region and along Panama's Atlantic coast, once occupied and dominated central Panama. Metallurgy and fine ceramics have been taken from their ancestors' graves (see Cocle pottery in fig. 1.5, p. 14). And like the mysterious Tupi script, their curious pictographs have a Panic ring, for they are similar to Easter Island's rongorongo* (which also compares with Indus Valley script). Kuna picture writing further resembles rongorongo in that both are boustrophedon (written "as-the-ox-plows," with alternating lines in opposite direction), syllabic, and inscribed on wooden tablets, for which reason author Frank Joseph points to "the Motherland from which both rongorongo and the Panamanian picture writing derived.

---

*The undeciphered rongorongo tablets are made from the *Podocarpus* tree, which does not grow on Easter Island but is found in Panama, suggesting their ancestors "got around."

Cuna place-names and the names of their leading deities abundantly reflect Lemurian origins" (2006, 72–74, 78). At both Easter Island and Panama, their sacred texts were recited at burials, accompanied by the use of "feather-sticks."

Cocle in Panama

Excavated back in 1927 but not often mentioned in the literature are the ruins of Cocle, including a great temple, stone monuments, massive columns, extraordinary colored ceramics, and statues with beards, rather unusual for indigenous America. Although the prehistoric inhabitants of Cocle were agricultural, today the area is unfit for farming. The ruins, as Verrill describes them in *Old Civilizations of the New World,* must be very old, perhaps twelve thousand years, for significant climate change (desertification) is indicated.

> This district once supported a teeming population . . . evident from the extent of village-sites, the size of kitchen middens, and the enormous number of stone columns, idols, and ceremonial objects. . . . Burials are numerous and closely placed. . . . Pottery fragments are so densely packed . . . they have become cemented by induration . . . form[ing] a brick-like mass six to ten feet deep. (Verrill 1943)

The stratification at Cocle in Verrill's view proves the antiquity of the culture. The columns and sculptured figures still standing are buried so deep that their tops are now 7 feet below the surface. "Prehistoric civilizations in America were most ancient in Central America.* The oldest remains . . . of a culture, which may be classed as semi-civilization, have been found within the boundaries of Panama" (Verrill 1943, 60). How old? Cocle ceramics depict a flying lizard rather like the pterodactyl!

Interesting and apt that Verrill uses the term *semi-civilization;* the

---

*This important insight is developed in chapter 5 of Verrill's *Old Civilizations of the New World* (1943, 206).

very thick crania of sixteenth-century Panamanian natives, some of gigantic size, are a sign of the more archaic type. Although advanced in certain ways, these early Panamanians do betray barbaric elements. The situation is not unlike that in Nicaragua, where Spanish chroniclers of the Chorotegans were astounded by their marvelous plantations, mixed in with unusually primitive customs. The Cueva Indians of Panama also have surprising skills; yet a "fierce, cruel, and irate" aspect dominates

Fig. 1.4. Map of Central Panama

Fig. 1.5. Dazzling Cocle pottery

their deities (Lothrop 1937, 41). Time and again, we will witness the ultimate degradation of people who were originally blessed with civilization; time and again has man traded faith in creator for faith in idols.

Idols and Barbarians

Whoever amongst you doeth sacrifice to the Lord are of his dominion; suffer none of my people to marry therewith ([saith] Abraham) . . . Moses being old, said . . . Was it not because the unlearned desired a form or figure to worship that the Lord (Osiris) ruined Egypt, making slaves of the Egyptians, both on earth and in the lower heavens? Pure spirits of the Faithist order . . . are not bound to idols, Gods, nor Saviors, but have faith in Ahura'Mazda, the Creator.

OAHSPE, BOOK OF SAPHAH: TABLET OF BIENE 22

AND BASIS OF VEDE 53

Evidence of sacrificial customs is not wanting in the Middle Kingdom. Flat-topped boulders at the base of the Cocle idols apparently served not only to support the stone monoliths but also as sacrificial altars. Other brutalities persisted up until the sixteenth century, at which time the Spanish found the Panamanians engaged in warfare with neighboring tribes, with captives often enslaved. The Cocle sites, as we will soon see, show a certain continuity with Peru's Nazca/Paracas culture, with its wonderful refined weaving and ceramics—yet figures do show men brandishing war clubs, betraying a culture of vaunted militarism among the regional Nazca, Mochica, and Chavin. The Nazca, like the Cocle people, were masters of polychrome pottery, many pieces showing bird figures (like Easter Island) and men carrying trophy heads! Gigantic intaglios at Nazca show people with missing fingers, as seen also at Tiahuanaco, which in turn has its own version of birdmen; its sun god wears a belt of severed heads at his waist. Civilized? Not very.

Easter Island brutalities centered around moai construction, which, as some observers have frankly inferred, "became a kind of social insanity" (Williams 2001, 167). At one time Easter Islanders also engaged in ceremonies involving human sacrifices to the god Makemake.

Fig. 1.6. Human sacrifice at a Tahitian marae. Numerous occasions demanded such a sacrifice, mostly in connection with auspicious royal events but also as part of war preparations.

Fig. 1.7. Sacrifices to their sanguinary deities were offered in seasons of war, at national festivals, during illness of rulers, and for the building of temples.

Neither was slavery unknown—the Long Ear aristocrats held in bondage the Short Ear commoners; other Polynesians regularly enslaved Melanesians to man their canoes. Tongans remember a time of eruption and assassination, people rebelling against the slavery imposed on them to build *marae* for the chiefs, one chief in the sixteenth century assassinated because he "compelled the people to drag great stones from the back of the island to the burial place Mooa" (Anderson 1928, 458–61).

Gory Glory

*During the early Neolithic age, beauty, sophistication,
and advances in technology and architectural design went
hand in hand with dark, sanguine activities.*

ANDREW COLLINS,
GÖBEKLI TEPE: GENESIS OF THE GODS

In ancient Panama burials, captives were sacrificed, while wives and retainers were made to accompany the chiefs to the next world; dead slaves, as a rule, were just dumped in the wilderness. In fact, the fiendish custom of sacrificing is actually thought to have caused the Flood, at least according to Arcadian legend, which emphasizes divine disapproval of that savage practice. In Mexico too deluge myths recount how the Toltecs grew licentious and corrupt. "Teotihuacan was apparently a despotic and extraordinarily well-organized city and capital of an empire. . . . Their warriors carry elaborate curved knives on the ends of which are stuck bleeding human hearts" (Adams 1991, 195, 211). And their armies were formidable—war captives were often fed to the gods. And the light of this people went out . . .

People have covered the earth over with cities; but where are they? [They] have been learned . . . but their knowledge is dissipated by the dread hand of war. Her people become wise in a day, but on the next, they are fools. One generation becomes skilled in knowledge of the sun, moon, and stars, and in mathematics . . . but a generation follows, and lo, her people are cannibals* again. And as often as they are raised up in light, so are they again cast down in darkness.

OAHSPE, SYNOPSIS OF SIXTEEN CYCLES 3:9–10, 15

---

*Cannibals were known in the Amazon Basin (Carib tribes), Peru, and Mexico and among the New Zealand Maoris. There were cannibal wars in Tonga and the Marquesas; cannibalism has also been noted in the Hervey and Pearl Islands, New Guinea, New Hebrides, Leper Island, New Caledonia, Fiji, Samoa, Australia, and Easter Island, where victors in warfare feasted on the corpses of the defeated. Cannibalism was also practiced along the Pacific Rim, at Sumatra, Vietnam, and Borneo.

Fig. 1.8. Painting by Albert Eckhout (1641) showing a Tarairiu cannibal woman from Brazil. Note the hand she holds and the foot in her basket.

Much of what comes to light through the efforts of archaeology, folklore, and protohistory represents, really, hybrid peoples; often enough this signals back-bred races and degeneration from a higher state. This regressive pattern probably explains why the *earliest* horizon at many, many sites shows the *finest* productions. At Teotihuacan—noted above for its elaborate but brutal customs—the *most archaic* sculptures entail a realism never again achieved in Mexico. Another classic example of cultural decline comes from the six-thousand-year-old Indus civilization whose efficient sewage works were superior to those of today's Pakistan! An Oceanic example: pottery shards are found by archaeologists at Nan Madol even though pottery is not made by the present inhabitants of the island; evidently some sort of regression has taken place. Indeed, a barbaric cruelty developed in the ruling class, and workers were virtually enslaved to build the (artificial) islets, the Saudeleur dynasty wielding absolute power. "Present-day Polynesians have lost much of their former culture. . . . Who shall say that, being barbarians, they have always been barbarians? They probably are the degenerate descendants of mighty peoples" (Perry 1968, 108).

But there is a method to this madness, and the cycles tend to follow a three-thousand-year rhythm: In Oahspe, we hear of the end of the Thor cycle (ca. 12,000 years ago), at which time men returned to a state of savagery. The Osiris cycle (ca. 9,000 years ago) also ended in barbarism.

> The kings took to war against one another. Anarchy ensued and men fell to destroying all the glories he had made. Thus again, after three thousand years, man went down in darkness . . . and became a barbarian.
>
> OAHSPE, THE LORDS' FIFTH BOOK 7:13–14

Thus did Tollan (as discussed shortly under "Toltec," p. 26), according to pre-Aztec history, fall because of its wickedness and degeneration. They glorified war.

> The Teotihuacanos . . . shifted [in]to glorification of warriors and rulers. . . . Later murals show armed figures with spear throwers, darts, and shields and even depict symbols of human sacrifice. . . . Warfare and ritual cannibalism were present in the final stages of Teotihuacan. . . . Murals show human hearts brandished by Teotihuacan warriors. (Adams 1991, 218–19, 224)

Chichén Itzá's Temple of the Warriors (with its "forest of columns") has the feathered serpent pictured on the royal banner that is held up in battle. The so-called sacred well at Chichén Itzá yielded dredged-up skeletons of youths brazenly sacrificed in times of drought.

> *Mayan rulers were . . . bloodthirsty lords.*
> BRIAN FAGAN, *WORLD PREHISTORY*

Avenues of the Ancients

Covering an area of almost a hundred acres, the central portion of Coclé consists of a number of *rows* of huge stone columns. Despite

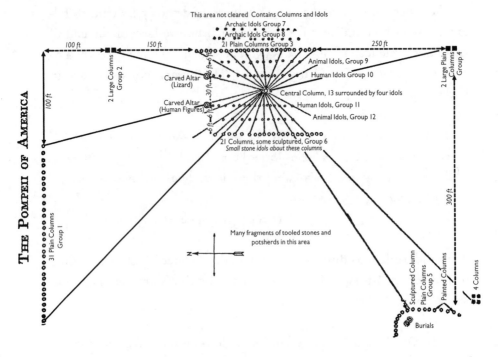

Fig. 1.9. Cocle, rayed out avenues, after Verrill

Fig. 1.10. The Nazca-line centers may have been places of sacrifice. On the jar is seen a Nazca priest clutching a trophy head, probably a sacrificial victim.

the state of ruin, the general arrangement is readily seen—lines radiating from the center like rays of the sun. Geoglyphs at Peru's Nazca share this configuration, some of the lines radiating from a central point. The Cipaya of highland Bolivia also used a system of radial pathways leading to far-flung points from a central place of offerings to their gods. The pathways can still be seen in aerial photos.

There are long rows of tall columns in Costa Rica as well. Such arrangements remind us of the avenues of stone pillars at Carnac, France, or Avebury's stones arranged in rows, or even pillars in the Australian desert, which run in a perfectly straight line. At Tinian, Micronesia, we again find avenues of stone pillars, some very tall. These *latte* litter the island, lined up in double rows facing each other; megalithic, they are up to 6 feet in diameter and up to 65 feet high, some weighing in at 30 tons. At Thailand's Anghor Wat there are again huge stone figures—in rows.

All of the above examples compare to Easter Island's statued avenues: one certainly gets the feeling of a common plan. On Rano Raraku, "the fallen images group themselves on either side of the ancient way . . . [along] which the funeral train of some great chief was to pass from the landing-place to his final rest" (Brown 1924, 5). These roadways remind some observers of the colonnades of sphinxes.

Temple ruins lying under Cocle's volcanic ash sport stone images oddly similar to those seen at Turkey's Göbekli Tepe, where massive engraved pillars also happen to be arranged in rows. Both sites were ritual centers. According to Oahspe's First Book of God (25.5) many cities once occupied the region that "extended from sea to sea in the Middle Kingdom (Panama). Here stood the temple of Giloff, with *a thousand columns of polished mahogany,* and with a dome of copper and silver. And within Giloff dwelt the Osheowena, the oracle of the Creator, for two thousand years" (author's italics).

As we will see in chapter 6 (regarding "Iram of the Columns," p. 225), self-gods enslaved hundreds in al-Yaman, Arabia, to build *a thousand columns of finest polished woods,* perhaps similar to the ruins of Waw al Adani in the Libyan desert, with its pillars and temple of the Sun. Both may be reminiscent of the Hall of Columns at Mitla (in Mexico's Zapotec region), the palace roof supported by huge monolithic pillars; here too a trained priesthood practiced human sacrifice and ritual cannibalism.

But pillars were originally built simply as a place to record great teachings and histories.* The strong pillar, in the first place, had only to do with endurance per se, insuring a legacy of wisdom to posterity. But later the establishment—that is, the sun kings—took to megalithic building and gigantic columns as a sign of their own power and glory. In the Society Islands, for example, at Opoa,

> the famous white stone pillar, nine feet high, five feet broad . . . is called Te-papa-tea-la-ru'ea (the white-rock-of-investment). . . . On to this pillar a prince or princess . . . was raised when proclaimed sovereign in the presence of a multitude, on the day of the regal inauguration ceremony. . . . Beneath each corner of the marae was placed a live man, whose spirit was supposed ever to stand firmly to his post as guardsman. The coral slabs that covered him were called taura'a-a-tapu, landing-place-for-sacrifice. (Henry 1928, 120)

One site of particular interest, off the coast of Callao, Peru, may prove to be a link to Polynesia: underwater expeditions have discovered the ruins of buildings and sculptured stone columns, some still upright. Lying about 50 miles off the mainland, at a depth of 1.2 miles, columnar structures were photographed in 1965 protruding out of the mud below. Inscriptions thereon were written in unfamiliar glyphs. More than a century ago opinion favored "the former existence of a connection between the coast of Chile and Polynesia," and, as Lewis Spence saw it, "between Peru and Easter Island there flourished at one period a great continental land" (1933, 144, 217).

As late as the nineteenth century travelers to Tiahuanaco (Bolivia) could admire and sketch imposing colonnades of which there is now no trace. When the Tiahuanacans erected the colossal Kalat-Sassaya "they first set up high columns, pillar supports which look exactly like

---

*See chapter 7, p. 306, discussing "Carved Histories" inscribed on pillars/tablets before the Flood to preserve knowledge.

menhirs . . . which Stonehenge made world famous" (Homet 1963, 159)—and not unlike the avenues of standing stones at Carnac in France.

> Connected in their history with other Celtic remains [are Peru's] Succanga [where] twelve pillars are set in order, at such distance the one from the other, that every month one of these pillars did note the rising and setting of the sun. . . . By means of these stones, they taught the seasons . . . and other things; they did certain sacrifices to these pillars of the sun. (Finch 1824, 83)

Pillars hide in the jungles of Hawaii as well: musician Merrell Fankauser, a great Mu aficionado, wrote me:

> *In 1973 I moved to the island of Maui with my band called MU. I learned from an old Hawaiian about some odd pillars deep in the jungle that were said to have been remnants of the people of Mu who lived there before the Hawaiians. . . . I found them and photographed them. . . . Here is a side view of one of the pillars . . . over 35 feet tall. There were four pillars in a semi-circle; one had fallen and was broken in pieces laying on a* Mayan-like platform. . . . *Everyone said the little Menehune Mu people built them.*

There are also pillars sunken in the deep at the other end of Oceania, off the coast of Panape* in Micronesia. Lying off Nan Madol's Madolanym Harbor are twelve stone pillars up to 25 feet high in *double rows*. Some weigh 10 tons and are up to 4 feet in diameter.

Due west of Panape on the island of Yap are lofty carved pillars, and just west of Yap, the island of Babeldaob again has several sets of stone pillars arranged in rows, fifty-two of them lining a hilltop in the north. Offshore, similar carved stonework was recovered by divers. And again,

---

*Although otherwise spelled Ponape (and officially Pohnpei), I'll stick with the earlier spelling of Panape, which 1) is probably phonetically more accurate and 2) better shows the connection to Pan.

Fig. 1.11. Broken pillar in the jungle of Maui (Photo courtesy of Merrell Fankhauser)

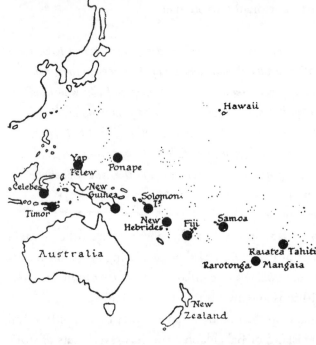

Fig. 1.12. Map showing Hawaii, Panape, Yap

several hundred miles southeast of Babeldaob, lies New Caledonia's Isle of Pines, with cement (lime-mortar) columns found inside tumuli of sand and gravel.

And let us not forget Australia's huge limestone pillars near Roper River, attributed to members of a white race—the site boasting streets and polished walls. Are the builders the same people depicted as bearded Caucasians in the rock art of central Australia near Alice Springs? Might they be the ancestors of the *Mu*rrian people of south and southeast Australia, possessed of a Caucasoid skull form, light skin, beards, and narrow noses?

And what about the Lak *Mu*ang column in Bangkok, Thailand? Frank Joseph, speaking of refugees from Mu, reports that their "ancient immigration is still commemorated in Thailand with a unique relic from their vanished homeland." As the Thai themselves recount, a "semi-divine people long ago dwelled on a distant island . . . until threatened with a global deluge. Three wise men were able to remove a central pillar from the chief temple and carry it away." Reaching their new home, "they erected the pillar and named it after the sunken realm: Lak Mu-ang, or holy stone of Mu" (all quotes in this paragraph, Joseph 2006, 225).

Ancient columns still stand at Tula, Mexico, while underwater cylinders/pillars in the Bahamas in limestone grooves run perpendicular to the shoreline. Criss-crossing in every direction, the similarities are striking. When that area of ruins off Callao, Peru, was again explored, rectangular buildings were seen fronted by columns that were similar to ruins at Chichén Itzá, where the Temple of Kukulcan, known as the Temple of a Thousand Columns, was founded by white strangers called Chanes who had landed at Vera Cruz and taught the people the civilized arts. Also in Mexico, Mitla's impressive colonnade is similar not only to Chichén Itzá's but also to those at Knossos and Tiryns.

Toltec

A Toltec site, Tula has many *cylindrical* columns dedicated to the god of the morning star (Venus). Tula, scholars say, is very old; the carvings include lion and elephant—long since extinct in America. The site of their ancestors' arrival in Hue Hue is very, very old. But confusion easily arises when we consider the "Cakehiquel Manuscript," which delineates four different Tulas, including one in the east and one in the west. Nevertheless, where the sun sets, "it is there that we came . . . from the other side of the sea . . . where we were begotten by our mothers and fathers" ("Cakehiquel Manuscript"). This of course points to a homeland somewhere in the Pacific Ocean.

From Mexico to Brazil there are signs of a people called Toltec (and their "Quiché colonies"), a race light in color, delicate of feature, imposing of stature. Cholula and Teotihuacan near Mexico City are considered Toltec sites, with remarkably engineered pyramids and

Fig. 1.13. Map of Mexico showing Tula; Toltecs are said to have landed at Panuco on the Gulf, proceeding inland.

Fig. 1.14. Tula anthropomorphic columns, not unlike Pan's moai. These human-figure columns (called "atlantes" after Atlas) of Tula, a.k.a. Tullan, still stand. Even though Toltec traditions and history are "a mass of contradictions" (Adams 1991, 271), it appears that the original Toltecs at Teotihuacan were unsullied, which is to say, not associated with the pomp of the sun kings; no statues of themselves or grandiose inscriptions on monuments bragging of their reign; and no palaces.

Fig. 1.15. Sculpture of bearded man from Teotihuacan

temples. Their work seems to extend to Cocle, Panama, with its huge *cylindrical* columns, excellent stone carving, ceramic art in a high state of perfection—and with its white founders. The San Blas of Panama excelled in woodcarving, just as the Toltecs, of whom the Aztecs spoke glowingly, were fine carvers, painters, sculptors, and potters. In fact, the word *Toltecatl* in the Aztec language means "artist." If anyone was the savage, it was the Aztecs, while all that was gentle and humanizing was Toltec. Say the Aztecs: "The Toltecs were a skillful people; all of their works were good, all were exact, all well made and admirable. Their houses were beautiful . . . clean and marvelous." Their architecture was cyclopean, their temples and palaces magnificent, their roads paved; these were a people with cities, hieroglyphic writing, papyrus, metals, and excellent goldsmiths. They knew the mines, they found the mountains hiding silver and gold, copper and tin.

Yet the *teachers,* the forebears, of the tall Toltecs had been the little people, the Ihins.

> The people of learning . . . survey the way for the canals; they find the square and the arch; they lead the Ihuan [first Toltecs] to the mines, where lead, copper and silver are buried. These are a great people. Without them the Ihuan* could not build his own house; he could not find the level for a canal; nor provide the square of his temple. The Ihins are the greatest people.
>
> OAHSPE, THE LORDS' THIRD BOOK 1:15–16

The Toltecs, under tutelage of the sacred people, were great singers, composing songs and singing among the people; for the Ihins had taught them hymns and rites and how to sit in circle to commune with Those Above.

> The Ihins . . . gave them rites and ceremonies, and taught them how to pray and dance before Jehovih.
>
> OAHSPE, THE LORDS' THIRD BOOK 3:23

More than twenty thousand years ago, the Ihuans became a very prolific people, and they spread rapidly over the Earth, mostly in the warm regions. And they prospered, becoming mighty in many countries (see "Sun Worshippers," chapter 6, p. 234).

---

*The name of the I-huan builders is evident in their works: Ta-huan-tisuyu, name of the Inca empire; *Huan*cane, pre-Inca site; Tia-huan-aco, Chavin de Huan-tar, Te-huan-tepec; not to mention Ik-huan, or brother(hood) in Arabic; and Tun-huang in the Tarim Basin, famous for its temples (*huang* means "chief" in Chinese).

But in course of time they began to war upon one another. And for hundreds of years they descended lower and lower in darkness. . . . Now the I-huans partly obeyed the Lord and partly obeyed the way of the flesh, and . . . they disobeyed God by inflicting the neutral gender on their enemies whom they captured in war.

OAHSPE, FIRST BOOK OF THE FIRST LORDS 4:5, 7

And they no longer obeyed the commandments of God, but mingled with the ground people [lower races], bringing forth heirs of darkness.

OAHSPE, THE LORDS' SECOND BOOK 3:10

Yes, the downturns are as critical to understanding protohistory as are the advances. We have been so busy looking for "evolutionary" progress that we have missed major cycles of regression entailing the dissolution of all gains.

Yet in the time of Apollo (ca. 18,000 years ago) the Ihuans "married up," this time crossing with the Ihins, thus producing a mighty race—called the Ghans.

God said: Your Lord provided for the light and knowledge that had been with the Ihins, to be merged into the new races, the Ghans and Ihuans.

OAHSPE, THE LORDS' FIFTH BOOK 6:1

Nevertheless, this race (Ghan) was only a fraction compared to the hundreds of millions of Ihuans and ground people [Neanderthal types]. . . . And the Ihuans were at war for more than a thousand years. They built great cities and established mighty kingdoms; but as soon as they were built, lo, the wars laid them low or dissipated them.

OAHSPE, THE LORDS' THIRD BOOK 3:16–17

These builders of great cities are, as legend remembers them, the giants of old, many described as blond or white, the race that was so fond of megalithic monuments in the Stonehenge era and earlier. They were none other than the Ghans and Ihuans, their large bones found throughout the Americas, as attested by excavations in Patagonia, Peru, Ecuador, Mexico, Alabama, Mississippi, Pennsylvania, and so forth. The name of the proud and stately Ghans became permanently fixed in such places as Af*ghan*istan, Fer*ghan*a (Uzbekistan), *Ghan*a (Africa) and in Europe as well, where the original clan name of the Celts was Eo*ghan*.

But exactly where the tall, white Toltecs came from no one seems to know. They were scattered far and wide, even into Canada. Tiahuanaco was their center in South America, Uxmal and Cholula in the Middle Kingdom,* with outlying settlements in Arizona, Texas, Florida, and California (*Tul*are). *Tul*a, according to Ignatius Donnelly, was the location of the North American flood hero Nanabozho (as seen in fig. 4.1, p. 140). Panama, as Verrill saw it, had far-flung congeners all over the Americas: "Even a cursory examination of the hundreds of specimens obtained [at Cocle] reveals . . . remarkable resemblances to . . . the cultures north and south of the Isthmus" (1943). All these resemblances speak of our far-flung Toltecans—whose magnificence was ultimately dissipated in war and profligacy, concerning which, it has been noted that the subject matter of *later* Toltecan art "is definitely weighted toward the martial and toward ritual violence . . . [also] showing the Toltecs as conquerors . . . sacrificing humans" (Adams 1991, 294–95).

A southerly migration of the Toltecs seems to have brought them to Brazil, where the Colloas and the Tapuyos people are distinctly pale and bearded—the latter culture boasting temples, textiles, sculpture, stone carving, gems, large towns, and stone palaces. But a clue to where they originally came from is found in the Mayan Popol Vuh, which records that the people had spoken but one language before their migrations

---

*The stone pyramids of Yucatán are comparable to the earthen pyramids of North America—the high mounds in the two regions are also alike as to their level summits, their shape, and their staircases. Indeed, some have thought the Toltecan lost land of Tlapalan was actually Ohio (Corliss 1976, 21). Related too are the cremation practices at Teotihuacan, Cocle, the Ohio mounds, Wisconsin, Iowa, and Tennessee.

began. "All that they had heard and understood when departing from Tulan [var. Tlapalan, Tollan] became incomprehensible to them. . . . Our language was one when we departed from Tula," which is to say, the language of Pan—called Panic.

Does this tie in with the Tower of Babel legend? Well, yes, to the extent that these Sons of the Sun were the great builders of the Mesolithic who erected high pillars and *towering temples* dedicated to the Sun. In fact, Toltec tradition revolves around the *zacuali,* a very, very high tower: Cholula?—which is more than 200 feet high. The legend of Cholula is similar to the biblical account of the Tower of Babel (and the ziggurats—or zacuali—at Tikal, Guatemala, are 212 feet high—more like towers, because so very steep).

In Sumerian belief there was a time when all mankind spoke one and the same language; interesting that among the Karens of Burma, *Pan*danman was the time before the confounding of languages. As Aztec legend recalls, giant brothers built a huge tower (zacuali), designed to reach the sky, after a cataclysm. But this offended the gods for some reason so they destroyed it; consequently people dispersed and they no longer spoke a common language. This of course is similar to the account in Genesis, wherein the Lord created a confusion of tongues by scattering the tribes of men. Nevertheless, Oahspe gives a different version of the "tower of words"—and the gods had nothing to do with it.

In the early days . . . one tribe said, ut (wheat); another tribe for the same thing, said, yat; and another tribe said, wat; and another, hoot; and so on. So, the later generations said, utyatwathoot (wheat), and this was called the Yi-ha language; and so great were the number and the size of words used, that the writings of the ancient prophets were lost, because none could understand them. The Lord spoke, saying: I desired to preserve the genealogy of my chosen, [but] . . . you have built a babble [babel; i.e., bah'bah'i —Ed.], a tower of words, so that your tongues are confounded one with another.

OAHSPE, THE LORDS' FIFTH BOOK 2:4–6

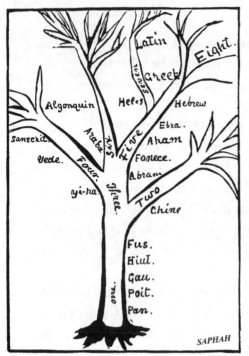

JEHOVIH said: As I cause man to grow, so I caused man's language to grow. Yea, even as the earth matur= in its place, so shall man look backward and judge what has been.

According to the time and place of the earth, so spoke man. And it was so. And the deviation in the progress of speech was even as the deviation of the vortex of the earth.

Even the words of man in ages past shall be revealed by My seers in the time of *KOSMON*.

And it was so.

Fig. 1.16. Yi'ha language as seen on the language tree (left), illustrated in Oahspe, Book of Saphah, Plate 63 (right)

The Weavers

The Hopi in Arizona, like the Panama people and the Toltecs, are great weavers and expert potters. In their heyday the Toltecs wove robes of fine texture; today we marvel at the splendid weaving of Panama's Kuna group. Their ancestors, the Cocle people, were very industrious, with unexcelled weaving and pottery skills, just as their descendants in the San Blas region are adept woodcarvers. All along the western coast of South America, in fact, weaving has proved to be a very old art: as old as Pan? Word lists in the Book of Saphah (Osiris 93) include the Panic word for cloth, or woven fabric: *shi*. Looms were used in Melanesia and Micronesia; in New Zealand, the fair-complected, golden-haired goddess Niwareka ruled over a people, all with fair skin, flaxen hair, and straight noses, and it was these people who introduced weaving* and

---

*We also find the lost art of weaving along the Pacific Rim; within a series of cathedral-like caves in the Subis Mountains of Borneo, explorers came upon prehistorical "fabrics of such fineness and delicacy that . . . one cannot imagine savages making them" (Von Daniken 1970, 88).

woodworking to the Polynesians, according to the myth relating to a lost race that once dwelled on a submerged island. Polynesian oral history says a fair-haired, weaving-and-carving folk lived there before the Submergence.

But *after* the Submergence weaving became a lost art, known only among the Ihins *until* 12,000 BP, at which time (Age of Osiris)

> great became the wisdom of man . . . greater than had ever been since the world began. . . . He excelled in building temples and palaces; and in all manner of inventions; in fabrics of linen and silk, and wool and fine leather . . . and in chemistry and botany.
>
> OAHSPE, THE LORDS' FIFTH BOOK 6:2, 7:1–2

As for the prehistorical weavers in South America, on Peru's Paracas Peninsula, these ancient textiles—having appeared on the illegal market in the 1920s—alerted archaeologists, who then made their move to explore the Paracas necropolis. Here they found mummies wrapped in rich garments, including some of "the finest examples of the embroiderer's art that any age of man has produced" (Stuart 1973, 164–65). These weavers used vivid colors and the rare "needle-knit" technique. The Nazca, Chimu, and Mochica peoples all lived in the same general vicinity. Before the region dried out, their civilizations produced the world's finest weaving and ceramics; the Nazca area was famous for the world's most beautiful fabrics, unsurpassed in technique and beauty. These brilliant-colored shrouds and tapestries are minutely stitched (500 threads per inch), obviously made by virtuoso weavers, spinners, and dyers. Legend says Mama Oullo, wife of Manco Capac, taught the women weaving; Mama and Manco were the heavenly founders who arrived in Peru after a great flood.

But these skills are not confined to South America. Near Fallon, Nevada, red-haired mummies at Spirit Cave dated to at least 10,000 years ago are carefully wrapped in fine woven goods. Similar were the Florida bog mummies, also with red hair and at least 8,300 years old. "The textiles found at this site exhibit a high degree of weaving sophistication, and like the textiles found at Spirit Cave, they fly in the face of the general understanding of weaving techniques at [such a] distant date" (Dewhurst 2014, 276, 295). At a kind of midpoint between Nevada and Florida, an advanced mining culture in Wisconsin 11,000 years ago boasted copper artifacts found in association with textiles and drilled beads (of which we learn more below). Farther east, the Ohio mound people also left exquisitely woven fabrics, one piece "in texture almost identical with cloth found among the ruins of ancient Babylon and Assyria" (Dewhurst 2014, 98, 243). Those Iraqi textiles were seemingly "embroidered with fairy hands" (Roux 1992, 353). Hmm. The Ihin little people were the race behind all the fairy legends of the ancient world.

> *Old and New World looms are remarkably similar in*
> *design, and the methods of weaving were strikingly alike.*
> *. . . Anyone seeing ancient fabrics from Egypt and Peru*
> *will immediately sense a relationship . . . [particularly in]*
> *highly specialized applications such as mummy shrouds.*
> CYRUS GORDON, *BEFORE COLUMBUS*

Peru's looms were almost identical to Egypt's—both had eleven working parts—a fact that has caused researchers to ask if "both areas benefitted from a common . . . central source" (Berlitz 1972, 177). In Egypt incredibly fine textiles are found, not coincidentally, in little people enclaves: at Helwan, Egypt, for example (where ground lenses of ancient manufacture were also found), archaeologists dug up a piece of cloth, the fabric so fine that today it could be woven only in a special factory (a single thread of their linen was composed of 365 minor threads!). "Dwarfs" seem to have been the producers, for they were traditionally the official overseers of linen and chiefs of the royal textile works. These dwarfs (little people, really) may have descended from the ancient Ihins who, tens of thousands of years ago, according to The First Book of the First Lords, made cloth of flax and hemp for covering the body.

The thirteen-thousand-year-old linen garments (Natufian) found at Beidha, Jordan (the region of western Asia's first towns), are also striking; these people dressed elegantly in tunics and skirts made from spun flax. The Natufians were agricultural, peaceful—and rather short of stature. Here in the eastern Mediterranean world Sumerian myth says agriculture and weaving were brought to them from the sacred mountain of Du-*Ku*—near the Taurus Mountains of Turkey.

Indeed, the Turkic-speaking people in the Uighur region (with its Caucasian mummies—of which we will hear more) were superb weavers, their textiles, according to James Churchward, seventeen thousand years old. One might surmise that this industry was continuous with that discovered in Russia, northeast of Moscow at the Sungir site: here fabrics more than twenty thousand years old were found in frozen burials.

It occurs to me that weaving alone would help scholars connect the dots that link Panama/Peru to Turkey and the Near East, a link that, as we will soon see, is further vouched by the megalithic ruins of Cocle, Panama. As for related ruins at Turkey's Çatalhüyük, here too one finds very finely woven cloth and pieces of carpet of supreme workmanship. The famous site boasts some of the world's oldest woven cloth and delicate fabrics dating to no less than nine thousand years ago.*

Tur, Tol, and Other Variations on the Theme

Is there a genuine historical link between *Tur*key (Ana*to*lia) and *Tol*tec? Let's not be surprised if there is; early postdiluvial peoples have shown similarities on every hand, and "Asia Minor was inhabited at a very early date by highly civilized peoples, tens of thousands of years before history began to be recorded" (Churchward 1931a, 141). There is a reason they say Noah's Ark landed near Çatalhüyük in Asia Minor. The oldest finely woven cloth (using biconical spindles) comes from Anatolia's Çatalhüyük. Judging from their wheel cross (see fig. 5.10, p. 198, and fig. 7.4, p. 279) and clustered housing (also seen at Troy), they shared an ancient heritage with the San Blas of Panama and the Pueblos of North America.

---

*Although 10,000-year-old linen in Turkey has been called the earliest known, others say fine cotton fabrics, "the oldest so far discovered," are to be found at the Indus site of Mohenjo Daro in today's Pakistan.

A terraced town of wheat farmers, Çatalhüyük had comfortable brick-and-timber houses and canal and irrigation works. This Hittite settlement is one of the oldest known cities in the world, boasting the earliest mural and landscape paintings, superb fired pottery, and cuneiform writing. Here animal sacrifice was substituted for human, which signals the suasion of a humane people, at one time a distinctly separate people. Indeed, the earliest Hittites practiced the levirate "to preserve the seed" of their own holy race. And the longer they preserved the seed, the more they continued to resemble their equally conscientious cousins, even in far-distant America.* As long as fifteen thousand years after the Flood the Faithists in widely separated parts of the world still shared some of their olden heritage acquired by their ancestors on Pan.

In time though, Çatalhüyük did lose the gentleness of the egalitarian sacred tribes, for they became socially stratified; they also left ornate weaponry (indicating a cherished warrior class), and they deployed bull effigies (symbolizing brute force, not "male fertility"). Too, they were somehow obsessed with birds of prey and also kept human skulls on display—all of which speak of a retrograde trend and not-so-delightful rule of law.

Speaking of weapons, the famous site contains some of the oldest known examples of metallurgy and smelting in the Near East. Old Turkey, all told, had the first wheel, first coins, good jewelry, and polygonal masonry. Among their ruins were examples of superb craftsmanship in wood (articles produced with lathelike perfection) and in obsidian (Turkey was a busy exporter of obsidian 14,000 years ago). Their colleges taught minerology, math, chemistry and assaying, and the rules for inventing chemical combinations (Oahspe, Book of Wars 21.20).

The *Tur* in *Tur*key is of special interest, for it may help us trace some of their long-lost cousins: peoples possessing the same advanced culture in the so-called Stone Age. *Tul* (which meant "eminent" in Old Hebrew) easily varies with *Tur*, depending on the dialect. In New Zealand, *Tur* again appears in Tur-oa, meaning "staff of authority" and conveying the

---

*Constance Irwin (147–8), for instance, spotted an "uncanny resemblance" in Hittite and Mesoamerican sculpture and dress styles.

Fig. 1.17. Temple porch with two pillars as seen in William Niven's Mexican Stone Tablet No. 50, more than 12,000 years old; it reminds us of the pillars that brace the entrance to Japanese shrines.

same sense of eminence as the Hebrew. Even *Tor* and *Tol* (as in Ana*tol*ia) arise as variants of the same stem: for example, in Spanish, which is the oldest European language next to Basque, tor-re = tower (it is *torri* in Corsican), which of course shares the meaning of "eminence" with the Hebrew *tul* and the Maori Turoa. In fact, dul = mound (i.e., another kind of eminence) in Sumerian (rendered today as *tel*), and this in turn resonates with *tur*ret in English. Tor, as in England's Glastonbury Tor, means "hill"; tor-ii, in Japan, indicates the gates where twin *pillars* stand at the entry to Shinto shrines. *Tur* is also evident in the city name Tyre, with its "impregnable fortress," the walls 160 feet high. *Tol*min (var. dolmen) implies "tall"; the tall *Tol*tec race seems to share the same stem, as does the very word "tall."

Mexico's Popol Vuh, as noted previously, says that after departing *Tul*an the people's speech diverged into many different languages. "Our language was one when we departed from Tulan . . . the country where we were born." Isn't that country Pan? In New Zealand the Haku-*Tur*i (the equivalent of Hawaii's Menehune people) are remembered as a white, fairylike people, probably related to the fair-haired *Tur*ehu of Maori memory, the people who lived way up in the mountains of Urewera. Note that the *wera* in Urewera resembles the Spanish word for blond: *huera*, pronounced wera. Also in New Zealand, *Tur*angi is the name of their fishing center and probably reminiscent of the Polynesian demigod/voyager *Tur*i (son of Tangaroa, the oldest god). Turi (whose

Fig. 1.18. Maori girl

Fig. 1.19. Frieze found deep in the jungles of Yucatán, the relief showing a temple destroyed, a drowning man, a tidal wave, and someone escaping in a boat. It is thought that the frieze illustrates the reason why the Maya left their homeland of Tulan. According to The Annals of the Cakchiquels *their ancestors arrived from "across the sea . . . where the sun descends, the west."*

name may also be associated with Turi-whaia, a heavenly power) was a great chief of Tahiti whose son was named *Tur*anga, his descendants living on the sacred island of Ra'iatea. Were they related to the *Tur*uwal people of Australia (New South Wales)?

> *Ua pau a'enei teie fenua i te miti (This land was deluged by the sea).*
>
> RAIATEA LEGEND

The name *Tur* is equally notable in the Orient, for it seems to follow the Jaffites (Noah's Far Eastern sons) in their westward trek out of Asia, establishing the *Tur*anians in the north; the *Tar*tar tribes in Siberia; the *Tuk*haras, a.k.a. Tocharians, in western China; and the Oasis of *Tur*fan in east *Tur*kestan. The movement continued on to Asia Minor: Troy itself, I suspect, may derive from Tur-oy. Next, into northern Iran we have *Tur*eng Tepe (much more on the sacred "Tepes" in chapter 8, p. 344). As they moved westward these light-complected Jaffetic people tarried in the North Caucasus, where legends of little people are still told around Nemrut Dag, an old burial mound. Long ago, they say, here in the Taurus (*Tor*us) Mountain* range, lived tiny people with white hair in whose memory some of the holy places were built. They were much "smaller than normal people."

Finally penetrating Europe itself, the sons of Jaffeth left their mark in Scandinavia at *Tur*ku, Finland, and in southern Europe at *Tar*tessos, the leading, most civilized city of Spain, founded by the *Tur*duli people. In Italy they became the mysterious Etruscans, a.k.a. the *Tur*usca people (the Egyptians called them *Tur*sha). A branch of the *Tur*anian Altaics, they migrated to Italy from Lydia (Asia Minor) and found the city of *Tur*sa.

Troy (Tur-oy?) was a layered city, city on city, (i.e., probably much older than we suppose). Situated on Turkey's west coast, it was the seat of an ancient aristocracy—the "blue bloods" of yesteryear. Indeed, the Trojans who founded London and Rome descended from people

---

*Are the Taurus Mountains named after "the hilly land of *Tau*"—a Hawaiian reference to their sunken homeland?

of very fair, almost translucent skin—hence the blue veins of these bluebloods. Every man of note and royal family, after the fall of Troy, claimed to descend from the noble line of Priam (king of Troy); even the French kings Dagobert and Charles the Bald traced their lineage to the illustrious Trojan race.

A Comparison of Turkey and America

How can we interpret Heinrich Schliemann's discovery that Trojan pottery shards are identical in chemical composition to those found at Tiahuanaco? And why does Turkey's highly refined art—for example, at Göbekli Tepe—remind us so much of Toltecan artistry? Göbekli's huge columns, like Cocle's, run in rows. Even though the Cocle beards indicate a modern race, the characteristic wide-set eyes seen on its statues points us to some of the oldest races on Earth: Pygmies' eyes, besides bulging, are often set wide apart, as are those of the Bushmen and the tiny Palauan specimens (in Micronesia). This morphology reminds us of W. Scott-Elliot's reconstructed Lemurians, whose eyes were set so far apart that they could supposedly see sideways without turning. The Ainu of Hokkaido, for all their Caucasian features, also have those primeval eyes: set far apart. And those ancient eyes (set in "modern" faces) also belonged to the little Etruscans of Italy—a civilized race of astronomers and builders representing an advanced civilization of the archaic era—yet so similar to the faraway master race at Cocle, Panama. If those wide-eyed Etruscans migrated to Italy from Asia Minor, it would explain why Etruscan and Trojan vessels are of the same stamp. But then how do we explain Etruscan urns that are identical to ones in North America and Brazil? (Homet 1963, 172). What about the Etruscan "false arch," which matches that found at Palenque in Mexico? The sprawling Cocle civilization is considered the oldest culture in the New World—"exceedingly ancient," making it easier to understand Cocle affinities with Turkey—and the further back we go, the plainer are the resemblances of these "cousins" whose roots are on Pan.

These two parts of the world—Asia Minor and the Americas—were somehow under a common influence.

Fig. 1.20. Turkey "Pueblo-style" house and ladder

- Their spirit huts are of the same type (more details in chapter 8, p. 348 under "Tholoi" and clustered housing).
- Many Incan words appear in the Turkic-speaking Chuwashen vocabulary (Von Daniken 1975, 208).
- "Laron" cases (white little people) have been found in both Ecuador and Turkey.
- The ceramic work at Troy and Tiahuanaco, as noted, is equivalent and made of the same composition of clay. Bronze vases among Troy's treasures of Priam were identical to Tiahuanaco's—same size, shape, and owl head.

The links extend back to the motherland: the large statues at Tiahuanaco correspond to Easter Island's in both sculptural technique and architectural style. Easter Island's founder, Hotu Matua, has the same story as Peru's Manco Capac. The construction of Easter Island's Vinapu "was not just similar, but identical to that of Cuzco, Machu Picchu, Sacsayhuaman, and Ollantaytambo in the high Andes of Peru" (Childress 1988, 317). Indeed, both Cuzco and Easter Island were called the "Navel of the World"—as was Göbekli Tepe! Easter Island's

Fig. 1.21. Left: Flat-head soapstone carving from ancient Nebraska.
Right: Flat-head figure in New Mexico's Cliff Dweller petroglyphs.

rongorongo tablets were their own version of the pillars upon which were inscribed diluvial histories. Consider also the flat-topped heads on Easter Island statues (moais): most of the monolithic statues discovered at the Cocle temple site in Panama had precisely the same flat-topped craniums.

> *In Guatemala and Mexico, in Colombia, Peru, and*
> *Bolivia, we find legends of . . . men with flat heads.*
> PETER KOLOSIMO, *TIMELESS EARTH*

We find the same flat heads in Colombia's Cauca Valley, reproduced in metal, stone, and even huge rock carvings; they apparently correspond to a flat-headed race that once inhabited Venezuela. Although the strange custom of head flattening has invited a lot of guesswork, there is good reason to believe that skull deformation was originally intended for the sake of prophecy.

> Then came the God of evil, I'tura (Ahura) ... before the prophets
> ... obsess[ing] the nations and tribes of men to worship him. ...
> And he set on foot a war of plunder. ... And he taught mortals to
> flatten the head, to make prophets, and, lo and behold, the land

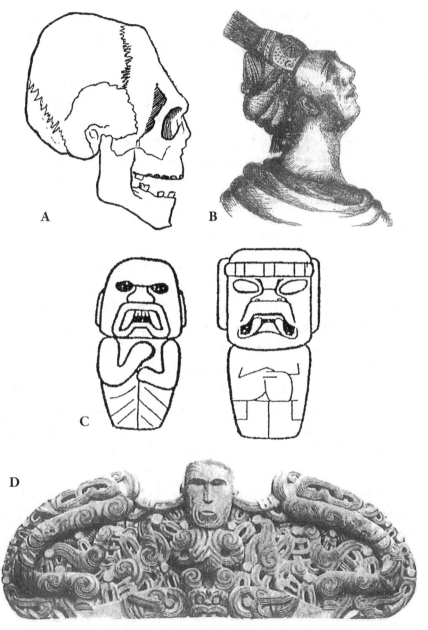

Fig. 1.22. a) Ancient flat head seen on a Swiss skull, from a cemetery near Lausanne; b) Flathead of North America: Took-shein, king of "Anagoomahaha, land of the flatheads" (plate 15, Oahspe, First Book of God 27.34); c) flat-head "jaguar men" in Olmec art of Mexico; d) Maori (New Zealand) door lintel

of Guatama [America] became a land of seers, prophets, and conjurers . . . consulting the spirits of the dead for war and for earthly glory in blood and death.

OAHSPE, FIRST BOOK OF GOD 24:24–26
(ABOUT 6,000 YEARS AGO)

In the days of Abraham,* a man or woman whose head had been flattened in infancy sat by a table covered with sand, upon which the spirits wrote with the finger. And this person communing with the spirits was . . . next to the Sun King in rank.

OAHSPE, FIRST BOOK OF GOD 11:21

Flat skulls also appear on stone images of the Pacific's Marquesas Islands, which boast processional avenues leading to a sacrificial altar built of monolithic stone (Spence 1933, 39). Head flattening was practiced in New Hebrides as well, by means of bandages, and in Hawaii and New Zealand and in the Cook Islands, where it is done by massage. In Penrhyn Island it is done with cradle boards.

In North America, head flattening continued to be practiced at the Adena Mounds in Ohio and among the Kwakiutal and Flathead Indians; almost universal, we see it also in Mexico, Peru (Aymaras), Bolivia, Brazil, the Caribbean, Crimea, Scythia, Austria, Scandinavia, Lapland, Finland, Caledonia, Basque country, Egypt, Crete, Arabia, Africa (Mangbetu people), China, Turkey, Australia, Borneo, and New Guinea. It persisted until recent time among the Turks and French. "Is it possible to explain this except by supposing that it originated from some common centre?" (Donnelly 1985, 270). Of course he means Atlantis, but not necessarily—for it can be explained by common inspiration.

Ahura sent tens of thousands of angels into *all the divisions of the earth* . . . Ahura's emissaries inspired thousands of experiments to be made, by which a prophet or seer could be made among the

---

*Abrahamic head flatteners at Tell Arpachiyah are described in Andrew Collins's recent book, *Göbekli Tepe,* pages 293–95.

Fig. 1.23. (Left): This figure appears in Oahspe, Book of Saphah (plate 75), Tablet of Fonece. "The brain and nerves of flesh could be changed in infancy by pressure to make the grown-up man of any character desired." Compare to (right) a lintel carving at Yaxchilan (Mayan).

mongrels [mixed races]. And [they] . . . discover[ed] that by pressing down the front brain of infants they could be made capable of su'is [clairvoyance]. And infants were strapped on boards, and another board strapped on the forehead to press the head flat; and every day the headboard was re-strapped tighter than the day before, until the forehead, which holds the corporeal judgment, was pressed flat, and the judgment of the brain driven up into light-perceiving regions at the top of the head.

OAHSPE, BOOK OF DIVINITY 11:22–23 (EMPHASIS ADDED)

Another common point is wrapped hands; sculpted idols at Cocle are seen with hands hugging the pillar. Cocle pots feature arms crossed over the belly. Yet this is quite typical of Polynesia's tikis—hands are seen clutching the stomach at Raivavae, near Tahiti, as well as in the Marquesas, on Pitcairn, and on Easter Island's moai, where the arms and hands were thus placed over the stomach, especially in the statues of the earliest period. This posture in turn is strangely reminiscent of certain sculptured columns at Tiahanaco (thought by some to be a "militaristic" pose).

The very same pose appears on statues at Göbekli Tepe, while

Fig. 1.24. a) Tiahuanaco column with arms wrapped; b) A'a;
c) carvings on Polynesian gateway and window frame;
d) Huastec statue of Mexico resembles Easter Island moais

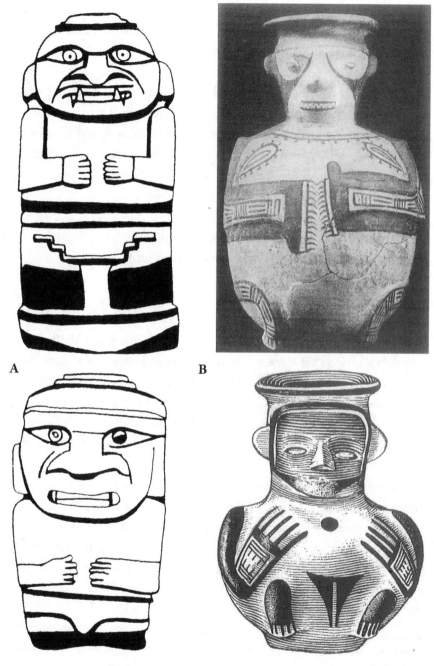

Fig. 1.25. a) Figures with cat-toothed faces and wrapped hands were placed inside the temples at San Agustin, Colombia. Hundreds of stone giants were found at that site. b) Two examples of wrapped hands seen on Cocle pottery.

Bulgaria, which is indeed adjacent to Turkey, also features cult figures with hands on belly. Statues at San Agustin, Colombia, also have the wrapped hands—*and* the long ears typical of Easter Island, the Incan Orejones, and the Chinese Buddhas.

The Polynesian technique of inlaid obsidian eyes on statues again ties these three far-flung regions together, for it is similar to work found in Mexico and central Turkey. Erich Von Daniken found figures on Mayan bowls rather like those on a vase in the Turkish Museum. Of course, the farthest southward reach of Mayan influence is Panama, and here Kuna pictographs resemble

- the figures in Peru's Nazca Lines (geoglyphs),
- the glyphs of Easter Island's rongorongo script,
- Egyptian hieroglyphics, and
- decorations at Turkey's Çatalhüyük.

Consider Çatalhüyük's ornamental stone beads, so finely drilled that a steel pin cannot penetrate them; the same technique* may have been used to drill the extremely small quartz beads taken from Peruvian mummies (Cuzco)—the tiny holes could not have been made by any commercial drill today. Ecuador's "granulated" beads of gold (Manabi culture) also matches Trojan work. Additionally, both ancient Ecuador and Çatalhüyük produced obsidian mirrors.

Mummies in Peru's Paracas necropolis are dressed in multicolored shirts and turbans. Archaeologists have wondered why Peruvian pottery figures wear a Hittite turban and a beard. A Hittite-style turban (of Turkey) is also worn by the Mexican Zapotecs and many other tribes in the Americas; it adorns the stone giants of Copan (Honduras), Tiahuanaco,† and images of Viracocha on Peruvian pottery (see chapter 5, p. 217).

---

*It has been suggested that here, and in Egypt, ultrasound was used to create perfect boreholes.

†Tiahuanaco reminds Peter Kolosimo of Israelites, for here are found "statues with aquiline noses [and] classic turbans . . ." (1975, 210) as worn in Israel more than 3,000 years ago.

Fig. 1.26. Upright stone at Copan depicts a turbaned rider sitting on what looks like an elephant of India

Turbans, made of fine feathers, are worn by women of rank in Society Island dances. The turban (*taumi-upoo*) was also worn by warriors. Most were made of plant leaves, while on the sacred island of Raiatea, brown-and-white turbans were made of tapa. Did the turban originate in the motherland? It seems significant that turbans figure in Copan art and that the Temple of Copan is "exactly on the same plan as that of Tahiti" (Lang 1877, 153). The name itself may be our biggest clue: Co-Pan.

WHITE MAN'S ISLAND

Samahtumi Whoolah

Copan, as it happens, is only one of many pan-named places in Central America, as seen in chapter 5, "Pan Names in the Middle Kingdom," p. 207. In other parts of the world, the name Pan adheres to tribes of remarkably short stature.

Name	Details
Panos	Bolivian tribe of little people (see chapter 7, p. 302 "Mysterious Scripts")
Pan-akhlamaichhlama	"Stick Indians" of ancient North America, tiny and fierce people who lived in the mountains
Pan-chiens	the little people who anciently lived near the Red Sea
Luchor-Pan	another name for Ireland's leprechauns
Pangan, Pantal, etc.	Negrito (i.e., short and dark) tribes of insular Southeast Asia

The great diaspora from Pan saw white little people, *Homo sapiens pygmaeus,* disperse to almost every part of the world. Prophets of God,

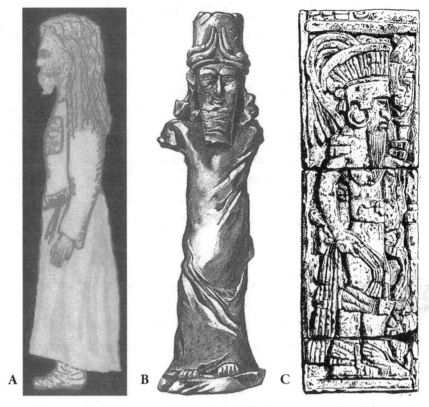

Fig. 2.1. a) The forefathers of all the bearded races were the Ihins, the little people, the chosen survivors of the Flood. b) A similar little bearded man is seen on an Assyrian amulet used for protection from evil. c) A comparable figure seen at Chichén Itzá, on door of Temple of Kukulcan.

the tiny Ihins had long white (or yellow) beards; hence those bearded men sculpted on the statues at Cocle. They represent the ancestors of the fully bearded natives of Panama first seen in the sixteenth century. Similar long-bearded figures are carved on Olmec statuettes as well as on the Mayan columns of Chichén Itzá. In fact, many of their deities, like Tlaloc, are bearded. And so observers have wondered how beardless brown Mexicans could have imagined a bearded white figure as their god. In the Andes too the Indian face is beardless, yet their ancestors built monuments to bearded gods and prophets.

In pre-Columbian America, the natives themselves were fairly beardless. Or were they? Tiahuanaco's redstone monolithic statue wears a beard; there have long been rumors of a white, bearded race living nearby on an island of Lake Titicaca. A bearded, white race in Bolivia was seen at Conquest time in the valley of Coquimbo around Lake Titicaca; today's Siriono Indians in Bolivia are different from other Indians. Bearded white people are also known to inhabit the forests of eastern Peru and the headwaters of the Amazon. Some of these "White Indians," along Brazil's Xingu River and the upper tributaries of the Amazon, supposedly inhabited cyclopean cities. There is a tradition in this region of a semi-divine Teacher named Samé who taught them agriculture and had a white beard. Is his name a clue to his origin?

Sam: The Sam-paya Indians near Lake Titicaca drew pictures of men resembling Old World types. Could this be an indication of an Old World missionary? After all, men were said to have come to Brazil from across the eastern ocean. In the Old World, *Sam* cognates are most prominent in the Jaffetic (i.e., Asian) branch of Noah's sons:

> Samar Island, Philippines
> Samarindo, Indonesia
> Shamo, Chinese name of the Gobi region
> Samoyed, Uralic-speaking people of Siberia; the Tungus sam-an ("priest") gave us the word *shaman*
> Sahm, father of the white-haired hero Zal in Persia's epic *Shah Nameh*
> Samen, the name of the little Lapps means "white"
> Samarra, in southern Iraq: blue-eyed Sumerians came from Samarra (Joseph 2014, 18)
> Samaria, old capital of the Ten Tribes
> Samarkand, north of Afghanistan
> Samsun, Turkey

In the forgotten world of Oceania, *sami* is a Polynesian word for the sea; and here too is *Samoa*, which may be the source of all our *Sam* names, as I will elsewhere suggest—that the tall Samoans are the oldest survivors of Pan. Just east of Pan, on America's northwest coast, there was an Okanagan myth of their lost land, *Samahtumi Whoolah*, "White Man's Island," that lay in the middle of the ocean and was inhabited by a race of white giants (Samoans?). Indeed, a giant who led important expeditions shows up in the Samoan legend of King Rata. In Sanskrit, *sama* means "chant or sacred verse"; in the Finnish epics, *Sampo* means "heaven itself."

Like many names that were devotedly retained for their ritual or sacred significance, Sam may have originated on Pan. Check Oahspe's Book of Saphah for its extraordinary word lists, especially the one detailing *Sam* words from the Panic language.

Let my prophets sit on the K'Sam and be oracles in My kingdom. An emblem of a miracle kept over the altar . . . [is called] Sam'tu, triangle. The sign of Soul-light, also an instrument for measuring . . . [is called] Sam'fong . . . Sam'miji . . . [is] the seventh emblem in the third degree of Faithist . . . Samuel, prophet . . .

TABLET OF SEMOIN 23, 25, 97, 12 (EMPHASIS ADDED)

BEARDED ONES IN THE MIDDLE KINGDOM OF THE AMERICAS

Who/What	Where	Details
Statues	Cocle	several statues
Zacatencos and Ticomans	Mexico	on ceramics
Figures	Chichén Itzá, Mexico	on door of the House of the Great Spirit
The Old Ones (*Huehue*)	Mexico	shown with "European" features
Statuettes	Mexico	Olmec figurines
God of Zapotec	Lambityeco, Oaxaca	found above the tomb of a deified ruler
Arawak tribes	Caribbean and beyond	men of light color with long hair and beards

A

B

C

*Fig. 2.2. a) Arawak; b) bearded profile, carved at Chichén Itzá;
c) carving of bearded little man, from Chinque, Guatemala
(Drawing [right] by Jose Bouvier)*

PALE, BEARDED MEN IN SOUTH AMERICA

Who/What	Where	Details
White people	Peru	a gentle people with beards, "the oldest race now alive" (Wilkins 2000)
White Indians	east of Cuzco, Peru	inhabiting El Gran Paititi
White people	Peru	at the Pucaras fortress
Nazca remains	Paracas, Peru	red-haired mummies
Indians	Brazil	in 1750 missionaries encountered white bearded Indians; the ancestors of the Shuaras were "man-like gods"
Assurini people	Brazil	white skinned, red bearded; spoke a distinct language
Carved in mountain	Havea, Brazil	head of bearded man

BEARDED MEN IN NORTH AMERICA

Who/What	Where	Details
Copper statue	Michigan	discovered in the seventeenth century near ancient mines (Coppens 2012, 112)
Great Stone Face	Illinois	a 10,000-year-old artifact, not Indian made
Pomo and Hupa Indians	California	remarkably abundant beards
Haida Indians	northwest coast	see more on Haida at end of chapter 3
White Inuits	Alaska	heavily bearded; blond Inuits

In the Far East the most heavily bearded (and most Caucasoid) people are the Ainu of Japan, their name a possible variant of the New World *Inu*it (or even Ihin). Blond Inuits were seen by navigator-explorer Sir John Franklin in the nineteenth century: an Alaskan people with blue eyes and full beards, the Inuits appear to be descendants of the "mummy people," a Caucasoid race who lived on Alaska's Aleutian Islands seven thousand years ago. Early in the twentieth century, explorers again encountered tribes of white Inuits, some with red hair, living on the shores of Davis Straits, their facial features "so well made."

Fig. 2.3. Ainu with beard

The forefathers of the white Polynesians of today, the
forefathers of the white Mayas of Yucatan, and the
forefathers of all our white races were one and the same.
JAMES CHURCHWARD, *THE LOST CONTINENT OF MU*

The Innuits themselves assert that the first men were white. Their ancestors, possessed of a complexion as fair as Europe's Cro-Magnons, enjoyed an unexpectedly advanced culture. Who exactly were they? Anthropologist Roland Dixon thought there had been a Neolithic race of blond people that extended from Asia to Siberia to the Bering Strait. Doubtless they were the very people who built an "arctic metropolis" in Alaska; their material culture was certainly distinct from the Inuit as we know them today. Lost arts abound; excavations at Ipiutak gave up astonishing ruins of this mile-long metropolis—long avenues of living sites, remains of eight hundred houses, thoroughfares, a population in the thousands. Whoever these pre-Alaskans were, their next-of-kin— blond and industrious—were forging a similar lifestyle in almost every other part of the globe.

And if hair type and beards have helped us reconstruct this Lost Ancestor, let's not forget the nose.

The Nose Knows

Although discussed more fully in chapter 5, it's a long way to chapter 5, so we'll preview here the five sons of Noah: Shem in India, Yista in Japan, Guatama in the Americas, Ham in Africa, and Jaffeth in China. And the point is this: these all were originally bearded whites with well-bridged, sometimes pointy, noses. Perhaps we will even find their predecessors among the scattered islands in the Pacific Ocean. The Ambats of Melanesia, for example, were white with aquiline noses. Carved images on Easter and Chatham Islands have the goatee beard (sported still by some of the Islanders) and aquiline nose. The latter feature is seen again to the west, among the fair-skinned "Redin," who came to India (Shem) from the motherland, stopping in the Maldives, where tradition describes them as redheaded. Also of the Shem family is Abraham, near whose birthplace is an eleven-thousand-year-old statue of a man with a prominent nose (Collins 2014, 55).

The Japanese (Yista branch) Jomon had equally prominent noses and light-colored beards. (The living Ainu are considered the last remnant of these Jomon people.) Yet the Jomon are so similar to their Guataman counterparts in Ecuador not only in their identical pottery but also in physical appearance—Von Daniken mentions Ecuadorian images that depict ancient engineers, "men with long noses" (1975, 20). This distinct type follows through to Mexico, where Itzamna, the bearded demigod of the Maya who brought writing and medicine, is pictured with a prominent nose. The sharp Semitic profiles seen in the art of Mexico have been compared to Sumerian and Egyptian faces. (Indeed, Itzamna's story has been linked to Egypt; see chapter 3, p. 95 "Egyptians in the Americas?"). In Europe we might note the long and narrow nose of the Basque (Jaffetic branch), likely descendant of the eagle-nosed Cro-Magnon and possessing the oldest genes in Europe. This closes the loop with Pan, for the native genes of Easter Island are said to match Basque genes.

Fig. 2.4. Vase from Tula, Mexico, showing long beard and pointed nose

Fig. 2.5. Note the long nose on Easter Island moais (left) and one of the five faces seen on the Ibn Ben Zara map (right): these pointy noses appear in medallions placed at the corners of the map; calm and aristocratic, they are perhaps of Greek Orthodox or Coptic type.

Marcel Homet thought he found his long-lost Celtic cousins in the Great Lakes region of North America and in Amazonia: on the Amazon, the Waikas Indians, "beautiful human beings," looked like Arabs with their aquiline noses and high foreheads. "These were men of the white race" (in Guatama). And in Hamitic Africa, in Dahomey, again we encounter "men with aquiline noses" (1963, 114, 181). Finally, in China (Jaffeth) is Cherchen Man with Celtic DNA, long nose, reddish hair, and ginger beard.

In Bolivia, Tiahuanaco's statues sport the aquiline nose and pointed beard, like that of the present-day Quechua inhabitants. Tiahuanaco tradition recalls a white-haired man from the East who raised temples and statues to the sun. The deified figure known as Viracocha ("Kon

Tiki Viracocha") appears on Peruvian pottery with beard and aquiline nose. Not coincidentally, Kon-tiki is the name of the *Polynesian* race founder, who was again bearded and white, as were the ancestors of the Easter Islanders and the Panapeans; here, on Sokeh's Rock, one can see the carving of a bearded man (Childress 1988, 221). In Hawaii too the original people, the Mu and Menehune, were little folks with facial hair. The *Homo sapien pygmaeus* Andamanese, living south of India in the Bay of Bengal—although themselves dark skinned—say their Supreme Being is white skinned with a long beard. Nearby are the Ceylonese Veddas, also little, pale, and heavily bearded.

Indeed, enclaves of little people with beards are found in numerous lands that are otherwise inhabited by glabrous people; they represent the ancestral type; that is, genes from the original Ihins. *Homo sapien pygmaeus* with beards have lived on almost every continent.

- Pure Negritos of Zambales, Philippines.
- Little people of Malaysia are more fully bearded than their Mongoloid neighbors.
- Central African Pygmies are more heavily bearded and lighter colored than the black African.
- *Pygmaioi* (*Homo sapien pygmaeus*) of ancient India were black and bearded.
- Short-statured and bearded priests of ancient Sumeria.
- In Europe, King Oberon of the dwarfs was only 3 feet tall with "a sunny beard."
- The magical gnomes of the high Alps are named *barbegazi* after their heavy beards.
- Alux, the Mayan little man, has a long, jet-black beard.
- Carved figures from Chinque, Guatemala, are bearded, squat figures (see fig. 2.2, p. 54).
- The short Mapuche Indians of Chile are pale and bearded.
- Bearded "dwarfs" along the Amazon are 4 feet tall, of classic Greek features.
- The tiny Nunnehi of the southern Appalachians were blue eyed and bearded, according to the Cherokee.

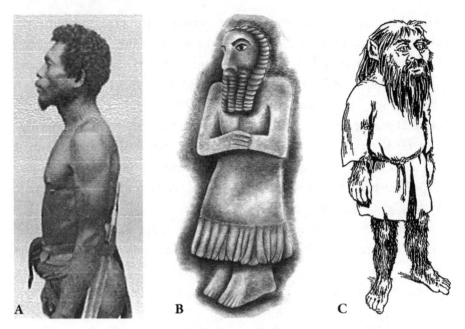

Fig. 2.6. a) A Zambal Negrito; b) short Sumerian priest;
c) Alux of Mexico (Drawings B and C by Jose Bouvier)

A pointed beard was the cardinal feature of the Egyptian pharaohs. The earliest Egyptians were reportedly "blond and bearded" (Charroux 1972, 127). Egypt's beloved dwarf gods Bes and Ptah were tiny bearded figures—probably representing nothing more than the deification of the Good Little People (Ihins). Osiris himself was bearded. All these figures stand for Noachic types, meaning the *mortal* initiators of Egypt who brought medicine, agriculture, learning, astronomy, and navigation.

Egyptian priests would put on a false beard for religious functions, just as it was worn by the pharaoh to symbolize his authority. Even Queen Hatshepsut had to wear a false beard during her reign. The same can be said for First Dynasty kings of Mesopotamia, with the king donning a false beard in imitation of the great ancestor. Odd as this custom may be, it is echoed in South America, in the same region where the Arica Mummies were found: here, in Chile's Atacama Desert, the Molle Indians, "a people unable to grow facial hair," wore false beards

Fig. 2.7. Bes and Ptah (Drawing by Jose Bouvier)

Fig. 2.8. Assyrian winged figure donning false beard

"made of ceramic by inserting it through a hole cut into their own jaw-bone. It was worn in painful imitation of ancestors who arrived from over the sea long ago, after the Great Flood" (Joseph 2006, 206).

The Long-Haired Ihins

More than fifty thousand years ago, according to Oahspe's First Book of the First Lords, the little people, called Ihins, were white- and yellow-skinned—that is, before the great amalgamations saw them blend with the larger, darker races. Ihins of all ages had hair white or yellow, long and silky. Such people were known to the Choktaw Indians, who sometimes encountered Pygmy beings called Kwanokasha, living deep in the forest—all with long white hair.

The Ihin race, standing no more than 3 feet tall, were the forefathers and foremothers of all the world's little people: *Homo sapien pygmaeus*. And they were the first people on Earth with long, straight hair. From Pan they spread out to the five divisions of the Earth—although they did leave behind (in Oceania) a few of their genes, as visitors have often admired the long-haired women of Polynesia. As Maori tradition has it, there were once "very small, fair people [seen] dancing in the sand with their slight fair figures and long yellow hair . . . fair and graceful, slimly built, with well-formed bodies. Their long light-coloured hair hung to their waists" (Anderson 1928, 288). And this is why the Tahitian god Tangaroa is represented as a man with fine hair reaching to the ground and why Hina (named after the I-hin ancestress) is pictured with hair that went down to her feet and why Temehara, their goddess of wisdom, has long shiny tresses.

Those genes persisted for fifteen thousand years in Guatama, whose Queen Minneganewashaka (in North America) had yellow hair, long and hanging down. The Cherokee remember the tiny Yunwi Tsundsdi as a handsome people with long hair falling almost to the ground. In the Pomo (California) creation myth, the First People were beautiful and very long haired. Indeed, the Pomo and Hupa, by their heavy beard (so unlike most Amerinds), appear to be genetically linked to those First People.

Long tresses, according to Charles Darwin in *The Descent of Man*, were so greatly esteemed by the American Indian that a chief was elected solely from the length of his hair.

The tall Ghans, a race that sprang from Ihin blends with the indigenous Ihuans,* inherited that long hair. Such were America's Ongwee*ghans,* who

> came suddenly into the world [due to that crossbreeding] and they had long hair, black and coarse; but their skin was brown, copper-colored; and their arms were short, like the |hins. . . . So, the Ongwee-ghan became a new race in the world, having all the symmetry of the |hin, and the savageness of the |huans.
>
> OAHSPE, THE LORDS' THIRD BOOK 2:2–3

Such a one was found in the nineteenth century—discovered in Mississippi were the remains of a giant with waist-length, jet-black hair, buried in a timber vault.

> Of the |hins, | provided testimony in all the divisions of the earth, with long hair belonging to the tribes that worshipped the Great Spirit.
>
> OAHSPE, THE LORDS' FIFTH BOOK 3:5

At one time these long-haired people existed worldwide. In India, for example, the legendary Dorani had hair of golden color, locks so long "it was often unbearable." Upon this long-haired race was, no doubt, based the story of Rapunzel, with her wonderfully long tresses, fine as spun gold. In the British Isles too the prehistorical Sidhe (mound people, see chapter 8) had blue eyes, pale faces, and long yellow hair, these wee bodies so like the handsome blond-headed Scottish fairies and the golden-haired imps who appeared regularly in King Arthur's court.

One French fable describes a dwarf 3 feet high with "hair yellow as fine gold." In Russia it is the Rusalky, very beautiful women who have pale skin, slender bodies, soft voices, and long wavy hair. Nor is she different from Austria's legendary Wilden Fraulin, *Homo sapien pygmaeus*, with long blond hair, or the beautiful Germanic women of the hills who

---

*When the Maori say Ihua-tamai was a husband of Hina, we understand that *Ihua*-tamai represents the Ihuan race that intermarried with the I-hins ("Hina").

possess uncommonly long and beautiful hair. A slender, long-haired beauty is also remembered in Scandinavia and Wales, while the Finnish epic *Kalevala* declares that the stature of their "hero from the ocean . . . [was] as a man's thumb"; his "hair reached down to his heels, the beard to his knees."

We might also recall the skillful little nixes of Germany, Iceland, and Norway who possessed delicate features and long, light hair, almost white; or the lovely nymphs of Europe's wild places with their silver hair. Northern mythologies remember these white-whites: "His flesh was as white as snow and his hair as white as wool," recalls one legend of Thule (Iceland, Greenland), referring to their awe-inspiring ancestor—perhaps Noah himself, who, says the Book of Enoch, was born with perfectly white hair.

In Asia Minor white-haired people lived in the Taurus Mountains; here in this ancient land the venerable Hittites were a short, white, and bearded people with long hair. In Malaysia the Great Ancestor Kari, God of Thunder, is depicted with long white hair. Similarly, among Mexico's Huichol, the white-haired earth goddess is called Our Grandmother. The Quechua of the Andes have hair almost to the ground; some of their ancestors, the Inca (mummies) had long *white* hair. No, it is not the white hair of old age, but of their Ihin forebears. In North America the Mandans (see "The Big Canoe" on p. 85) had numerous children with white hair.

Fig. 2.9. Cartoonish white dwarf of the North recalls the legendary Ihins.

Fig. 2.10. Mummified Jivaro Indian head with very long black hair, like that of the Venezuelan "crater people"

In the jungles too there have been rumors of Pygmy-like beings such as those seen among the hardwoods of British Honduras; "two little people" were sighted by a government timberman who described the pair as about 3 feet tall, the man heavily bearded and the woman with extremely long hair. This matches James Churchward's account of his time in British Honduras: "I was informed that hunters and explorers occasionally meet them back in the dark valleys of the mountains. They are about three feet tall with . . . an abundance of very long black hair" (1931b, 20).

Local tribes in Venezuela speak of strange people sometimes seen in the woods, their skin the color of yellowed ivory, their long hair of different colors. British explorer-theorist Harold T. Wilkins reports seeing white people with long black hair in canoes, and dwarfs with hair that reached almost to their feet (2000, 46). The Arawaks grow long hair, as did the sixteenth-century women of Panama—and of eastern Mexico.

Because all people on Earth have some Ihin blood, it is not surprising to find even the most savage tribes, like the (now extinct) Nittevo of Ceylon, possessing a few of the distinctive *Homo sapien pygmaeus* traits; in the case of the little Nittevo it was the long straight hair. North of the Nittevo, in India, the ancient Negritos were said to have hair down to their knees and heavy beards. In China the mummy called the "Loulan Beauty" (in the Lop Desert of the Tarim Basin) had long, light hair; her people were blond and bearded. As Chinese legend goes, an ancient land by the name of Fu Sang had white women with beautiful long hair and the gift of clairvoyance (see "Irin and Irihia" on p. 73). Historians have been spinning their wheels, attempting to determine the true location of Fu Sang.

Ihins, the Sacred Little People

A friend of mine was in Japan and mentioned the name Ihin to a Shinto priest who recognized it, saying that is the name of the people mentioned in their history books; he pronounced it Ine, as in *wine*. Which, indeed, sounds like Ainu (pronounced *eye-new*), who are the short, original white people of Japan.

The unusual name Ihin is in fact many tens of thousands of years old. Indeed, the Wyandot Indians of Ohio said that the little people were old enough to remember the Flood; the Choctaw say the same, that there lived on Earth "before us the Little People" (like the above-mentioned Kwanokasha). Similar recollections are echoed in eastern Europe, where the Serbs and Poles remember the *ludki,* the little people who "lived before humans." In western Europe's folk belief, the "fees" (who stand between 2 and 4 feet in height) are held to be the oldest beings on the planet; they were called the Old Ones.

In Oceania too they were known as the Before-Time people. In the Society Islands, *man-ihin-i* means "guest." (The Society Islands were so named by the British after the Royal Geographical *Society,* which sponsored Captain Cook's expeditions.) Little people on Fiji were also reckoned the original islanders. There are also "pygmoids" in New Hebrides, Easter Island, Palau, and Raiatea (Henry 1928, 202). On Nan

Fig. 2.11.
Little people of
Polynesia fishing
at night

Madol tradition holds that the island was originally inhabited by a race of *nani* (little people) before the continent was submerged. Hawaii's own Menehune were likewise the pint-size aborigines of that land.

Theopompus (in the fourth century BCE) wrote about a faraway continent with a city called Eusebius whose people had been pious and peace loving and so just that the gods vouchsafe to converse with them. There are modern historians too who think the first civilizers in the Pacific Ocean "generated purpose, peace, prosperity, and character growth" (Valentine 1975, 27). These first human beings, as Abraham Fornander so faithfully recorded the Hawaiian traditions, were "situated in a large country or continent . . . a sacred land. . . . A man must be righteous to attain it; he must prepare himself exceedingly holy who wishes to attain it" (1969, 1:77).

Likewise does today's protohistorian understand that "a blue-eyed, fair-haired race . . . formed the spiritual features of the world" (Chouinard 2012, 104). But where are their traces? As my colleague David Pitman explained, "The Ihins wouldn't have built much out of stone because they wouldn't have wanted to be bound to the earth. . . . Perhaps this explains why there is so little physical trace of these people" (personal communication). Pittman's view is reflected in the opinion of yet another protohistorian: "One thing is certain: the reality of an advanced race which was not recorded in history. That nation could have passed its scientific tradition to . . . Egypt, Babylon, Mexico, and India and to the philosophers of Greece and China" (Tomas 1973, 165). Don't you agree?

The sum total of my own research points to the little Ihins (and even their mixed offspring) as that advanced race. And I think it is time to stop calling these worldwide whites "anomalous." Is Bactria, in Iran, really the birthplace of the Aryan race, as we are taught? Did the Aryans really originate somewhere between the Baltic and Black Sea? Or even in the Pamirs of Central Asia? Looking over the literature, it occurs to me that the term *Aryan* has become a confusing, worthless, even treacherous term. Instead, let us look to the history of the Ihins, the true Initiators of mankind. White people did not originate from any single point in Eurasia but rose to prominence in *all* the divisions of the Earth where the sons of Noah settled after escaping Pan.

> *Their legends say that the head and front and beginning*
> *of the Polynesians lay in a white (the Arian) race; and I*
> *found this . . . confirmed by referring to their language*
> *. . . as well as some customs and modes of thought . . . a*
> *chip of the same block from which the Hindu, the Iranian,*
> *and the Indo-European families were fashioned.*
>
> ABRAHAM FORNANDER,
> *AN ACCOUNT OF THE POLYNESIAN RACE*

The root of the word *Aryan* is *Ari,* as in French *ari*enne or English *ari*stocrat. I believe *ari* originated on Pan: ari-nga ora was an early name for Easter Island's *moai*, which means "king." Arii means "king" in the Society Islands. In Hawaii, ari-ki means "regal," while in the Ladrone Islands, departed chiefs are called ari-ti. In other parts of Polynesia it indicates priest; Ari is a god of Rarotonga (Aria = founder of Rarotonga). And Arii is a Polynesian name for the sun. There are several such derivatives as shown here:

Ariki = priest in New Zealand; Burma was long controlled by "an alien Ari priesthood," according to John Cohane (1969, 115); chief in Rarotonga

Ari'i = "admirable" in New Zealand; it means "sovereign" in Tahiti

Ari-oi (var. areoi) = Polynesian men's society

Ari-ari = the figure from whom sprang the races of man in Polynesian myth

Ari-hi = Tahitian hero, in their sagas; the word also means "enchanted"

> *White skin and red hair were once highly prized among many Polynesian societies.*
> ROBERT SUGGS, *THE HIDDEN WORLDS OF POLYNESIA*

The aristocracy in most of Polynesia "blanched" their daughters by keeping them out of the sun. In Mangaian legend the maiden Tonga-tea "was the envy of all Marua on account of her fairness. . . . In Tahitia a fair skin was esteemed, and women, and men too, would live as much in the shade as possible in order to retain the fairness" (Anderson 1928, 14, 318, 324).

Hawaiians remember the Sea of the Deluge, when the land was overwhelmed by the sea and only two humans survived. The event is called *Kai a Kahin-arii,* which also happens to mean "place of origin." It is then not surprising that the same root, *ari* (or *arii*), took hold in the different parts of the world to which the survivors dispersed:

Arii: oldest Celtic tribes, from which name Erin (Irish) seems to have derived

Ariti: Central Brazilian tribe with Semitic-looking alphabet, according to French explorer Marcel Homet

Ari-kara and Ar-awak Indians: the latter of lightish skin tone

Ari-juna: among the Guajiros, an Arawakan tribe, means "white person"

Ari-conte: in Brazilian mythology, one of the twin brothers who survived the Great Flood

Pac-ari Cave, Peru: Lodging of the Dawn, out of which the first people emerged

Ari-ca: 8,000-year-old mummies in Chile; their Great Ancestor is said to have arrived from "over the sea"

Bish-ari: an African people with lighter skin, hair not woolly

Ari-ha: Arabic name for Jericho

Ari-bah: ancient pure blood Arabians

Ari-yaneh: old name of Iran

Ari-maspians: tribe of ancient Scythia

Ar-arat and Ar-menia: region from which the term *Caucasian* came; their hero and god of vegetation, Tammuz, was also known as As-ari

Ari-nna: Hittite Sun goddess; her Russian counterpart is Ari-na

Ari-cia: name of goddess Diana's sacred grove

Ari-mi: Latin name of the Aramanians

Hina, the All Good

Though based on the entirely forgotten name Ihin, words and names all over the world incorporate the sacred *hin*. Hino, to the Wyandot Indians, was a beneficent god linked to the Land of the Little People. Across the western sea, the Hin name of the little ancestor is just as familiar: in Hawaiian, hini-hini means "small" and po-hina means "whitish." Hina also means "white" on Tonga and the Marquesas, sometimes implying "pale or pure." The name Ihin, shortened to Hin, is found idealized, even deified, in Tahiti, where Hina is the Earth and all-good wife of the Creator. In many parts of Polynesia, Hina is understood as the ancestress of the race.

Hina takes so many forms and meanings in Oceanic myth: she may be the Moon, she may be First Mother, or the goddess of childbirth; she may be the wife of the god Maui (or his mother or his sister), or the goddess of fishes, or a "sky fairy," and so forth. In Ceram the word for mother is ma-hin-a, in the Teluti language ihina means "woman," while in the Society Islands the queen is Ma-hin-eva-hin-e (Ma-hin-e is king). In Mangaia, Hina was the daughter of Ku-i.

Yet we also find the idealized Ihin or Hin a few continents away—in North Africa: Tin Hin-an is the legendary matriarch of the Tuareg Berbers. In Hebrew, She-hina means "God's presence." In fact the I-Hin name is distributed throughout the entire world, often indicating the deified ancestor (or perhaps "ghost," as in Etruscan hin-thial). Elsewhere it might stand for a place of pilgrimage, or simply a land, like Hin-dustan.

ILLUSTRIOUS BEINGS NAMED AFTER (I)HIN, IN ALL PARTS OF THE WORLD

Name	Meaning	Where	Details
Kua-hin-e	rain goddess	Hawaii	
Kihawa-hin-e	mermaid	Hawaii	
Hin-amoa	ruler of the Sea	Polynesia	reflecting the navigational skills of the early Ihins
Hin-aura	legendary ancestors of the Maori	New Zealand	
Hin-epoupou	ruler of the Sea	New Zealand	according to the Maori
Hin-erangi	woman in epic	New Zealand	Hine is also name of king's daughter
Telk-hin-es	first children of Ge & Pontos	Rhodes	mythic ancestors of mankind
Hin-o	thunder god	Iroquois Indians	also called Grandfather
Hin-uno	a god	Paiute Indians	
Kac-hin-a	surrogate deities	Hopi Indians	protectors of the people
Hasts-hin	First Beings	Apache Indians	
Hin-nah	the ancients	Algonquin Indians	
Cruit-hin	builders of the raths	Scotland	a pre-Celtic "dwarf" race
Tin Hin-an	ancient queen	Hoggar, North Africa	in Tuareg legend

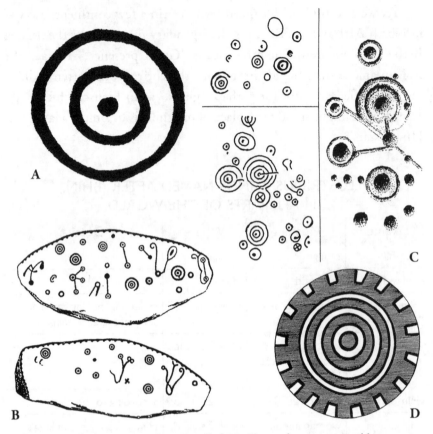

Fig. 2.12. a) Concentric design, called Hin'kwa, designates Es (the unseen part) within corpor, which is to say, spirit within body, or more broadly, something within something. The Ihins were the first on Earth to possess soul power, an inner connection to the cosmos. Engraved hin'kwas have been seen in the Pacific at megalithic sites on Wewak and Fiji. In New Guinea, shells incised with concentric circles are considered sacred. b) All epigraphers are familiar with the sign of Hin'kwa, frequently seen in petroglyphs such as these two from Forsyth County, Georgia. c) Irish cup-and-ring marks, also seen in Brittany; "archeologists can only guess that it probably had some religious significance" (Thorndike 1977, 46). Still undeciphered, though believed to be a shamanic symbol, this sign is virtually universal, inscribed in rocks and standing stones in Scotland, England, Wales, Brittany, France, Portugal, Spain, Italy, Greece, Palestine, Turkey, Syria, Algeria, Egypt, Switzerland, Mexico, Panama, Brazil, Peru, Colombia, China, Mongolia, and India. d) Hin'kwa on Cocle ceramic.

PLACES OF IMPORTANCE WITH *HIN* EMBEDDED

Name	What	Where	Details
Mi-hin-tale	city of pilgrimage	Ceylon	shrines, sanctuary
Hua-hin-e	place	Society Islands	with a distinct flood legend
Hin-apsan Islands	with latte megaliths	in the Marianas	
Sec-hin	early ceremonial center	Peru	
Wai-hin-d	kingdom	Persia & Afghanistan	first "City of Man"
T-hin-is	place	Egypt	home of First Dynasty kings
Rusa-hin-a	ancient name of Toprak Kale	Armenia	Kingdom of Urartu

Spiritual things carry the sacred *hin* in words such as Hin-ayana, the school of Buddhism that emphasizes the self-denying aspect, and To-hin-ga, the Maori rite of purification.

Irin and Irihia

Not every tribe could pronounce "Ihin." In some dialects the aspirate *h* becomes a lateral *r*. Among the Tupis of Brazil, for example, a man named *Irin* Mage was the sole survivor of a "violent inundation," thus linking Noah to Irin and ultimately to the Ihins, who alone survived the flood that sundered Pan. In Spain the feminine name Irina (our Irene) means "Peace," recalling the nonviolent society of the little people. Off Brittany, on the island of Gav*rinis,* concentric designs (hin'kwas) in megalithic art are thought to be part of a cult honoring a powerful goddess whose stone idols are also found in Spain. Is it coincidental that on the sacred island of Raiatea in the Pacific, na-*i'iri* means "nymphs of power"?

In the Aegean, Ayia *Irini* is the ancient name of a Bronze Age settlement in the Cyclades; today called Kea, this place was the home of poets, philosophers, and physicians, clearly indicating an elect seat of

intelligence, as seen again in Hu*zirina,* the Assyrian center of learning. Here in ancient Mesopotamia, *Ir* had the meaning of "guardian."
We find this in the *Epic of Gilgamesh,* where the protective goddess is
called Irninis—cousin, I believe, to the angelic Hebrew *Irin:* Hebrew
legend mentions the Holy Watchers, a class of angels inhabiting the
sixth heaven. These angels, as the saga goes, descended from their holy
mountain to the plains and proceeded to mate with the Daughters of
Men (read: they came down from the *mounds,* see chapter 8). Otherwise
known as Sons of God (Bene-ha-Elohim), these angel-men called Irin
had "long white hair and pale skin" (Collins 2014, 276). Just so, the
Polynesian "gods" are depicted as fair, with red or sandy hair (Spence
1933, 75). Not really gods, they are more likely the deified ancestor.

"Irihia," says New Zealand oral history, is the name of what was once
"the most sacred spot in all the world." (Was the New Guinea province
of Irian named after it?) Maori chants describe this bygone country of
Irihia, famous for its sacred mountain and temple of learning. What's
more, the name Irihia "appears to apply to a continental land, not an
island . . . [it] is the site of the Deluge" (Smith 1921, 102–3, 132), the
land from which the Maori ancestors came.

Irihia was only one of many names in Polynesia for the sunken land
of their ancestors. Other Oceanic names for the lost lands include Hiva,
Haiviki, Avaiki, Hoahoamaitu, Helani, Fenua Nui, Bolutu, Kalu'a,
Humari Nadu, Kahiki, Papa, Hau-papa-nui-a-tau, Uru, Marae Renga,
La-Mu-Ra, Mu Dalu, Mutuhai, Pali-ilu, Kapakapaua-a-Kane, Nirai-
Kanai, Horaizan, Rangi-motia, Ta Rua, Nakauvadra, Koro, Kahoupo-
o-Kane, and Atia-te-varinga-nui. The many other names of the lost land
are too numerous to list exhaustively: Mu, Tien-mu, Lumania, Lemuria,
Rutas, Pacifica, Adoma, Patulan-Pa-Civan, Peng Sha, and so on.

Fig. 2.13. Easter Island glyph representing Hiva, the motherland

Havaiki, fanaura'e fenua! Fanaura'a ta'ata! (Havaiki, the
birthplace of lands! The birthplace of people!)
SOCIETY ISLAND TRADITIONAL SONG

Pan, as recorded in Oahspe, was called Wagga before it was submerged. Perhaps a dialect variant of Wagga is Wawau, which is "a very
old Polynesian name, like Havaiki . . . [it] applies to places, in memory of a more ancient land" (Smith 1921, 38, 257–58). It was also
called Whanui: *Wha,* the land, and *nui,* great. Wahi, in Hawaiian,
means "distant place." Wagga (var. Whaga or Waga) is also similar to
Moti-whawha, an island of unknown location in the Rarotonga epics;
and to Whaka-tane, New Zealand ("the old-time people" of the Maori),
which also has its whaka-rewa-rewa (boiling springs) and whaka (island)
(Anderson 1928, 206). Whainga-roa, according to Maori myth, was a
country submerged by the sea; whole tribes perished.

That name Whaga is apparently recalled as well in the Wahgas tribe,
the civilized white-skinned people on the Pacific Rim, on America's
northwest coast; they lived around the Klamath River *before* the Yurok
Indians, and they became their teachers. There is also the Wagogo tribe,
near the source of the Nile and Waga-du, the ancient name of Ghana.
The Wahgi Valley is in New Guinea's highlands; here Ta-*waga* is the
highest mountain in the New Guinea deluge tale. Wagawaga is another
cognate, at New Guinea's Milne Bay.

The name Wagga Wagga also remains as (1) the name of an
Australian city on the *Mu*rrumbidgee River of New South Wales, (2) a
district in Iwate, Japan, and (3) a province in the Punjab of India.

Pacific (Rim) Whites

A native white race once dwelt in the Pacific.
LEWIS SPENCE, *THE PROBLEM OF LEMURIA*

The Polynesian is regarded as the Caucasian of the nadir.
JOHANNES ANDERSON,
MYTHS AND LEGENDS OF THE POLYNESIANS

The diversity of features and complexion in the Polynesian
family—the broad forehead, Roman nose, light olive
complexion, wavy and sometimes ruddy hair—attest its
Arian descent.

ABRAHAM FORNANDER,

AN ACCOUNT OF THE POLYNESIAN RACE, VOL. 1

All the way Down Under, the Australian Aborigines, especially in the west-central part, show a high frequency of yellow-to-brown hair, occurring in many children and quite a few women, some with outright blond hair. It is likely they descended from the "Caucasian" type who inhabited Australia (Lake Mungo) more than twenty thousand years ago, corresponding to ancient paintings at Prince Regent River of "European" people.

Whites, say the Aetas, settled Mindanao (Philippines) after a great deluge that drowned all but three people, who then intermarried with the natives; those offspring are the ancestors of the Aetas; indeed, the forebears of these Aeta folk, according to a thirteenth-century Chinese account, had yellow eyes. The Bagabo people, also of the Philippines, say their creator god, Melu, is white. There is some blondism here still among these Filipino Negritos. Small framed, curly haired, small nosed, the Aeta are counted as the earliest inhabitants of these islands.

Especially pale are the Abenlens, living deep in the isolated Zambales Mountains of Luzon. They are a strange, small people (no more than 4½ feet high), light in complexion, with light-brown eyes. Most possess fine features and wavy hair. The Abenlens' fair coloring may be taken as representative of the earlier type, for they are reclusive and never mixed their genes with neighbors or conquerors.

Malaysia too has its pale people in the Senoi, Semang, and Sakai. Fair-skinned folk, the Rampasas inhabit the Indonesian island of Flores. They have their own white Noah, the forefather of their tribe who was "saved from a flood in a ship." Farther east, into Oceania itself, some natives of New Caledonia (with numerous signs of an advanced culture) and Fergusson Island, though primitive types (hairy, heavy brow ridges and jaws), are light brown and blond in coloring. In East New Britain (Tolai people) and in the Ellice group and Omba, the people are markedly light in complexion. Remarkably pale people abide at Baie des Français and Mangea, the latter described as "the fair-haired children of Tangaroa" (Perry 1968, 306); Nagaru, a demigod of the Mangaia, has golden locks.

In New Guinea as well, "we saw men of a light, nearly yellow, colour. . . . The hair of young children is often quite fair. . . . [A] pygmy people, known as the Tapiro . . . [have] skin of a lighter colour than that of the neighboring Papuans, some individuals being almost yellow. The stature averages 4 ft. 9 ins." (Wollaston 1912, 48, 110). The Tarifuroro, with their marvelous gardens, are another yellow-skinned people of New Guinea.

Italian prehistorian Egisto Roggero in *Il Mare* observed that "the great Oceanic race, an ancient people of whose story we know nothing . . . [were striking in] their resemblance to the white races of the west." Polynesia's tall redheads are also notably akin to the stately Inca nobility with their wheat-colored hair. The Polynesian demigod Tane is red haired, his people "white" (*karakako*). Pumotus and Tahitian legends speak of redheads with blue eyes who came up out of a lagoon (Emergence?). The Tahitian Chant of Kualii sings of the ancient land of Kahiki inhabited by white men (*haole*)—and "he is like a god" (Anderson 1928, 69). Tokelau Islanders say their own ancestors lived in the land of the white people—*Papalangi*.

In fact, there are pale-skinned people living in almost every part of Oceania, including New Hebrides, the Solomons, Vanuatu, Rotumah, Suuna Rii, and Fiji; a three-thousand-year-old skeleton of a Caucasian male was exhumed on Fiji in 2002. The Marquesan Islanders first seen by Europeans were white skinned.

In the Tuamotu creation legend we find the human race descended from Hoa-tea, "light-skinned Friend." On Paea, the tutelary god was Tamatea, "Blond Child" (Henry 1928, 241). Motu Island also has a white culture hero named Knat. The famous Polynesian race founder, Kon-tiki, is, again, said to be bearded and white, while Lono, Hawaii's culture hero from sunken Hiva, was white skinned and golden haired; fair-skinned people of unmixed blood are still to be met with among the natives of Honolulu. Maui genealogies call this light-colored family *Poe ohana Kekea,* a people with bright, shining eyes, their descendants still living on Oahu, around Waimalo.

One Hawaiian account has the Polynesian family descend from the

Fig. 2.14. Left: A Marquesan chief. Tall, light-skinned Marquesans were encountered at Contact in 1596. Painter Paul Gauguin is buried in the Marquesas. Another Frenchman, Eric De Bisschop, recalls how "French navigators were astounded to discover that in the middle of this vast ocean there was . . . a type of man . . . who seemed to belong to a race somewhat similar to their own. . . . There was an unmistakable white element among the islanders" (1959, 5). Right: A young Maori woman of almost "Western" countenance.

Fig. 2.15. Nineteenth-century sketch of a Hawaiian woman

Menehune people who in turn had Nuu (Noah?) as their ancestor (for more on Nuu as Noah, see chapter 4, p. 139; Nuu is also the Arabic Noah, similar to the Chinese Nu Wah). To Lua Nuu, tenth in descent from the Polynesian Nuu, is ascribed the custom of circumcision. If you ask the Marquesans, they say they got this custom from their ancestor A-pan-a (note the *pan,* probably suggesting a prediluvial origin).

Circumcision

Circumcision as practiced in Malekula and the Marquesas is a relic of the holy tribes, for "the Lord commanded the male Ihins, old and young, to be circumcised . . . for it was the testimony of the Lord to woman that seed of their seed was born to everlasting life" (Oahspe, First Book of the First Lords 1.20). Oahspe further explains that circumcision was given "as a measure of the boundary of my chosen"; that is, to keep them separate from all other people (The Lords' First Book 1.28). Nevertheless, even after their mixing produced the statuesque Ghans, "the Lord sent Ihin priests to circumcise the new race, the Ghan. And he commanded the Ghans to marry among themselves. . . . And the Ihins gave them rites and ceremonies, and taught them how to pray and dance before Jehovih" (The Lords' Third Book 3.22–23). It may interest the reader that Oahspe concludes these histories by stating, "There was a law of circumcision; but I render judgment against that law, for it has fulfilled its time" (Book of Judgment 35.14).

In olden times, Fijians and Tongans overran parts of Melanesia, and from these conquerors today's higher aristocracy of New Caledonia claim descent; circumcision is practiced among them. In addition, "it has always been the custom of the Tahitians to practice circumcision (*tehera'a*) . . . the operation performed by adepts . . . upon lads generally fifteen or sixteen years old, and it was formerly a religious rite accompanied with prayer" (Henry 1928, 188). Elsewhere, circumcision has been practiced among the Jews and Arabs, Inuits and early Algonquins, in Egypt, Arabia, all over Africa south of the Sahara, Australia, and Indonesia.

> *All the legends of Hawaii, the New Hebrides and New*
> *Zealand talk about a white-skinned race with fair hair.*
> PETER KOLOSIMO, *NOT OF THIS WORLD*

The extinct Mu folk of Hawaii's Kauai forest have been described as people with Caucasian features, ancestors, some say, of the present-day Aryans. The Mu were civilized, a numerous and unrivaled race famous for their temples. They had shiny yellow hair, as told in the Hawaiian Song of Creation. In the Tahiti group, the island of Moorea, opposite Papeete, is traditionally called "the island of fairy folk with golden hair." They were, to modern interpretation, "an agile race of dwarfs" (Williams 2001, 147). In parts of Polynesia, there is the story of an indigenous golden- or red-haired race that, having crossed with "some of the conquering immigrants, left the *uru-kehu,* or light-haired families" (Brown 1924, 236). (*Kehu* means "pale.") The Maori term for *European* is *pa-keha.*

Some Oceanic traditions remember the white race as master builders.

1. White giants, recalled in the legends of Kosrae Island in the Carolines, are also remembered by the New Guinea Kai people, who associate their megalithic sites with white giants who lived before the deluge; the legend seems to be corroborated by light-skinned mummies found there.
2. In the New Hebrides are the blondish Takopia people and the Malekulans, who attribute their megalithic-building tradition to five culture-bearing brothers, white men with aquiline noses; these were the Ambat people.
3. On New Caledonia live the pale descendants of an unknown race who left hundreds of tumuli and great pillars on the landscape.

In the Solomon Islands is a tradition of red-haired people who migrated long ago to their island; there is still a sprinkling of light-haired people there. The Gilbert Islanders in Micronesia speak of

Matang, a legendary land of blond people who migrated from their lost homeland after a cataclysm; their pale descendants are occasionally seen in the villages, especially in Malaita. It is well known too that Easter Islanders are largely Europoid in type, with "many indications of a blond race" (Brown 1924, 236): straight nose, thin lips, large eyes, light skin with a tinge of copper. Their culture hero, Rongo, was white.

Far south of Fiji, "in the very heart [of New Zealand], light or golden-coloured hair may occasionally be observed where no mixture with European races could have taken place" (Spence 1933, 76). Their legends, moreover (as well as those of Hawaii and the New Hebrides), talk about a white-skinned race with fair hair who survived the Submergence. New Zealand lore has the long-sunken land Hawaiki peopled over by a Caucasian race with fair skin and hazel eyes. One such group was the Mori-ori;* they were in New Zealand long before the Maori and built great monuments, hill forts, and irrigated terraces.

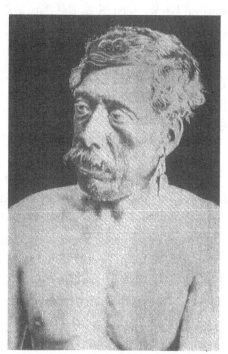

Fig. 2.16. A Moriori descendant in the Chatham Islands; a peaceful people, they said that all fighting had been prohibited in the days of their ancestor Nunuku (Noah?).

---

*This name means "anointed" in Polynesian. *Mori* shows up in Ainu/Jomon sites such as O-mori near Tokyo City and Mori-machi on Hokkaido, noted for its huge stone circle, 110 feet in diameter.

Another name of New Zealand's prehistorical whites, the purest of blonds, is Patupaiarehe, a people said to have come from sunken Hawaiki. Their sacred places on Mount Rangitoto are still guarded. The most ancient Pacific stock, the Patupaiarehe were "more advanced in culture . . . [and] occult knowledge . . . a godlike race . . . peaceful" (Spence 1933, 79–81). Also called Iwi Atua, these folk had red or gold hair and eyes black or blue. And it seems that they were little people, for legend depicts them as fairies, otherworldly beings who taught the Maori the art of making nets. "The general name for these little beings . . . was Patu-pai-arehe, or Turehu. They are also called Nuku-*mai*-tore* in the legend of Tura" (Anderson 1928, 126). They guarded the sacred places and kept the temple of learning—*wharekura*.

Today, when "the occasional albino" is born among the Maori, they are "said to be the children of the Patu-pai-arehe . . . denizens of an unknown land. . . . Such a land was Raro-henga, where dwelt the Turehu, a race of fairies or supernatural beings related to the Patu-pai-arehe" (Anderson 1928, 288). Fairies, I have come to realize, are mythology's naive, even ignorant, way of remembering the very spiritual little people, *Homo sapien pygmaeus*.

White Indians

The Flood hero Manabozho, a.k.a. the Great White One, is, generally speaking, the common ancestor of the North American tribes. You won't find it in your history books, but millions of Caucasians lived and thrived in North America tens of thousands of years ago. For this land called Guatama was settled by the sons of Noah after the destruction of Hawaiki (a.k.a. Whaga, a.k.a. Pan, a.k.a. Mu). The Noachics were the only race among whom were born white-haired children, though many of them were yellow haired. A nineteenth-century homesteader in Jennings County, Indiana, happened to be digging a cellar out of the hillside when he came upon the skeleton of a little child. The hair was

---

*While *Nuku* looks like a Noachic name, *mai* represents a Panic province, explored in chapter 9; *tore* may be a reference to their tallness or their tall monuments.

white. The "hillside" was actually an Indian mound, but the child had obviously "belonged to a fair-complexioned race of people" (Dewhurst 2014, 36).

We have already seen that the Choctaw Indians had a name for these people with long white hair: Kwano-kasha. Out West, the Mandan Indians (discussed shortly in "The Big Canoe") were themselves of this type. Not only did they have the silky hair of the Ihins ("as fine and soft as silk") and their short stature ("below the ordinary size") and finely proportioned bodies ("beautiful symmetry of form")—but there were very many, according to a nineteenth-century report, "of every age, from infancy to manhood . . . with hair of a bright silvery-gray, and in some instances almost perfectly white" (Donnelly 1985, 186).

So too in the Maidu Indian (California) creation myth, are the First People described as "white as snow." Hence the twenty-four-thousand-year-old Caucasian-like skeletons found in the region (Goodman 1983, 98). And what about the controversial Calaveras skull? Hotly contested and rejected as an early anatomically modern human (AMH), the California specimen, found in 1866 at a decent depth of 30 feet, rested in Pliocene gravels; the skull had the appearance of the modern type. In keeping with this find, West Coast Indians like the Yurok said that a white-skinned folk occupied the land before them; today, some of their remains are still kept in California museum collections. Offshore, found on Catalina Island in 1929, though quickly "written out of the history books," were the remains of "a fair-skinned, tow-headed, highly intelligent race." A series of digs revealed "strands of hair [proving] that all these people were blondes" (Dewhurst 2014, 302–3). And they carried forward the name Mu in the Pi-mu and Li-muw tribes; these people, as sixteenth-century explorers documented, were fair of complexion and fine of form and demeanor. The Gha-las-Hat people, said another sixteenth-century report, were also fair complected, living on San Nicholas Island, off the coast of California.

Then, in the seventeenth century, expeditions reported white Eskimos in the Canadian Arctic living on the shores of Davis Straits, many with perfectly blue eyes, red hair, and blond eyebrows. Surely they have something to do with the Alaska mummy people—archaeologists have discovered that seven thousand years ago the Aleutian Islands were inhabited by a Caucasian race that used a decimal system, manufactured white parchment, and left mummies. The Kutenai Indians in that region along the northwest Pacific had beards and light skin; in fact, *Kutenai* was the Blackfoot word for "white men" (and *Ku* in the first syllable is distinctly Panic in origin, to be spotlighted in chapter 4).

One recurrent theme in Amerind lore is that white people were *there,* on the land, *before them.* Shawnee Indians, for example, knew nothing about the origin of the long stone wall and large statue on Mount Carbon in West Viriginia; "when questioned about who built the wall, they replied in the same manner of South American Indians asked similar questions, that a white race had once lived in the valley before them" (Berlitz 1972, 146). Meanwhile, in Nevada, at both Spirit Cave and Lovelock Cave, "the Indians' own native lore speaks of the original inhabitants of the area as being white-skinned," the claim later confirmed by DNA testing of cave mummies in 2006 (Dewhurst 2014, 296, 278). Other tribes like the Nez Percé hold that white men once came among their ancestors and taught their people many things.

Fig. 2.17. Shawnee Indians may carry genes of their white forebears.

Among the Menominee, Dakota, Mandan, Zuni, and Arkansas Indians is the occasional individual with pale skin, auburn hair, and blue eyes.

FURTHER EXAMPLES OF WHITES IN ANCIENT NORTH AMERICA

Who	Where	Details
Brown Valley Man	Minnesota	12,000-year-old Caucasoid male found in grave
Pelican Rapids Woman	Minnesota	8,000-year-old skeleton with Caucasoid features
Flagstaff Skull	Arizona (near Hopi rez)	60,000-year-old Cro-Magnon type
Ioskeha*	Iroquois territory	culture-bringer of the Iroquois, a White One
"Our white ancestors"	Algonquin territory	according to the Abenaki Indians
Lenni Lenape Indians	Pennsylvania & Delaware	tall and white
Cave burials	Cairo, Tennessee	fine, auburn hair, blue eyes, white skin
Nunnehi	Cherokee territory	legendary little people with pale white skin; William Bartram found some Cherokee females "as fair and blooming as European women."
Acoma Indians	Southeast	said their ancestors were white
bog mummies	Florida	red haired, up to 14,000 years old

*Most interesting that the *keha* in this Amerind name Ios-keha corresponds to the Polynesian word *keha*, meaning "pale."

The Big Canoe

Ignatius Donnelly described the Mandan Indians of the Upper Missouri as "a strange people and half white . . . with the most pleasing symmetry and proportion of feature, with hazel, gray, and blue eyes" (1985, 186). Not long before smallpox and other disasters decimated them, the artist

Fig. 2.18. Benjamin West's painting of William Penn's treaty with the Lenni Lenape Indians (top); the seated warrior is actually the lightest-colored person in the scene. Early sketches of New Mexico Pueblo Indians (bottom).

George Catlin* stayed with the Mandans and learned that "their first ancestor was a son of the *West,* who preserved them at the flood" (Brinton 1976, 200; emphasis added). Indeed, the flood legend was strong among the Mandan, who virtually organized their ritual life around it. An actual image of the ark was preserved from generation to generation. Called the Big Canoe, this large structure at the very center of the village stood as an object of veneration, central to the annual religious ceremony in which one man impersonated Nu-mohk-muck-a-nah (the First and Only Man). Painted with *white* clay so as to resemble this ancestor, he enters the medicine lodge and goes through some mysterious ceremony—in the course of which he narrates the sad catastrophe of the land inundated with water.

The Sioux legend calls that Lone Survivor Nu-Hohk-A-Nah; he is dressed in a white wolf fur in their ritual enactment. Similarly among the Navaho, an actor wears a white-faced mask to impersonate "Grandfather," he who survived a flood in the western sea, the birthplace of First Man and First Woman. Their neighbors, the Hopi Indians, preserve a tradition of Emergence from the previous world, a sunken motherland. In commemoration of their deliverance, the ritual entails retelling the drama of escaping from their flooded homeland on stepping-stones (i.e., islands). Still held at Oraibi, Arizona, the rite recalls the rising water, the frightened people, and the miracle of their escape.

If skeptics argue that the lost motherland of man is nothing more than woo-woo occultism, they will also have to discount the many tribal rites that commemorate it, like the Hawaiian Kumulip Chant, recalling the lost lands. It has been said that the pyramids in Shansi, China, were built to commemorate the mountains that saved humanity after the Flood (Charroux 1972, 67). And not just in China. Churchward calls the Xochicalca pyramid (in Monte Alban, Mexico) "a commemorative monument to Mu" (Churchward 1931a, 241). In fact, on Pan itself, the

---

*It was in one of Catlin's wonderful paintings that John Lang discovered that a "singular custom that obtains equally among Polynesians and Indo-Americans is their mode of disposing of the dead." In that painting of a Mandan village, "the cemetery struck me exceedingly . . . for it was exactly similar to what I had seen in the village of Kororadika in New Zealand—a series of trestles or stages on which the bodies of the dead, wrapped up in the skins of wild beasts, had been left to putrefy in the open air" (1877, 178–79).

Eimeo Islanders say that when the floodwaters subsided, their ancestors erected a marae as a thank-offering to their god. Likewise in Japan,
the Ama people conduct an annual ceremony, right on the beach, in
remembrance of Nirai-Kanai (their lost island kingdom) and the souls
who perished there. All of which resonates with the Greek festival called
Hydrophoria, celebrated in memory of those who perished in the Flood.
The Lapps also make prayerful offerings, based on the terrible sky-fall
recalled in the *Kalevala*.

Now Churchward further informs us that

> the aborigines of Yucatán, Petan, and other countries of Central
> America . . . are wont, at the beginning of November, to hang . . .
> cakes made of the best corn . . . for the souls of the departed. . . .
> [Similar festivals are] held at or near the beginning of November
> by the Peruvians, the Hindus, the Pacific Islanders, the people of
> the Tonga Islands, the Australians, the ancient Persians, the ancient
> Egyptians, the northern nations of Europe . . . the Japanese . . .
> and the ancient Romans. How was this uniformity in the time of
> observance preserved? Between the columns in the Temple of
> Sacred Mysteries at Uxmal* there was a grand altar . . . [where] they
> were wont to make offerings to their Manes [ancestors]. . . . The
> sacred rites and ceremonies practiced at the temple came from the
> Motherland. . . . The Egyptians, like the Quiche Mayas, symbolized
> the destruction [of Mu] in their religious ceremonies. The initiate
> . . . symbolically passed through the scene of the destruction of his
> Motherland . . . to keep her in memory. (2011, 289–90, 307)

Whites in Central and South America

And as Churchward further asserts, correctly I think, "the Empire of
Mayax was made up of . . . peoples coming from the Motherland. . . .
All the kings and queens of Mayax during the twelve dynasties were of

---

*Old chronicles tell us that Uxmal's House of Dwarfs was erected in honor of their white
god.

the white race . . . with flaxen hair. . . . Temple inscriptions in Yucatán say they came there from lands that lay to the west of America" (1931b, 81, 204, 233).

The Aztecs seem to be named after these "white men who came from the sea" (as described in the Popol Vuh): Iztac, meaning "white." Oral tradition of the Aztecs (Nahuas) says that they arose from darkness by virtue of a "white god" (read: fair-skinned mentor, deified ancestor). Carved figures of Caucasian men turn up all over the Middle Kingdom at ruins like Chichén Itzá and La Venta. A thirteen-thousand-year-old exemplar of this white race (the skeleton of a female) came to light during a building excavation in Mexico City. But even today, "White Indians" abide in small villages among the forests of Guatemala and Honduras. In chapter 1 we met with a few of the surprisingly fair-skinned natives of Panama, especially the Scandinavian-like Chukunaque. Leaving Panama, and continuing south, the phenomenon persists, all the way down to Chile.

SOUTH AMERICAN NATIVE WHITES

Who/What	Where	Details
Arawaks	Caribbean and beyond	men of light color, resembling Polynesians
Akurias	Suriname, British Guiana	not much darker than Caucasians
Statues	Colombia	European appearance
The White One	Colombia	bearded figure who represents the first civilizer
Los Paria (White Indians)	Venezuela	villagers in forest near Rio Apure
Yuracaras	eastern Cordillera	very pale-colored people
"Laron" people	Loja, Ecuador	small and white people
Nazca mummies	Peru	blond and reddish hair, with fine features
Mochica (Chimu) graves	Peru	some skeletons of white race
The ruling Incas	Peru	fair-skinned, hair "blond as straw"

SOUTH AMERICAN NATIVE WHITES (*cont.*)

Who/What	Where	Details
Chachapoya	Peru	white, with blue eyes, builders of cities
Uros Indians	Lake Titicaca	white and bearded, exterminated by the Colloas
Tupis	Brazil	named after the first man Tupa, flood survivor, of fair complexion
Tapuyas	Brazil	"fair as the English," with delicate features
White Indians	Brazil	around the Xingu River
Tahuamanu	Brazil	pure whites, red hair, blue eyes
Lower Assurinis	Brazil	white skinned, red bearded
Pygmies and White Indians	along the Upper Orinoco bordering Brazil and Venezuela	
Chilotes	Chiloe Island, Chile	red-cheeked little people, light skin, black hair
Punta Arenas and Chono people	Chile	some blonds
Mapuches	Chile	pale and bearded

Old World Whites

Even though the Ainu are in the extreme Far East (and have always been there), they are made to represent an "ancient migration" from Europe—simply because of their Caucasian appearance. Oh, how the experts love to invent migrations that suit the official version of history. The same strategy was imposed on the red-haired mummies found in western China: they "must have" been migrants from Europe. But most of Europe, in the throes of barbarism ten thousand years ago,* did not even *have* white people when the Ainu spread through Japan or when the now-extinct Tocharians entered China twenty-four thousand years ago. Some kind of Paleo-Caucasoids, rather like the Ainu, also inhabited *northern* China at ChouKouTien at that time; a non-Mongoloid people of the modern type.

---

*See story of Uropa in chapter 7.

While paleontologists seem content enough to chalk this up to a "mystery" (and leave it at that, though *mystify* would be a more apt word), it is not really surprising to find archaic whites—Noah's children—settling any part of the world twenty-four thousand years ago.

Like all the early Ihins, the sons of Noah called Jaffeth—who, escaping Pan, fled to China—were white and yellow: "The original inhabitants of the region [China], far from being Mongoloid, were actually Caucasian" (Chouinard 2012, 156). Neither are the Sichuanese Han-Dropa people of a Mongoloid caste, but they have blue eyes like the ancient Wusuns of China or the pale mountain people called Miao-Tse or the Uighur of western China. I find it disingenuous when scholars declare that today's blue-eyed Uighurs of Xinjiang have nothing to do with the ancient Caucasians who inhabited that region, or nothing to do with Churchward's Uighur Empire of some eighteen thousand years ago, the earliest colony of Mu.

China's Red-Haired Mummies

There are hundreds of blond- and red-haired mummies in China with Europoid features. They of course bring to mind their congeners in other parts of the world: red-haired mummies at Nazca, Peru, and others in the Canary Islands, Egypt, Kentucky, Florida, New Zealand, and Russia—cousins all. Fair-skinned, carrot-topped skeletons in western China have been known since the 1930s, though not announced to the Western world until 1994 (for political reasons). These are naturally mummified corpses in the Takla Makan Desert of the Tarim Basin, between Tibet and Mongolia (recall the Cherchen Man and the long-haired Loulan Beauty). Here, Ying-pan Man (note the *pan*) was blond and bearded. These well-dressed people had light eyes, substantial noses, ginger beards, "European" DNA, and long hair (some blond, some dark). They were fairly tall with Western-shaped faces, the females quite pretty. Dating them is tricky: 4000 BP? 6000 BP? Some even say 10,000 BP. Similar light-haired mummies were found in the Gobi and other parts of Mongolia (the Gobi is northeast of the Tarim Basin).

On the Asian mainland, "from the end of the flood onwards, we begin to see settlements all along the . . . coast of China" (Oppenheimer 1998, 477). Chinese legend says that the Gobi Desert was once a great sea, and there was an island in this sea inhabited "by white men with blue eyes and fair hair . . . [originally] inhabitants of Mu . . . who imparted civilization" (Kolosimo 1975, 57). It is from this region that "the Uighur people arrived after the collapse of [their] Kingdom in . . . Mongolia" (Coppens 2012, 240). The region—including parts of the Himalayas—still has tribal groups with white-rosy skin and gray-blue eyes.

It is also a fact that members of Genghis Khan's family had reddish hair and blue eyes (Lissner 1962, 255). As I see it, Gobi, Uighur, Tocharian, Tarim, and so forth all carry expressions of the same non-Mongolian root stock whose settlement of Asia will be scrutinized in chapter 5 under "Jaffeth," son of Noah, p. 191.

Moonlike and Zarco

South of China in Nepal the Newars are an anciently civilized people with light yellow skin and delicate features. The fair Lepchas of Sikkim too are noted for the beauty of their women, while white populations in eastern Tibet were seen and described by G. F. Wright early in the twentieth century. In Pakistan the Kalash tribe has some blonds, as do India's Kashmir people. Here in India, the *Pan*davas are the five heroes and brothers of the Mahabharata, their name presumably based on Sanskrit *pan*du, "white, yellow-white, pale." They of the moonlike complexion were sovereigns of India's divine dynasties.

Here in Mother India we find the qualities of holiness, whiteness, and deepest antiquity combined in the person of Sarasvati, consort of Brahma himself and goddess of writing, knowledge, and the arts—in short, the personification of higher mind, higher self. In Sarasvati we perceive the embodiment of that early race of fair-skinned teachers, the sacred and learned tribes of yore. Famed for her transcendent nature, Sarasvati is, iconographically, a beautiful woman with snow-white skin. Her book in hand represents her love of learning.

West of India, many groups of Central Asia, particularly between the

Fig. 2.19. The Lady of Elche. This "Spanish Mona Lisa," a 21-inch-high, fourth-century BCE limestone bust of a priestess, is said to resemble the Mexican rain goddess, Chalchihuitlicue. The face always struck me as classic Ihin.

Black (Pontos) and Caspian Seas, are of light complexion with varying color of eyes and hair: some natural blonds are found in Kazakstan, as well as among Afghanistan's Pashtun and Nuristani (*Nur* means "light") in the northeastern mountains, where one in three are light haired. Many Tajiks and Sarts in the same general region are light eyed, like the green-eyed Shikak tribe of Kurdish Iran; indeed, the ancient Iranians thought that "the First Man was white and brilliant" (Heinberg 1989, 68). The same *Sar* (in *Sar*asvati and *Sar*ts) recurs in *Sar*acen, the talented builders of Arabia, artificers who came to Spain bringing their "light-eyed" Zarco strain; such people in the North African Rif are called zar-kan.

*Sar*ku is also a Hittite divinity (pronounced almost the same as Spanish *zarco*, which means "light eyed"). There must have once been a more or less continuous chain of white tribes throughout northern Asia. This great family of pale-skinned civilizers, though lost in the fog of prehistory, is tens of thousands of years older than those latecomers history calls Aryans. In Southeast Asia we find a remnant in the "white Caucasian race . . . still to be found in the Khmers of Cambodia" (Fornander 1969, 3:33).

And when we find them in North Africa, they are ancestors of the Egyptians, the small and fair Badarians, or the ancient people of Libya called the Garamantes, who are painted on walls and cliffs as fair-skinned, blond charioteers living in the Sahara. Although numerous writers would have us believe that the lost civilization of white founders and their high arts—especially of pyramidal Egypt—originated in a land called Atlantis, I have come to view such reckoning as popular history, even pseudohistory. So let us step into that controversial zone known as Atlantology.

SINKING ATLANTIS—
ONCE AND FOR ALL!

For quite some time now, certain writers have been feeding us resemblances between Mexican and Egyptian pyramids as "important confirmation of the Atlantean theory" (Kolosimo 1975, 174). The geographical logic is that "Atlanteans emigrated eastward to the Nile Valley or westward to America, building colonies" (Drake 1968, 113). Hence, the lost continent of Atlantis is made the glorious source of both Mayan and Egyptian civilization. But there is more than one way to skin a cat.

Egyptians in the Americas?

It is true that, of all the many cross-cultural comparisons ever noted by keen observers, none hold a candle to the remarkable analogies between Egyptian and Guataman civilization. Queen Moo of the Mayan Can Dynasty, according to one interpretation of the "Troano Manuscript," visited the Nile colony in Egypt sixteen thousand years ago. Or was it the other way around? After all, it is assumed that Egypt was once a naval power, probably at least five thousand years ago (Perry 1923, 458–59). And further, ancient strains of American corn have been found in Egypt.

"My grandmother was fond of telling us the Tarascan [Mexico]

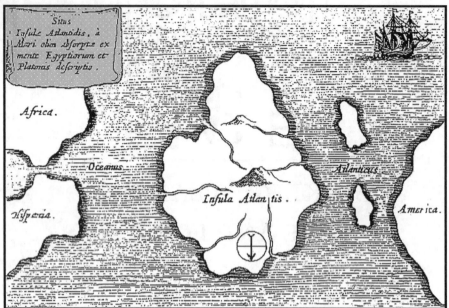

Fig. 3.1. Father Athanasius Kircher's 1644 map of Atlantis based on a literal reading of Plato's writing. It was a mistake from the start to read too much into Plato's clever allegory.

story of an ancient queen from a faraway land who sailed the great sea. . . . She landed in the land of the Tarascan Indians and married the great king Itzamna" (Caunitz 1993). Yet Itzamna himself, the fair-skinned Mexican god of medicine and writing, is associated with lands to the east of America—Egypt? His prominent nose and beard are certainly not typical of Mexico. A related point of interest was Mexico's sixteen-thousand-year-old mausoleum frescoes depicting the life of a Mayan prince: such work is echoed in the burial chambers of Egyptian kings. And speaking of mausoleums, mummy shrouds in Egypt and Peru are of almost identical fabrics.

Back to Mexico—one might also wonder if the Temple of Palenque has anything to do with the Egyptian Temple of Paaleq. The similarity was underscored when Palenque was found to enclose a *tomb* (as in Egypt). In 1950 a grave was indeed found inside the Temple of Inscriptions, the first Central American pyramid found to serve as a royal tomb. There was also a facsimile of the Egyptian gold death mask* used by the chiefs at Palenque. Also, Egypt's and Mexico's God of Joy icons are identical, while some even said the thirteen letters of the Mayan alphabet correspond to Egyptian hieroglyphs. Epigraphers have pointed out that Mayan script was phonetic and syllabic, just like Egyptian writing. Egyptians and Olmecs, moreover, used comparable symbols, such as the ankh, feline heads, and ritual axes; similarly, the Olmecs wove garments from a strain of cotton of Egyptian type.

Long ago people in Florida *and* Egypt embalmed the dead and decorated their graves with pearls. Artifacts recovered from North America's mounds, including the scarab tablet taken from an Ohio mound, have been compared to similar ones in Egypt. Historians have also wondered why the rituals of the Ojibway Midewiwin Society are so similar to the Egyptian Book of the Dead. The comparisons seem endless: Egyptian inscriptions in New Mexico, and Egyptian armbands in Arizona; Mi'kmaq and Aztec ideograms and headdresses that resemble those of Egypt; and headdresses worn in ancient Egypt that can also be seen in Brazil. "Many early Egyptians wore on their heads the same feathers that you still see today on the Brazilian Indians" (Homet 1963, 68), comparable also to those seen around North America's Great Lakes—where they ventured for Michigan's copper mines (see pp. 247–48).

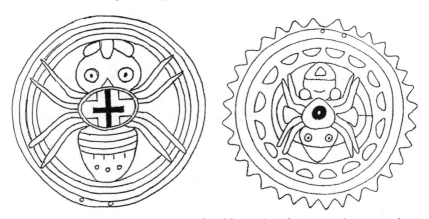

Fig. 3.2. North American scarab tablets taken from an Ohio mound and tablets from Egypt are strikingly similar.

---

*The death mask and sarcophagus found in an Illinois cave also look like Egyptian work.

Fig. 3.3. Teotihuacan

Much has been said about the resemblance of Mesoamerican and Egyptian pyramids. The base of Mexico's Teotihuacan Pyramid to the Sun measures 740 by 725 feet, as does that of Egypt's Cheops. As Ignatius Donnelly points out, both Teotihuacan and Cheops have galleries many feet above the base that terminate in a well or chamber. Teotihuacan further resembles Egyptian pyramids in construction of the steps, dedication to the sun, a small mound adjoined to one face, analogous interiors, and sides facing the cardinal points. Also, the huge obelisk at Egypt's Temple at Heliopolis has architectural features in common with Teotihuacan, which has also been compared to Egypt's Karnak.

In Egypt the crocodile was anciently a sacred symbol, called s-b-k; in Nahuatl (Aztecan) it is similar: cipak-tli. There was also a sacred crocodile in Cocle, Panama, and Brazil. In fact, crocodile gods are seen everywhere from Costa Rica to southern Peru. Crocodiles were also important in Southeast Asia at Timor and carved as well on New Zealand's pre-Maori lintels.

Fig. 3.4. Cocle crocodile god

Speaking of animal gods, Egypt's Horus is shown with a hawk on his head, just like the Mexican "firebird." In addition, Egypt and Mexico shared similar methods of cataract surgery, removal of ulcers, as well as skills in dentistry. Both the Egyptian and Mexican years begin on February 26. The parallels extend to metallurgy, religious beliefs, and art motifs: their murals and their vases show faces "with a ruthless verisimilitude" (Drake 1968, 113). It was actually the opinion of archaeologist Augustus Le Plongeon that *Muvians* were the common ancestors of both the Egyptians and the Maya. For this, we do not need Atlantis.

These parallels are particularly striking in the Andes. Like the Egyptians, the ancient rulers of Peru and Colombia took their own sister as wife. Peruvian stonework is another instant reminder of Egyptian work: Sacsahuaman (near Cuzco) evokes Egypt's Khufu; Moche Valley temple architecture evokes that of Egypt; Tiahuanaco (Bolivia) evokes Medinet Habu; and Kalasasaya (at Tiahuanco) evokes Abydos's Temple of Seti. The sarcophagus of Peru's Prince Capac, perhaps seven thousand years old, "was an example of most beautiful Egyptian execution" (Homet 1963, 169). Peruvians and Egyptians used the same techniques to mummify their dead. The death barge in Egypt and the Amazon are identical in appearance. Wilkins matches Brazilian pictograms with Egyptian ones. And think of the word *Andes* itself: *andi* in Egyptian meant "high ground." To top it off, there was a racial resemblance between the ancient Egyptians and the inhabitants of Tiahuanaco.

Catnip and Catchall

Keenly aware of all these marvelous correspondences across the pond, the father of modern Atlantology, Ignatius Donnelly, proposed a common origin for the civilizations of Egypt and the Americas: Atlantis! Nevertheless, he makes this double-edged statement: "In Yucatan the traditions all point to an eastern and foreign* origin for the race . . . [Yet] it was also believed that part of the population came into the country from the west. . . . The smaller portion [came] . . . from the east and *the greater portion . . . from the west*" (1985, 167; author's italics). West is the Pacific.

The mystic protohistorian in our own day and time (Donnelly lived in the nineteenth century) tends to have two speeds: Atlantis and ETs (UFOs). Talk about legends. Urban legends and lost continents. But let's share a sober moment with that erudite polymath L. Sprague De Camp, who, dauntless amid the mystique, was not afraid to diagnose "Atlantism [as] a form of escapism that lets people play with eras and continents as a child plays with blocks." De Camp goes on to remark, incisively, that "there is no mention by any writer before Plato of any sunken island in the Atlantic." Nor does De Camp find any mention of Atlantis in "the surviving records of Egypt, Phoenicia, Babylonia, or Sumeria." Plato's little story, argues De Camp, was a fine-tuned play on Athenian politics: "Classical Alexandria was a hotbed of the vice of allegorization. . . . Interest in Atlantis," he goes on to comment, "revived with the discovery of the Americas, and since then has grown to the proportions of a neurosis" (1975, 3, 12, 30).

Indeed, one opinion poll dared to conclude that "the people in the United States would rank the discovery of Atlantis as a greater news story than the Second Coming of Christ" (Steiger 1974, 54). Catnip to writers and publishers alike, Atlantis has managed to "become a catchall for the idea of a lost legacy from the very distant past" (Robert Schoch, quoted in Chouinard 2012). Atlantis, the wannabe lost continent, is then the proverbial escape hatch—and the New Orthodoxy. Don't

---

*Chapter 6 takes up those people from the east.

know the origin of something? Solution: it came from Atlantis. No one can prove it. No one can disprove it. But it sure comes in handy. "There is so much universality of culture . . . around the world that we feel the Atlantean influence was extremely far-reaching" (J. M. Valentine, quoted in Steiger 1974, 61). "My own hunch," reveals another true believer, "is that we are looking at Atlantean when we look at many of the undeciphered ancient languages" (Asher 1974, 30).

European esotericists, especially aggressive Celtophiles, like Atlantis a great deal, because it puts their own Western culture at center stage. "The Atlantic Ocean and the British Isles [are] the home base from which the Phoenicians, the Celts, and others went forth to show the world how to sail ships, to produce food, to make beer, to mine minerals, to erect pyramids. . . . The Atlanteans colonized the world" (Trench 1974, 20). Beer? Alright, have another! Inebriated with the same Eurocentric bias, even the Nazis loved Atlantis, as it could be made to fit "the Nordic-Aryan myth" (Kreisberg 2012, 83–84). Our Western lands, according to a leading Celtocentric writer, "have inherited the civilization of Atlantis . . . [which] was the true and original source of the science and the arts, the gods and the traditions of the white races, whose world was born in the West" (Charroux 1972, 64). Atlantology thus places the very cradle of civilization right in the heart of the Anglo-American sphere—all great things supposedly stemmed from Atlantis, the source of all the world's advanced cultures, agriculture, metallurgy, writing, and mathematics. But as prehistorian-cartographer Charles Hapgood so correctly pointed out, "Some 20,000 or more years ago, while Paleolithic peoples held out in Europe, more advanced cultures existed elsewhere on the earth" (1996, 194). That elsewhere, for the most part, was in the Far East.

Eastern, Not Western, Beginnings

Many of the similarities between the Old World and New World that theorists seize to prove Atlantis as the connecting link could just as well result from the overlooked *worldwide* maritime culture of the Neolithic and beyond. Such transatlantic correspondences may well have arisen from the oceangoing culture of the prehistorical era. "Donnelly based his conviction of a common source in Atlantis 'primarily on his belief that ancient man was incapable of crossing long stretches of open ocean by sailing ship. . . . Such voyages were made at far earlier dates than has been generally accepted'" (Cohane 1969, 27).

> *I believe the Cretans to be Atlantean survivors.*
> MAXINE ASHER, *DISCOVERING ATLANTIS*

Crete is often cited as an offshoot or colony of Atlantis—which is nonsense—one must look eastward not westward for her antecedents; Crete, with both Arabic and Turkic roots, was settled some eight thousand years ago by people with *Anatolian* genes (according to DNA research), having come across from Turkey (Asia Minor) easily on stepping-stone islands in the Aegean. The thesis of a Western (i.e., Atlantean) "homeland" blithely and rebelliously ignores all evidence of civilization streaming from the East. Protohistory as a whole points to oriental origins.* China and Japan are the oldest of cultures.

> *When the Motherland [Mu, Pan] started out to people*
> *the earth . . . [it was] eastern Asia . . . where she planted*
> *her first colonies. . . . We may look for the earliest records*
> *of man not in Europe, Egypt, or Babylonia. They were*
> *the tail-enders.*
> JAMES CHURCHWARD, *THE CHILDREN OF MU*

Churchward elsewhere calls these tail-enders "the dying embers." The children of Mu produced a great civilization "tens of thousands of years before those pesky, old monkey men of Europe scattered their bones around very promiscuously to baffle and mystify future scientists" (Churchward 1931a, 82). Another keen prehistorian—athough himself an Atlantist—the Scots mythologist Lewis Spence is on record as admitting that

---

*I spent some time, in the last chapter of *The Mysterious Origin of Hybrid Man* making this point (against the current Afrocentrist romance).

traditions . . . tell of the transmission of the ancient Atlantean wisdom to initiates in both Europe and America. But to speak frankly,
I have always been suspicious regarding these, because . . . the tradition did not square with archaeological fact. [Moreover, despite]
many hundreds or even thousands of automatic writings relating to
Atlantis . . . none of these agrees with the other. (Spence 1933, 204)

The comment by Spence betrays the sorry fact that much of
twentieth-century Atlantology was jump-started by pseudoprophecy
that exploited and misused the pure devices of Spiritualism. Messages
conveyed by untrustworthy "entities" through automatic writing is
one case; supposed "past lives" lived on Atlantis is another. "Perhaps,"
offers Maxine Asher, "the single most startling psychic proof for the
existence of the Atlantean culture complex is the astounding 'memory'
of many people around the world who recall one or more prior lives
on Atlantis." Asher further lays on the psychic twaddle by confiding
that "the records of Atlantis may already be known to certain select
groups and are buried in secret archives . . . off limits to almost all
historians." And if substantial evidence for Atlantis is not forthcom-
ing, there is a reason: "The Atlanteans apparently will not allow us to
validate the remains of their island continent until we have attained a
mind set which can fully understand and interpret their deeply spiritual culture" (Asher 1974, 23, 28, 70–71). And if you believe that, you
can believe anything.

My guess is that if there *were* great islands or lands in the
Atlantic, it was millions of years ago, before man ever walked the
Earth or devised outlandish theories of his past. De Camp reasons
that the wannabe homeland in the Atlantic "would have left remains
in the form of shoals, which it has not done . . . [it] may have existed
10,000,000 years ago . . . long before civilization arose. . . . A land-
bridge probably did exist once upon a time . . . sixty or more million
years ago" (1975, 171).

Many Atlantists, furthermore, are convinced that Atlantis is the
sunken continent that is behind the story of Noah and the Flood! The
Great Deluge. To give a single example: "About 12,000 years ago a

catastrophe occurred . . . in the island continent in the Atlantic Ocean . . . that destroyed the cultural center . . . a memory kept alive in all races by legends of the Great Flood" (Berlitz 1984, 162). Otherwise put, "Noah was a survivor from Atlantis . . . the Ancients venerated Noah as an Atlantean" (Drake 1974, 140). However, be it noted that when Europeans used the word *Atlantean* they were, as a rule, not talking about a lost continent, but about the distinctive races of coastal western Europe and Northwest Africa. For instance, it was said that "the Bretons . . . both in morale and physique present the type of a southern race—of the Atlanteans. By Atlanteans [one] refers to the inhabitants of the Barbary States . . ." (Donnelly 1985, 389).

Was Atlantis Wiped Out by a Catastrophe?

Lots of clever theories have come and gone to explain the ruination of a fatherland that *never was;* these, we realize, are all "could haves": Venus *could have* brought on "the cataclysm that destroyed Atlantis" (Charroux 1974, 27). Or some other planet *could have* entered Earth's field, disturbing its axial shift and submerging Atlantis (Von Ward 2011, 123–24). Some speculate that the fabled continent—by blocking the warm Gulf Stream—*could have* been the cause of the last ice age in Europe and America; then, when it sank, it ended that ice age! Yet others spin this around, saying it was *melting ice* that drowned Atlantis. Up until twelve thousand years ago sea levels had supposedly been lower; then, with the world coming out of the alleged ice age,* the sea levels rose, "so for a civilization to be swallowed up by the ocean . . . is not only possible, but we ourselves have seen this occurred [*sic*] to a number of places" (Coppens 2012, 162). Another approach (favored by "disastrophiles") argues that the Earth's previous moon (assuming the existence of a pre-lunar satellite) could have split up and fallen, crashing into the ocean and submerging its lands. One more "could have" is tidal

---

*See chapter 3 of *Delusions in Science and Spirituality,* where I challenge the veracity of ice age theory itself.

waves: "Atlantis was submerged by great tidal waves" (Scott-Elliot 2000, 140). Take your pick.

When Did All This Happen?

At one end of the wildly conjectural spectrum are Atlantean dates in the millions of years: Edgar Cayce's readings assumed a highly civilized Atlantis ten million years ago. A bit more conservative is Madame Blavatsky's date of 850,000 years ago, though French writer/explorer/Celtophile Robert Charroux thinks the Ica Stones in Peru (see fig. 3.12b, p. 130) depict Atlantis "hundreds of millions of years ago" (Charroux 1974, 29). Meanwhile, Frank Joseph thinks "the profound antiquity of Atlantis" should be shelved at 350,000 years ago. Where is a consensus in all this? Joseph actually goes on to quote the contradictory idea that "the Atlantic tidal waves enveloped the continent of Atland and smashed into the Mediterranean" in the much more recent year 2193 BCE (Joseph 2013, 2), which date is not too different from Velikovsky's, a date based on Plato's account. "The most probable date of the sinking of Atlantis would be in the middle of the second millennium" (Velikovsky 1965, 147). Still others inform us that Atlantis sank in the seventh century BCE. But most say it is the very same event as the Great Flood itself and happened some 11,000 or 12,000 years ago.

Ignatius Donnelly cited the Dolphin Ridge as the key relic of Atlantis, even though most of that mid-Atlantic ridge is under two or three miles of water—"and there is no known way to get a large island down to that depth in anything like the 10,000 years required" (De Camp 1975, 180); besides, after many years of exploring the ridge, they have found no trace of sunken cities. And Donnelly's assumption that Atlantis was located mid-ocean is contradicted by more modern oceanographic observations of the seabed, which indicate no evidence at all of such a cataclysm or such a continent.

According to the late Phillip Coppens:

of course, it was 12,000 years ago that Atlantis sank. . . . Yet all the information we've gleaned so far suggests that it ended sometime

around 1200 BC. . . . Some argue . . . that Atlantis was actually
a memory of . . . the Thera eruption that signaled the end for the
Minoan civilization on Crete in c. 1450 BC. (2012, 194, 162)

And so it goes, round and round, as far from any agreement (or
even coherence) on the demise of dear old Atlantis as we were a hundred years ago.

Exactly Where Was Atlantis, Anyway?

That underwater ridge in the Atlantic Ocean "has been gradually built
up from the ocean floor . . . [and] is not the remains of a former continent, but evidence of fissures in the earth" (John Algeo, in Scott-Elliot
2000, xii). Another prefatory comment (this one in Chouinard 2012, x)
by Robert Schoch reminds us that generations of writers have "placed
Atlantis in virtually every imaginable location on earth, from one pole
to the other, on every continent, and in every sea and ocean." Whew.
Patrick Chouinard himself rides (at least) two horses in suggesting that
"there may in fact be more than one Atlantis [huh?] whether it be near
Tartessos, Helike; or Palvoperti in Greece; Dwarka, off the coast of
India; or the sunken pyramids at Rock Lake, Wisconsin" (Chouinard
2012, 43). Honestly, does that make any sense? How far are we willing
to stretch logic just to keep the idea of Atlantis alive?

I do wonder how a large or even medium-size "continent"* could
be located in the various proposed sites of Atlantis, including the
following:

the city of Sens, France, or perhaps Cyprus (Coppens 2012, 184, 180)
the isle of Crete (Dewhurst 2014, 9)
the Persian Gulf (Chouinard 2012, 192)
the British Isles (Trench 1974, 33)
Africa's Gold Coast (Leo Frobenius)
Mongolia (according to eighteenth-century astronomer J. S. Bailly)

---

*Even Plato called it "the *island* of Atlantis," not a continent.

A quick survey reveals that the lost continent of Atlantis has also been "found" in Ceylon, the Caucasus, Malta, Tunisia, Nigeria, Palestine, Morocco, Russia, the South Pacific(!), Netherlands, Indonesia, South Africa, Greenland, Iraq, Sweden, and so forth, as culled by De Camp, who, by the way, aptly comments on "the patriotic desire of some Atlantis-hunters . . . to prove their own land the source of all civilization" (1975, 193, 326–31).

So . . . was Atlantis a city? An island? A continent? It all depends on which author you are reading or which "breakthrough" is shouted the loudest. There is no telling what the Atlantis oracle will come up with next—like, "Atlantis was never a stationary landmass at all but rather a massive UFO or floating city!" (Kreisberg 2012, 137–38). Now let us come down to Earth for a moment.

> The existence of these [ancient] maps is further evidence
> for . . . a worldwide civilization. This would explain
> why researchers seek in vain for an isolated location
> of the original "Atlantis" or mother culture. . . . Those
> who seek a marvelous "Atlantis" in any one place are
> doomed to disappointment. The whole world was highly
> civilized at a certain period in the remote past. . . .
> The fact that different accounts from all points of the
> compass have led people to believe that Atlantis existed
> in the Mediterranean, the Atlantic, Spain, Greenland
> or Iceland, America or Tibet . . . merely points to a
> civilization that was worldwide [and] . . . not limited to
> one mysterious island or continent.
> RICHARD E. MOONEY, GODS OF AIR AND DARKNESS

Sure, man-made structures have been found in the shallow depths of the North Sea as well as off Helgoland, France, and any number of other places; coastal regions are likely to show some subsidence. None of this, however, indicates a continent out there in the Atlantic. Just because there are subsided lands off Ireland or the Mediterranean or anywhere else does not imply a continent thereof. Nevertheless, I would bet that lost islands along the eastern coast of America (and western coast of Europe) have contributed to the Atlantis myth.

When Europeans "discovered" America in the fifteenth century, some thought that the riddle of Plato's Atlantis was finally solved. "Plato must have heard of real transatlantic continents and based his romance upon it" (De Camp 1975, 30). Atlantis was simply America: those Happy Isles, the Islands of the Blessed. Diodorus had told of a vast land in the ocean many days to the west, with mountains, beautiful plains, and great rivers—America. As far as Cyrus Gordon, professor of ancient languages and cultures, was concerned, "it is futile to dwell on the lost island of Atlantis . . . and then to forget his [Plato's] plain reference to the continent that seals off the Atlantic Ocean on the West. This continent . . . can only be America" (Gordon 1973, 108).

> They had communication with America. The Atlantic
> Island must mean America, and its disappearance in the
> ocean must mean the discontinuance of communication
> with it.
>
> JOHN D. BALDWIN, PRE-HISTORIC NATIONS

In Plato's time (ca. 400 BCE) the Greek historian Theopompus wrote of an enormous continent named Meropis, with great and splendid cities, located far beyond the Pillars of Hercules, on the farther shore of the ocean. The name Meropis gives us pause. The hero of the deluge, in parts of Greece, was named Merops, while Merope was the daughter of Atlas, in their mythology. The actual land of the Meropes was believed to be west of Ireland; Theopompus called it a great continent *beyond* the Atlantic. Moreover, Plutarch's Kingdom of Meropa (mentioned in his *On Lunar Spots*) was South America; we can trace the origin of that name to the Peruvian Quechua language. Twentieth-century South America enthusiasts include the English explorer Harold T. Wilkins, who thought he found Atlantis in "the unknown hinterland of the Andean cordilleras . . . [and] in the splendid and mysterious ruins of Brazil" (Wilkins 2000, 10–11).

More recently, the late archaeologist-epigrapher David Allen Deal, studying plate tectonics and undersea structures, concluded that no continent *ever* existed in the Atlantic. He simply states, "The large island continent was the Americas. . . . The whole fanciful story of lost Atlantis was the invention of the Phoenicians in order to keep others away from their private continent Aztlan* . . . even driving them to sacrifice any vessel which was being followed" (1984, 59).

Just after the Flood, the world's people

built ships and sailed abroad on the seas, and inhabited its islands, north and south and east and west.

OAHSPE, THE LORDS' FIRST BOOK 2:20

It is interesting that Augustus Le Plongeon placed the "sunken continent" in the Gulf of Mexico and the Caribbean; indeed, the eastern sea from which the Maya say their forefathers hailed is not the legendary Atlantis but rather subsided islands just offshore in the Antilles. Isn't this why Portuguese tradition calls the lost islands to the west "Antilla"? In fact, whole tribes were driven to the mainland from the gradually subsiding lands of Antillia, according to Mexican oral tradition. Carib groups of the Lesser Antilles even penetrated to the heart of Brazil; and this is why they "strongly resembled the Maya in appearance and culture. . . .The Maya language, too, has been classified as of Antillean origin" (Spence 1933, 232).

This is also why man-made structures abound in the waters of the Caribbean and neighboring areas. When the water is clear, causeways and roads can be seen along the coastal seabottom off eastern Yucatán and British Honduras. In the second half of the twentieth century it became well known that the floor plan of Mexico's Uxmal Temple of the Turtles/Dwarfs is a duplicate of the underwater stone structures found at Andros and Bimini Islands east of Cuba. Nevertheless, *ultimate* origins were from the West not the East, Uxmal an early

*Aztlan being the Mexican name for North America, or, more specifically, for Michigan's Upper Peninsula. The name Aztlan also denotes "a semimythical place to the west of Mexico" (Adams 1991, 398) said to have been the homeland of the Chichimecas.

offshoot from Pan. At Uxmal, Churchward found a ruined temple bearing inscriptions commemorative of the Lands of the West, "whence we came."

Roadbeds and 4-foot-thick walls under the waters of the Bahama Bank are also just like Tiahuanaco's,* their square-cut blocks so similar to those in the Andes. Bimini, after all, is Arawak country, and the Arawaks "may have been Polynesian" (Gladwin 1947, 234). Like-named are the Arawe people in Melanesia and the Arawa subtribe of New Zealand's Maori. Old customs die hard. In the northern Amazon, "when gorgeous wreaths of flowers were laid around our necks I was most astonished for I thought that this festive custom in greeting" was Polynesian (Homet 1963, 68). One of Polynesia's most famous canoes was called Arawa.

Even when the location of sunken lands is close to the *Pacific* (not the Atlantic) Ocean, writers still call it *Atlantis*! For example, the northwest coast Okanagan Indians (3,000 miles from the Atlantic coast) in Washington State have a legend of a large island in the remote past that sank into the sea (their legend is told in chapter 4). "This sounds like a version of the catastrophe that befell *Atlantis*," says Mr. Wilkins (2000, 17; emphasis added). And to this he adds the *Alaskan* myth of a great flood—equating it too with Atlantis! These are obviously Pacific not Atlantic locations! In such cases where the locale is obviously in the *Pacific* region, still they call it "Atlantis"! Even concerning animals that normally live in the lowlands of the Andes, and that face the Pacific not the Atlantic, Peter Kolosimo explains their presence in the uplands by reasoning that "the creatures must have died in their natural coastal habitat, which was laid waste and pushed up to its present altitude by the cataclysm which destroyed *Atlantis*" (Kolosimo 1975, 150–52; emphasis added). On the other hand, the interaction of the plates joining Easter Island and South America can probably explain how the Andes arose.

---

*Tiahuanaco may have been settled by the Arawaks of Pan via the Caribbean. Panic origins may show in the name itself: *Tia* (*underworld,* Polynesian) + *huan* (Ihuan) + *aku* (*spirits,* Polynesian).

Mortarless Joins Traced to Mu,
Not Atlantis

Speaking of Easter Island, David H. Childress, commenting on the mortarless masonry and interlocking blocks at Vinapu, Easter Island, remarks, "As in Cuzco and the underwater sites at Bimini and Morocco, this type of construction is sometimes called Atlantean" (1988, 336). But why call it Atlantean when its provenance is more consistently tied to the *Pacific*?

- Easter Island: cyclopean walls of precise unmortared masonry, the only cement is "gravitation"
- Tahiti marae: megaliths constructed without cement, carefully fitted together for perfect joins
- Marquesas: great stonework of the carefully fitted type
- Tonga: matching Peruvian work, the colossal unmortared stonework at Tonga is notched to fit like a puzzle piece

Fig. 3.5. A marae on Tahiti

- New Zealand: 6-foot-long blocks of the Wai-ta-hanui, cut and fitted without mortar
- Hawaii: The Menehune* Wall, finely cut and shaped like intricate puzzle pieces to withstand the most violent cataclysm

In fact, mortarless joins are worldwide; so why call them Atlantean?

- Cuzco, Peru: stone blocks cut to exact size and positioned without mortar
- Tiahuanaco and Ollantaytambo: masterfully notched joins
- Bimini: stone blocks fitted together by means of tightly notched joins
- Guatemala: subterranean structures with stone blocks dovetailing into each other
- Cambodia: Anghor Wat blocks made an exact fit without cement
- Yonaguni, Japan: perfectly cut and fitted stones
- England: stones at Stonehenge tongue-and-grooved to one another
- Greece: peg-and-socket joins on Mycenae stone gateway
- Malta tomb: blocks fitted together without mortar, earthquake resistant
- Zimbabwe: drystone fitted work

Was Atlantis a Supercivilization?

One explorer of Bimini, J. Manson Valentine, believed Atlantis had "reached an advanced state of technology. They certainly had the capability of heavier-than-air flight." In fact their supertechnology is blamed for their downfall. Valentine agrees with those who say that "the sink-

---

*The extinct Menehune were known for their high-level work. Known as the Small Sacred Workers, only 3 feet tall but strong and stout, these bearded people were *Homo sapien pygmaeus,* "much like leprechauns" (Childress 1988, 338). Agriculturalists, master architects, and engineers, they are credited with the ancient canals, irrigation tunnels, and petroglyphs in the Hawaiian Islands. They built the *lokoia,* the fishponds of cyclopean structure along the coast of Molokai and elsewhere. Expert stone crafters, they built some of the *heiau* temples.

ing of Atlantis was due to runaway energy and a terrific implosion. This was what we saw in one psychic reading" (Valentine interview, in Steiger 1974, 61).

At this point speculation tends to shift from Plato-based to Sanskrit-based vindication; in which case, India's epic dramas speak of supernuclear blasts that shattered whole cities, even countries, titanic jolts presumed to have smashed Atlantis down to the deep, indicating some sidereal force like that described in the Mahabharata. The theorist now extrapolates that Atlantean scientists—or a split-off of Black Magicians—"were playing with forces capable of the most terrible destructive potential . . . [that] unleashed a chain-reaction of lethal power. . . . This holocaust resulted in seismic disturbances that . . . [destroyed] the greater part of Atlantis" (Trench 1974, 21).

Although all knowledge, science, and arts of civilization have been attributed to elusive Atlantis, we are never told how the Atlanteans got so smart in the first place. Unless . . . it was ETs. Mounting guesswork solves the riddle: "Occult tradition *infers* that the Atlanteans had *probably* reached a very high degree of technological achievement. . . . Undoubtedly they had space ships and were in communication with other planets" (Trench 1974, 21; emphasis added). But such writers seem unable to decide if these smart "men were from outer space or astronauts from Atlantis. Some . . . suggest that the curious headgear seen on some statues is . . . a space helmet" (Kolosimo 1975, 158).

Helmets

On Mexico's icons, Quetzalcoatl wore a helmet, which the Spanish conquerors thought quite similar to their own. In South America, Mochica jars picture helmets with metal crests; a favorite subject of these people "was their warriors' making life miserable for the savages. . . . There is no mistaking the warriors who always wore crested helmets" (Gladwin 1947, 281). Copper helmets were also found in the North American mounds. But in the case of the turquoise helmets worn by the peaceful Hopi kachinas, the distinctive headgear denotes spiritual guardians, not warriors.

Fig. 3.6 a) Drawing on reverse side of a mirror found near Vera Cruz, Mexico, the headgear resembling that worn by Cretan gods and Phoenician warriors. b) Helmeted Libyan nobleman. c) Nigerian plaque showing seated king with helmet like the helmeted warriors of Benin. d) Olmec giant head with helmet, found near Tenochtitlan, whose grand markets sold everything from flowers to slaves to helmets with crests of animal heads. e) A feathered helmet from Hawaii, similar to those worn by ancient Greeks. The fau, *war helmets, were worn by men of Hawaii, Tahiti, Rurutu, Society and Austral Islands. The Hawaiian Menehune are sometimes pictured wearing* mahiole, *the ancient helmets of the island chiefs.*

Fig. 3.7. Egyptian helmet with horns; in Egypt we see carvings with horned helmets, rather like the boar tusks on the leather helmets of armored men described in Homer's Iliad, *and also resembling Athena's helmet with two horns, and the horned helmet worn by Sardinia's warriors.*

Quite a few writers would have us believe that these are the helmets of spacemen! For example, a grotto drawing in Uzbekistan, with a helmet, must be "a prehistoric astronaut" (Charroux 1967, 48). Or, Stonehenge's carved figure wearing a helmet "is perhaps a member of a space crew" (Kolosimo 1973, 140–41). And with helmeted stone heads at Tiahuanaco, the nearby truncated pyramid must have been their landing pad! In Australia, at the source of Prince Regent River, among strange cave paintings of European types is one round-headed figure with no facial features but with a helmet, perhaps a space helmet. Examining the rest of the drawing, this author wonders, "Does the spiral represent an orbit and the horseshoe object a spaceship in flight?" (Tomas 1973, 118). But the round head with a dot in the middle is not a helmet; it is an ancient Celtic symbol of dead warriors. Not spacemen! Earthly warriors like the Alaskan Mummy People and the Ainu both wore wooden armor and helmets—like the Scythian battle helmets. Helmet and dagger are found together in a royal Sumerian tomb.

Equally dependent on the fancies of occultism or psychic readings, author Raymond Drake states that "some psychics reveal that Celestials from Venus taught their wonderful science to the Giants of Atlantis"; but maybe not so wonderful, for Drake himself elsewhere suggests that "maleficent invaders from Jupiter . . . enforced a tyranny provoking earth's Giants to revolt. . . . The Atlanteans rebelled against the Space Overlords. . . . Possibly the titanic war between the Gods and the Giants [was] revealed in the [Sanskrit] *Ramayana*" (1974, 140; and 1968, 2).

We are further informed by the ET proponent that Atlantean artifacts (actually found off the coast of Tunisia) show "what can only be described as a space rocket . . . an astronaut's cockpit with two antennae . . . [along with] fantastic drawings related to atomic energy and the conquest of space" (Charroux 1967, 210). Space Lords notwithstanding, it is still widely and wildly rumored and depicted in occult novels, science fiction, and speculative history that Atlantis had aircraft, TV, radio, air conditioning, and monorails, having mastered the superscience of "vril" or "mashmak" or some other kind of "psycho-electrical force" unknown to us. Channeled information from the explorer P. H. Fawcett called it blast electricity:

> You will think me mad . . . but I have . . . descended into the great subterranean world wherein electricity and air are combined and fused. . . . [They] knew more about matter and light, about the ether and its properties, than the scientists of the twentieth century can ever know or imagine. (Stemman 1976, 56–57)

These scripts went on to claim that it was not a natural force that brought down Atlantis but rather massive explosions in these subterranean reservoirs of electricity.

More of the same, this from Maxine Asher, "Atlanteans apparently harnessed energy sources drawn from the cosmos . . . [that] produced such astounding developments as the laser, nuclear power and advanced atomic submarines" (1974, 71). Asher's idle conjecture is then matched and exceeded by the asininity of her hunches.

Many Semitic people were involved in the manipulation of the occult on Atlantis, which contributed to its decline. . . . It has occurred to me that the great purity and morality of the Jewish religion upheld for thousands of years may have been an effort at group redemption for having misused the energy forces in the later days of Atlantis!" (Asher 1974, 71, 84).

While I certainly agree that the etheric force* was known and harnessed by ancient science, there is no reason to call it Atlantean; in the postdiluvial world it was the Egyptians—not Atlanteans—who revived the lost science of the ancients; and they

excelled in building temples and palaces; and in all manner of inventions; in fabrics of linen and silk, and wool and fine leather; in writing books and tablets; in mathematics; in laws and reciprocities; in navigation, and in inland travel; in making thermometers, barometers, magnetic needles, telescopes and microscopes; and in chemistry and botany. Truly the philosophers of those days knew the mysteries of heaven and earth.

OAHSPE, THE LORDS' FIFTH BOOK 7:2–3,
IN THE AGE OF OSIRIS

In Frank Joseph's excellent book on Lemuria, I came across an intriguing interpretation of ancient technology, which lends itself to the present discussion specifically because its setting *is in Mu—not Atlantis.* "A leading theme repeating itself through Pohnpei's [Panape's] stark ruins [is] electricity. At Nan Madol and Insaru, tons of magnetized basalt . . . were constructed into great enclosures, towers, walls, rooms, and canals . . ." (2006, 38–39).

There were also watertight "coffins" made of platinum, thus possessing electrical resistivity.

The installation of platinum in a powerful electric field tends to dampen the accumulation of more energy. . . . Let us consider its unique location, where eastern Pacific typhoons originate. . . .

---

*My own website, www.earthvortex.com, goes in to great detail concerning the etheric force.

Tempests are born within the 300 miles separating [Panape and Kosrae]. Meteorologists now recognize an essential electromagnetic component in tropical storms and believe such dangerous weather phenomena can be mitigated . . . in the first stages of development by somehow diffusing the electromagnetic core of a hurricane before it gains strength. (Joseph 2006, 38–39)

And that is what the Muvians, according to Joseph, were doing.

In Egypt the higher degrees of Anubi initiation might help explain certain aspects of lost technology.

Anyone (who desired to learn heavenly things) was eligible for the degree of Anubi. . . . And the angels taught mortals . . . the secrets of falling water; and the application of lotions to the skin, that would make poundings and rappings.

OAHSPE, BOOK OF WARS 7:6

Raymond Drake has Atlantean adepts "conjuring aid from elementals in other dimensions" (1968, 112), which would explain how certain technical skills or knowledge depended upon clairvoyant faculties (especially where whole populations were obsessed with cranial deformation, as illustrated in chapter 1).

But I believe some of these powers and capacities actually belong, not in the mortal realm, but in the spiritual. Let me explain, much of the speculation about ancient high tech is based on passages from India's classic works such as Mahabharata and Ramayana, and as we will see in chapter 5 (in "Shem," p. 180), it was India that was entrusted with the names and titles of the heavenly powers. Only India preserved records of these gods and goddesses (Vishnu, Durga, Krisna, etc.) and even of the wars in heaven. I will illustrate this with a single example, the term *Das,* which translates in India as "Servant of God, devotee, initiate." In heaven, the rank of Das, as described in Oahspe's Book of Fragapatti, is brought to bear for the containment and deliverance of drujas, the abject spirits who form horrible "knots" in hell.

And Fragapatti stationed sentinels with power, near the walls of fire ... [to] prevent the drujas from escaping. ... A million ethereans [higher angels], with rods of water and rods of fire, came in answer to Fragapatti's commandment. And he said to them: "Behold, I have established one signal center in hell. It will require a thousand more centers before we have broken them up and delivered them. The marshals shall select from among you ten thousand of the rank of Das, to remain in this center and complete the work. ... Now the das are those who have attained to power with the rod [wand] with water, and the rod with fire. ... They go among the denizens of a signal center (in hell) with the two rods, casting water with one and fire with the other. And the hosts of spirits in darkness [drujas] run for them, like cattle for salt. ... The lowest spirits go for the rods with water, and the highest for the rods of fire. Because the lowest spirits dread the light; and because the highest desire to be rescued from the lowest. ... Such, then, is the labor of the das in hell, baptizing and selecting; and it continues until all the people are taken beyond the walls.

OAHSPE, BOOK OF FRAGAPATTI 11.17–22

Now the Mahabharata speaks of great weapons like the Narayana missile, "Scorcher of Foes," used to destroy whole cities. And although "Kapilla's Glance," another superweapon, could supposedly burn whole populations in a matter of seconds, the prophet Capilya (after whom it is named) lived no more than 3500 BP, which is to say in Moses's time, and is therefore hardly likely to be an Atlantean. Yet these are the weapons that come in to play in the Indian epics, which presumably describe a war between the Rama Empire and Atlantis, a war waged with fantastic nuclear weapons, aerial craft, and laser death rays, allegedly bringing on the cataclysms that shattered civilization and scattered survivors to the ends of the Earth!*

---

*But again, the timing is off. The idea that civilization was shattered 12,000 BP with the demise of Atlantis does not compute. Writers mistakenly have the world relapsed to barbarism with the sinking of Atlantis: "The final sinking of Poseid removed the last vestiges of civilization from the face of the earth" (Trench 1974, 68). But it is quite the contrary—12,000 BP is when Egyptian civilization blossomed (Age of Osiris).

The *vimanas* airships (*vimana* literally means "temple-dome") are also taken from the Indian epics and thought to have been man-made flying machines—aircraft of the ancient scientific elite. Childress, for example, suggests that "the fantastic piece of architecture known as Vinapu" at Easter Island could have been an "ancient Vimana platform from the Rama Empire" (1988, 336, 342). He adds, "Are the bird man glyphs representative of men who came in airships? Ahu Vinapu was possibly an ancient vimana landed [*sic*] pad. . . . On Moloka'i is the gigantic stone platform of 'Ili'ili'opae Haeiau' . . . [which] like those at Malden Island, Tonga, Tahiti, and elsewhere, is stepped, like a large flat pyramid. Was this a vimana platform for the 'Bird Men'?" (1988, 336, 342).

He also mentions the Atlantean *vailxi,* another aircraft that "could go anywhere they wanted," an aerial ship described as harnassing a balance of forces between gravity and levitation, something like today's zeppelin, but cigar-shaped and electromagnetic in nature, indeed anti-gravitational in nature. Yet it is interesting that the most impartial reports of man-made flying devices come, not from the direction of Atlantis, but from genuine traditions in the motherland. Here, Childress informs us, south of Tahiti in the Gambier Islands, the aboriginal inhabitants recount how in the very remote past a flying canoe with great wings was operated *by the priests** who flew great distances—as far as Hawaii, for example (1988, 342). One village actually has an artist's model of the ancient flying canoe. If the people said the Tahitian kings could fly, consider this explanation for the claim: in passing from one district to another, His Majesty must not touch the ground, so he arrives on the shoulders of his bearers. This is called *mahuta*—meaning "to fly"; it was then customary to say "the king flew from one district to another." (Also, there was flying of man-lifting kites here, as mentioned in chapter 1.)

Churchward, also basing his comments on the Ramayana and

---

*Weren't priests and shamans, after all, the masters of flight? It has been supposed that the famous Nazca lines and drawings (geoglyphs) of Peru may have been guides to the *shaman's* flight (rather than UFOs). Medicine men everywhere have been credited with flying through the air and visiting the sky world.

Mahabharata, describes the vimana as "independent of all fuel. . . . The power is taken from the atmosphere in a very simple inexpensive manner. The engine is somewhat like our present-day turbine in that it works from one chamber into another. . . . It had two stories and many chambers with windows and was *draped with flags and banners.* It gave forth a melodious sound as it coursed along its airy way" (1931a, 188–89; emphasis added). Well, this description (not to mention their designation as "celestial cars") sounds less like airships of the Hindus and more like the chariots of the gods. The gods "really did move about the skies in flying machines" (Charroux 1972, 121). Such are the fireships of the high-raised angels, as so thoroughly described throughout Oahspe.

And now the builders, who had measured the elements lying in the route to the earth, formed their crescent ship of fire, and equipped it; and with *mantles, curtains and banners* created of it a vessel of beauty. . . . Hardly was the ship completed when . . . what was beautiful before, was now illuminated, sparkling and bright as a sun* . . . for such was the quality of the ether of the heavens. . . . Sue [God of Earth] said: "Cut loose, you Gods, and you, O ship, born of heaven, to the red star, the earth, Go!" And . . . lo, the mighty ship of heaven turned on its axis, cutting loose from the high firmament. And it turned, with its great *curtains and banners* sailing gracefully and swiftly through the blue ether. The music of her es'enaurs swelled and rolled along on the spheres of many worlds . . . where live countless millions of spectators viewing the marvelous speed, power and brilliant colors of the great ship.

OAHSPE, BOOK OF SUE 2:3–8 (EMPHASIS ADDED)

The Soviet astronomer Kazantsev once suggested angels could be men from space. After all, legends generally call the drivers of these vehicles "the gods." Some authors, like Philip Coppens, assume, correctly I

---

*"It was as if two suns were shining"—description in Ramayana of vimana, the "fiery chariot."

heavenly musicians, singers & instru-
mentalists. The hosts of heaven come
in a ship of fire.

Fig. 3.8. Glyph for es'senaurs, heavenly musicians. "Some propelled their ships by music alone; the vibratory chords affording sufficient power in such highly skilled hands, and the tunes changing according to the regions traversed" (Oahspe, Book of Cpenta-armij 2:19).

Fig. 3.9. Etherean host descending. "Down to the lower heaven I come in ships of light, curtained about with etherean mantles . . ." (Oahspe, Book of Sethantes 19:22).

think, that vimanas were simply "ancient UFOs" (2012, 237–38), and he centers them in the Gobi Desert—not Atlantis. When we hear of these fireships in Oahspe, the mechanism involves vast etherean vortices of light, which can be formed into any shape. Thus are UFOs sighted as eggs,* carrots, donuts, cigars, cones, triangles, arrows, saucers, crescents,† ovals,‡ cylinders, spindles, tops, even straw hats—in other words, every conceivable shape.

> As I taught corporeans [mortals] to build ships to traverse corporeal seas, so have I taught ethereans to build vessels to course My etherean seas ... [and] so did I create My heavens for the spirits of men, that by manufactured vessels they could course My firmament.... But, to My exalted etherean angels, I have given power to clothe their hosts with ships of fire.
>
> OAHSPE, BOOK OF LIKA 6:2–3 AND BOOK OF APOLLO 10:12

The heavenly ships are of no earthly substance, but rather etheric (pre-atomic) in nature. In a 1942 address titled "Etherean Ships," George Morley in London explained that UFOs do not "have a physical origin, but are spiritual vessels temporarily materialized" (1955). Morley then gave the swift-rising Ometr as an example: "This particular one goes up quickly; similarly the Abattos had the power to withdraw very quickly out of the earth's atmosphere" (1955). Doesn't this sound like the aerial object sighted by Bob Oechsler in 1990, from his Maryland home? "I first saw it at a distance, then it moved out straight toward me over the field behind my house. After about thirty seconds, it took off—straight up.... The object ... at its closest approach [had] a kind

---

*The avalanza was "egg-shaped ... the propelling vortices were within the center" (Oahspe, Book of Lika 17.2).

†The starship of Sue was a crescent ship; a UFO sighted in California was crescent shaped. "A light appeared in the firmament ... a star-ship from Nirvana ... like a crescent it came, a very world of light" (Oahspe, God's Book of Eskra LX, 1–3). The arrowship is also described in Oahspe.

‡"And when the whole airiata [fireship] was completed, it looked like an oval globe of light" (Oahspe, Book of Thor 3.14).

Fig. 3.10. Found on every continent, the ball and cross was originally the universal sign of the Creator. The added leaf (maple) stands for Life.

of Celtic cross clearly visible underneath" (Good 1994, 235). I might remind the reader of the numerous ball-and-cross references and figures (a.k.a. Celtic Cross) shown in this book. "Well, the Celts may claim pride of name, but this most ancient symbol . . . is still one of Africa's most powerful signs of . . . communication with the Creator" (Kreisberg 2012, 175).

When provided with ballast, an etherean vessel can stand at any point within the Earth's vortex. This halting in midair is familiar to UFO buffs. Standing or hovering, even for hours on end, is not unusual, like the ethereal ships or "visiting stars, halting at the boundaries of the earth's vortex to form in rank" (Oahspe, Book of Aph 16:1), or like the port-au-gon, described in the Book of Ah'shong.

> Thus Ah'shong, well skilled in the course and behavior of worlds, gathered together his millions of angels. . . . Quickly they framed and equipped an Orian port-au-gon, and illuminated it with fire-lights and bolts. . . . Embarked, they sped forth . . . and stood close above the earth . . . here they halted, so that . . . their magnificence may awe the men and angels of the earth with the power and glory of My emancipated sons and daughters.
>
> OAHSPE, BOOK OF AH'SHONG 1:18, 2:1

Linking (and Confusing) Atlantis with Mu

A certain tendency arises among those smitten with Atlantis to deny the existence of Mu. These, for example, are the words of Philip Coppens in his last book.

Mu . . . is a mythical civilization. . . . The first person to write about Mu was nineteenth-century traveler Augustus LePlongeon, who claimed Mu was at the origins [*sic*] of the Egyptian and Mesoamerican civilization, which he claimed were [*sic*] created by refugees from Mu. Though LePlongeon located Mu in the Atlantic Ocean [!], in the early twentieth century, traveler James Churchward moved it to the Pacific, claiming to have found evidence for its existence in a series of secret documents in Indian temple libraries. Almost a century later, there is no evidence to suggest that the story of Mu has any historical foundation . . . there are no ancient, openly available texts that document the existence of . . . Mu—

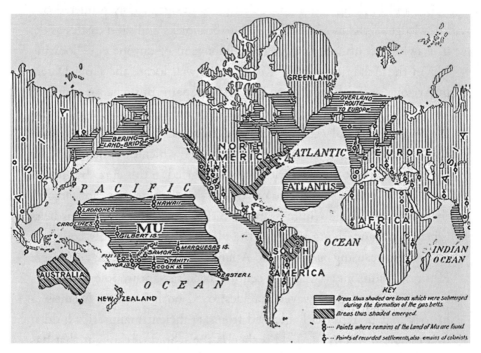

Fig. 3.11. Map including both Mu and Atlantis, after Churchward

unlike Atlantis, which was written about more than 2,000 years ago. (2012, 287, 236)

The same dismissive tone is adopted by another writer of Atlantis books, again dumping on Le Plongeon, who, incidentally, was not a "traveler" but a pioneer archaeologist—with plenty of dirt under his fingernails. Criticizing the Frenchman's translation of Mexico's *Codex Troano,* Charles Berlitz comments:

Le Plongeon thought that . . . [Troano] described the sinking of the "Land of Clay Hills, Mu . . . in the ocean, together with its 64,000,000 inhabitants," calling to mind the phrase historian Robert Silverberg applied to a similar instance: "It has about it the fascination of lunacy, like some monstrous bridge constructed of toothpicks." (1972, 39)

I find it interesting that Berlitz chose to quote Silverberg, whose skepticism and burking of the lost-race theory has grievously hindered our knowledge of the moundbuilders. But toothpicks and sand castles aside, it is awfully confusing to hear of Le Plongeon or anyone else "locating Mu in the Atlantic Ocean"! We might as well locate the Gobi Desert in Arizona or Tahiti off the south coast of Spain. But when it comes to lost continents, the most extraordinary mental acrobatics have entered the printed page. Blavatsky aficionados, for example, have been known to identify Atlantis as a peninsula of Lemuria, which extended from the Indian Ocean into the Atlantic. No holds barred in this crazy business.

Every conceivable scenario of Atlantis-Mu-Lemuria has appeared in the literature. In the Churchward rendition it was the Earth's gas belts (great caves underlying much of the planet) that supposedly collapsed disastrously, causing *both* Mu and Atlantis to sink. According to George Hunt Williamson, a twentieth-century occultist-anthropologist, it was earthquakes and tidal waves that destroyed both Mu and Atlantis (a history that he reportedly gleaned from an ancient manuscript hidden in a temple in the Andes). This then is the school of thought that has Atlantis and Mu suffering a mutual, contemporary demise: "Two mighty continents vanished, apparently almost in a day and a night and at the same time" (Wilkins 2000, 190). But you can't ride two horses; you can't have both Mu and Atlantis as the motherland of man. It has to be one or the other. No attempts to combine the two have amounted to anything.

Then too there is the "view that there was an atomic war between Mu and Atlantis, a view supported by the Vedas and the Popol Vuh, the sacred book of the ancient Mexicans." This war supposedly caused a worldwide cataclysm, the event having occurred "more than twelve thousand years ago . . . [when] two antagonistic blocs, one in Atlantis, the other in the Land of Mu" clashed so disastrously. "The rivalry of the two blocs led to an atomic war, which caused the destruction of mankind" (Charroux 1967, 59, 16).

But there's more than one way to sink a continent, and so the vision easily shifts to the following scenario: The sinking of Mu lowered the world's water level, with the result of joining the alleged islands of the Atlantic into a single continent. As once source, the Stelle Group, explains it, when Lemuria/Mu went down, sea levels diminished drastically all over the world "as water rushed into the newly formed Pacific Basin. The relatively small islands that had existed in the Atlantic during the time of the Lemurian civilization were left high and dry by the receding ocean, and the newly emerged land joined the Poseid Archipelago of the Atlantic Ocean, into a large continent" (White 1980, 313). Is this history—or pseudohistory? Hey, last time I checked, when an object is submerged in water, the water *rises,* rather than lowering and inviting the rest of the world's water to rush in and take its place. Besides, if we use this model, the sinking of Mu 24,000 years ago[*] hardly accords with the flourishing of Atlantis 350,000 years ago!

Avoiding these pitfalls, and playing to the Lemuria audience, the Atlantist has conjured a kind of compromise history, staging migrations out of Mu to settle Atlantis. Hopefully this will make everyone happy. Smacking of Blavatskyan hype, the reconstruction runs something like this: Prior to Lemuria's destruction, migrants to Atlantis developed a civilization in their new home. Some say it was only missionaries from

---

[*]See "The Land of Pan Went Down Twenty-Four Thousand Years Ago" in chapter 9, p. 378.

Mu who settled Atlantis, or that "the wisdom acquired in Lemuria through many millennia . . . inspired the priest-scientists of Atlantis" (Drake 1974, 36).

Lewis Spence, on the other hand, turns all this around and has the Atlantis culture finding its way via America *to* Oceania.

> The narrow isthmus . . . in Central America would readily lend itself as a point of departure for the dissemination of that culture through-out Oceania. . . . We find many instances of . . . the Atlantean culture-complex in the Lemurian area . . . such as head-flattening . . . [which was] an Atlantean custom. . . . Indeed we find most of the "apparatus" of the Atlantean complex in Oceania. (Spence 1933, 232–33)

But as we saw in chapter 1, head flattening came under a common inspiration, *with no single place* serving as its source or center of diffusion. Nevertheless, Childress, in line with Spence's thinking, entertains the idea of "'the Atlantean League' . . . who sailed the world's oceans . . . and carved an empire out of the Pacific Ocean" (Childress 1988, 268).

The most popular spin-off from this school of thought has (as alluded to in the first sentence of this chapter) Atlanteans emigrating "eastward to the Nile Valley." Even Churchward has Egypt settled by Atlanteans (actually, by Muvians who had previously moved eastward through South America to Atlantis!). Pure speculation. Atlantis, the brat reared by permissive parents, turns its sassy back on world history, which well knows the fountainhead of culture streamed westward from the Orient. This seems to be confirmed by the very latest archaeological finds that credit China with "the earliest modern humans" (*Time,* 17).

> *We must turn to Asia to discover the earliest*
> *manifestation of civilized life.*
>   JOHN D. BALDWIN, *PRE-HISTORIC NATIONS*

In this respect, I must abandon my alternate-history contemporaries and even the trailblazing Colonel Churchward himself and stand instead with such thinkers as the German explorer Leo Frobenius, who thought that civilization began on a lost continent in the Pacific Ocean and spread from there to Asia, and from there again to the West. The Frenchman Louis Jacolliot interpreted the Sanskrit sagas as referring to a great landmass that once covered the region of Polynesia. Jacolliot argued that Plato's Atlantis was merely a stand-in for that forgotten continent in the Pacific Ocean.

Now it is well known that the Greeks—including Plato—got their story of Atlantis from the Egyptians, who had preserved a record of the Flood on the temple walls of Edfu. Yet the Egyptian story does not actually *name the ocean* where this missing continent once stood. In fact, for the early Greeks the Atlantic Ocean was nothing less than a huge body of water that completely surrounded the *world*. "The Greeks, and therefore Plato as well, were only familiar with the Atlantic Ocean . . . and may have assumed the flood and sunken continent stories . . . had taken place in the Atlantic. . . . Then from that misunderstanding arose the fictional account of Atlantis written by Plato, and since taken up by many others" (Jones 2008, 244). De Camp, for his part, recommends that Atlantists read the rest of Plato's writings, in which case they would "realize what a fertile myth-maker he was; [then] they might be less cocksure about his reliability as a historian" (De Camp 1975, 252).

Nor can we omit the politics of the thing. Elsewhere in this book we look at unrecorded voyages of mariners/miners like the Phoenicians, whose trade routes were, literally, *deathly* secrets. This time frame fits with Plato and with his student Aristotle, who thought his teacher's Atlantis parable "poetic fiction" and who acknowledged instead a certain land with navigable rivers that had been discovered by the Carthaginians. And here's where the politics come in: "to prevent an exodus that might shift prosperity from Carthage to that 'island' they . . . announced the death penalty for any planning to sail there" (Gordon 1973, 38). The secret land of course was America itself—with all her great rivers* and

---

*Carl Lehrburger traces ancient Old World coins that are found in America and are "directly tied to . . . ancient Mediterranean naval powers, including the Carthaginians. . . . The distribution of these coins shows a strong correlation with coastal and navigable river waterways. . . . The third largest distribution . . . is in the copper mining regions of Michigan" (2015, 40).

untapped mineral wealth. That island (America) was described by Diodorus as many days' sail from Libya westward. There, he added, the Phoenicians found stately buildings, fountains, and an abundance of precious metals; as John Baldwin concludes, "the land reached by the Phoenicians," who had good maps of the Western Hemisphere, "is likely to have been some part of Central America . . . where stood the great cities now in ruin" (1869, 398–99).

It has been supposed that perhaps up until the Mesozoic period all the lands of the Earth lay together in one massive supercontinent named Pangea. The idea became amenable to twentieth-century scientists once the theory of continental drift—and soon after, plate tectonics—took

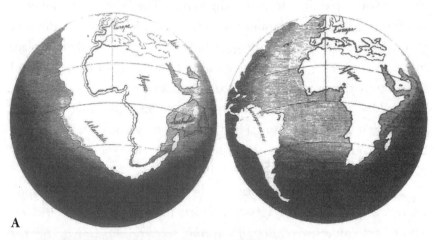

A

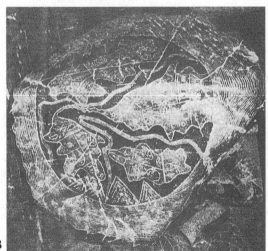

B

Fig. 3.12. a) Maps showing hand-in-glove fit of the continents; it is thought that Europe and America "split apart" early in the Pleistocene. b) Pangea map on Peru's Ica Stones, shown in process of separating.

hold. This gradual spreading out of landmasses seemed to make sense in light of the hand-in-glove appearance produced by the coasts of western Europe/Africa and the Americas.

If Atlantis, as De Camp argues, was simply North America, then "continental drift has nothing to do with Plato's Atlantis" (De Camp 1975, 168, 170). But the peculiar thing about the map of Pangea is a rather large gap in the shape of a triangle between Laurasia and Gondwana. That gap has been called the Tethys Ocean. Gondwana (the southern part of Pangea) shows a gap in the Pacific area. That triangle (as if from a pie with a wedge missing) cannot be explained by continental drift. But Polynesia is shaped like a triangle, with Hawaii, New Zealand, and Easter Island at the points. Ian Cameron, not coincidentally, has described the world's islands as mostly confined to the Pacific Ocean, a "triangle whose apexes are Tokyo, Jakarta, and Pitcairn" (Cameron 1987, 21). Pan, as illustrated in Oahspe, is again of triangular shape—and it sits just where the Tethys Ocean should be. Pangea was like a pie with one wedge (Tethys) cut out.

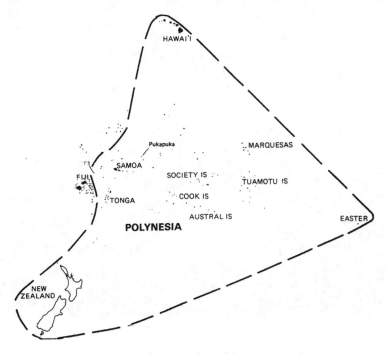

Fig. 3.13. Polynesia, shaped like a triangle

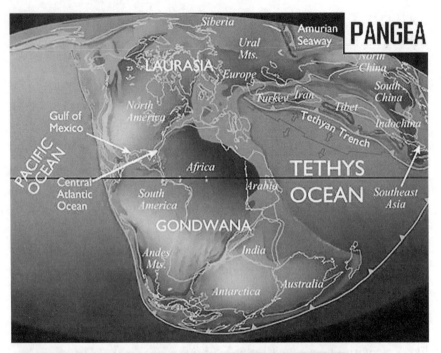

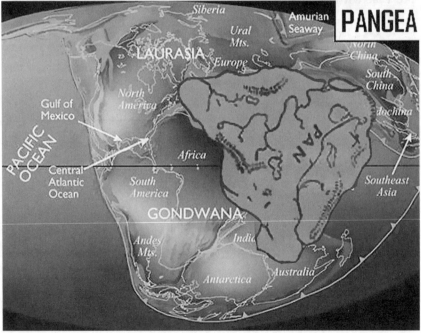

Fig. 3.14. The Tethys Ocean must be Pan itself,
courtesy of Oahspe Standard Edition

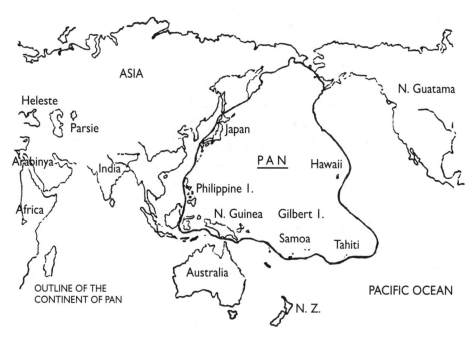

Fig. 3.15. Pan map from Oahspe, seen to be triangular in shape, connecting in the northeast to the northwest coast of America

The connection to the northwest coast gives us pause . . .

Northwest Coast

Rand and Rose Flem-Ath give the Haida Indians, whose dialect is the oldest branch of the Na-Dene language family, at least twelve thousand years in British Columbia's Queen Charlotte Islands; before then, the Haida say, their ancestors lived in a distant land where "the great heavenly chief decided to punish this great village. . . . He caused the river waters to rise. . . . Only the high mountain peaks showed above the swollen water" (Flem-Ath 1995, 54). The flood story is made more interesting by a tradition called the Haida Texts, which are the myths of the *Caroline Islands*—in Micronesia! All along America's northwest coast native traditions of a lost Caucasian race abound. White people dwelled here more than fifteen thousand years ago, as attested to by craniofacial measurements; there are no Mongol traits here. British Columbia's oral traditions speak of red-haired ancestors. Northwest coast Indians, even today, retain certain Caucasian features.

In Haida tradition itself five tiny brothers, the First People, came out of clamshells (dugouts? arks?). The art of the Haida appears to "have originated from some older Oceanic art" (Spence 1933, 186). Curious that the Haida name for their land is *Gwaii* ("Islands of the People"), sounding a bit like Hawaii. Well, in Hawaiian tradition Lono was the white culture bringer whose emblem, the *Lonomakua,* was a tall wooden pole. The features of these wooden images have appeared throughout the Pacific Islands, and they "are as easy to trace and account for as the totem poles of the northwest coast of America" (Spence 1933, 120–21)— which also resemble Polynesian masks. *Ti'i-potua-ra'au* were the long fierce figures carved one above another on all sides of a single log and

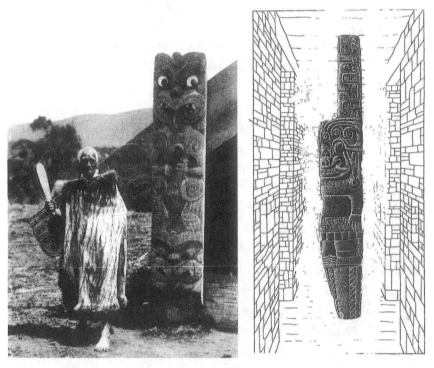

Fig. 3.16. Left: Maori totem pole. Right: The Lanzon god of Peru carved on a pillar in the temple of Chavin de Huantar. In North America, ototeman is the Ojibway totem pole representing clan groups.

erected with great pomp in Tahiti. Students of Inuit designs say that the designs are almost identical to Maori and Melanesian ones (Cohane 1969, 62), while Alaskan animal figures are clearly a match with those found in New Zealand and Micronesia.

In the Society Islands, special affection or regard is shown by rubbing noses; this was the old Polynesian way of kissing, called *ho'i* in Tahiti (Henry 1928, 518). In Hawaii it is called *hongi;* pressing noses together was a traditional form of greeting, as it was in New Zealand—and among the Inuits. Also, the double-bladed paddle, the sacred drum, and the Marquesan dancing club are "found amongst the American Indians . . . one of many features of Polynesian culture that seem to point to the North Pacific" (Brown 1924, 156). The 60-foot-long dugout canoes of these different cultures are again almost identical.

Finding Atlantis has been a wild goose chase. It's time to throw in the towel. Until we give up on Atlantis as the answer to history's mysteries, the record of ancient culture and all antiquity will remain sealed. Frankly, Atlantis has made it through on celebrity status and a mountain of inferences. Hundreds of years of Atlantology have been but a warm-up for the truth—about Pan, the real lost continent. Now let us explore the catastrophe itself—the Submergence, a.k.a. the Great Deluge.

RIDING OUT
THE STORM

The sea of Iku has enclosed us . . .

HAWAIIAN SONG OF THE DELUGE

"Sam Lono said the islands were a larger island thousands of years ago . . . it was the theme of several Hawaiian chants including the Kumulip," musician Merrel Fankhauser told me in an e-mail. The *Ku* in Kumulip and Iku is probably not coincidental—if we recall the continent's acclaimed Temples of *Khu*. The Marquesans also had a chant of the deluge; it was called *Te-tai Toko*.

> Give them words in heaven and words on earth, pertaining to matters of [the flood], and make these sounds sacred, so that it shall be proven in Jaffeth, Shem, Ham, Guatama. . . . So, accordingly, were they enjoined to sing the song of the flood; and they thus established its history to endure forever on earth.
>
> OAHSPE, BOOK OF APH 12:7–8

In the lands of Shem it was the Gilgamesh epic of Babylonia that recounted flood times; the legend was told in song and consisted of twelve cantos of about three hundred lines each. And in the lands of Guatama the Hopi song of the flood brings them from their motherland on stepping-stones (islands), accompanied by spirits (kachinas) whose songs and dances helped them establish the New Earth and which the Hopi later performed in their ceremonies. Also in North Guatama recorded in the nineteenth century were the songs and chants of the Delaware Indians, comprised of very extensive histories both before and after the flood.

In South Guatama as well, the Tupis of Brazil were named after First Man, Tupa of fair complexion, he who survived the flood; they sang of destruction by violent inundation that occurred a very long time ago. In Inca tradition it is said that the Creator gave to each nation the language that was to be spoken and the songs to be sung. These songs, among Peru's Indians, were handed down from ancient times, telling of the flood and the coming of the Teachers. "All these provinces filled up . . . six hundred years after the deluge," said one local historian; "this can be gathered from the poetry and ancient songs of the Indians" (Bandelier 1905, 250–70).

> *In Tuscany and in Egypt, in India and in China, and even in the South Sea Islands and in both Americas, we behold the evidence of a civilization which runs its course anterior to the age of Homer. . . . [This] ancient civilization was originated by the antediluvians, and brought through the Deluge to their successors by the family of Noah. . . . To find its starting-point and write its early history, we must be able to explore the obscurest deeps of antiquity.*
>
> JOHN D. BALDWIN, *PRE-HISTORIC NATIONS*

Once upon a time, God looked about the Earth and found one noble and good man, Noah, whom he saved with his family from a terrible flood. Or so the legend goes. Nevertheless, distinct personalities, individuals, do not go back much earlier than the prophet Zarathustra, nine thousand years ago; so when we speak of "Noah" from twenty-four thousand years ago (concerning that date see chapter 9) it must be metaphorical, standing for a people, not an individual. Noah represents then not a single person but an event really—and a time: the arc of Noe.* Indeed, we find that term *Noe* in Chinese, where Noe-ji means "spirit"; in Japan, Noe means "lord"; it was in the arc of Noe that Aph, then god of Earth, oversaw the entire "project" of the flood.

> In the time of the world twenty-four thousand years before the kosmon [current] era . . . in the arc of Noe . . . the earth and her heavens were in great darkness. But the spirit of Jehovih moved upon His high-raised God, Aph, in etherea, to consecrate new dominions on the earth and her heavens.
>
> OAHSPE, BOOK OF APH 1:1

> And God's sons in [the arc of] Noe took . . . the living [Ihins] . . . to keep their seed alive on earth. . . . And the fountains of the sea came up on the lands. . . . And man and beast alike . . . died, for the land was no more. But the heirs of Noe [the Ihins] suffered not. . . . And by the sons of Noe was the whole earth overspread.
>
> OAHSPE, BOOK OF WARS 29:37–43 (THE QUOTE IS
> ACTUALLY AN EXCERPT TAKEN FROM THE OSIRIAN BIBLE.)

The world, say many traditions including our own biblical one, was depopulated by the Flood. "None of the flood accounts leaves one with the impression that the survivors met any other survivors to form a new community for the repopulation of the area. They alone escaped" (Balsiger 1976, 25). But no, I don't think the world was depopulated, for the Flood was not universal—but only on Pan. And the survivors did indeed find many populations wherever they landed. After all, how could Noah, who was white, be the father of all modern races? "The strongest argument against the descent of the present human race from one pair [of survivors] has hitherto been found in the peculiar character of the Negro" (Higgins 1991, 28).

---

*The "arcs," as delineated in Oahspe, cut up cosmic time into approximately 3,000-year cycles, the arc of Noe beginning 24,000 years ago during the reign of Aph, god of the flood.

Nuu is the name of the Arabic Noah—as well as the Polynesian Noah: "In the time of Nuu . . . the Flood came upon the earth" (Fornander 1969, 1:94). Nuu Mehani, says Hawaiian tradition, escaped the flood and repeopled the Earth. Let's have a quick look at a sample of the many names of Noah.

Name	Where/Tribe
Nu Wah	Chinese
Nouh or Yima	Persia
Oki-ku-rumi Kami	Ainu
Xisuthros or Tag-tug	Sumerian
Utnapishtim	Babylonian
Atrahasis	Assyrian
Menes	Egypt
Minos	Greek
Dardanus	Samothrace
Deucalion	Greek-Roman
Mannus	Lithuanian
Manu or Vaisvasvata	Hindu
Minabozho	Ojibway
Oklatabashih	Choktaw
Nichant	Gros Ventre Indians
Tapi	Mexico
Tezpi or Coxcox	Aztec
Nata	Mexico (in Codex Chimalpopoca)
Marerewana	Arawak
King Makonem	Brazil's Makushi Indians
Tupa	Brazil's Tupi Indians
Bochica or Kikina'ku	Colombia
Viracocha	Peru

Fig. 4.1. The Amerind Nanabozho in the Flood

In the American Southwest, along Arizona's Gila River, is the tribe of A'a-tam (Pima) who say a great flood once overwhelmed the Earth. I think the *tam* in this name A'atam is especially significant, for it appears all over the Americas (and the world), and as I hope to show, probably originated in the lost Pacific lands. Tamma-nend was the name of the Delaware Indian god who brought them knowledge and wisdom. This beneficent *Tam* turns up again in Tama-ndare, the Guarani (Brazil) and Paraguayan flood hero, which seems related in turn to Tam-u, the Carib deluge hero, a white man. Indeed, the Tam-anaco people of southern Venezuela say that long ago a bearded white man came among them. This resonates with Peru's Tam-potocco, the cave where survivors of an earlier civilization took refuge.

The Chorotegans of Nicaragua named their main god Tam-agastad, and he too was white and connected with a great flood. And what about Mexico's legendary place Tam-oan-chan, "land of mist," far to the west? Is that Polynesia? In Hawaii, Tama is the name of a major personage in their genealogical songs; he is worshipped in most of Polynesia as their first god, who brought the people fruits and vegetables. Actually there are a whole bunch of Tamas in the islands.

Tama-rua is an ancestor of the Rarotongans.

The **Tamahani** Mountains in Raiatea are considered the abode of departed spirits.

Tamari'i is an honorary name of the high chief in Tahiti.

King **Tamatoa** I was the first *areoi* on Earth (on Opoa).

King **Tamatoa** was also the name of Tahiti's chief at time of Contact.

Tamapouli-alama-foa is the King of Heaven in Tongan mythology.

Tamaya is the god on BukaBuka (Danger Island) who is associated with the creation of first man.

Tamakaia was the first man in New Hebrides (but also the creator of the world!).

Tama is the Polynesian god of surgery; generally, *tama* means "son"; in Melanesia it means "father."

Tama is the savior god in Paumotu.

In the epic of their migration from Hawaiki (the lost homeland), Tama-tea (literally, "white child") heroically led the Maori people to New Zealand, carefully preserving the sacred knowledge of their homeland. The Maori's earliest known voyager, Tama-rereti, "explored a large part of the world" (Smith 1921, 115–16). Is this why Kota *Tam*pan is the name of the very first settlement in Malaysia? For that matter, Thama-nin is said by local tradition to be the first settlement by Noah on the Turkish-Syrian border. Indeed, the map of Mu produced by a group called the Lemurian Fellowship shows a Tama Valley in the north. Today there is a Taman Island, west of Kiribati, Lake Tamai on the Eimeo Islands, Tamapua Island, and Tamarua in Mangaia.

Tam, in the Old World, includes Tham-iasadas, the Scythian Neptune (i.e., sea lord), while the Canaanite sea god was Tamm, and Tammuz was their god of vegetation—his "whiteness" indicated in his alternate name: As-ari (see *Ari* in chapter 2). Tamra means "bright, gold" in Sanskrit; Tamil in southern India also means "white or stranger"

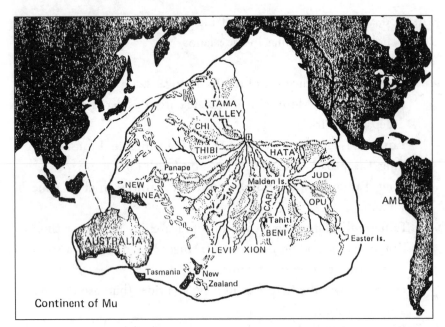

Continent of Mu

Fig. 4.2. Map of Mu published by the Lemurian Fellowship in the 1940s. Explorer Mark Williams thinks this map "corresponds almost exactly to the boundaries of the Pacific Plate. But the map first appeared long before geologists even knew of the plate's existence. . . . Pacific islands do look suspiciously like mountain peaks of a much larger area" (Williams 2001, 69).

(Cohane 1969, 207). In fact, the old Egyptian word for the white race is *Tam-hu,* which resonates with Tama-chek, the name of the Tuareg language (this Saharan tribe is famous for their light eyes and Europoid look).

In some Chinese texts Tam is the name of the king at the time of the flood. Tama is also a chiefly title in Borneo among the Madang. In Hebrew tam simply means "pious," reminding us of the holy tribes who were the *only* survivors of the Flood.

Spiritual Condition of Men and Angels
Twenty-four Thousand Years Ago

But Hebrew legend speaks of the sinful generations of the Deluge just as God in Genesis 6:12 looked abroad and saw how corrupt the Earth had become, mortals leading depraved lives. Echoingly, the Apaches say that the world became so wicked that the Great Spirit sent a terrible flood. Hopi legend too mentions that the "Third World," before its demise, had been corrupted into wickedness and evil.

To put this in a cyclic perspective, the Flood came, not coincidentally, at the end of a three-thousand-year cycle, the final years of which are typically dark and degenerate. The Earth had been in a'ji (a cosmic state of density and low light) for several hundred years.

> The earth and her heavens were in great darkness. . . . They have turned away from My God and My Lords; they have shut themselves up in conceit and darkness. They have peopled the air of the earth with . . . drujas and cannibals.* Have they not made it a place of everlasting destruction? They visit their evils upon mortals . . . [who] became void of direct purpose because of the confusion of soul. . . . They do not desire wisdom and resurrection. Their love lies in darkness. To eat, to sleep, and to devour are the delights of their souls. The first lesson of life they have not learned. . . . Hear My judgment upon them. . . . I have raised them up again and again[†] . . . but they fall the moment My Gods leave them alone. . . .
>
> And it came to pass that . . . the wickedness of man became [so] great in the earth, that the desires of his heart were continually evil. . . . And the Lord God said: Behold, I will bring a flood of waters. . . . But my covenant is with my chosen [Ihins], who shall not be destroyed.
>
> OAHSPE, BOOK OF APH 1:1, 1:10, 1:15–16, 1:20–21;
>
> BOOK OF WARS 29:34–36.

Although Pan (a.k.a. Mu) was often portrayed in legend as a land of prosperity and harmony, many traditions nonetheless aver that it was submerged due to the corruption of its people and the gratifying

---

*Oahspe's mention of cannibalism in Waga (Pan) corresponds to historical cannibalism in Malekula, Rarotonga, Paumutua, Marquesas, and so on.

†This is an implicit reference to that 3,000-year cycle, which typically begins with heaven-sent renewal but ends in downsliding and degradation.

of selfish desires. In Africa, for example, on the Gold Coast, their hero Anansi made the First Men, but they were ungrateful, so Anansi created a small man [Ihin?], and he became the pride of the race. A similar story in South America has Monan as the Author of All among the Brazilian Tupis; upon seeing the ingratitude of men, Monan caused a conflagration of fire, which nonetheless filled him with such pity that he sent a deluging rain on Earth to put it out. The South American tale resonates with one told in the holy book of the Maya, the Popol Vuh, wherein the people forgot their Creator, so Hurakan, the Heart of Heaven, brought a great flood and drowned them all.

> They sacrificed by means of war and death.
>
> OAHSPE, THE LORDS' FIRST BOOK 1:20

Greek legend recalls that men became so wicked that the Earth was soon wet with slaughter; it was then that Zeus sent an immense flood. "Men of blood and brawls had turned it [life] into almost continual fighting" (Wilkins 2000, 28). And there was "no place left for . . . the upright and virtuous in heart" (Oahspe, Book of Aph 1:21). This degeneracy corresponds in certain ways to the infamous Fall of Man.

Giants as Cause of the Flood

> There were giants in those days . . . and their flesh became corrupt and . . . they were worthless on the earth.
>
> OAHSPE, THE LORDS' FIRST BOOK 1:29

To judge from mythology alone, it was the sins of the giants, in great measure, that caused the Flood; but one race was preserved—*Homo sapien pygmaeus,* the sacred little people. The good were chosen and saved, recount the Mayan priests, and they were brought to a new land. *Mayab,* in fact, means "Land of the Chosen Ones." Likewise does the Pima (A'atam, above) creation myth involve the salvation of *chosen beings* from the Flood, while the Skokomish Indians of Mount Rainier relate that the Great Spirit was displeased with the evil in the world, and secluded the good people before causing a massive deluge. Finally, among the Arikara Indians, it is said that the Creator caused a flood to get rid of the unruly giants but saved the little people by storing them in a cave.*

Just as Genesis 6 recalls a time of depraved, murderous giants, the Book of Enoch declares that they, the giants, were at their worst in the time of Jared (antediluvian). What's more, these goliaths were twice the size of men today, men double our size (according to Theopompus). And they "were without judgment and of little sense . . . [though] strong and prolific. . . . Too prolific is the earth . . . [with its] imperfect giant stalk" (Oahspe, Synopsis of Sixteen Cycles 2:13, 3:11, 11). And it was these outsized men who drove the faithful into hiding, despoiled and slaughtered them. Myth is replete with this shameful giant who troubled the Earth, like Loki of the Norse: wherever he came trouble followed. Hither and yon, the Earth's giants are remembered as wild, unreasonable, incestuous, blind to heavenly things, like the impious Titans—corrupt, idolatrous, criminal.

In New Guinea the NeMu are remembered as the rulers of the world before the Flood; the Kai tribes say that these NeMu were much taller and stronger than any people today. But they were all destroyed in the Flood. A great many other sources "attribute a tall stature to those who were submerged in the Deluge—and a small stature to the races which [survived]" (Norman 1973, 131).

South American legends have Tiahuanaco built by giants, an impious lot who, angering the gods, were turned to stone; similar stories in Peru have the giants destroyed by fire from heaven, killing them all. Just so, from temple ruins in Guatemala, inscribed on a piece of antelope skin, comes the story of an island that split open in a burst of flame, whereon a great serpent from the sea swallowed all the giants on the island along with their golden palaces. Toltec tradition relates how our Earth was peopled by giants in the Second Age. Called Quinametzin, they disappeared when the world was devastated by earthquakes.

---

*All these tales agree with Louis Jacolliot, who adduced that the survivors of the lost continent were an elite group.

GIANTS IN THE FLOOD,
ACCORDING TO WORLD MYTHOLOGY

Source	Account
Legends of the Hebrews	The sins of the Nephilim (giants) brought the Deluge upon the world.
Arabian lore	The race of giants was destroyed by the Lord.
Roman mythology	Jupiter banished the Titans to Tartaros.
Greek mythology	Giants were riveted in the sky (i.e., sent to eternity) by Orion, as punishment.
Britain	A boiling ocean, long ago, engulfed the race of godless giants.
Scandinavian Eddas	Giants were effaced by the Deluge.
Pawnee	The giants, too proud, had to be destroyed in great floods.
Okanogan	White giants on an island in midocean, through their wickedness, were destroyed.
Bolivia/Tiahuanaco	The impious giants angered the gods who turned them to stone.
Pre-Incan myth	The god of creation was displeased with the giants and sank them in a deep flood.

Was the Flood a Punishment?

In Raiatea legend the Polynesian deluge was occasioned by the wrath of Lord Rua, god of the ocean. *Wrath?* Do the gods really get angry or spiteful? A Chibcha legend (in South America) records that the spiteful moon goddess, Chia, caused a lake to overflow, bringing on the flood. The Peruvians imagined a wrathful deity unleashing a catastrophic flood upon the wicked, disobedient world. Thus do many traditions, including our biblical one, have a furious god drowning mankind for his sins. The Hebrews saw it as punishment by the Lord, provoked by the rebellious generations of Adam. Likewise did the Babylonians regard the flood as a mighty chastisement—blind fury at the degradation and corruption of their great cities.

But most of these tales are childish and naive, or at best, admonitory lessons, preachy in tone, warning us to be good—or else! As recalled in Oahspe's Book of Aph, however, it was not God's wrath at all, but actual strategy—to save the Earth!

> Shall man of earth say that the Creator was angry, and so sent the land beneath the ocean? He [man] does not have wisdom to comprehend that in this day I cast out hell and destruction. . . . For behold, I [brought] a flood of waters . . . even above the highest mountains [to] . . . destroy its corruption, and purge it of all uncleanness.
>
> OAHSPE, BOOK OF APH 1:29;
> THE LORDS' FIRST BOOK 1:36

> *The Flood was a merciful amputation.*
>
> GUS CAHILL,
> *DARKNESS, DAWN, AND DESTINY*

The Flood Was Ordered by the Gods

> I smote the earth and broke it as an egg.
>
> OAHSPE, BOOK OF GOD'S WORD 1:12

> *The flood is roaring.* God wills it.
>
> MARQUESAN CHANT OF THE DELUGE
> (EMPHASIS ADDED)

As we have seen, in Arabian and other traditions, giants were destroyed *by the Lord*. In the same vein, a northwest coast Indian tableau recounts that the Creator desired the destruction of the motherland of Mu. And with the advent of the Oahspe scriptures late in the nineteenth century, we can now study in great detail the run-up to that conflagration, events that entailed the universal persecution and ultimate genocide of the sacred tribes twenty-four thousand years ago.

Fig. 4.3. Map showing the prediluvial names of the Earth's major divisions. The continents were called by these names for 48,000 years, until the sinking of Pan, in the arc of Noe.

In four great divisions of the earth, Vohu, Jud, Thouri, and Dis (Africa, Asia, Americas, Europe) they did not leave one alive of the Ihin race. In Whaga (Pan) I had a remnant; and they were scattered far and near, in separate places hiding away from their evil pursuers.

OAHSPE, THE LORDS' FIRST BOOK 1:25

God, who was Neph,* said: Hear my prayer, O Jehovih! . . . The Ihin has been destroyed in all the divisions of the earth except Whaga. More than thirty billion angels [former mortals] are gathered on the surface of the earth, and they are too low in grade to be delivered. What shall Your God do, O Father? . . . Cities are destroyed, and they [mortals] live in the manner of four-footed beasts. The inspiration of Your God and his angels can no longer reach them. When they die and enter these heavens they are like festering sores on one another, billions of them.

OAHSPE, SYNOPSIS OF SIXTEEN CYCLES 2:1–8

---

*Neph, the god of Earth in the 3,000 years previous to Aph, is also the name of a great god of Egypt.

Such passages help us to understand the "Why" of Pan's destruction and also to eradicate a few of her myths along the way: for example, all was presumably well and good in that happy land, thought Churchward, until gas belts and volcanic outbursts unleashed mayhem on this prosperous people. Churchward (and almost everyone else) assumed that *natural* forces were at play. Yet there is nothing in geological time to compare to the vanishment of an entire continent. Conversely, there is abundant testimony from the world's people that the destruction was wrought by *the gods* to erase abomination from the face of the Earth and her heavens. "The whole point of the Flood was to lay to rest the savage futility of human nature" (Pilkey 1984, 54).

Viracocha sent the Flood to destroy mankind, says Andean legend. In Sumer too, as in so many other places, flood myths are infused with the unshakable conviction that the gods themselves convened in privy council and resolved to obliterate mankind. Men were continually fighting, says one Polynesian legend, until the gods finally decided the only thing to do was to drown them all beneath the waves. Thus in Tahitian epics, it was the god of the winds who broke the continent (Fenua Nui) into scattered islands. On Easter Island the legend of Hotu Manua has Uoke stirring up the bottom of the sea, undermining the land; Rapa Nui (Easter Island), they said, was once much larger, but because of the sins of the people Uoke broke it all up with his crowbar.

Likewise did the ancient Maya record that Homen, of strong arm, caused the Earth to tremble. He, the wizard who makes all things, simply kicked it, and it was sacrificed that very night (Codex Cortesianus). In the same way does the Popol Vuh portray the flood as agitated "by the will of Heaven." In North America too, according to the Hopi, Taiowa the Creator ordered that the world be destroyed.

Hear My voice, o ye managers of corporeal worlds, for the red star [Earth], in her pride and self-glory, flieth toward the point of My whetted sword . . . Jehovih hath decreed a pruning-knife to a traveling world.

OAHSPE, BOOK OF APH 2:6–8

My Decree Has Gone Forth

While volcanoes, earthquakes, and tsunamis can do vast damage, they have never been known to plunge whole continents beneath the waves. But gods and goddesses, working in great phalanxes, can accomplish the inconceivable—well beyond the local tremors of the natural order. In Gopi Krishna's view, "Those apparently menacing geophysical cataclysms would be instrumentalities by which the Creator keeps his creation in balance . . . [to insure] growth to a higher state of being" (quoted in White 1980, 269).

With this in mind, let us consider a few of the intriguing passages in Oahspe that describe how and why the gods "cleft asunder" the continent of Whaga. First: Why?

> Man forgot his Creator; he said: "No Eye sees me, no Ear hears me." And he neglected to guard himself against the serpent [corporeality; self-satisfaction per se]; and the serpent said to him: Partake of all things, for they are yours. And man heeded, and, lo and behold, the race of man descended into utter darkness. And man did not distinguish his sister or mother; and woman did not distinguish her brother or father. And God saw the wickedness of man, and he called out, saying: Hear my voice, O man! . . . But because of man's darkness he could not hear the voice of God.
>
> OAHSPE, SECOND BOOK OF LORDS 2:12–15

> So the Most High said, "I know what is for their own good"; and My decree has gone forth. . . . These druj [earthbound spirits] return to mortals and fasten upon them as fetals or as familiars, and inspire them to evil.
>
> OAHSPE, BOOK OF APH 1:17

And in the next breath, he commanded his gods and goddesses to

> go now to the earth and find . . . where most of these druj congregate, for I will uproot their stronghold. . . . The drujas and fetals

shall be . . . cast into walls of fire . . . kin shall be torn away from kin, friend from friend, mother from daughter, and father from son; for they have become like absorbents, sucking one another continually. And the walls of the fire shall go up around them without ceasing, and they shall not escape* . . . [but] shall be stirred up and made to know that they are alive, and can exist independent of fetal [sucking].

OAHSPE, BOOK OF APH 1:18, 30; SYNOPSIS OF SIXTEEN CYCLES 3:15

The scenario then focuses on the Pacific continent and its heaven.

And the council deliberated and caused the records of the earth to be examined and they discovered that the heaven of the land of Wagga was beyond redemption because of the great numbers of spirits of cannibals and of the multitude of fetals. . . . So Jehovih said: Behold, the division of Whaga shall be hewn off and cast beneath the waters of the ocean. Her heaven shall no longer be tenable by the spirits of destruction, for I will rend its foundation and scatter them in the winds of heaven.

Go, therefore, down to the earth and provide nets and vanchas for receiving the spirits of darkness, and for receiving the spirits of mortals who shall perish in the waters. Also provide a place in My exalted heavens suitable for them; and you shall put walls around them in heaven so they cannot escape,[†] but can be weaned from evil. And when you have come to the earth and its heavens,

---

*"They shall not escape" reminds me of the Tibetan story of Kunzang At Muwer, who hurled a gigantic rock to the Earth that landed in the Pacific Ocean; it was only then that "the deities and the demons of the nine dimensions trembled with fear, fainted and were paralyzed" (Joseph 2006, 282). In other words, it broke the anchorage of the drujas. As absorbents and sucking fetals, their behavior is somewhat similar to what we call *co-dependents*.

†Rarotonga cosmogony has a corrupted version of these nets of no escape. Souls after death could get caught in the *net* of Muru; certain "souls had no means of escape from the fatal nets of Muru. . . . We have reference to souls struggling to escape the nets. . . . The fate of souls that fell into one of the nets was simple; they were taken out of the nets, their brains were dashed out . . . and they were carried off to the shades to be eaten" (Williamson 1933, 2:26–27).

acquaint My God and his Lords with My decree. And say to them: Thus says Jehovih: Behold, behold, I will sink the land of Whaga beneath the waters of the ocean; and her heaven I will carry away to a place in My firmament, where she shall no longer engulf My people in darkness.

OAHSPE, SYNOPSIS OF SIXTEEN CYCLES 3:16–19

The Polynesians seem to know something about these "walls of fire" and "nets" and even the trick of "paralyzing" demons. In one Tuamotu legend of revenge, the hero Tahaki finds his way to "the house of the goblin band who tortured his father. He conjures upon them 'the intense cold of Havaiki' (the other world), which puts them to sleep. Then Tahaki gathered up the net . . . and carried it to the door of the long house. He set fire to the house. When the goblin myriad shouted 'Where is the door?' Tahaki called out: 'Here it is.' They thought it was one of their own band who had called out, and so they rushed headlong into the net, and Tahaki burned them up in the fire" (Santillana 1969, 175). The nets, in a similar tale, are in the possession of the gods of the Pleiades. The strategy portrayed in Oahspe, though, is a bit different.

And you shall spread a net around the borders of Whaga, against the line of the ocean and to the high north mountains; and the net shall encompass the continent of Whaga, and its height shall be a thousand miles, and in thickness, so deep that no spirit of darkness can escape and find the way abroad. . . . The seine of My fishing pole is stretched; countless millions of druj and fetals will fall into My net. . . .

I [Aph] formed the tube of transit . . . where I planned to deliver the drujas and fetals of those who were to perish in the ocean . . . and of these spirits there were more than twenty-four billion four hundred million, of whom more than three billion were fetals, familiars, and spirits in chaos. . . . And now Neph came, his ship*

---

*Concerning these etherean ships, see chapter 3, p. 120, on vimanas and fireships.

filled with his long-laboring hosts. And I greeted him and said to him: By the power and wisdom of Jehovih, the continent of Whaga is to be cut loose and submerged, and her heavens carried away. Return to the earth; and from all the divisions of earth and heaven, *bring all the spirits of darkness to Whaga,* so that I may carry them away. Then Neph and his hosts viewed the imposing scene and returned back to earth.

OAHSPE, BOOK OF APH 3:15, 2:11, 3:19, AND 32, 4:3 [EMPHASIS ADDED]

Bringing all the dark spirits to one manageable place is actually a theme found in Okanagan myth, which recounts the long-ago time when the quarreling among the "white giants" grew into a war. This made Scomalt, their leader, very angry, so she *drove the wicked giants to one end of the island,* and when they were gathered together she broke off that piece of land and pushed it into the sea.

The Lord said: A wise physician amputates a diseased limb and so preserves the trunk to become healed. Did I not see the rankness of the tribes of darkness, the druks;* and that the proceedings of man would render the earth void? . . . Behold, I saw that my chosen had become exterminated on all the divisions of the earth except Pan. And I saw that those who had been their destroyers had, in turn, nearly exterminated one another. . . . Indeed the land of Whaga (Pan) was already in the throes of death. The druks had become a festering sore; and the spirits of the dead, tens of billions of them, would not quit their hold on mortals. . . .

And I sent my angels around the whole earth, and gathered in the spirits of darkness; gathered them to the land of Whaga. And when my work was ready, I raised up my hand, as a surgeon that would lop off a diseased limb, and I cleft asunder the continent of Pan and sunk it beneath the waters. And my angels conducted my chosen out of that land, and not one of them perished.

OAHSPE, THE LORDS' FIRST BOOK 2:1–9

---

*Druk is the mortal; druj is the spiritual equivalent.

The Chosen People

Those with the higher light were called Faithists, because they perceived that Wisdom shaped all things. . . . And the Faithists were also called the chosen people, because they chose God.

OAHSPE, THE LORDS' FIRST BOOK 1:19–20

Antiquarians may not know their exact name or place, but know at least of the existence of an "enlightened race saved from a great catastrophe" (Higgins 1991, 33).

God said: I preserved the Ihin race to be without evil, as the foundation of my light, from whom I could reach forth to the tribes of darkness.

OAHSPE, BOOK OF APH 4:1

By now it should be plain that, at the time just preceding the flood, the only virtuous culture left in the world, albeit a minority, was on the continent of Pan. "The Tongans have traditions of times when wars were not. . . . A highly civilized people . . . of a peaceable nature [once] occupied the South Sea Islands. . . . They were gradually pushed back . . . by various people who . . . were constantly fighting and killing" (Perry 1968, 156). And so it was. Thanks to the druk and Ihuan warriors, "the Ihin hath been destroyed off all the divisions of the earth save Wagga [Pan]" (Oahspe, Synopsis of Sixteen Cycles 2:2). War, genocide, and retrobreeding in both the New and Old Worlds had left the prediluvial civilization in ruins.

Thou killest my prophets.

OAHSPE, BOOK OF GOD'S WORD 1:9

In the New World the extermination of a South American white race was recounted to Pedro Cieza de Leon, who was told that before the time of the Incas there were two powerful lords who "conquered many of the *pucaras** . . . one of these chiefs, Cari, entered La Laguna de Titicaca and found there a white people who had beards. They fought with them in such a manner that all were killed" (Wilkins 2000, 49, 117). In North America the Menomonee Indians had a similar tradition of a fierce tribe in the Long Ago that wiped out a white-skinned population, just as Cherokee lore recounts that their own ancestors waged war against a 3-foot-tall race of moon-eyed white people. Africa, China, Scandinavia, and Scotland share similar histories of a harmless people whom their ancestors exterminated.

Indeed the chosen people, the Ihins and their Faithist followers, had everywhere been persecuted and despoiled, like the Zarathustrians of ancient Persia who "fell into constant persecution . . . [and] were nearly destroyed . . . millions of them put to death" (Oahspe, Book of Saphah: Earthly History 16, 17, 20). Now it is interesting that Lewis Spence made the keen observation that most regions of the Pacific *Rim* have a mystery religion and ancient arcane wisdom, from Kamtchatka to Chile to Alaska, even the Australian Aborigine. Yet the Pacific area *itself* is virtually bereft of such systems. "This," says Spence, "can only be accounted for by the fact that they were suppressed. . . . The professors of the ancient Lemurian Mysteries found a refuge in . . . lands surrounding the Pacific Ocean" (1933, 204).

> They lived in hidden retreats.
> DAVID CHILDRESS, *LOST CITIES OF*
> *ANCIENT LEMURIA AND THE PACIFIC*

By twenty-four thousand years ago then, the land of Pan had become peopled over with men raised up to deeds of blood; yet a remnant of the peaceful Ihins hid out from their evil pursuers. The theme is a familiar one.

---

*The vocable *puc* (or puk or puck), as in *puc*ara ("stronghold"), is, in the universal language, a designation for sprites or more correctly the oldest races of little people, *Homo sapien pygmaeus.* Puuc was the capital city of these little people before the Maya came. In North America as well, the Puk-alutumush is the race of little people remembered by the Mi'kmaq Indians. One finds it also in Japan, where Koro-*puk*-guru, an "underground" race (i.e., living in the mounds), was also wiped out.

Since the time of the ancients to this day the worshippers of the One Great Spirit have been persecuted and abused by idolaters of Gods and Saviors.

OAHSPE, BOOK OF SAPHAH: PROLOGUE 55

Genocide, in fact, is the real story behind Cain and Abel (druks versus Ihins).

My chosen were persecuted and hidden away in the valleys and mountains, even on the tops of mountains.

OAHSPE, THE LORDS' FIRST BOOK 1:25, 32

This reminds us of Hawaii's Mu and Menehune* people and all the other peaceful "fairylike" tribes known for their isolation from the rest of humanity. "The fairies dwelt away in the wooded mountains," says New Zealand legend (Anderson 1928, 135). "The descendants of the Mu [people] in the Hawaiian Islands did not welcome their Polynesian guests. . . . They refrained from making war against them, but kept their distance. . . . They were sworn never to reveal any of the[ir] rites" (Joseph 2006, 175). So when Hawaiians say that a wise "dwarf" race of supernatural powers inhabited the mountaintops, living in seclusion, we recognize the characteristics of *Homo sapien pygmaeus.* As far as living memory can recall, the majority of these little people were massacred by the Polynesians,† and, as Spence sees it, "it is only in the more spacious localities like Hawaii and New Zealand that they could find refuge and hiding-places. These islands are especially rich in legends of them. . . . They were worshipped as gods" (Spence 1933, 74).

Yet they were oppressed by the very ancestors of these Hawaiians and New Zealanders. I wonder if certain recent practices are a leftover from the time of the Ihin persecutions: in Mangaia (Cook Islands), it

---

*The tiny "Manahune" are also recollected in New Zealand, Tahiti, Rarotonga, and Mangaia.

†As mentioned in chapter 2, a blond fairy people called the Turehu were driven to the mountains by the invading Polynesians.

was only *golden-haired* children who were sacrificed, not too long ago, to the god Tangaroa.

The Peach of Immortality

According to the Yuroks of California, when the Earth was new the immortals lived in harmony with the cosmos. It is a theme not unfamiliar to world mythology.

> The chosen of God, called Jhins, because they were the fruit of both heaven and earth, were taken, under the protection of God, his Lords and angels, to all the divisions of the earth for the fulfillment of man on the earth. The Jhins were preserved by the Gods . . . for they are like leaven, prepared for the resurrection of all the races of men. . . . They do not kill . . . nor are they given to lust, war, or quarrelsomeness. . . .
>
> The Jhins were my living examples of righteousness. Do not think, however, that the Jhins were the perfection of manhood and womanhood. They were not a developed race, nor righteous because of their own knowledge. By the constant presence of my exalted angels, they were obsessed to righteousness, being restrained away from evil. They were my sermon before the tribes of druks and cannibals that covered the earth over.
>
> OAHSPE, THE LORDS' SECOND BOOK 1:2;
> BOOK OF GOD'S WORD 18:20 AND 19:13;
> THE LORDS' FIFTH BOOK 4:8–10

The "chosen" of Pan were chosen—to survive—for the same reason that the biblical Noah was esteemed the only blameless man of his time; his people bore the light of Immortality. Isn't this why the Finns claim that first man *radiated light*? And why the Babylonians said "his plane of wisdom was the plane of heaven"? (Heinberg 1989, 65). Studying these Babylonians and their Gilgamesh flood epic, we learn that when Gilgamesh, King of Erech, was devastated by the death of his dearest friend, Enkidu, he went off to find the secret of immortality from his ancestor Utnapishtim, the Babylonian Noah, who along with his family had been the only survivor of the debacle; they were afterward *made immortal by the gods.* Decreed henceforth to be one with the gods, they dwelled in the Far Distance. Stripped of its mythic garb, this immortality was nothing but the force of soul, the capacity for everlasting life—made possible through the influence and genes of the Ihin people. Sole survivors of the Panic deluge, they were "seed" and spark of all future humanity. Theirs was the "blood of the gods"—just as the first kings of Tibet did not really die, but "mounted into heaven."

Isn't this conveyed as well in Japanese lore, which has the Peach of Immortality bestowed as a result of contact with those from the drowned motherland? Indeed, Boluto (i.e., the lost land) was known to the New Zealand Maori as the Island of Immortality. Coming close to the truth of the matter, the Cup of Immortality, as the Persians averred, was simply given to *all the faithful.* As for China, the emperor Qin Shi Huang died while still searching for the legendary Islands of the Immortals—*off the eastern coast of China.* (It is he who is buried together with the famous Terra-cotta Army.) Also in China is Kuan Yin, the beloved goddess who held the secret of Eternal Life in the Kun Lun Mountains, abode of the Immortals.

He Blew His Breath upon the Ships

And Jehovih blew His breath upon the ships of His sons and daughters, blew them about upon the ocean; blew them to the east and west and north and south . . . my angels conducted my chosen out of that land [Pan].

OAHSPE, THE LORDS' FIRST BOOK 1:45–46, 2:9

A certain mystique still infuses the Great Ancestors' miraculous passage from their ruined homeland. As the Yucatecans tell it, god delivered them by opening twelve paths through the sea, an event that the Macus Indians of Amazonia say was a miracle performed by the "king of the floodtime." In India too a similar notion of divine intervention takes the form of a giant fish (an avatar of Vishnu) that *guided* the ship

Fig. 4.4. The god of the flood from Nineveh. The Indian version has the fish-god helping Manu over the Mountain of the North.

through the Deluge. In a related Polynesian version, the god Maui pulls the canoe of the migrating folk across the ocean—as does Uitzilopochtli in the Aztec legend.

> With me, I [Aph] took Neph, Son of Jehovih, and another thirty thousand Gods and Goddesses, besides ten million ethereans, who each had thousands of years' experience in heaven and on various corporeal worlds; and we came back to the earth, to the ocean where the land had gone down.
>
> And when I came to the ships in which the Ihins had escaped, finding the Gods who were in charge of them . . . Your voice, O Jehovih, came to me, saying: Bend the currents . . . O My Son; shape the course of the ships so that they fall into groups. . . . So I divided my hosts, making four divisions of them. And I said to Neph: Direct them, O God, to those countries Jehovih has shown you, for you know all the earth; remember, you are still God of earth. Now those in charge of the wind currents divided the ships and drove two of them off to the northern land [Japan]. And the Gods and angels turned the currents about and drove the four groups of ships in four different ways, according to the directions of God.
>
> OAHSPE, BOOK OF APH 7:3–8

Did the Deluge Destroy a Great Civilization?

In all this we perceive a serious departure from what we have been told about the lost race and their civilization. For example, it is often said that "titanic forces . . . some appalling catastrophe . . . utterly destroyed the great civilization" (Wilkins 2000, 137, 185). French writer Robert Charroux fueled this legend with his various declarations that "our Superior Ancestors . . . the earthly intelligence . . . was totally destroyed by a great cataclysm" (1974, 70), or that "an unknown civilization had been destroyed by a sudden cataclysm. A long period of ignorance then followed . . . in the post-diluvian world . . . nations of the earth were struggling painfully back to knowledge and civilization" because "a very highly developed antediluvian civilization . . . had been obliterated" (1972, 99, 117).

Reversing this depiction of the flood, it was, I dare say, the "highly developed" ones who were saved—not destroyed! Standing the actual nature of the event on its head, such writers have portrayed the calamity as one that *reduced* civilization to a state of savagery, "thrusting those who survived back into a barbarism from which it would have taken centuries to recover" (Mooney 1975, 155). Yet another protohistorian argues that "only a huge disaster can explain the sudden disappearance of cultures present in the most distant epochs of North America. . . . Why had [the horse in America] gone? As a result perhaps of that same force which shook the United States back into barbarism and killed off its original inhabitants" (Kolosimo 1973, 90–91). Likewise has it been written as fact that "people fled in panic from their shattered cities to be swept by raging seas down to the sunless deep. The few stricken survivors plunged to barbarism" (Drake 1974, 90). The flood, says yet another writer, "destroyed everything but vestiges of an advanced civilization" (Von Ward 2011, 125).

Thus has it been repeated many times in the literature that the high culture and golden age of the remote past were utterly destroyed. Much of this accords with the equally fictitious romance of Atlantis, which declares that knowledge was lost and a dark age ensued, "decimating the population . . . and condemning the survivors to take refuge in caves" (Kolosimo 1975, 11). Leaving only a few survivors, the disaster allegedly ended a great technological civilization, which also held the secret of paradise on Earth.

Again and again we are told of a golden age destroyed by a cataclysm. But in my view *not a scintilla of knowledge was lost because of the*

Great Deluge; quite the contrary, the Noachic man-gods who escaped the sinking of Pan (which was indeed the flood) brought the arts of civilization (agriculture, writing, navigation, mining) to the savages among whom they settled in all the divisions of the Earth. In fact, a new golden age (postdiluvial) *followed* that flood: the dispersal from Pan brought a veritable renaissance of culture to the Old and New Worlds. It was the greatest of all diasporas, and it brought the "reign of the gods," the era known among many people as the golden age.

And because the Ihins of Pan are our spiritual forbears, the signature of Pan was impressed, hither and yon, on all things pertaining to the growth of the soul. In ancient America, for example, there was the holy rite of Annubia-*pan* (Oahspe, First Book of the First Lords 27, 24). In the Alps, *Pan*tegani was the legendary species of blessed little people, protectors. In France, Montes*pan* is a Cro-Magnon shrine with cave paintings; Maka*pan* is a cave shrine in South Africa. In India the district of the Holy Pan was *Pan*dimandalam. *Pan*chaia was the legendary utopia in the Arabian Sea. Pan-oh is the séance hut in Malaysia (see chapter 8, p. 348, "Tholoi"), while tam-pan are the ceremonial cloths of Sumatra. Pan-et means "temple" in Hebrew. But it was Pan's own temple district, Khu, that left its most enduring mark on the languages of the world.

The Holy Khu

... the temples of Khu shall sink to rise no more ... in the deluge.

OAHSPE, SYNOPSIS OF SIXTEEN CYCLES 3:28

In the Pacific the word for *temple* on the island of Ongtong-java is *hare-a-iku* ("house of light"). *Iku* also serves as the oldest royal appellative in Polynesia. "Mu, the Motherland, was also called . . . Kui Land . . . [with] great carved stone temples" (Churchward 2011, 26, 157). This resembles Mexico's Cuicilco (phonetically Kui-cilco) pyramid, considered perhaps the oldest monument in the Americas. In fact, *kue* meant "temple" in Mexico, at the time of the Conquest, while k'ul means "divine" in Yucatecan. In California kuksu is the Pomo Indian rite of renewal.

The motherland, Hiva, says native lore, was a land of temples, called *Kua*-i-helani by the Hawaiians. In the Maori chant for that lost country the *whare-kura* was the temple of learning. Now *kura* means "light," and the Maori founding hero, discoverer of New Zealand, had a similar name—Kupe—while the first maiden formed by the gods was called Kurawaka. What's more, Ku is the architect-god; Kupua, a demigod; and Kuila-moku, the god of medicine in Hawaii.

Khu names pertaining to ceremonial life abound not only in Oceania but in the Old World as well.

KHU WORDS OF RITUAL SIGNIFICANCE IN POLYNESIA

Name	Where	Comment
Ku	Hawaii	a ritual honoring the phases of the moon; ku also refers to an "upper place"
Kuma	Hawaii	leader of ritual dance commemorating the flood
Kuakeahu	Hawaii	a spirit land
Kuasha	Hawaii	private altar
Kuahu	Hawaii	shrine
Kumulipo	Hawaii	the legend of creation
Kuni	Hawaii	a ceremony
Aru-ku ku-renga	Easter Island	the wooden tablet on which rongorongo is written
Aku-aku	Easter Island	ghost, spirit
Kuhane	Marquesas	soul of priests and chiefs
Ma-ku-tuo	Polynesia	black magic
OLD WORLD		
Mizuko ku-yo	Japan	a ceremony
Khu Mueang	Thailand	holy district
Ku	China	Shang era ceremonial goblets: kuang are vessels for offerings
Kushana	Central Asia	mythical "bird-serpent"

Name	Where/Who	Comment
DuKu	Babylonia	creation chamber of the gods; also "holy mound," indicating the place of the founders
Ku-durra	Babylonia	commemorative monument, sanctified by the gods
Ku	Sumeria	meant "holy" (Collins 2014, 260)
Khuzistan	Southwest Persia	a religious center
Kushta	Iraq	Mandean term for earlier ideal world
Kusha	India	sacred grass
Kudr	India	ceremonial grouping among the Toda clans
aa-khu	Egypt	"spirit," "light
Rite of Khu	Egypt	propitiating the dead (*khu* meaning "intelligence of the spirit")
Khuit & Khufu	Egypt	temples of light* (i.e., Gizeh and Kheops)
Kurru	Egypt	site of kingly tombs

*Ku also appears as symbol of light in Peru: cuyo (kuyo), a kind of glowworm, is the name of an insect that produced a penetrating light used by Incan surgeons.

KU AS HERO OR DEIFIED ANCESTOR

Name	Where	Comment
Kuihi-kuaha	Easter Island	names of two gods of the original homeland
Haku	Society Islands	"lord"
Pan Ku	China	first man and Creator
Nu Kua	China	first human beings
Nu Kua Shih	China	goddess of creation
Kuei	China	discarnate spirit
O-ku-ninushu	Japan	semidivinity, Ruler of the Land
Khu'an	Thailand	guardian spirit

KU AS HERO OR DEIFIED ANCESTOR (*cont.*)

Name	Where	Comment
Kut	Kamchatka	God; Kur is supreme God of the Siberian Gilyaks
Ku	Hawaii	creator deity
Kupua	Hawaii	demigod, like Hi-ku
Ku-mu-honua	Hawaii	first couple
Ku-hine	Hawaii	goddess of rain
Kulabob	New Guinea	culture hero, initiator
Kuchi	Australia	supernatural beings among the Dieri
Khub	Hottentot	the Lord
Khuzwene	Bantu	a god
Kumaras	India	sons of God
Kubera	India	epic hero of Ramayana
Kuha	India	god of good fortune
Khullakpa	India	among the Nagas of Assam, hereditary priests
Khumbaba	Babylonia	Lord of the Forest
Khusar	Byblos	ancient god who taught divination
Ku Roi	Ireland	King of the World
NEW WORLD		
Kumpara	Jivaro	Creator
He-kura	Yanomamo	ageless spirits
Kulimina	Arawak	goddess, race founder
Kukumatz	Maya	the Great Spirit
K'hu	Maya	deity
Kukulcan	Maya	founding father
Zakuk	Chiapas, Mexico	Royal mother of Palenque
Kumash	North America	Modoc god

NEW WORLD (cont.)		
Kumastambo	North America	Mohave Creator
Kutoyis	North America	Blackfoot culture hero

I noticed too that numerous *ku* names refer to mountainous areas. Were the Temples of Khu situated on eminences? Many of Polynesia's maraes are indeed built on elevated ground. For example, Kukii is the *heiau* (temple) of hewn stone on the Hill of Kukii, in the Puna district.

Mountainous places with *ku* in the name* include:

Name	Place	Meaning
Kumuele	Molokai	mountain
Kula	Maui	mountains
Mount Ikurangi	Tahiti	mountain
Khu	Egypt	mountain
Ku	Serra do Joelho, Brazil	"mountain" in Indian language
Kiberai de Ku	Serra do Sapo, Brazil	a mountain in the Tupi region
Kucapah	northern Mexico	mountain range
Kumawa	New Guinea	mountain range
Ko-ku-shi	Gobi	mountain range
Kuen Lun	China	mountains
Kulen	Cambodia	plateau
Lawu-Kukusan	Java	mountain
Kurkura	Mesopotamia	mount where ark landed in Chaldean legend; kur = "mountain" in the language (Collins 2014, 261)
Du-ku	Turkey	sacred mountain, first farmers in Near East

*See appendix A on more *Ku* words.

Name	Place	Meaning
Kuruman	South Africa	hills
Kula	Vedic	slope
Kunoy	Faroe Island	one continuous mountain

A Grateful Heads-Up

If we were to profile the many Noahs of world mythology, one point of agreement in legends from Persia to Polynesia is a heaven-sent *forewarning* of the destruction to come. The Coxcox and Aztecs of Mexico recount that the Creator taught this pious man, Tapi, to build a boat to escape an imminent flood of waters. In another Mexican legend the god Titlacahuan told Nata and his wife, Nana, to hollow out a big cypress tree and enter it when the big waters came. The hollow-tree motif appears again in the far-distant Banks Islands in the myth of Quat: the land of Gaua was swamped, so Quat made himself a boat from a very large tree. While he was building it he was often laughed at by his brothers; this derision echoes right back to the Mexican Tapi, who also was mocked by his neighbors. Even the North American Zuni have a comparable tale of being scoffed at by the profane. In Algonquin tradition the ancestors had warning of the flood and built ships to escape. It is the same among the Navajo of Arizona and the Bochica of Colombia, who say their ancestors somehow knew of the Deluge in advance.

It is always interesting to see how local flavor is injected into universal legend. For instance, in Arizona the Pima flood hero was warned by an eagle, while in Greece it was the cry of a crane that alerted the people (at Megaros). The bird becomes a fish in India—the Hindu Noah, Vaivasvata, was warned by Vishnu (who took the form of a fish) and told him to build an ark. In cultures with a mystical bent you sometimes find the flood hero acquiring his foreknowledge in a paranormal way: the classic flood story, that of the Sumerians, has Ziusudra/Xisuthros (their Noah) described as a pious and god-fearing king before whom Cronus/Ea appeared in a dream-vision, warning him to build a vessel and save his people from a coming inundation.

Sometimes it is God himself who issues the warning, as in the Persian version; in the *Shah Nameh,* Yima and his pure flock were given directions by the god Ahura Mazda, who foresaw the coming catastrophe. Yima was told to build a *vara* accommodating 1,900 people, "as long as a race course . . . nine avenues must be laid out." The Greek rendition is similar. Deucalion and Pyrrha, king and queen of Thea, a pious couple, are warned by Zeus. Their ark floated for nine days before coming to rest on Mt. Parnassus.

As for the patriarchs, the Book of Enoch recounts how Enoch warned his son Methuselah of a great judgment that would come upon the Earth; but his grandson Noah would survive. "The experiences attributed to Enoch appeared spontaneously in a dream . . . or a trance. . . . Another person of whom the Old Testament says 'he walked with God' was Noah. . . . Could it have been that Noah in trance . . . had a premonition of the imminent flood?" (Ryzl 2007, 72). Indeed, some theologians are convinced that God talked directly to Noah and told him how to build the ark. God speaks to people in visions, or in dreams, or by a voice they can hear. Did Noah hear the voice telling him what to do? In Genesis 6:14–16, God gives Noah instructions: "Make yourself an ark of gopherwood, put various compartments in it, cover it with pitch," and so on.

In Oahspe it is the angels who give the warning to the Ihins. "And the angels of the Lord went to the Faithists and inspired them to build ships. . . . For two whole years builded they them" (The Lords' First Book 1:38). On Wagga, those chosen people had been hidden away on the tops of mountains. This seems to be confirmed by the Tahitian epic of King Rata Rata that, curiously, has a number of ship-building "elves [living] in their mountain habitation" (Henry 1928, 490).

Deliverance

Because you have kept my commandments, come forth and hear the word of the Lord your God. And they came out from their hiding places, thousands and thousands of them. And I sent my angels to them, saying to my angels: Say to my chosen: This is the

Fig. 4.5. Hopi petroglyph carved on a rock near Oraibi

word of the Lord your God: Go and build enough ships . . . and get within, where none can pursue or destroy.

OAHSPE, THE LORDS' FIRST BOOK 1:33–35

As for those hollowed-out trees, legend, depending on local flora, has them variously made of cypress, balsamwood, eucalyptus, gopherwood (acacia), and so forth. In one version of the Hopi Emergence the faithful were sealed into hollow tubes, which then floated upon the water.

The land was swallowed up, valleys and mountains; and all the living (on Whaga) perished, except the Ihins, who floated off in the ships. And there were twelve thousand four hundred and twenty; and these were all that remained of the first race of man that walked on two feet.

OAHSPE, THE LORDS' FIRST BOOK 1:43–44

Although the flood legend that we are most familiar with has *Mesopotamian* people (and animals) embarking in one grand ship and disembarking on a not-very-distant mountain (Ararat), I believe the demythologized version of this great event would entail 1) *many* ships (not a single monster ship), 2) no animals aboard (*Sorry, No Pets*), and 3) landing places in *several* parts of the world, though not including the Near East (Mesopotamia).

The Lord said: I will name the fleets of my chosen, and their names shall be everlasting on the earth. And the Lord named them Guatama, Shem, Jaffeth, Ham and Yista. . . . The Lord said: From these, my seed, I will people the earth over in all its divisions.

OAHSPE, THE LORDS' FIRST BOOK 1:48–49

Of course, if the legend is indeed about the escape from Pan in the

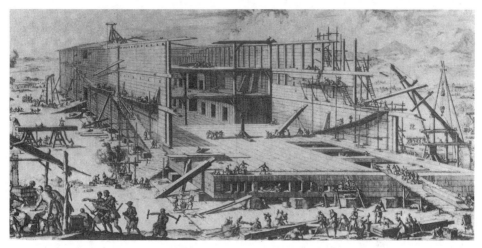

Fig. 4.6. From an old European book, artist's reconstruction of the monster ship built by Noah's people. A few biblicists have calculated that the grand ark contained a total of more than 100,000 square feet.

Pacific, the survivors might well have scattered in different directions. We might recall that Johann Friedrich Blumenbach, known as the father of physical anthropology, divided the human race into five types: American (Guatama), Caucasian (Shem), Mongolian (Jaffeth), Ethiopian (Ham), and Malayan (Yista). This fivefold classification dovetails with the five* land-ing places of the sons of Noah (which is the subject of the next chapter).

In Peruvian myth "this cataclysm was followed by a peculiar incident. On a high mountaintop appeared five eggs. . . . The egg is the equivalent of the Ark in which the universal Noah embarks. . . . I believe these Peruvian

Fig. 4.7. Left: Five men in a raft, Oahspe sign of Pan, signifying the five fleets radiating out of the lost lands. Right: Near the Haida are Alaskan groups. What do you make of this Inuit drawing of five men in a boat?

---

*Is it coincidental that "five" is *panj* in Farsi and *panca* in Sanskrit? Maybe, maybe not. It is also interesting that the Armenian word for ark is *Tapan*.

Fig. 4.8. a) Mayan glyph from Bishop DeLanda's alphabet. b) Undeciphered Maori writing. c) Colombian gold horde unearthed at an old Spanish mission on the outskirts of Bogota, showing five men on raft of golden logs; the two figures in the rear are out of focus.

'eggs' symbolize the great arks or ships of the Lemurians washed up by the flood. . . . From the ark of the Flood, humanity is, as it were, rehatched and born anew" (Spence 1933, 192). Five arks or eggs become clamshells in the tradition of five brothers among the Haida Indians of British Columbia, who say the first people came out of clamshells (dugouts?), and they were "five little bodies," which is to say the Ihins, *Homo sapiens pygmaeus*.

It may be significant that the Malekulans of Melanesia attribute their megalithic-building tradition to five culture-bearing brothers, white men with aquiline noses. In India as well the five heroic brothers of the Mahabharata are the *Pan*davas; it is likely that the name is based on the Sanskrit *pan*du (i.e., "white, yellow-white, pale").

By the will of God, the ships were congregated into four fleets; *thirty-four* ships into each fleet.

OAHSPE, THE LORDS' FIRST BOOK 1:47 (EMPHASIS ADDED)

The Irish *Book of Invasions* records that the Nemhedh were five brothers who, bringing order, justice, and prosperity, established the five provinces of Ireland. These Nemedians, says the book, "had *thirty-four* [emphasis added] ships that traveled the open sea in search of new lands." The name *Nemedian* seems to be an anglicization of Nemhedh (var. Neimhidh), being a "noble, sacrosanct, worthy people" who arrived in Ireland some time (600 years) after the Deluge. It is the same lineage that produced the king's poets—the forefathers of Ireland's diminutive Tuatha de Danaan, a "divine" race.

Genesis has the waters overwhelming the Earth for 150 days before the ark came to rest on the Armenian mountains of Ararat (Genesis 8:4), presumably on Luba, one of its twin peaks that rises 17,000 feet. However, the Bible "omits any mention of how Noah led all those animals . . . from those dizzy crags in the clouds down to terra firma" (Drake 1974, 149). Surveying the flood literature we find the "mountains of Noah" not in Armenia alone but in *every part of the world*.

Country	Landing Place
Iraq	Mount Nisir (according to the Epic of Gilgamesh), otherwise situated on Mount Korkura
India	Himalayas
Ethiopia	Illubabut Mountains
Yemen	in the mountains west of Marib
Taiwan	Mount Ragasan
Rotti (near Timor)	Lakimola Peak
Philippines	Mount Amuyao or Mount Kalauitan
Indonesia	Mount Pokis
Greece	Mount Parnassus
Samothrace	Mount Ida
Southeast Turkey	Cudi Dag
Colombia	Altiplano of the Andes
Peru	Mount Vilcacoto
Bolivia	Tiahuanaco
Mexico	Culhuacan
North America	Rocky Mountains
Hawaii	Mauna Kea Peak

The First Thanksgiving

If Genesis tells us that Noah afterward built an altar to the Lord and offered burnt offerings, the Hawaiian Noah, Nuu, offered a pig and coconuts after being rescued from the flood. Traditions may vary, but the theme of a thank-offering remains constant—the ancient Athenians threw wheat into a hole in the ground at the place where Deucalion's flood had erupted. In Mesopotamia, after the waters abated, Utnapishtim came out of the ark and poured out a libation to the gods, followed by an offering. In North America the Mandan rite was culminated with offerings that are thrown into the river, just as Hebrew, Chaldean, Sumerian, and Central American legends of the flood end in a solemn sacrifice of thanksgiving. Five figures appear on the Sumatran ceremonial "soul ship"—the frequency of boats of the dead in this region appears to be memorials to the land of their ancestors. Sometimes it is rafts.

Colombia's Chibcha (a.k.a. Muysca) in the northern Andes gather around Lake Guatavita in a similar ritual—on the appointed day the king goes to the lake to give offerings to the gods. A raft of rushes

Fig. 4.9. The king is anointed before sailing out on the lake on a raft of rushes.

awaits him. He anoints his body with gold dust and boards the raft. At the center of the lake the gilded king makes the offering to the gods, the treasures thrown into the water.

When the ships made landfall in the five divisions of the world, in each of those places the survivors alighted and gave thanks to the Creator, swearing oaths to maintain the rites and customs of their fathers. "Let us build an altar unto the Lord and sing and dance because he is with us" (Oahspe, Book of Aph 7:11).

The story of riding out the storm ends in the greatest diaspora of all time. "Drive the groups [fleets] of ships, and bring them to the different lands of the earth . . ." (Oahspe, Book of Aph 7:6). So let us now take a close look at those five divisions of mankind.

DIASPORA

The Garden of Pan

Why were the South Seas once called the Summer Isles of Eden? "The Garden of Eden was not in Asia but on a now sunken continent in the Pacific Ocean." This is the first sentence in James Churchward's outstanding still-in-print classic, *The Lost Continent of Mu*. Like Churchward, Leo Frobenius, the German explorer, believed that civilization first emerged on a lost Pacific continent and spread to Asia, then farther west to Egypt and the Mediterranean. "Nowhere on Earth," agrees Frank Joseph, one of today's leading protohistorians, "do as many indigenous versions of Garden of Eden–like accounts exist as among the native peoples of Indonesia and the Pacific realm" (2013, 44).

In Tahiti, "Queen of the Pacific," the cradle of the human race was said to be Fenua Nui, a great continent that the god of wind broke up into myriad islands.

> Pan said: I am the earth, the first habitable place for man.... By the tribes of Faithists I was carried over all the world . . . I am the first spoken words. Before me, man uttered like a beast.
>
> OAHSPE, BOOK OF SAPHAH: PAN 1:1, 2:3–5

Thus do we find *Pan* words so often indicating "first things."

- Co-pan is considered the first Mayan city (Perry 1968, 100).
- The Sumu people of Central America say that two brothers created the world, the *older* one named Pa*pan*.
- Peru's Pan-yos tribe, thought of as the original people, is traceable to a lost white race.
- *Pan* means "head" in the language of the Mandan Indians.
- Olel*pan*ti was the home of First Man among the Olelbis (California Indians).
- The first quinoa in the New World is found at the *Pan*aulauca cave site in Peru, at least 12,000 years old.
- Po*panopan*o is the Hawaiian word for the first egg-laying animals.
- Legend says *pan*danus was the first food available in Polynesia and Malaysia (*pan* means "bread" in Spanish).
- *Pan*a means "elder (first) brother" among the Malaysian Lanoh (Negrito). *Pan* is prefixed to a name to indicate "elder" also among the Filipino Zambales Aeta.
- In New Guinea, pan-gua is a reference to the common ancestor.
- The supreme god at Sulawesi (Indonesia) is *Pan*g Mats, "Old Lord."
- Pan-chalas is the name of the earliest kingdom in northern India.
- The Chinese called the Creator *Pan*ku, the same as First Man, while Ci*pan*gu is the Chinese name of a legendary Pacific land.

Five Fleets

Most accounts of the submersion of Pan/Mu leave out the all-important story of its survivors, or, as is often the case, suppose that only one man or one couple or one family escaped the disaster. But a great many did escape from the devastated homeland.

The ships were congregated into four fleets . . . except two ships, which were carried together in a fleet by themselves. The Lord said: I will name the fleets of my chosen, and their names shall be everlasting on the earth: Guatama, Shem, Jaffeth, Ham and

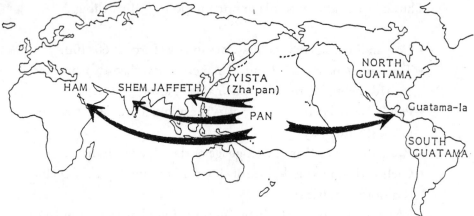

Fig. 5.1. Map of the diaspora from Pan

Yista. The Lord said: Behold I will carry them to all the divisions of
the earth, and people it anew with the seed of my chosen.

OAHSPE, THE LORDS' FIRST BOOK 1.45, 1.47–49

Shem, Ham, and Jaffeth are the classic names designating Noah's
Old World descendants. Genesis has Jaffeth and his people eventually
settled around the Black and Caspian Seas, one branch extending westward to Spain and others to Greece and the Germanic areas. As for
the sons of Ham, they went to Africa, then northward to the land of
Shinar and Assyria (Nineveh, Akkad, and so on); Ham's son Canaan
also settling along the Mediterranean from Sidon to Gaza and eastward.
Finally, the family of Shem is said to have occupied the area north of
the Persian Gulf—Elam, Ashur, and so forth, these illustrious generations leading to the prophet Abraham.

According to Oahspe, the mother tongue, the Panic language,
actually remained in use up to the time of Thor (15,000 years ago) by
these sons of Shem, Ham, and Jaffeth: "They speak and write with
Panic words" (The Lords' Fourth Book 2:7). Which is to say, even
nine thousand years after the diaspora Panic remained the common
tongue for a good portion of humanity. Isn't this the reason why protohistorians have observed that "unknown races all over the world, some
20,000 years ago, had a sort of lingua franca" (Wilkins 2000, 141).

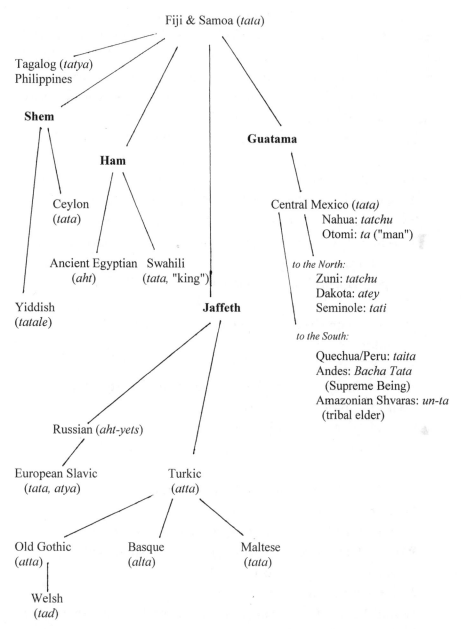

Fig. 5.2. Chart showing the word "father"—tata—as dispersed from the Samoan center of the homeland to places like Bolivia where tata *still means "father." In the Society Islands,* ta'ata *means "men." Tino Tata *means "progenitor" in Tahiti, and in New Hebrides* tata *means "father" while in other parts of Melanesia* i-tata *means "father-in-law."*

I was most intrigued when a colleague (Peter Hartgens) told me the meaning of *tan* in Panic was "power." I soon discovered that *tano* still means "powerful" in the South Seas (Ellis 1931, 291). In Samoan legend Tan-galos was the god who dredged up the archipelagos of the Pacific for the survivors of the flood. Indeed, Tan-garoa is the Supreme Deity and Upheaver of Islands in most of Polynesia.

Power or supremacy is reflected in other Pacific *Tan* names:

Tan-e: Maori progenitor
Tangata manu: embodiment of divine power in Easter Island
Tan-i: legendary progenitor of the Marquesan islanders
Tan-giia: Polynesian demigod of voyages and great ancestor of the Raratongans
Tan-go: "support," or a primordial deity of the Cook Islands

Out of the homeland, a *Tan* progenitor or Creator is seen in world-wide divinities:

Tan-goi: Malaysian ancestress, taught the useful arts
Chai-tan: spirits of the Gilyaks
Sou-tan: creator god in Borneo
Tian Tan Buddha: here Tan signifies "big" or "great"
Tan-ayitnu: the Sanskrit Thor—the Thunderer
Tana Penu: Earth goddess of India's Sakiti cult
Pesho-tan-u: the Persian Poseidon
Tanen: ancient Earth god of Egypt's archaic matriarchy
Wo-tan: Old World (Germanic) god of storms and battles
Ti-tans: primordial giants in Greek legend
Tan-it: great goddess of Carthage
Wakan Tan-ka: Creator, among the western tribes of North America
Kich-tan: god of the Massachusetts Indians
Tanga-tanga: a principal deity in South America
Gua-tan: god of whirlwind along Peruvian coast

Tan words in some languages may also entail powers on the dark side:

Fig. 5.3. Maori monster Tan-iwhas, a "mysterious power that attacked man from within" (Anderson 1928, 139)

Sa-tan: the evil one, English
Ta-tan-is: devils, Easter Island
Tan-has: clinging spirits, Sanskrit
Gu-tan-u: destructive bull of heaven, Mesopotamian
Tan-niyn: dragon, Aramaic
Tan-iwhas: terrifying monsters (of the mind), something like alligators, whom epic heroes fought in New Zealand

Tan may also refer to strictly earthly powers or the stamp of authority:

Tan-gata-Whenua: the culture bearers to New Zealand
A-tan-ua: first queen of the Marquesans, fair and beautiful
sul-tan: chief, Middle East
Tan-ausu: last prince of the Guanches
Chen Tan: chief of the (Mayan) Lacandons
Nico-tani: priestly dynasty, Cherokee
Tan: hero, Chinese

Fig. 5.4. Chen Tan, chief of Lacandons

I have also found *tan* embedded in the names of strongholds or places of power:

Tan-cah: Mexican site with a series of watchtowers
Tui-tan: Toltecan fortress
Tan-ach: Canaanite fortress
Tan-Zoumiatak: Sahara, ancient citadel with art depicting war chariots
Mi-tan-ni: on the Euphrates, stronghold of the Hurrians
Nan Tan-ach: "Place of Lofty Walls" on Panape
Tan-a Toraja: Celebes (northeast of Java), ancient megaliths

Shem

The sudden arrival of these mighty fleets helps us understand why so many traditions say that civilization was brought *from the sea* (the great initiator sometimes outlandishly portrayed by the mythic mind as a fish god).

> The fleet named Shem landed to the south . . . [the land] called Vind'yu [India] to this day.
>
> OAHSPE, THE LORDS' FIRST BOOK 1:59

The Hindu epic Ramayana speaks of white settlers arriving *from the east*—not to be confused with the much later Aryan invasion from the *north*. It is therefore no surprise that India's main genetic markers indicate "a movement of peoples outside Southeast Asia. . . . The so-called incoming Aryans have failed to turn up in the genetic record. . . . The Puranic view is that the Vedic people hailed from the south of India after a great flood" (Kreisberg 2012, 35). And *these* are our first "Aryans."* *Pan*du (obviously reminiscent of Pan) is the Ceylonese name for the white race to whom they trace their descent; Ceylon is just south of India.

Another name of special interest is Manu. "Manu-ka is the original land from which we sprang"—Rarotonga recitation (Smith 1921, 94). Teoni-manu = sunken homeland of the Solomon Islanders. Known as "the sacred hearthstone of the race," it holds the same distinction in Samoan history, where it was fondly remembered as a land of peace inhabited by "a race of heroes . . . children of the gods [who] ruled by subtlety and skill" and whose culture was "much closer to that of the archaic civilization than that of the rest of the eastern Pacific" (Perry 1968, 140, 157, 298).

Indeed, the southerly route out of the Pacific at the time of diaspora might be traceable through the holy name Manu, which turns up as the flood hero of the Vedics; in the Puranas the sages and rishis, represented by the figure called Manu, came from the south. India's Manus were thenceforth considered the Great Regents of a planetary world, the doctrine set forth in the Vedic Book of Manu.

In the Admiralty Islands, Manu-ai is the name of the first man. In the South Seas manu-tahi are the red feathers that symbolize the gods, worn only by the sacred chiefs; thus does manu-nu mean "of kingly bearing." In Syria too manu is a kingly title. Sumerian inscriptions refer to the Lake of Manu, a "cloud lake" located in the "Mountains of the Sunset"; Lake Titicaca, say some scholars, is the only lake that fits the description. Not too far from here are the Tahua-manu people, with white skin and blue eyes.

---

*The very name Aryan, as we saw in chapter 2 (*Ari*) has its roots in the ancient *ari*stocrats of Oceania.

Manu was an important place-name in the Pacific Islands as well:

Enua-manu: Polynesian name for New Guinea
Noku-manu: place in Melanesia
Manu-ae Island: in Cook group
Manu Kau Harbor: in New Zealand
Manu-ka: in Samoa
Motu Manu: in the Marquesas
Enua-Manu: southwest of Polynesia
Tabuae-manu Island: in the Society Islands
Hana-manu: districts in Polynesia

In Fiji is Manua Levi, which features a monolith with writing on it. Indeed, writing seems to be the principal theme that ties India to the Pacific (see chapter 7, p. 296, which compares India's glyphs to Easter Island's rongorongo). On Easter Island is Tangata *Manu,* the bird-man who represents the god Makemake. Probably not coincidentally, the Lithuanian flood hero is named Mannus. The people of Shem, "the Aryans of India, [also] claim descent from Manu" (Perry 1968, 204).

Maybe because I lived for a while in Poona, India, I noticed another linguistic similarity between the subcontinent and Oceania in the name of Puna. *Puna*ouia district in Tahiti is the grand place of assemblage for all souls. "Moulded stones"* (i.e., rock with imprints of hands, as if once soft like clay) are found near Punaouia, the area legendarily inhabited by a pure white race. In Tahitian epics King Puna's name indicates water-spring. Similar place-names in Oceania include Puna-he (in the Marquesas), Puna-ru'u River (Tahiti), Puna Pau (Easter Island), and Puna (in Hawaii near Kilauea) where Puna was also the name of the popular ruler of Kauai in olden time; it was also the name of the great dynastic family who ruled Oahu and Maui. After all, *puna* means "source" (fountainhead, wellspring) in Tahitian. By extension, Puna-avia means "royal residence," while on Tuamotu, Tu-puna means "ancestor";

---

*There is also a South American counterpart: the *puna* grasslands of the Peruvian Andes, a landscape of rolling hills and stunted trees, where *Pan*aulauca cave deposits date to 13,000 BP. There are also moulded stones here, in Peru and Bolivia.

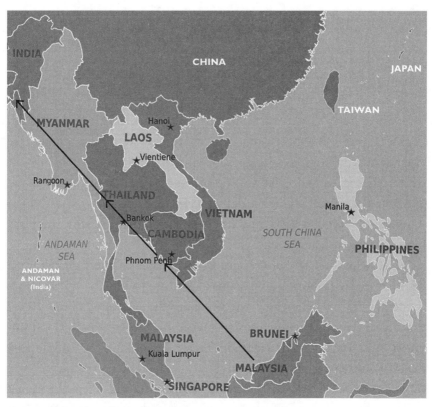

Fig. 5.5. Map of Southeast Asia showing possible route to India. Smith notes that the eleventh century in Polynesia was a time of wars and migrations (Smith 1921, 15).

it is also the name of the queen of Hiva. In the Society Islands the family temple that honors the ancestors is called Tu-puna.

In Tahiti, according to legend, the god of the winds and sea, Hiro, a being of the white race, was the first to set foot on the island, just as Hiro is the first king of Raiatea. Islanders also remember Hiro as the great navigator and explorer who brought in timbers from the kingdom of Puna ("source"). Now Hirto was the Lord of Shem (India), yet that name sounds rather like the Polynesian ancestor, Hiro.

"Linguists can't find the proto-language of Dravidian [in South India]. Solving that mystery would surely unlock a lot of doors" (Williams 2001, 69). Let us unlock the first door by looking at the spread of Austronesian languages "spoken by peoples ranging from the Himalayas, through India and Indonesia, right out into the Pacific . . . it is also spoken in . . . Burma . . . and by the Selung* and in the Nicobars" (Perry 1968, 95). Such a language map shows the sons of Shem following a route through Southeast Asia, where, says Churchward, they carried their sacred tablets to and through Cambodia and Burma. Along this route they left monuments like Angkor Wat, decorated with symbols of Mu. And this is probably why the frescoes at Angkor Wat are said to have a Semitic (Shem-itic) style, and why there are Polynesian dance styles in Cambodia, and why the Khmers are linguistically related to Polynesians, and why the Jaray have Caucasoid features and pale skin.

Then there are the pre-Hindu Redin people in the Indian Ocean who left ruins (mounds) and names associated with the motherland. Remembered as a blue-eyed race, these are the people who established the city of Ayodhya, whose founder traced his descent to the flood survivors who long ago arrived in Southeast Asia. This was India's first dynasty of divine kings.

Divine? Well, yes, to the extent that India did keep the sacred commandment—not to kill; they are primarily vegetarians. Yet it is not the cow alone that is sacred, but all life. The early Indus culture, according to Danish ethnologist Birket-Smith, was not marked with the taint of either "absolute monarchy or theocracy. Neither palaces nor temples were as great as those of Mesopotamia and Egypt, nor are weapons or defense works prominent. . . . Here are the remains of a peaceful farming and trading people . . . with a marked sense of cleanliness" (1965, 446). These were a holy people.

Now the Hindu pantheon is chock full of deities, named and illustrated, assuring a record of the presiding angels and heavenly places particular to the arc of Speta, at which time Cpenta Armij (later remembered as Spenta Armati) was goddess of Earth.

---

*The Selung of Burma (through which country the migrants from Mu reached India) say that their ancestors came from a land far across the Pacific Ocean, "the land of their birth in the East" (Ramayana).

And I went to Vind'yu and established a mighty people . . . for I had a work for them to do, which was to preserve My revelations of some of the divisions in My heavens above; and to prove, in aftertime, things which I had revealed to the ancients.

OAHSPE, BOOK OF ES 20:36

It is in India more than in any other country on earth that the traditions of an ancient great world civilization are still preserved.
CHARLES HAPGOOD, *MAPS OF THE ANCIENT SEA KINGS*

In the Upper Book of Oahspe we can find a number of the names of divinities and sanctities preserved only in India, names like Shiva, Durga, Daeva, and more such as these:

Vishnu: "renowned for his labor in [India] and her heavens." The story of the god Vishnu, the Protector, is told in Oahspe's Book of Divinity, chapter 14; see also the First Book of God, where Vishnu is the god who inspired Abraham (Book of Cpenta Armij 5:8–9).
Samadhi: Samati is the Ihua Mazda with Zarathustra, the atmospherean god of the Ihuan people (Book of Fragapatti 28:25).
Bakti: Bakhdi is the "third holy place in heaven . . . revealed by the Vedan gods, thence into Vede and thence into Sanskrit" (Book of Saphah: Ahura Mazda 1:2).
Chakhra: Wheel, disc, force-center in body. "And Ormazd created combination, which is strength, chakhra" (Book of God's Word 11:8).
Nirvana: A state of bliss, because of uniting and creating perfect union of all the faculties. The eighth stage of yoga is said to enable a state of ecstasy and trance tantamount to nirvana consciousness.

Many of the names of spiritual mountains are retained in the Vedic scriptures (see Oahspe, Book of Saphah: Basis of Vede 56). In the

Fig. 5.6. Ancient sign of
nirvana: that holy word
preserved only in India

Avesta, we learn how the God of Light planted the tree of Immortality on Mount Haraiti; in Oahspe, "the third grade of plateaus [up] from the earth's surface is called Haraiti. . . . Jehovih said: Here, O My Son, Fragapatti! Here in Haraiti I have laid the foundation of your kingdom" (Book of Fragapatti 3:16, 4:1). The heavenly mountains "extend over the earth mountains of Shem (India), and have an altitude above the earth of one hundred miles. These are the oldest inhabited spirit worlds since the submersion of Pan" (Book of Fragapatti 6:23–24).

Leaving India and moving west there is also much of Shemitic culture to be found. As Churchward explains, in a later migration the Naacals left India and went to Babylonia, there to teach the religion and sciences of the motherland. Such a migration might help explain why the holy cosmic number of the Vedas, 432,000, appears again in Mesopotamia, where Berossos made the Babylonian "Great Year" to last 432,000 years. The Chaldeans also got the sacred number 10,800 from India, of which 432,000 is merely a multiple. Also, Arpachad, son of Shem, "is said to have been the progenitor of the Chaldeans" (Collins 2014, 338), again showing a branch of India's Shemites in lands far to the west.

Note that *Shem* (var. Shum) became the Vedic word for land or country—hence Shumeria. (*Sumer* is the ancient Indic word for flat lands or plains.) Although of Jaffetic stock, the Sumerians, once settled in the Fertile Crescent, took over many Semitic words. Shem names in the region include Abi-shemu, a Phoenician king of Byblus; Shem-shara, Armenia—an eight-thousand-year-old archaeological site in northeastern Iraq; and Ras-Sham-ra (or Ugarit), an ancient Semitic city of great archaeological interest.

India, then, was also the starting place of the Hebrews, parts of their scriptures traceable to Hindu sacred writings. *Jud,* in fact, is an ancient name of Asia (see fig. 4.3, p. 148). Megasthenes identified the Hebrews as an Indian sect called Kalani; indeed, the early Judeans apparently passed through Afghanistan, where they are called Yadus. On the way from Afghanistan to Persia are places such as Shem-shak in Shem-iranat County (Tehran province) and Shem-shad Poshteh (in Gilan province).

The Land of Ham

Even though Africa has few flood myths, the Pygmies nonetheless knew of a hero named Mu-gasa who escaped a great destruction of his homeland *in the distant east*. White people (*Umlungu*), it is said, came from the sea; shamans still train underwater with the little people who are white. The white Pygmies of Africa (the Yumboes) and of Madagascar (the Vazimba)—and even the small and fair Badarians (of ancient Egypt)—were among the last, now extinct, traces of those "little people who are white."

> The fleet named Ham landed southwest, and the country was called the land of Ham for thousands of years, and is the same as that called Egypt and Africa to this day.
>
> OAHSPE, THE LORDS' FIRST BOOK 1:60
>
> (SEE ALSO GENESIS 10:6–14)

And this is why there is so much Caucasoid blood in Africa, the Fulani, Tuareg, Hausa, Berber, and others of the region, so Europoid in appearance. Indeed, the blondest people of Africa in the northern Rif (in Barbary, Morocco, and Algiers) are said to be Africa's most ancient inhabitants. In fact, the Fulani say that their ancestors were white, as do the Masas of Sudan. Noting a Caucasoid strain in the aquiline noses of the Sudanese Fula, Carleton Coon took this as representing "the amalgamation of Caspian [Caucasoid] and Negro peoples in the distant past" (1965, 84). A further example is the Tibbus tribe of the Sahara, a mixture of proto-Negroid and Caspian—tall and very black, yet the hair is not woolly, the nose is aquiline, and prognathism is absent. "All Negros are partly Caucasoid by interbreeding" (Thorndike 1977, 225), which is further indicated by common blood groups and architecture of the teeth.

[The |hin arrivals] mixed greatly with the |huans . . . being of mixed colors, they did not become impotent. But they broke the law of God more than all other Faithists, being of warm blood. . . . And they retained the name of Ham to the end of their line, when they ceased to exist as a separate people because of their amalgamation with the |huans.

OAHSPE, THE LORDS' FIFTH BOOK 5:13

The Somalis have black skin and frizzy hair combined with facial features of the European mold. Between Cairo and Khartoum we find nothing but an intermediate series bridging the southern European type with the Negro. From Senegal eastward, while the people are very dark skinned in the west, they become lighter as we go eastward—and also shorter. Both paleness and shortness are signs of Ihins; in this case, the Hamite Ihins who settled Africa twenty-four thousand years ago.

The tribes of Ham were of all colors (black, white, yellow, copper, red and brown); nevertheless, they were |hins, having flat nails and short arms, and desiring to acquire knowledge.

OAHSPE, THE LORDS' FIFTH BOOK 3:4

We can see this in Egyptian drawings—men of both dark and light skin—but the earliest dynastic line of Egypt was a race of short, light-haired people with gray eyes.

We sometimes find the name Ham varied with Hem (as in Sek-hem, Egypt) or in the name Kem or Khemet, which was indeed the ancient name of Egypt; there are also the mountains of Hem-acute, Egypt; Chem-mis, a.k.a. Panopolis, Egypt; and Wadi Ham-mamat, between the Red Sea and the Nile. Kem is at the root of Al-Khemet, or alchemy, for all people of the ancient day went to Egypt to study the science that became known as chem-istry. History also knows this civilization as Cushite, centered in Ethiopia, though John Baldwin argues that the original Land of Cush was Arabia. Nevertheless the Ethiopians claimed descent from the sons of Cham, and "wheresoever they went, they inoculated the barbarous tribes with their knowledge . . . [proving] the influence and intellectual activity of this wonderful Hamitic-Arabian race with its widespread influence in prehistoric times . . ." (Fornander 1969, 1:38).

Iraqi settlements with Ham or Chem in the name include Zawi Chemi Shanidar, the well-known thirteen-thousand-year-old site; Ham-man, the Chaldean ruins in southern Iraq near the Gulf; and the Ham-rin basin of lower Mesopotamia. Urk-ham was the earliest royal name in Chaldean inscriptions; Hamite tribes that retained the ancestors' name include the ancient Jur-ham (Thamudites) of Arabia, where Aham was the name of the sacred language of Arabinia (Oahspe, Book of Saphah: Interpretation 29). Other occurrences include Him-yaric, inscriptions of ancient Arabia; Kharek-ham, ancient port of Arabia with ruins (now El Belid); Jebel duk-ham in Bahrein, with its mound fields; and even the dir-ham, the coin of Arabic currency.

The famous Egyptian Sphinx was known as Ham-achis. Te-ham-a is the coastal region of the Red Sea, a 1,000-mile-long stretch off northeast Africa. Farther along the east coast of Africa, where the Hamite fleet made landfall, under three habitation layers lies a city of great antiquity with glazed earthenware. No study had been made of it in Churchward's time (Churchward 2011, 244).

I should add that while Fornander accounts for Polynesian-Cushite similarities by positing the influence *from west to east* (i.e., from Africa), I think it was the reverse, from east to west: the Sons of Ham. When we wonder how the African Dogon got their star knowledge, let us remember that the Dogon god Amma (from Ham-ma?) is said to have "landed in an ark." This Amma may be related to the Ama-lala, white tribes of the Zulu region. Though the Arabs (Cushites) are *linguistically* Shemite, they actually trace themselves back to Ad, son of Ham. In chapter 6 we will look at one story in the *Arabian Nights,* set in the desert of Ad-an and centered on a king named Ash Shed-ad, son of Ad. In fact, the Arabs call the first settlers of the land Adites. (The Dead Sea Scrolls have the Adites as great-great-grandsons of Ham, through Sheba, Raamah, and Cush.) The figure named Shedad, it is said, conquered all of Arabia and Mesopotamia, hence the appearance of Hamite populations from Sidon to Syria and beyond: the Ham-athites of Canaan; Nahal Hem-ar in Jordan; Abu Kem-al in eastern Syria; Ham-ath, ancient city in upper Syria; Ham-ra, Lebanon; Ham-adan, old Ecbatana; Ham-zan Tepe, Turkey; and Ham-mamet, Tunisia. Cham-ba, the solar god of Syria, was called Hama in Persia, while the name Ham itself was the Zeus of ancient Greece. Eraoran-ham was the Supreme Being of the Guanches on Hierro Island.

But the Hamite is predominantly a son of Africa. A telling tradition of the African Herreros, a Bantu tribe, says that long, long ago the Greats of Above let the sky fall on Earth and only a few people survived (a reference to the sinking of Pan). After that, say the Herreros, white men came and mingled among them. Local legends of white newcomers are known in other parts of Africa as well. In a twentieth-century report on Kalahari cave art in Damarland, Henry Breuil declared that this art was unmistakably the work of a mysterious race of white people.

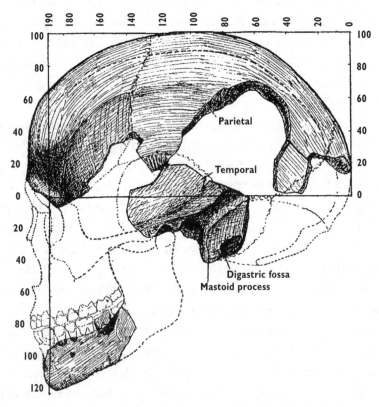

Fig. 5.7. Boskop skull; this race is thought to have had deep tan or yellow-toned skin.

Yet not really mysterious, as these protohistorical white settlers were none other than our deluge survivors.

The Kalahari Bushmen of southern Africa are short and well proportioned, built on the model and scale of the "symmetrical" Ihins. Today Bushman babies are born pale pink. Even full grown, the Bushmen are the lightest and shortest people in Africa, probably related distantly to prehistorical "Boskop Man," a large-brained, unusual Caucasoid type—a puzzle to paleontologists. The Boskop skull was delicate, the teeth small and graceful. We can suppose that after white people (the Hamitic sons of Noah) entered Africa, new blends quickly arose. Boskop Man, found in the cliff shelters of South Africa's Transvaal, was a splendid hybrid—dated to anywhere between forty thousand and ten thousand years ago.

A composite of white Ihin (Ham) and African Ihuan (the latter signaled by his supramastoid crest), Boskop Man, found in 1913, possessed a forebrain 50 percent larger than ours, a total of 1,800 cc! Yet there were primitive traits as well—thick skull wall and slight chin. Loren Eiseley's doggerel that Boskop Man was "born by error into a lion country" is nonsense. No error, only an offshoot of those Hamite refugees who mixed so freely with indigenous Africans. Boskop Man's location of course was on the southeast African *coast*. Isn't this a clue to the landing place of those arrivals from Pan?

Jaffeth

*The voice of history informs us that at a period of time
very shortly posterior to the deluge, the eastern parts of
Asia were occupied by a people comparatively civilized.*
JOHN D. LANG, *ORIGIN AND MIGRATIONS OF
THE POLYNESIAN NATION*

Chinese records, like those of Mesopotamia, say that the progenitors of their race came from across the sea (Donnelly 1985, 427). The sons of Noah (Jaffeth branch) who fled to China were white and yellow men. "The original inhabitants of the region, far from being Mongoloid, were actually Caucasian" (Chouinard 2012, 156). Neither are the Sichuanese Han-Dropa of a Mongoloid caste, but have blue eyes, like the Uighur of western China and the "Paleo-Caucasoid" Tocharians who entered China ca. twenty-five thousand years ago.

> The fleet named Jaffeth was driven to the westward and north, and the country was called Jaffeth for thousands of years thereafter, and is the same as is called Chine'ya [China] to this day.
>
> OAHSPE, THE LORDS' FIRST BOOK 1:58

In the Chinese language, Jafung is the original name of their country. The Moguls traced their pedigree to a progenitor named Japhet. "All Asia knows that the Khan [king] of Cara-corum is the lineal descendant of Japhet" (Higgins 1991, 2:359). Now this *Cara,* as in Cara-corum, appears again in the Bayan *Kara* Ula Mountains of Sichuan, Tibet-China, where a most unusual set of stone discs were discovered. Those mountains are inhabited today by the aforementioned Han and Dropa Pygmies (4 feet 2 inches)—*Homo sapien pygmaeus.* There were 716 stone discs in those caves, each with a hole in the center and a double groove of spirals, apparently a writing system no less than twelve thousand years old. The twentieth-century Han Dropa king was named Hueypan-La (my instincts tell me that name breaks down as Huey = old, Pan = Mu, La = distant). Legend has these small Han Dropa people dropping down from the sky, descending from the clouds with air gliders, which resembles Hopi cosmogony wherein the first Earth Initiate came down from the sky on a feather rope. In Orinoco legend it is a cotton rope. In Indonesia it is a vine; sometimes it is a spider's web. There are many variants.

Cara Words

This vocable *kara* (*cara*), as in Cara-corum or Bayan-Kara-Ula, also turns up in one esoteric name for the lost land, Mas-kara, and in Kara-wanimakin, a disappeared island in the Central Pacific. *Kara* appears to be a Panic word, still seen in the Polynesian island Fa-kara-va and in the Kara-kako of New Zealand, a race of white people with blond hair who lived under the red-haired demigod Tane; they are related perhaps to Kara-nga-iti, a mythical place in Mangaia cosmogony or to the Karitehe in the Bay Islands or to Kar-iahn, the burial place for priests on Nan Madol. There could also be a link to Kara-na, the capital of ancient Minoei of Arabia, which Fornander connects to Kalan-i-Havola, the Hawaiian paradise (1969, 1:56).

In Churchward's scheme Cara Maya was the language spoken in southeastern Mu; he thought Easter Island was occupied by Car-ians, a people who struck out for Central America after the Great Disaster. From Central America they made their way south—sixteen thousand years ago, which Churchward believes is shown in "many ancient remains . . . along the frontier between Venezuela and Colombia. . . . One of their present-day tribes, which have come down from the ancient stock, is the Godjiros [*sic*]" (Churchward 1931a, 87). I think he meant the Guajiros who live on the border of Venezuela and Colombia.

Ecuadorian Indians, in fact, say that their remote ancestors were called Cara; Caragues, Ecuador, seems to carry that ancient name. In Brazil, Cara-iba is the appellation of white people among the tribes of Matto Grosso, just as the Yura-cara are White Indians in eastern Cordillera. There are many Cara names in the New World (Guatama). For example:

Ari-kara Indians, with an excellent flood story
Ni-cara-gua
Cara people of Honduras
Bu-kara, in eastern Honduras, with megaliths in the jungle
Pa-cara, Panama, south of Cocle (see fig. 1.4, p. 13)
Ma-cara-cas, in the Asuero Peninsula of Panama
Venezuela's capital **Cara-cas**
Peru's **Caral,** with pyramids older than Egypt's
Cara-huirazo, mountains in the Andes
the high hill **Cachapu-cara** in the Cordillera
Pu-kara, ancient city and ceremonial complex near Lake Titicaca
Kara-ya Indians, with a distinctive flood legend
Cua-kara Indians, Brazil, as well as the Brazilian **Cara-i** Cataract
   on the **Urari-Coera** River
Cara-hybas of Paraguay, descendants of Caribs, with legends of a
   great deluge

Fig. 5.8. Photos of Guajiros taken by author in 1969

Kara is also prominent in the Jaffetic branch, spreading ever westward (as did Churchward's Uighur empire) from the Orient. Its original meaning may have been "place of building" or "enclosure."* In Africa, the Kara-nga people built the Great Enclosure, the imposing stone capital at Zimbabwe. In the Akkadian language, Khar-sag translated as "fenced enclosure." In Polynesian, Koro-tuantinim means "place of many enclosures." *Koro,* which means "enclosure" in Rarotonga, is probably cousin to the English *corral* and South African *kraal* (the village enclosed by a fence). Kara-ka meant "prison" in Sanskrit; karana in old Hebrew meant "boundary."

Now, in Oceania, kara-kia means "incantation,"† often including genealogies and performed in *special buildings* (enclosures). The people tended to associate the activity with the special clubhouse devoted to it; for example, among the nanga societies, nanga was both the building and the gathering itself. Kar-iei, in Rarotonga, is the house of amusements, a meeting place; koro means "fort." Koro-tuatini is a temple enclosed within a stone wall, a meeting place for gods and men.

Irish stone circles (which of course form enclosures) were called Car-rich Brauda; while in Wales such structures are known as Cer-rig Brudyn, meaning "astronomer's circles," similar to "sacred circles of stone" in Peru (Cuzco) whose pu-cara indicates "stronghold." In fact, Chu-car ("House of the Sun") was the original name of Tiahuanaco. Also in Peru is Huas-cara-n, "mountain of the Incas," with storied enclosures (storerooms) in caves.

It is especially in the Orient, among the sons of Jaffeth, that we find *kara* in place-names such as the following:

- Kara in Swat (Pakistan) means "place" as in But*kara,* place of Buddhist (statues).
- Samoyed, where karra means "village" (similarly, kara means "town" in the language of Chilean Indians, and caer means "town" in Welsh!).

---

*Just as caracole is the shell or enclosure of a snail and carapace is a shell or covering (of an animal).

†In some dialects *karakia,* by extension, means "priesthood."

- In Mongolia, khara means "city"; Karakal Valley is also in Mongolia.
- Kara Khota in Tangut (Gobi), with a tomb 50 feet below the ruins, was thought by Churchward to be the ancient capital of the Uighur Empire.
- Korea is Kara in the Japanese language.
- Karafuto is the Japanese name for Sakhalin Island.
- Karaganda, Kazakhstan.
- Kara Kalpak and Bukhara, Uzbekistan.
- Kara Kamar, Afghanistan.
- Kara Korum Desert and Kara Su River, Turkmenistan.
- Kara Kirgiz is the proper name of the Kirgiz people.
- Kara Sea, north of Russia.
- Kara-hunj, Armenia, a megalithic site; Surb Karapet is also in Armenia.
- Tell Karassa, Syria.
- Karabakh, Azerbaijan.

Concentrated in Turkey* are the following:

- An-kara, the capital
- Kara Dag, volcano
- Karamursel, city
- Kara Tepe, Hittite site in Cilicia, with monumental gateways
- Kara-han Tepe, in the Tektek Mountains, with 11,000-year-old carvings similar to Göbekli's stone pillars
- Kara-cadag, a mountain near Göbekli Tepe, with the first domesticated cereals, 10,000 years old

---

*In other parts of the East as well, *Kara* is prominent: Bida-kara, Java; Kara-chi, Pakistan; Karan River, north of the Persian Gulf; Karaj, Iran; Karak, Jordan; and in Egypt, Sak-kara, oldest pyramid and Kara-nis, the place where ancient lenses were found, plus Karamis Temple in Fayyum, where people would consult with the oracle. Karanovo in Bulgaria was a major Neolithic culture. At the other end of Europe, Eus-kara is the name of the equally ancient Basque language, with its Jaffetic roots; in a different part of Spain is El Cara-mbolo (near Seville). In Scotland, too, we have S-kara Brae. Cara-pito is the name of a dolmen site in Portugal.

Fig. 5.9. Karanovo early script. Bulgarian is the earliest Slavic language.

Churchward, as noted, uses the name Cara Maya to indicate the language of Mu that was brought to India, just as he has the Cara-Maya language brought to Central America. Indeed, the Lemurian Fellowship map of Mu (fig. 4.2, p. 142) shows a region called "Cari" near the center of the lost continent.

Kara

Allow for the elision of the final vowel, and *Kar/Car* opens up a new set of possibilities, yet still with the Jaffetic stamp. Caria is the name of a region in western Anatolia, colonized by the Greeks; "a white race known as the Caras or Carians are the Greeks today" (Churchward 1931a, 23). The Carians, on the shores of the Aegean, were migrants to Greece, and Crete was their maritime base (Cares is a site in Crete). The classic writers, Churchward notes, called the Caras a war-like seafaring people. Perhaps, then, the word cara-velle came from this, or coracle (a round boat). As we saw, a people called Carians settled Tiahuanaco. Andrew Lang was one who pointed out the affinity of the names "Carib" and "Carian"; he thought it meant "brave." This would fit with Abu Karib, the conqueror and great sun king of Arabia who fought his way through Central Asia. Indeed, in Quechua, Carib means "man of energy, brave"—probably referring to a warrior class.

The Car-pathian Mountains are Europe's oldest center of culture; on its rocks are unusual sculptures of the "Masma" type (see chapter 11, p. 459). "Exactly the same kind of sculptures" may be seen on the banks of the Nile, on black basalt rocks (Charroux 1972, 92); Ar-kar is the name of the Egyptian Old Kingdom; there is a Carnak in both Egypt and Brittany. Other examples include the following:

Carkini: 9,000-year-old settlement in Anatolia

Karim Shahir: Mesopotamia, a sight with ancient engravings

Mu Karib: Sabean priest-king (Arabia); the Syrian version is Kariba-il

Karen people: Burma

Kari: Malay god of thunder, with white hair

Westward-Moving Jaffeth

Have you noticed that the name Gobi is embedded in Turkey's Göb-ekl-i? Is this a coincidence or a linguistic clue to the westering Jaffites? *Kara* Khota in the Gobi, thought Churchward, was the capital city of the Uighurs. That seventeen-thousand-year-old tomb 50 feet under the ruins of Kara Khota contains two bodies; the sign of a circle twice cut appears on the sarcophagus.

When the Uighurs were in the Gobi, the region was fertile. But

A   B   C

Fig. 5.10. Even as they moved west, the Jaffites kept the wheel cross, sign of Creator, to decorate their pottery: a) pottery of southern Iraq at Eridu, perhaps the earliest settlement in the land later known as Sumeria (the sign is also seen in Sumerian pictograms); b) Hacilar painted pottery in Turkey shows influence from the east (the sign seen also at Troy and at Çatalhüyük, see figs. 7.3, 7.4a, 7.4c, and 7.4e, pp. 278–79); c) bowl from Susa I, now at the Louvre.

then, with the aridification of Central Asia, Jaffetics began moving westward. Today's Taklamakan Desert, part of the Tarim Basin between Mongolia and Tibet, once had large rivers; the people grew melons, corn, cotton, wheat, and grapes—but the climate changed, and today there are only dunes where once cities and farmlands prospered.

Remains of people dug up in the Gobi who look like northern Europeans should not be treated as a mystery. These were Noah's sons who settled Asia. Lewis Spence, after all, was able to trace the European race to southern Siberia; we know that the languages of the Finns and Hungarians relate back to the Ostyak of Siberia. In addition, recent evidence gave us Caucasian mummies with blond and reddish hair in northwestern China, which is today's Uighur region. In 2004 hundreds of these Caucasoid burials were found by Chinese archaeologists; among them is the Europoid "Loulan Beauty," who, according to the Uighur today, is the "mother of the nation." But the real question is, "in which direction the Caucasians traveled. Could . . . they be native [to China], rather than European visitors?" (Coppens 2012, 245).

The westering Celts and Scythians did leave remains of their culture in Russia; archaeologist Marija Gimbutas traced Indo-European migrations out of the southwest Russian steppe. Indeed, these herders and pastoralists can be tracked by their cranial morphology, Russia being the hub of the round-headed (modern) race. This brachycephaly, as it is called, is the distinctive head shape of the little people (Ihins) and of the Mongoloids who made their way from Pan. The closer to "Hiva [Pan], the more the people become brachycephalic" (Schwartz 1973, 157).

Some of these migrations brought the Jaffites to Bactria and Persia; Gobi tablets are written in an unknown language from which Zend (ancient Persian) was derived. The Jaffite influence is also seen in Mesopotamia, and this is why "remarkable likenesses existed in the number systems of Babylonia and China" (Hapgood 1996, 238). When these people moved into Mesopotamia they became known as Sumerians, whose ceramics and burial customs are essentially Central Asian. But whereas we are told that "the descendants of Noah migrated slowly *eastward* from Ararat . . . and soon repopulated the world" (Drake 1974, 152; emphasis added), it is actually just the other way around.

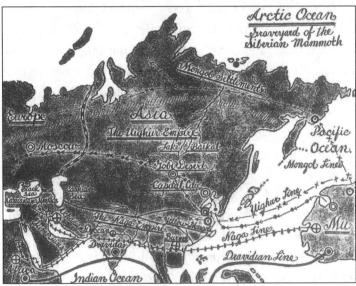

Fig. 5.11. Top and middle: Maps of Uighur Empire, according to Churchward (2011, 105; and 1931); he placed the western boundary around Moscow, but with outposts extending farther throughout Europe. Therefore, wheel-cross images continue on to Scandinavia, Wales, France, and so forth. Bottom: Seen here are drawings of a wheel cross from Spain and Italy.

Movement into Turkey was from the *east:* for example, the Cimmerians of Asia Minor said they descended from the son of Japhet. "Turkish tribes had previously lived in Mongolia . . . Chinese writers describe a powerful people in these regions . . . identical with the Huns . . . whose invasions the Chinese turned westward" (Birket-Smith 1965, 435).

Thus do we conclude that, in time, the Jaffites became the Turks, Celts, Germanics, Slavs, Basque, Bretons, and Teutonics. Indeed, the now-extinct Tocharian language of western China was close to the languages of western Europe. Discovery of those Tarim Basin mummy people gave us a "straightforward link . . . to the Celtic inhabitants of Europe. . . . They spread from this region to other regions—specifically Europe" (Coppens 2012, 242–45). The woolly sheep that provide the twill of the Scottish kilt came from Central Asia, where the Urumchi people originated both the twill and plaid design; this style of weave eventually turns up in ancient Austrian cloth as well.

Japheth was the leading influence over Celtic origins.
JOHN PILKEY, *THE ORIGIN OF THE NATIONS*

Professor J. Macmillan Brown even found here a direct linguistic link to the motherland, for "primeval Aryan as it is seen in Tocharish has the same range and number of sounds as Polynesian. . . . Its fundamental vowel was 'a' and so it is in Polynesian . . . [which] is an Aryan language itself" (1920, 23). According to Turkish flood legends Noah's son Iapetos (Jaffeth) escaped to Mount Ida (var. Ina) in a boat of skins; Iapetos then went on to found the great city of Troy—which was quite a bit older than we think as more than five successive cities underlay the Troy of Mycenaean times, Homer's Troy. This decidedly Paleolithic date for the settlement of Troy by one of Noah's great sons accords with Churchward's time frame, which establishes the occupation of Asia Minor and the Caucasian Plains thousands of years before 14,000 BCE.

But much of Turkey also dried out in the millennia to come, so movement west was resumed, explaining why one of the oldest names of Europe is "Japetia." DNA, another clue, "seems to indicate a migration from Anatolia into Europe during the last 10,000 years

. . . [plus] 103 Indo-European languages seem to have originated in Anatolia" (Stoecker 2014, 6). In Italy the migrants became known as the Etruscans. Eastern influence has long been recognized in Etruscan arts and culture—and physique: the low round skull, the long almond eyes, the rounded chin. On their terra-cottas, the pose is Asian. Eastern origins are also stamped in their vessels, which are so typically Trojan, and in their artwork as well—so like that of Tell Halaf (see chapter 8, p. 348). Archaeologists do wonder if Greek* civilization itself came from Asia Minor. Crete, Libya, and Basque (Spain) have Jaffetic roots too; Arabs called the ancient Turkish maps "Jaferiye." Finally, the Cimmerians ("Cymry") of Asia Minor were led into Britain/Wales by Hu Gadaru, just as ancient chronicles of Ireland have their ancestors descended from the son of Japheth.

Fleet to Guatama

The fleet named Guatama was carried eastward, and the country where it landed was also called Guatama.

OAHSPE, THE LORDS' FIRST BOOK 1:53

The Chikasaw people say that they came from the west where "many people came out of the ground" (i.e., *emerged* from places of refuge). Algonquin culture hero Nanabozho was a survivor from a sunken land, "the first land," beyond the great ocean (see fig. 4.1, p. 140).

The Lord inquired: Where is the place and boundary of the sacred people, the Jhins, whom I delivered in the time of the flood? And man answered, saying: From the head of the Ca'ca'tsak, the mountain river of rivers [Amazon] . . . and the mountain plains of

---

*Aristotle and Philostratus speak of little people descended from Pygmeus, son of Dorus, whose tribe brought iron into Greece. This points us to the Pontos area, joining Europe and Asia. Anatolia/Asia Minor, with her Hittites, Trojans, Lydians, Lycians, Cimmerians, and Phrygians, gives us the Jaffetic branch of Noah's sons, leading to the Etruscans, Greeks, Britons, and other founding populations of Europe. And *these* are the Asianic whites who are eventually known to us as Caucasians.

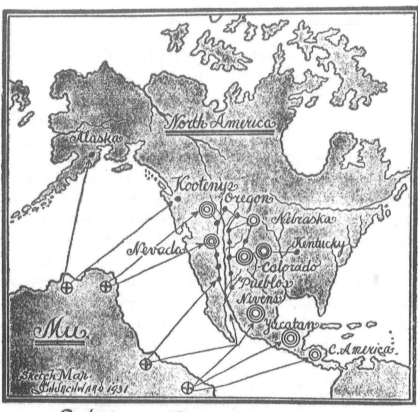

Fig. 5.12. Churchward's Map of North America

Fig. 5.13. Sign of Guatama (America), from Oahspe,
symbolizing the Meeting of the Nations, several tribes united
in one. "Middle America is among the most naturally tolerant
parts of the world, largely because from the start it has been the
meeting ground of many races" (Gordon 1973, 137).

Om [Mexico] ... and by the lake Owane [Nicaragua]. ... And to the north land ... where the still river [canal] Eph'su begins ... Vid and Sajins [Lakes Superior and Michigan].

OAHSPE, THE LORDS' THIRD BOOK 1:5–6

Guatama, the ancient name for the Americas, turns up at Mount Shasta in California, where mysterious white-robed inhabitants are said to have commemorated the time when their forebears were saved from the Submergence. Their particular ceremony was called "Adoration to Guatama." Occultists have claimed that Shasta was the secret headquarters of a Lemurian Brotherhood, a sect of sages with hidden enclaves in other parts of the world. At Shasta the Mayan-style buildings appear to be constructed of marble. But the structures and the people cannot be filmed. Some inquirers have testified to seeing peculiar boat shapes flow out of the mountain, then continue on to the Pacific Ocean as vessels!

According to the Hopi, Maya, and Nahua peoples, the previous Age of Man went out with a bang. Overnight. Aztec legend has the Fourth Sun (Age) destroyed in a cataclysmic flood, while the Hopi speak of the Third World from which their ancestors emerged as survivors of a sunken motherland. Different groups of these True White Brothers, as the Hopi call them, went separately into the world at that time, each with the same purpose and the same sacred stone tablet of knowledge. But the forebears of the Hopi, the Anasazi Cliff Dwellers, seem to have come from Mayax twelve thousand years ago. "The Pueblo region was colonized from Mexico" (Perry 1968, 66). It was in the very center of the Americas that True White Brother landed.

The Hub: Central America

Knowledge of domesticated plants and even the seeds themselves came to the American Southwest from Mexico. "The oldest American agriculture derives from Mexico whence maize reached north to the Great Lakes— and all the way south to the lands of Peru and Chile" (Birket-Smith 1965, 154, 473). The venerable Tarascan language of Mexico is linked to Zuni (in the north) and to Quechua (in the south). Words like *zi* ("hair") and *ahka* ("take") in Zuni are identical in the Otomi (Mexican) language, just as Zuni *pu'a* ("break") and *tachchu* ("father") are also Aztecan words. In fact, the Keresan language family of the North American Pueblos is Hokan-Siouan, which originates in Mexico and Nicaragua.

> *One can take the Pueblo Indians as . . . sharing in a*
> *common inheritance with the civilization of the Maya.*
>
> JACQUETTA HAWKES, *MAN AND THE SUN*

> *The Quiches originally came there [Peru] from Central*
> *America . . . [and] the Pueblos [in North America] have*
> *many Maya words in their language.*
>
> JAMES CHURCHWARD,
> *THE LOST CONTINENT OF MU*

While buried cities and stone floors found in Texas and Oklahoma have been attributed to Mexican founders, the design of Florida's Crystal River plaza and pyramid platforms calls to mind identical layouts at Chichén Itzá and Tikal; the Florida complex "is actually typical of a lowland Maya city," not to mention "identifiably Mayan flints" excavated in Missouri and Oklahoma (Joseph 2014a, 46–47, 72).

The key, the hub, of the Americas was at its center; "from the Motherland . . . the particular spot where they landed was Mexico" (Churchward 1931b, 21). The capital city of the Quetzals was established thereabouts—in Guatema-la (i.e., Guatama-la).

> The Lord said: From this place [Guatemala] shall my chosen spread
> out north and south.
>
> OAHSPE, THE LORDS' FIRST BOOK 1:53

> *From this center [Mexico] their arts spread north and*
> *south.*
>
> HAROLD T. WILKINS,
> *MYSTERIES OF ANCIENT SOUTH AMERICA*

It was through the *interior* of the Western Hemisphere that they moved, never reaching the coasts. "Through the inland parts of Central America a white race [once] predominated" (Churchward 2014, 118). This is why the White Indians of Guatemala and Honduras are in the interior and also why the densest settlements of the moundbuilders were in the interior; that is, near the Mississippi. "There is no evidence that they had reached the Atlantic coast; no authentic remains of the Mound Builders are found in the New England states. . . . The civilization of this people . . . did not cross the Alleghany Mountains" (Donnelly 1985, 370–71). "The mounds . . . soon disappear once the Mississippi is crossed in the westward direction" (Perry 1968, 68). This is also why the *oldest* cultures are in the interior—for the migrations followed a north–south axis; the coasts were not explored until much later.

G. C. Vaillant, formerly of the American Museum of Natural History, found ceramic styles in Guatemala that eventually reached both north to the Mississippi Valley and as far south as Peru. A most interesting Jesuit manuscript, kept at the British Museum, states that the Peruvian Manco Capac's ancestors were colonists from Central America, and they were called Quichés. The name is familiar: Balam-Quiché was one of the Mayan founders. The Maya were indeed "related to the Incas [whose] civilization probably originated in what is now the Peten province of Guatemala." What's more, Peru's "Chimu empire, with Chanchan as its capital . . . [comprised] a people descended from inhabitants of Mexico" (Kolosimo, 1975, 215).

In the sixteenth century, everywhere along Peru's northern coast one "found wooden or stone statues of a god named Guatan . . . [whom] the Mayas 'exported' to South America" (Kolosimo 1975, 172, 215–56). The Chimu themselves say they came from the north: their customs, their crania, their pictograms, their spiral staircase of the caracole style, are all like the Maya's. On the eastern slopes of the Andes, in the Chachapoya* region of Peru, the medial moldings, T-shaped glyphs,

---

*The Chachapoyas were white skinned, their blond and blue-eyed descendants still living in the vicinity of the old ruins. The almost Armenoid-type Chachas, as they are called, represent the tail end of the legendary light-haired Cloud People of Peru, residents of a lost city deep in the rain forest (Utcubamba Province, northern Peru).

and aquatic designs on their circular buildings are fundamentally the same as those found at Chichén Itzá in the Yucatán. Archaeologists also believe that the stirrup-shaped jars in the Andes originated in the Valley of Mexico.

> *In the marketplace at Cuzco [Peru], Pizarro found everything Cortes had seen at Tenochtitlan [Mexico].*
>
> PETER KOLOSIMO, *TIMELESS EARTH*

> *True civilizations were first developed in Central America . . . rather than in the areas to the north or south . . . [it] was the cradle.*
>
> A. H. VERRILL,
> *OLD CIVILIZATIONS OF THE NEW WORLD*

Pan Names in the Middle Kingdom

This of course explains why there are more Pan names in Central America than in any other region of the Western Hemisphere, or of the world for that matter. Sites in *earliest* Central America named after Pan include the following:

- Santa Izabel Ixta*pan,* one of the earliest known cultures in Mexico, dated to 18,000 years ago
- Caula*pan* in Puebla, with a 22,000-year-old stone scraper
- Kich*pan*ha, a Mayan site with first signs of writing
- Co*pan,* oldest Mayan site in Honduras
- Tepex*pan,* near Mexico City, one of the oldest known (12,000 BP) cultures in Mexico
- Ahuacha*pan* Pass, which opens Chalchuapa (Salvador) to the Pacific, earliest Olmec populations here
- Tlalla*pan,* the land that the legendary Quetzalcoatl came from
- Hon'yapan, oldest name of Central America
- Waneo*pan*ganosah, another old name of "the Middle Kingdom," Central America

Other Pan Names in the Middle Kingdom

- Tepantitla, palatial residence famous for its murals, near the Pyramid of the Sun
- Xolalpan and Teopancaxco, elite districts in the central sector of Teotihuacan
- Mayapan, name of the ancient capital of Yucatán
- Teopantecuanitlan, Olmec archaeological site recently discovered
- Pijijiapan, Olmec site with massive sculptures
- Chiapanec region, east of the Isthmus
- Totonicapan, Mayax
- Matacapan, in the Tuxtlas Mountains
- Haluepantla, Mexico
- Tlacopan, Aztec city and Nahua tribe
- Ochpanitzli, Aztec harvest festival
- Topan, the Aztec World Above
- Teopanzolco, Aztec ceremonial center at Cuernavaca
- Tlanepantla, a sacred Mexican site
- Tecpanec Empire (Nahua tribes), in Basin of Mexico
- Palpan, hill above Tollan ruins
- Tuxpan, in the Gulf Coast area
- Comapan, fortress/cemetery, and Tuzapan, fortress, both in Veracruz
- Ajalpan in Tehuacán Valley
- El Totonacapan, land of the Totonacs
- Tuscapan, pyramid site, and Papantla, in province of Cempoala
- Atizapan, site in Valley of Mexico
- Tecpan, Guatemala
- Cuilapan, Mexico
- other archaeological sites: Iztapalapan, Tlayacapan, Tzompantitlan, Tenenepanco, Uruapan, Actopan

Central Americans with a distinct legend of the flood include Aztecs, Mixtecs, Zapotecs, Tlascalans, Michuacans, Toltecs, Nahuas, Mayans, and Quichés. The Aztecs say that they hail from the seven tribes of

Chichimecs who came from a place to the west of Mexico. Only the Pacific Ocean is west of Mexico. At Uxmal temple inscriptions commemorate "the lands of the west whence we came." This temple, according to Le Plongeon, memorialized the loss of those lands. Legend also recalls that the Mayan dwarfs of the First World built their cities after everything was destroyed in the first great flood and that God had delivered those first people through paths in the sea. Mexico's Cholula Pyramid, it was further said, had been built to protect against another flood.

Quiché

Let's get back to that Mayan name—Quiché; also spelled Kiché (as in Kich-pan, a formative Mayan site) or Kish as in Ma-kish-ko, near Mexico City. It is pronounced the same as Sumerian *Kish,* which was, according to their King List, the first capital after the flood. Considering flood times and the far-flung diaspora from a common homeland, it is only natural to find linguistic similarities in very different parts of the world. (There is a Kich tribe also along the Nile, as well as a Zambian ceremony called Mac-kish-ee.) Now the Kish of Mesopotamia is a well-known Sumerian city (a.k.a. Ur) with an important group of *tells* (mounds, see chapter 8); it was the birthplace of Abraham and the main port of Sumer. Here the cult of Kish and Temple of the Mother of the World once flourished; in fact, Kish-ar was the parent of God Ea in Chaldean tradition.

Iconography (as well as extant groups) show these Mesopotamian people as the *same racial type* found among the Quiché of Central and South America: long, high-bridged nose; pale skin; large head; bearded chin; and large, round eyes. In fact, Churchward thought the writing on William Niven's Mexican tablets was related to Babylonia (see "Sumerian–South American Comparisons," p. 210). The Quiché people of Central America were southwestern neighbors of the Yucatecan Maya and authors of the Popol Vuh,* whose histories relate how Balam-*Quiché*'s

---

*Popul means "book," Vuh means "counsel," which I believe derives from the old meaning of Vohu, "voice." Zarathustrian *Vohu Mano* meant "voice, engraved word" as received from the presence of the Lord Vohu.

people migrated, some from the west: "many came hither to Guatemala." Quiché dialects are still spoken in the Guatemalan highlands; also, the people of Chiapas (touching Guatemala) claim to be the first arrivals in the New World, led by one Nima-*kiche*. From whence?

Sumerian–South American Comparisons

Six thousand years ago the Sumerians, having migrated from the east, spoke an agglutinative (Jaffetic) language (resembling the tongue of drowned Lemuria). In this respect they were like their Guataman cousins, the Native Americans, whose languages are also agglutinative (sometimes with very long words). I keep coming across these American-Jaffetic affinities. People of the Caucasus and the Maya of Mexico have Rh-negative blood; Lapp and Algonquins share blood-type A. There are many other Asian-American comparisons, such as words held in common.

Sumerian	Peruvian	Shared Meaning
Goa	Goya	mother goddess
Mica-iah	Micay	like unto Jehovah, godlike
Panesa	Panaka	royal family
ilu	illi	talisman, God's proxy
pacha	pacha	sacred vessel
kosher	kocha	pure or holy
apu	apu	lord
mami	mama	earth mother
lak lak	llake llake	heron
lul	llu llu	lie
sug	soco	reeds
kasher	kusuru	basket

*From the ruins of the Sumerian cities we watch the shadows of
the cat-men whose emblems of stone look at us from the ruins
of pre-Colombian America.*

PETER KOLOSIMO, *NOT OF THIS WORLD*

Cuneiform inscriptions have been found in Brazil at Havea, Marajo, and Mato Grosso (Kolosimo 1975, 36). Marcel Homet also speaks of the ancient walls in Peru as identical to those of the eastern Mediterranean; most striking are the metal clasps that held together the stone slabs of Tiahuanaco, "found only in one other place in the world, namely, in the Assyrian palaces in Mesopotamia" (Homet 1963, 160). In those two places the terraced pyramids are as alike as two brothers. What's more, the Chaldean technique of embedding a mosaic of chips in asphalt is found also at the Olmec capital, La Venta (23 feet down) (Gordon 1974, 131). Mesopotamian-type seal cylinders are found in Middle America. Drake also notes a "surprising kinship" between Hebrew and Mayan dialects, arising, he supposes, either from Atlantis or Mu (Drake, 1974, 253).

The cradle of the Aztec race, says the mythology of the Quichés, was called *Pan*-paxil-pacayala, the place where "the waters divide in falling, or between the waters parceled out and mucky." That name *Pan* (representing the motherland) again appears in legendary Teotlal*pan,* the "Land of the Gods," with its white and yellow corn from which was made the flesh of man. Where was that land? Well, the Aztec goddess of that excellent maize had her home in the *west.* Even in North America, the Chippewas say that maize was brought to them by the sacred *Quichés* (pronounced *keesh-ay*), the first men who were molded from it (i.e., whose civilization thrived on it). *Kisha* Manito is the name of the Creator himself among the Menomini Indians of North America—similar to the Koryak Siberian name for the Supreme Being: Gich-olan. The Algonquin word for "lord" was *Gitche.* The god of the Massachusetts Indians was Kich-tan.

South America

*In Peru, the Quiche, who originally came there from
Central America, are now known as Quichuas.*

JAMES CHURCHWARD, *THE LOST CONTINENT OF MU*

The mountain-dwelling Quichuas (var. Quechuas) of Peru, a peaceful
and docile people, with their strong Ihin heritage, are shorter and lighter
than the Aymaras. Quechua is also the name of the language spoken by
these long-lost cousins of the Central American Quichés, a relationship
that the orthodox historian either ignores or denies. Yet the Chimu of
Peru do indeed say they came from the north. And doesn't Cha-Cuna
Valley, their home, reflect the *Cuna* tribal name of Panama? Interesting
too that the first Inca king was named *Pan*aca (title) Chima. Central
America also has its Chima: Chimal-huacan, in the Valley of Mexico, as
well as Chimal-tenango in Guatemala. Mexico's Codex Chimal-popoca
preserves the history and mythology of the Aztec civilization—detailing
the story of their founder's immaculate birth by a virgin mother named
Chimal-man. Descended from the inhabitants of Mexico, the Chimu in
South America founded the Mochica culture, with monumental architecture, excellent roads, irrigation, reservoirs, surgeons, and goldsmiths

*Fig. 5.14. A
Quechua man*

Fig. 5.15. Chimu walls

of great skill. The capital of the Chimu Empire, covering 18 square miles with immense pyramids, massive walls, amenities, and everything well organized, was called Chan Chan. On the walls of Chan Chan's palace is depicted a sunken homeland; fish are seen swimming *over* the summits of its step pyramids.

Chan Chan

The reach of Chimu-style culture is astounding. The fine reliefs at Chan Chan are reminiscent of almost every known civilization. Chan Chan, with hot and cold running water, for example, reminded archaeologists of the startlingly modern bathrooms of ancient Crete. The Chimu moon goddess, Sin An, is answered by her counterpart at Nineveh, Sin, and Akkadian moon god, Suen. Were the founders of the Sumerian Temple of Sin (at Khafeje) little people? Its chambers were of diminutive size. Sina is also the Polynesian goddess of the moon.

There are prominent Chans in Mexico as well, such as Chan Bahlum, king of Palenque (seventh century). I wonder if *Can,* as in Can-cun and La-can-don, is indeed a variant of *Chan.* In the book of Chilam Balam, the first people in the Yucatán were called Ah-Can-ule.

Fig. 5.16. Note the striking similarity of Chimu (left) and Egyptian (right) rulers. Thor Heyerdahl cites "such reed boat centers as Chan Chan . . . and Egypt as centers for [a] worldwide trading culture" (Childress 1988, 315), which would certainly help explain so many of these East/West resemblances.

The Mayan king Can, says Churchward, may go back as much as thirty-four thousand years. Indeed, the Xicalan-*can* people were *predecessors* of the Toltecs in the former civilization called the Third Age; they settled Poton-*chan*.

In South America are the Can-aris Indians of Ecuador—whose origin myth has twin brothers escaping the deluge on high mountains. Among the Bolivian Chané the flood hero escapes in a floating pot! Maya called the white strangers who landed at Vera Cruz, Chanes; these Chanes taught the civilized arts and founded Chichén Itzá. The Chan-e of Paraguay show influence from Mexico (Lothrop 1937, 27), while the Chan-es culture of Panama tallies strongly with that of Chimu. In Colombia too are the Tu-can-os and Sutumar-chan (with megalithic standing stones) as well as Ga-chan-tiva (Mochica), where "Chan Chan!" was an invocation to the gods. Some scholars have trans-lated Kan (var. Can, Chan) to mean "upright, favored, priest"—which would apply to Kukul-can and Kan-tule, the Kuna high priest. The

Mexican Chan-e were a priestly caste too, founded by Ahau *Can*.

As J. M. Brown saw it, Polynesians founded the great city of Grand Chimu. Sunken off the coast of Peru is a dock large enough for an oceangoing craft. Brown thought that these early voyagers came from the Marquesas, the only place in the Pacific with both megalithic work and statuary similar to what we see in Peru. Was the first Chan Dynasty in the Pacific? "The true lineage of Hawaiian kings came from Kane" (Santillana 1969, 164)—and the people named Kan-aka are white men. Is it just a coincidence that Tamoa-*chan* is the name of the legendary land west of Mexico?

It may also be relevant that the *earliest* language group in California is Ho-*Kan,* said to belong to the Austronesian languages of the Pacific. When *chan* or *can* is suffixed, it seems to indicate "kingdom" in many place-names in the Valley of Mexico: Xalto*can,* Acolhua*can,* Tenayu*can,* Teculhua*can,* Coatli*can,* Coyohua*can,* Culhua*can,* Amaqueme*can,* Michoa*can.* In the Panic language Chan meant "city" (Oahspe, Book of Saphah: Tablet of Kii, 2). Old World counterparts of all these Chans include the pyramid of Chan-pa-Chan in Turkestan, being the cradle of their people according to the Tartars, whose tradition says it was their first settlement *after a great deluge.*

Neither should we ignore the Mongolian word for "king"— *Khan,* as in the famous Tartar Genghis Khan. Yet on Panape, in the Caroline Islands, *chan* also means "king." Chan-te-leur, for example, means "Kings of the Sun," just as Chan Bahlum was the onetime ruler of Mexico's Palenque, whose deluge hero built the great city called Na-Chan (Palenque). Also in Mexico, Chan Kin ("King Sun") was the title of the La-can-don chief. Not too different in the Old World, *chun* meant "prince" in ancient China, while in ancient Europe, Can designated a *war* chief, a conqueror; for example, the Iberians called Si-Can-es colonized Italy several millennia BCE.

The founder of Peru's Chan Chan, at Trujillo, was Tay-can-amu. Where exactly did he come from? Peruvians say the first empire was ruled by a race called Chan-cas, who came to Titicaca from Amazonia's Golden City (Manoa); these Chancas, according to Churchward, came directly from the motherland (southeastern Mu).

Polynesians in South America

The portion of the human race that the Indo-Americans
most resemble in their craniological development was
decidedly the Polynesian. . . . [They] are one and the same
people . . . connected with each other by mutual ties of
parentage and descent.

JOHN LANG, *ORIGIN AND MIGRATION OF*
THE POLYNESIAN NATION

Legends of flood persist among South America's Muiscas, Quichuas, Tupinamba, Achaguas, Araucanians, and Guari, the latter saying that their ancestors came from the west, across the Ocean. Some coastal peoples recall the arrival from parts unknown of a strange and entirely different race, whose land in the South Seas was submerged. The ancient songs of the Tupis of Brazil recount "destruction by a violent inundation . . . a long time ago" (Brinton 1976, 226). Significantly, the Tupi people are leptorrhine and brachycephalic (narrow nosed and round headed) like the Ihins; this race, thought British explorer Colonel P. H. Fawcett, was of Pacific origin.

It was Professor J. Macmillan Brown, former chancellor of the University of New Zealand, who most resolutely championed a lost continent in the South Pacific inhabited by white men; he believed it lent its culture to Peruvian civilization. It was, he thought, these Polynesians who brought the mound culture to America. Workers have since been able to connect Tennessee, Kentucky, and Ohio moundbuilders to populations in Fiji and the Sandwich Islands, their artifacts "clearly of a Polynesian character. . . . The North Americans [and] Polynesians . . . were formerly the same people, or had one common origin" (Ellis 1931, 122).

In the Andean highlands, according to Brown's contemporary, the American anthropologist A. H. Verrill, "we find tribes, which it is difficult to believe have anything in common with those of other portions of the New World. . . . Many of the Central and South American tribes are far more . . . Polynesian than Mongolian in appearance." In South America, Verrill goes on, "we find words . . . identical

Fig. 5.17. Panpipes from
the Solomon Islands
and from Bolivia.
Interestingly, the pipes
have tonal identity and
the same pitch.

with words of the same meaning in Oceanian dialects. In their arts, habits, and religious beliefs there is [also] great similarity . . . many astonishingly alike." The bearded, blue-eyed Bolivian Sirionos, for example, with their "typically Oceanian features, bear no faintest resemblance to any other known Indian tribe" (Verrill 1943, 12–13). In Peru, H. T. Wilkins found a "shy, furtive and gentle" race of white people with beards whom he dubbed "the oldest race now alive" (Wilkins 2000, 117), rather like the white Tapuyos, who were thought to be refugees from a former civilization.

North America's bearded Kennewick Man specimen was also a non-native type with Oceanic overtones; neither was Spirit Cave Man in Nevada particularly Amerind in type. It took the work of Walter Neves (University of São Paulo) to establish links between the skulls of Polynesians and North American Paleo-Indians; just as anthropologist Marta Lahr matched Patagonian skulls to those of the South Pacific. Earlier, Baron Erland Nordenskiold had compiled about fifty items mutually used in South America and the Pacific Islands; if this correspondence was due to actual migrations, they were of "exceedingly remote date"—very remote indeed, as the flood and diaspora occurred twenty-four thousand years ago.

South America and Oceania share any number of comparable

customs: pile houses, men's societies, slit-log drums, fish weirs, slings, blowguns, swizzle sticks, grooved mallets, short clubs, battle stilts, five-pointed stone mace, raincoats made from palm leaves, wooden clubs and paddles, bark corsets, knuckle dusters, and signal gongs, not to mention the ancient arts of trepanning and tattooing. Chilean canoes are virtually identical to Polynesian ones; "sword clubs" of South Sea origin have been found in several Peruvian graves. Polynesians and Peruvians elongate their earlobes in just the same way. Quipus, moreover, were used by both peoples (see below, "The Shining Cuckoo"). The poncho worn from Mexico to Argentina matches the *tiputa* of Polynesia. "The umu or earth-oven of the Pacific penetrated South America . . . the stone axe was also adopted in the Pacific regions of South America" (Spence 1933, 190).

The Shining Cuckoo

The Andean quipu finds its counterpart of knotted cords on Oleai in the Caroline Islands and in New Zealand as well. Rongorongo affines, as we've seen, also link up these far-flung islands.

I have found equivalents of quipu in Vietnam and Babylonia; in the

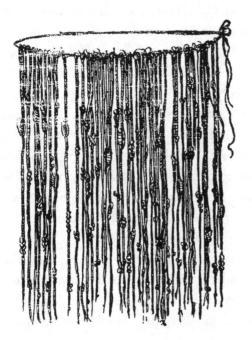

Fig. 5.18. Quipu: Peru's system of colored knots served as a mnemonic device for figures, facts, histories, calendars, songs, and chants.

latter, the economic overseer (the master accountant) was called *qipu*. Quipu-type record keeping with strings and knots was also known in China and the Ryukyu Islands. According to Chinese chronicles, an emperor had replaced ideographic script with one based on knots. Knotted strings for records were also used in western North America and still are used in Tibet (Birket-Smith 1965, 400).

In Hawaii, to collect tribute from outlying islands, King Kamehameha's tax collectors kept accounts on knotted cords. *Kipu* is actually the Hawaiian word for (administrative) "lands." In the ancient Polynesian empires the knotted cord was used for the communication of the wishes of the government. In Polynesia and Easter Island they also recited genealogical lists using knotted cords, each knot corresponding to the name of an ancestor. The knotted strings are made of coconut fiber in the Marquesas, where the priests make a fresh knot for each new death, these being their mortality statistics.

In New Zealand quipu is called *tauponapona,* the knots conveying a message or command. "Whatonga, a pioneer of migration to New Zealand . . . when voyaging from Hawaiki, had to rest in . . . the Society group. . . . His grandmother at home, wanting to know what had become of him, sent off a *Tame Pipiwharauroa,* or bird of Long Voyage, with a message in knotted cords tied round its neck. . . . This bird, the Shining Cuckoo, arrives in the north of New Zealand early in November. . . . Evidently the Society group lies in its line of flight. We have here a development of the *quipu* that goes far in the direction of the Easter Island script. . . . That the *quipu* was used in the Society group centuries before Pomare moulded it into an empire points back to the Polynesian fatherland as its source" (Brown 1924, 83).

The link between Peruvians and Maoris is also linguistic (see appendix C, p. 474).

In fact, it is the *oldest* Peruvian languages that show greatest similarity to the Polynesian, leading us to suspect that "the migration must have taken place in very early times; and there can be no question of these immigrants having transmitted a higher civilization" (Honore 1964, 188).

Fig. 5.19. Polynesian carving (top) and Maori lintel (bottom) showing faces with protruding tongues, so often seen in South American art—as well as in portrayals of deities in China's Yangtze region "Ch'u Silk Manuscript." In Tibet it is a traditional manner of greeting.

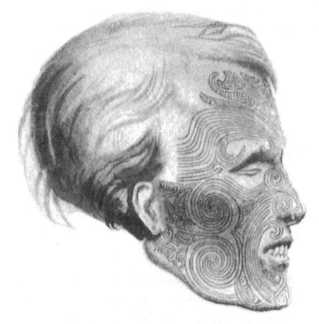

Fig. 5.20. Maori facial tattoo. Observers have commented that Brazilian Indians could pass for New Zealander Maoris (Lang 1877, 130).

TRANSPACIFIC WORDS IN THE ANCIENT LANGUAGES OF THE AMERICAS

Word (Place)	Word (Place)	Meaning
gata (Samoa)	gatuc (California)	worm
sua (Samoa)	dzu (South America, Cayriri)	snake
muna (Maori)	munay (Peru)	love
taki-taki (Maori)	taki (Peru)	chant, song
toki (Maori)	toki (Peru)	ax (of chief)
poorok (Australia)	poroko (Brazil)	thunder

Researchers Pierre Honore and Macmillan Brown thought immigrants from Oceania must have reached America, remains of which migration Honore found principally in Brazil. Comparable customs shared by Brazilians and Melanesians include the following:

communication by "drum language"
method of bleeding (venesection)
panpipes almost identical (see fig. 5.17, p. 217)
penis sheaths and nose ornaments
the habit of chewing lime mixed with a narcotic
the ikat style of weaving
comparable palisades built around the village
dimensions of prehistoric skulls
cat's cradle

I must admit though that most of these similarities devolve on contacts made many thousands of years *after* the great diaspora. The next chapter brings us further into the question of our globe-trotting ancestors.

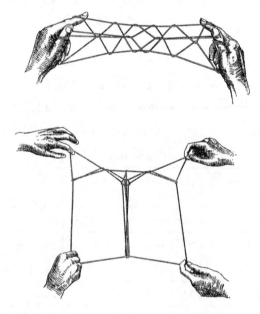

Fig. 5.21. The Maori game of whai is played with a loop of string, the configurations representing different mythological events. Cat's cradles are also popular among the Marquesans and Papuans.

INTERLUDE

The Era of Saviors

In every great city of earth there is a false god and the spirits of the dead are his slaves.

OAHSPE, BOOK OF THOR 1:11

Beware of spirits and Gods who profess to save the souls of men, saying: Only through me shall you . . . arise to Chinvat [upper heaven]. I declare to you that all such spirits and Gods belong to the lower heavens, where they have kingdoms, and they are the tyrants [thus warned Zarathustra]. . . . They [men] catch at the promises of Saviors, hoping to fly from the earth direct to Chinvat. . . . [But] unless you have learned to perfect your own selves in wisdom and goodness you shall not rise to Chinvat.

OAHSPE, BOOK OF SAPHAH: SE'MOIN 1:21

In short, there are false gods that lurked among the ancients, each competing for man's devotion in order to enrich their own heavenly kingdoms: Charles Fort famously said, "I think we're property." In a way, this tallies with the Sumerian belief that people were created to serve, to labor for the gods—which included waging war for the gods. All this is against a backdrop of the supposedly "divine" kings of the Near East, conspicuous consumption, lavish palaces, and vassal states forced to pay tribute. Even in today's counterculture the name "Babylon" stands for outré materialism and the entrenched interests of a notorious but established elite; it also stands for a place of polar haves and have-nots. In a word, the state in Egypt and Mexico "functioned for the benefit of a minority—privileged rulers and nobles to whom all wealth and power flowed" (Fagan 1999, 192).

There are kingdoms and principalities in heaven [that] are ruled over by both good and bad Gods. . . . Whoever worships Buddha shall go to Buddha to be his slaves; and whoever worships Brahma shall go to Brahma, and be his slaves . . . giving their own souls into bondage. For they shall . . . understand that the Great Spirit, the Ever Present, is not an idol in the figure of a man, sitting on a throne. . . . The time shall come when angels and mortals shall know in truth [when] the Lord God is a false God, and a vain-glorious usurper . . . and they shall see and understand that man of himself never invents

Fig. 6.1. Assyrian king— note the pomposity of his imagined size compared to commoners, mere mortals.

a God in the figure of a man. . . . Only through the inspiration of My enemies, who build kingdoms for their own glory, has any people ever fallen from My estate to worship a God in image of man.

OAHSPE, GOD'S BOOK OF ESKRA 40:14–15 AND

BOOK OF WARS 21:11

Iram of the Columns

Those savior-kings of yore, worshipped as gods especially in the era of the sun kingdoms, were, as a colleague of mine, Tom Veigle, once remarked, "egotistical maniacs." South America's Viracocha (as discussed below) was a figure of bloated pomp, the father of New World despotism and courtliness, builder of huge majestic cities. In Oceania "the royalty and aristocracy led an existence of the most luxurious character. . . . The traditions of the wickedness of these people is perhaps a memory of [this] soulless selfishness . . . glutted with power . . . almost identical with that of Incan Peru . . . bent above all things on the erection of large megalithic buildings, the exaltation of royalty and the priesthood" (Spence 1933, 217). These firmly entrenched oligarchies that commanded the megalithic cultures also characterize most of prehistoric Mexico and the classic Mayan culture. All such economies of the ancient world "depended upon the compulsion of its people to heavy tasks [moving monoliths] and would have safeguarded itself by the formation of a large standing army" (216).

> They not only waged war, but in times of peace they maintain armies ready for more war. Come, therefore, away from them . . . and I will deliver you into another country [quote Abraham]. Rather than being impressed into war, come where I will lead, and dwell in peace [quote Brahma].
>
> OAHSPE, BOOK OF SAPHAH: TABLET OF BIENEI 4

When writers ask *why* such huge monuments and idols were built, they tend to ignore or downplay the manifest vainglory of those ancient regimes, perhaps because such "economy," along with standing armies, inflated ego, false gods, and love of power is indeed *not a thing of the past.*

The Arabian legend "Iram of the Columns" is a cautionary tale, similar in some ways to the Tower of Babel.* Here we see one Ash Shedad, son of Ad, inspired to build an earthly paradise in the desert of Adan (al-Yaman: Yemen) that would rival the celestial one. Told in *The Arabian Nights,* this parable of the sun kings speaks of the extravagance and splendor of Adan's terrestrial paradise, built by slaves: gem-encrusted monuments, throne of gold, *a thousand columns* of the finest polished woods, skyscrapers. Indeed, one Yemenite chronicler claimed that there was once a twenty-story palace in the city of San'a, today's capital of Yemen.

We build up mighty kingdoms, and our places are replete with great magnificence; in search of what? While that which costs nothing, love, the greatest good of all in heaven and earth, we leave out in the cold.

OAHSPE, BOOK OF WARS 44:7

These builders, in a word, were self-gods, men of tall stature. All such legends describe what became of the race of Ghans, large men, warriors, wealthy, proud, and profane, unbelievers in the Great I Am. Their sun king nine thousand years ago declared: "It cannot be that there are Gods or spirits. . . . These things were suited to the dark ages. They [merely] frightened men to justice" (Oahspe, Book of God's Word 16:27).

So, inevitably, there came a "noise" out of the firmament, and lo, the builders of Adan were struck dead by the noise, and the many-columned palaces fell in a heap of ruins; for these men had "become as gods." Fallen was the Adite nation, "except a very few who escaped because they had renounced idolatry. . . . Ad had married a thousand wives. . . . [It was] a nation, in short, with whom material progress was allied to great moral depravity and obscene rites . . . an ancient, sun-worshipping, powerful and conquering race [that] overran Arabia at the very dawn of history" (Donnelly 1985, 276–77).

---

*As John Lang saw it, the Tower of Babel "was evidently intended to subserve the purposes of personal ambition . . . to enslave the rapidly increasing population . . . [and] to pave the way for the establishment of a universal and despotic monarchy" (1877, 144).

The story of Iram reminds us of Mexico's comparable lore of "giants"—actually, just tall men, like the Toltecs, the Ihuans, and Ghans who wanted to raise themselves up to the sun. Easter Island too, as David Childress points out, was anciently inhabited by very big men (not really giants). The tall and stately Ghans lent their genes to the royal families of Polynesia, Africa, Sumeria, and Peru.

> Lo, the race of Ghans . . . now stands triumphant on the earth . . .
> Not like lambs are the Ghans, but lions untamed, born conquerors.
> . . . And when they die, and enter heaven . . . [they are] still full
> of inherent stubbornness and *self-will* . . . set[ting] up heavenly
> kingdoms of their own, in darkness. . . .
>
> OAHSPE, BOOK OF OSIRIS 1:11–12 (EMPHASIS ADDED)

More than twelve thousand years ago the oracle of Baugh-*Ghan*-Ghad declared, "I go forth. . . . My name is Might" (Oahspe, Saphah: Baugh-Ghan-Ghad 1).

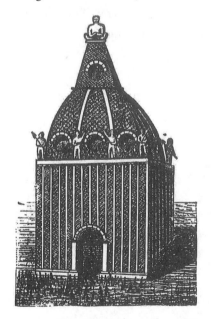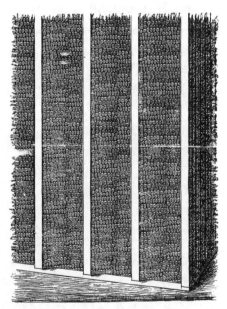

Fig. 6.2. Oahspe plates 85 and 86 showing distant view of the Baugh-Ghan-Ghad Temple and a sectional view of the temple. Note the hundreds of skulls embedded in the wall.

Having built a glorious tower (or zacuali), an astronomical observatory really, they were admonished by the Lord of Creation, "It is not right that mortals should lift themselves to us." So, says legend, with thunder and lightning the gods destroyed the giant tower and confused their languages—at least according to Mesopotamian tradition. But what was the real point or moral of these stories? The problem was not that man presumed to storm heaven or become "too godlike" or grab the secrets of heaven; rather, the reverse, for he had become a nonbeliever in, a despiser of, the All Highest, making a god of *himself* instead. They said of themselves, "I am the highest."

> Because of unbelief in the Great Spirit, man has set himself up as the All Highest, and his trade has become war and destruction.
>
> OAHSPE, BOOK OF GOD'S WORD 18:17

We see here how gods or angels became false by proclaiming themselves to be the embodiment of All Knowledge.

Iram's "thousand columns" have an echo in the New World: those columns of Panama and Mexico—all signaling the ancient era

Fig. 6.3. A depiction of Osiris the False, plate 90 from Oahspe

of ostentatious gods at work. But "was it not so in all times on the earth? Out of the mouths of my chosen . . . come words of truth, love, wisdom, kindness. . . . But from those who deny me come corruption, war, avarice, and the love of earthly things for self's sake" (Oahspe, The Lords' First Book 1:9).

Egyptian Pomp and Circumstance

Despite all, writers today still play to the grandeur of yore, to the work of those autocrats and privileged few who controlled the lowly masses. In Egypt, Luxor's Sphinx-lined avenue "still manages to inspire and awaken those emotions of grandeur and pompous ceremony. . . . The avenue terminates at the Temple of Luxor [which is] a truly magnificent structure built by various pharaohs" (Roberts and Ward 2014, 56)—who, incidentally, enjoyed lavish private harems (not too different from the extravagant Adites who "married a thousand wives"). And how do you like the steps of Amenhotep III's palace, covered as they were "with images of bound enemies so that as Pharaoh walked upon them, he was symbolically crushing them beneath his feet"? (Roberts and Ward 2014, 112). Is this to be admired? In the New Kingdom construction work was done by enforced servitude, "a veritable slave caste," some consisting of prisoners of war. Yes, Egypt's colossal monuments "existed for the sole purpose of recording . . . the glories and accomplishments of the Pharaoh, trumpeting his triumphs and vaunting his valor" (Roberts and Ward 2014, 94).

Why does the adulation of these monuments continue to this day? Megaliths, say some, "evoke some instinct for the sacred" (Zink 1979). But what is so sacred about "the pyramid, a monument of stone that is a witness of the futility of selfish human aspiration? The colossal folly of the building of [tomb] pyramids is typical of man's desire for his own preservation and also of the ruthlessness with which he will encompass that desire" (Perry 1968, 438).

The great author Herman Melville was once invited to Cairo to see the pyramids. After climbing to the top of one, Melville—a sensitive and justice-loving soul who played a significant role in ending the practice of flogging in the Navy—was overcome with nervousness and terror. The great monuments, the author would later confess, left him with the impression of "something vast, indefinite, incomprehensible and awful."

Dazzled by the scale of these mighty works, we have somehow overlooked the traditions of the world's people, which tell us that the great builders of old, the "giants," were also great *ruiners,* obsessed with might and power. It is almost as if the more majestic the display, the more despotic and crueler its creator!

Practically Slaves

The builders of the China Wall and the pyramids of Egypt used enforced labor. It took three million workers and thirty-seven years to build the Great Wall. D. H. Childress compares the work at Panape's Nan Madol (walls 12 feet thick and 30 feet high) to "the building of the Great Wall of China and the Great Pyramid of Egypt in sheer amounts of stone, labor and the gigantic scope of the edifice" (Childress 1988, 214). In J. M. Brown's view, Panape (in Micronesia) was built by an entrenched slavocracy. To Harold T. Wilkins there was "an aura of ancient evil" at Easter Island, whose master builders "conscripted, for the work of raising these mighty stone blocks into position, slave-labor. . . . Almost every face [on Easter Island's moai] is arrogant and masterful—men of a race of world-conquering imperialists and militarists" (Wilkins 2000, 25). Concerning these moais, recently a Finnish tourist accidentally knocked off the earlobe of a moai statue. He was arrested and forced to pay a $17,000 fine. The ancient hype continues . . .

Brown, like Wilkins, perceived the moai as "arrogant and resolute [in their] ruthless majesty, haughty scorn, and imperious will." Oozing from these monuments is a sense of "limitless power . . . the capacity for organizing great masses of men . . . to haul, raise, and place the blocks. Wherever there are megalithic monuments there was absolute power controlling tens of thousands of toilers who were practically slaves" (Brown 1924, 14, 17, 258).

Sometimes I wonder why we are so drawn to whimsical theories that posit magic or some supertechnology to raise the monuments *effortlessly* rather than concede that ambitious tyrants enslaved thousands of workers. It has been estimated that seven hundred men were needed at Stonehenge to shift a monolith of 35 tons and that as many as eight thousand men would be needed to move a 130-ton block. Traditions also speak of "foreign invaders making them [California Indians] into helots . . . [and] similar prehistoric invasions of the South American west coast. These invaders . . . made the ancestors pile up stones for a great temple whereon these great lords might take refuge" (Wilkins 2000, 16).

Sun kings in the Mariana Islands may have been such foreign invaders. Concerning their mushroomlike monuments, "the Taotaumona [are] . . . characterized by the indigenous Chamoro as *alien builders* who arrived from over the sea during the ancient past" (Joseph 2006, 109; emphasis added).

In Phoenician legends of Baal (see Baal the savior, discussed in "Sealed in Blood," p. 255) he conquers the races of distant lands; we will soon get back to those globe-trotting Phoenicians and the forty-nine saviors who, like the later Apostles, were sent to the ends of the Earth. Bochica, Colombia's prehistoric savior, supposedly sent by God, was different from any race known to them; he appeared suddenly from a land to the east, built great towers, and introduced the worship of the Sun. In Mexico too the men who built Cholula Pyramid were foreigners. The Toltecs, who built beautiful houses, temples, and palaces, all of the greatest magnificence, did indeed colonize many other parts of Central America—hence, foreigners.

> *Phoenicians were sailing on westward, out beyond the*
> *Pillars of Melkarth, seeking new sites for colonization.*
> *(These religious zealots are known to have carried their*
> *cult practices with them out to distant colonies.)*
> CONSTANCE IRWIN, *FAIR GODS AND STONE FACES*

But the Ihins, the original white founders, were of a humble disposition and never were inclined to build palaces or grandiose monuments.

Wherever you find a privileged class, you have left the chosen people behind.

> God said: Where are my chosen? ... You have shown me the Jhuans [giants], their great cities and kingdoms. ... But the greatest of all, you have not shown. ... These that build temples of hewn stone, and cover them with polished copper, are not my people. These warrior kings, that fortify their cities with soldiers, are not my people. They are not great.
>
> OAHSPE, THE LORDS' THIRD BOOK 1:9, 13

Blood and Idols

The barbarous priest some dreadful God adore,
And sprinkle every stone with human gore.

QUOTED WITHOUT ATTRIBUTION BY
JOHN FINCH (1824, 149)

The Popol Vuh remembers the sacred tribes of yore: "They prayed to neither wood nor stone." But then, as Churchward explains, "a great blot ... disfigured the ancient religions. The Mayas, Egyptians, Phoenicians, and other of the ancients ... turned the pure worship of God into horrible forms of idolatry ... the crowning horror and disgrace—human sacrifice" (Churchward 2011, 285). "Mine bow down not before idols" was the Zarathustrian code (Oahspe, Book of Saphah: Faithists in the East, 11). This firm belief was held because "the Great Spirit ... [was] an inconceivable entity, Whose form and extent no man could attain to know; [nevertheless] He was now transformed and declared to be in the form of a man ... merely an idol; and so began the overthrow of the holy doctrines" (Oahspe, Book of Saphah: The Basis of the Ezra Bible, 28).

Some of us have heard the famous story of the prophet Mohammed destroying the people's idols. Indeed, Africans are known to dismiss the ancient dolmens found on their continent as tombs of the idolators. And these builders of megaliths, menhirs, dolmens, and *sacrificial* stones are thought to be the world-traveling Phoenicians and Carthaginians, with

Fig. 6.4. A 4½ ton sacrificial table: The incised rectangle at Mystery Hill is thought to have served to collect the blood of sacrificial victims. Phoenician or Cretan connections are suggested by the inscriptions seen here.

Baal their idol in heaven. For example, the sacrificial stone at "America's Stonehenge" (a.k.a. Mystery Hill) in New Hampshire bears an inscription written in Phoenician proclaiming their deity Baal: "To Baal of the Kanaani, this is dedicated." Similarly, the Punic inscription on the Pontotoc Stele at Oklahoma reads, "When Baal-Ra rises in the east, the beasts are content. . . ."

Wilkins notes "a very definite lunatic twist" in monolithic sun cults like "eerie Stonehenge. . . . Each year, a procession of skin-clad priests . . . along an avenue between monolithon pillars . . . [followed behind] a fair youth and maiden . . . the victim [then] bound to the slaughter-stone. . . . Priests, with knives of stone killed the victim, in prehistoric Britain, just as they did in old Mexico" (2000, 115). In Teotihuacan ritual, the precious Sun could be fed by blood and blood alone; while the priests at Tenochtitlan, wrapped in cloaks made of human skin, slaughtered the youth of noble families by strangulation, throat slashing, or burying alive in the pyramid. The inauguration of the temple required the sacrifice of fifteen thousand people. Chroniclers tell us that the Tenochtitlan district had more altars and sacrificial stones than anywhere else in America; the pyramid itself was dedicated to the war god and literally drenched in blood.

In Australia tall, white pyramid builders sacrificed virgins to the Sun (Childress 1988, 98). Samoan history also has humans sacrificed to the Sun, just as Tahitian temples sacrificed humans to the gods. Up until the twentieth century (1930s) dolmens were still used in the Pacific at the New Hebrides Islands in rites of sacrifice. Humans were offered up to the planet Venus in Polynesia, according to Immanuel Velikovsky (Velikovsky 1965, 179).

Often noted is the phobic avoidance of old ruins on the part of various Pacific Islanders who claim that those places are inhabited by ghosts and evil spirits (*mauli*). Even today the people have a superstitious fear of these rows of megalithic stones. Surely this fear and dread hark back to the not-so-distant day of horrid human sacrifice. In the Society Islands human sacrifice was part and parcel of the divine right of kings. Here it was believed that when a person died violently, his agitated spirit remained in place. "Hence the belief still that certain places, especially marae . . . are haunted" (Henry 1928, 200).

Sun Worshippers

They made an idol of the sun, an idol who must, often enough, be appeased, be fed. In Richard Dewhurst's recent book *The Ancient Giants Who Ruled America*, I was struck by what the archaeology of three Amerind sites revealed about solar religion. In Tennessee, for one, the Children of the Sun, "compelled by despotic power to obedience," consecrated human victims in a wood fire "for the use of the deity" (Dewhurst 2014, 328). At another site, this one on Catalina Island, off California, were found skeletons of sixty-four children, beneath whom lay the remains of a 7-foot man—a Ghan! Here, stone circles were aligned with the sun god, Chinigchinich; their "child sacrifices were made in wholesale fashion" (308). Finally, in Illinois, three hundred burial sacrifices were uncovered south of Monks Mound, where the sun calendar is similar to that of Stonehenge; signs of ritual execution abound (mostly young women in

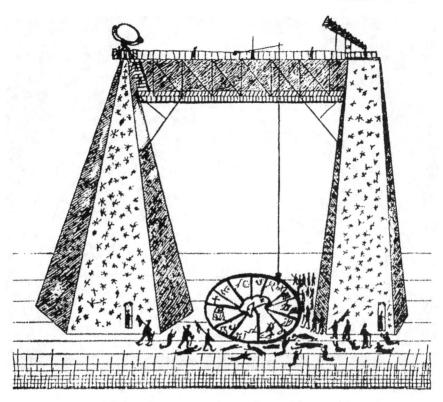

*Fig. 6.5. Megalithic observatory, plate 8 from Oahspe, star worshippers
in the time of Osiris. Are the prostrate figures victims?*

mass graves). The ruler reposed on a blanket of twenty thousand beads,
surrounded by the bodies of his hapless attendants. "The extensive public
works and human sacrifices are evidence of a class society in which rulers
held sway over life and death and labor" (139–42).

From Fonece (proto-Phoenician) records comes this interesting
excerpt:

> In ancient times long past, were worshippers of idols and Gods
> who professed to save the souls of men. . . . Their pride and glory
> lay in ships of war and mighty weapons of death. . . . An ancient,
> ruined pot read: "Because I am a Faithist in the Great Spirit, I am
> enslaved by these idolaters. Alas, what is my crime?"

OAHSPE, BOOK OF SAPHAH: FONECE 31–43

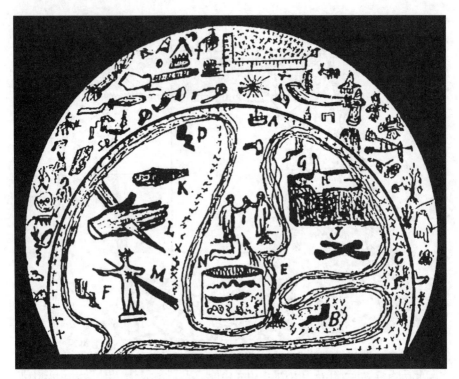

Fig. 6.6. Book of Saphah, plate 70. Ceremonies in Sun Degree: J = place of death, represented by bones and skull. K = coffin. L = proof of spirit-power to overcome pain. M = submission to have the body run through with a lance. N = testimony that the initiate could endure all corporeal torture unharmed. These are excerpts from the initiation rite led by saviors and idolaters of the heliolithic age, calling for man to prove his devotion by torturing his flesh. All of which reminds us of the tortures of the Sun Dance among the Plains Indians, and indeed of Quetzalcoatl's bloody "penance" (as discussed later). "Quetzalcoatl . . . Bochica and Viracocha were sun-worshippers" (Wilkins 2000, 24). Bochica's protégés (the Mochica) employed earplugs and other forms of self-mutilation, including the custom of removing the entire upper lip. Reminder of Easter Island's virtually lipless moai?

I would like to point out that the prehistorical Empire of the Sun has mistakenly been thought of as the *first* religion of man. But according to David Zink, the solar religion of Egypt, headed by the sun god Ra (or Re), did not become dominant until the Fourth Dynasty

(Zinc 1979, 67). Allow me then to take a closer look at these sun-worshipping theocracies, still rather glorified by the (supposedly democracy-loving) reading public and also by writers of alternate history, such as Raymond Drake, who regales us with "the wonderful Sun Empire of Mu" (Drake 1968, 183), which built the large stone structures in the Caroline Islands.

These marae of Micronesia were built in connection with the Areois secret societies (see chapter 10), which William Ellis exposed as a privileged fraternity whose exhibitions were "most disgusting . . . dissipated" (Ellis 1931, 236). Areois and megaliths tend to go together, for the sun cultists were apparently the very ones who introduced the art of megalithic building. Nan Madol on Panape, where gigantic human bones have been found, seems to have been built in accordance with the annual changes of the sun; "an organized society of traders and navigators worshipped the sun and built great megalithic cities, pyramids, and platforms throughout the Pacific" (Childress 1988, 268).

In South America stories were heard by the Conquistadors of erstwhile gigantic white men, Sons of the Sun. The royal Inca claimed direct descent from the sun god, as did the Natchez, Mexicans, the pharaohs of Egypt, the Hindus, Chinese, Assyrians, and Cretans, as well as the Japanese, who say they hailed from the sun goddess Amaterasu. It was a worldwide phenomenon—the "Heliolithic Age" led by worshippers of the sun and builders of megaliths. In most of these places the sun king's decree was infallible, for he was, as we've seen, held as the All Highest. In the Andes he was "the center of an iron paternalism, a benevolent tyranny that makes the citizens of present-day Russia seem all but free" (Hawkes 1962, 126).

"There were," from a Faithist point of view, "many Middle Eastern peoples whose understanding of . . . the Creator had deteriorated into the worship of Shamash, the sun or sun god" (Jones 2008, 135). Have we been looking at these sun worshippers and what Heyerdahl calls "the fraud of sun-descent" (Heyerdahl 1953, 264) through rose-colored glasses? In Africa the Zimbabwe sun king had a harem of three thousand women! Just as Peru's sun king was entertained by a bevy of beautiful concubines. Even though the Sons of the Sun were declared the

Fig. 6.7. Shamash. Hammurabi received the Laws straight from the mouth of the sun god Shamash. Thus did the king of Babylon take the name Shamash-shumukin.

divine fathers of mankind, in many legends they are seen to turn from good to bad. The corruption of Plato's "Atlanteans" is really the story of the global sun kings, the arrogant and mighty Ghans. It was especially under Egypt's Osirian materialism that the sun became the All Highest, when man, abandoning the unseen powers, took to worshipping the sun and stars. Indeed, Childress traces the sun-worshipping societies to the Osirian dispensation: "As tall white navigators of the world, they were probably a combination of Libyan, Egyptian, Phoenician, Ethiopian, Greek and Celtic sailors . . . formerly the . . . Osirian Empire" (Childress 1988, 268). In Egypt the chief ruler was called the sun king, or king of the sun. The central kingdom was called the sun kingdom, and the others were called satellites.

Churchward deplores the ambitious priesthood who "degraded the pure, simple, beautiful Osirian religion . . . to accomplish their ends" (Churchward 2011, 100, 277). Similarly, Godfrey Higgins pointed out in his awesome work *Anacalypsis* that adoration toward the rising sun became "corrupted by the Arabians, and in order to avoid this very corruption and preserve the worship of one God . . . Moses established a law against bowing to the east" (where of course the sun rises) (Higgins 1991).

No, sun worshippers were neither our greatest nor our earliest ancestors. Yet a group called the Lemurian Fellowship did identify Mu's Empire of the Sun as the first civilization on Earth. But it was not the first, for the Children of the Sun were simply the *inheritors* of a yet older legacy—that of the Ihins, who were the "forefathers and foremothers of the great Ihuan* race" (Oahspe, Book of Wars 19:2). The very *first* civilizers were neither sun worshippers nor kings and queens, nor warriors and sacrificers, nor slavers or builders of great monuments.

Nor did the faithful ever have kings. The Zarathustrians had no kings. The *earliest* Hebrews had no kings; they owned nothing, giving everything to the *rabbah* (spiritual headman) for the public good. Nor did the Tua Git (the godlike people) of China have any king, serving the Lord only. It was the same in earliest America; the little Akuria people (*Homo sapien pygmaeus*) were utterly without kings or emperors, tyrants or despots in North America. The sacred people as well as their faithful Ihuan followers "lived without kings or governors. . . . And the tribes were made into states, with chief rabbahs as representatives, and these states were united into the Algonquin government, made and maintained for the benefit of the tribes" (Oahspe, God's Book of Eskra 10:12).

> These warrior kings, that fortify their cities† with soldiers, are not my people. . . . My chosen live in mounds. . . . They do not dress in gaudy colors, nor ornament themselves with copper, silver and gold. They are the people of learning.
>
> OAHSPE, THE LORDS' THIRD BOOK 1:13–15

---

*Hindu scriptures address the origin of the Ihuans. When the druks (the ground-burrowers) and the Ihins *interbred,* "the newborn people [the Ihuans] became the mightiest of all people in the whole world, because they came out of both darkness and light" (Oahspe, The Lords' Fifth Book 1:21).

†Tiahuanaco's Kalat Sassaya, built by the Sons of the Sun, was a fortress. Indeed, these sun kingdoms were usually at war. "They kept standing armies, trained in the labor of death; and this for the glory of the Sun Kingdom" (Oahspe, Book of God's Word 12:25).

The royalty that engendered the sun kingdoms of the Incas and Easter Island were "a race of conquerors . . . that great stone-building aristocracy who imposed . . . a species of slavery unequalled for its severity before or since. . . . There was no such thing as personal freedom. . . . Individual enterprise was unheard of" (Spence 1933, 197). And so it was that "the King of the Sun, King of Kings . . . sent his proclamations to the chief cities of Jaffeth, Shem and Ham, commanding that . . . certain presents must be sent to him every year, among which were thousands of subjects (slaves)" (Oahspe, Book of God's Word 16:6; referring to western Asia about 9,000 years ago—indeed, researchers at sites like Göbekli Tepe are finding evidence of more than 10,000-year-old power elites behind the megalithic projects in Asia Minor).

Let us better understand the bite of this elite "stone-building aristocracy." In Polynesia, on Raiatea, death was the penalty laid on any commoner who dared to approach the most sacred rites at the marae. And in Tahiti, if the king walked on a footpath, it was death for a plebian to walk on it afterward. In Hawaii commoners were excluded from the temple cult, and only kings and priests could bathe at Rongo's marae. It was hardly different at Peru's Sacsahuaman (meaning "royal eagle"), which only nobility were allowed to enter.

Fig. 6.8. Temples in the South Seas were called maraes.

Ra

Ra was the name of the great sun god of this global heliolithic civilization.

- *Ra* was the word for sun (and day) in New Zealand.
- Ravi meant "sun" in Sanskrit.
- Ra-mi was the Peruvian festival of the Sun.
- RaMac was a godlike race represented on Tiahuanaco's colossal statue.
- There was a sun goddess named Ra in Brazil.
- Arawak incursions brought with it sculptures of their Mother Goddess, Ra.
- In Mexico, Ra-na was a Toltec god.
- In the Near East, Ra-yan was a Yemeni god.
- Ammon-Ra was the sun god of Egypt.
- Babylon was called Ka Ra, City of the Sun.
- In India, King Ra-ma of Ayodhya dedicated his temple to the ancient solar religion.

Fig. 6.9. Egypt's sun god, Ra

On Pan itself the head of the Empire of the Sun was RaMu. Ra is still the god of war at Huahine and Raiatea, while Ra-uti is the orator (cheerer) of battle—just as in Egypt the goddess Hathor, at the command of Ra, waged war on mankind.

We might even ask, Did it all begin in Oceania? Nowhere is *Ra* so prominent. Ra'a means "sacredness" in the Society Islands. In Tahiti rara means "tribute," including *human* tribute: rara roroa. The word for chief or wealthy landowner is *Ra-atira*. Raa is the name of the sun clan on Easter Island, where the despotic Long-Eared lineage had their statues at Ra-vavai. Rapa Nui (the name of Easter Island) also has its Ra-no Rara-ku statues. Also, in the Austral group there was Rapa Iti, with a dozen pyramid palaces. Rarotonga, Raraka Island (east of Tahiti), and Ra-iatea are other Ra-named lands in the Pacific. "Raiatea," reports Childress, "is the religious center of Polynesia. . . . It is sometimes thought that the ancient and mysterious Havaiki was the island of Raiatea" (1988, 268). In fact, La-Mu-Ra is a Polynesian name for that lost country.

Yet for all its implied holiness, Ra is a tetract!*—a Member of the Beast, as it is called.

God said: Behold, my chosen shall remember the seven tetracts: Dibbah, the enticing evil, slander; Ra, the flesh evil, delight in being bad; Zimmah, wickedness, the joking evil; Belyyaal, worthlessness; Aven, vanity; Anash, persistent stubbornness, delight in destruction; and Sa'tan, desire for leadership, which is the captain of death.

OAHSPE, THE LORDS' FIRST BOOK 1:68

"The flesh evil," Ra, is elaborated in the Hindu language as rabhu, seizing spirits (Vedic), as Ra-ti, desire, and also as Ra-jas, all the lower passions. Rawan was the demon king in Ceylon; rabies is madness in Latin. In Hebrew, Ra-hab is the enemy of the Most High, and Yeser Ra

---

*Reuben's tetracts appear in the Holy Bible; Reuben was the first of the twelve sons of Jacob. As portrayed in related mythologies, the tetracts are the "seven evil spirits" or the "seven deadly sins."

is "the evil inclination" (Talmud)—recognizing that men and women are born with these tendencies but bound to master them.

Almost lost to history are the liberating words of one of Peru's most enlightened kings. When the Temple of the Sun in Cuzco was newly built, Inca Yupanqui himself rose before the multitude with this startling message: "Many say that the Sun is the Maker of all things. But he-who-makes should abide by what he has made. Now many things happen when the Sun is absent; therefore he *cannot be the universal Creator*. . . . He must have a lord and master more powerful than himself, who constrains him to his daily circuit without pause or rest" (Brinton 1976, 56–57). According to Balboa this was also the general opinion of the Indians. Indeed, to honor the Most Powerful, a temple was constructed near Callao, where his worship was to be conducted *without images or human sacrifices.*

It is most interesting that a comparable speech was given in Mexico by the Prince of Tezcuco. "Verily, these gods that I am adoring, what are they but idols of stone without speech or feeling? They could not have made the beauty of the heaven, the sun, the moon, and the stars which adorn it, and which light the earth, with its countless streams, its fountains and waters, its trees and plants, and its various inhabitants. There must be some god, invisible and unknown, who is the Universal Creator." The same prince who gave this speech went on to erect a temple that he dedicated "to the Unknown God, the Cause of Causes" (Brinton 1976, 56–57). This temple, he ordained, should never be polluted by blood (i.e., wanton sacrifice).

Phoenician Voyages

In the Americas, Australia, Spain, South Africa, the Indian Ocean, and Oceania, one finds traces of these sun-worshipping, seafaring Phoenicians. Accomplished metallurgists and skilled craftsmen, these are the ancient mariners who built faraway cities and colonies starting in the second millennium BCE. Thus do inscriptions on South American menhirs and dolmens contain letters from early Mediterranean alphabets. Some Phoenician and Carthaginian vessels,

Fig. 6.10. Mexican terra-cotta image strongly Phoenician in type. The Phoenicians are famous as the stonemasons sent to Jerusalem to build King Solomon's Temple. Helmets worn by figures in Mexican friezes and statues are also Phoenician in type (see chapter 3, "Helmets," p. 113).

weighing more than 1,000 tons, were stoutly built with huge square sails and capable of carrying 250 men.

In their wake were left hundreds of inscriptions cut in stone tablets along the banks of Brazilian rivers; rock paintings at Serra do Machado and Pedra de Gavea show Phoenician letters. Phoenician glass beads also turn up in Brazil, just as Phoenician designs appear on Brazilian Arawak stone hatchets. Ideograms associated with the Phoenician sun god Baal have been found in pre-Incan parts of Peru, whose amphitheaters are suspiciously like Mediterranean ones.

> *Transoceanic navigation flourished . . . throughout the Bronze Age, and probably earlier. . . . The winds and currents facilitate crossings from the bulge of Africa to the bulge of Brazil.*
>
> CYRUS GORDON, *BEFORE COLUMBUS*

Professor Gordon dates the first Phoenician crossings to the sixth century BCE, based on the Paraiba inscription of 530 BCE.

This controversial stone tablet in Paraiba, Brazil, reads, "We are sons of Canaan* from Sidon. . . . Commerce has cast us on this distant shore. . . . " Recording that ten ships had sailed from the Gulf of Aqaba on the Red Sea, the inscription goes on to state, "We set [i.e., sacrificed] a youth for the exalted gods and goddesses. . . . [after being] separated by a storm . . . from the hand of Baal."

The same sacrificial cult may have found its way to the Far North as well. At Mystery Hill, New Hampshire, the four thousand-year-old site called America's Stonehenge has megaliths and observatory alignments typical of those in Europe; inscriptions here appear to be in Phoenician or Celtic (Ogham) letters, which also turn up in other parts of New England, such as Massachusett, as well as at Mechanicsburg, Pennsylvania, Oklahoma, and Nevada. Celtic expeditions seem to have also left Ogham inscriptions in Arkansas, Kentucky, and off the coast of Maine, the latter script making reference to Carthaginian rulers. Also about four thousand years old, the Metcalf Stone of Georgia is inscribed with an Aegean or eastern Mediterranean script.

> *Phoenicians, Carthaginians, Greeks . . . could have sailed across the Atlantic . . . there to become the Quetzalcoatls and Viracochas.*
>
> CONSTANCE IRWIN, *FAIR GODS AND STONE FACES*

If I had to bet, I would wager that these voyages from the Old World—*not Atlantis*—explain why so many Amerinds say that their culture founders came from the east. "Atlantologists find the [Mexican] Quetzalcoatl-Kukulkan legend an important keystone of what might be called the arch of the Atlantean theory, while others consider that he may have been Minoan, Phoenician . . . [or] Carthaginian" (Berlitz 1972, 134–35). Is it simply a coincidence that ancient harbor construction in Florida is comparable to work of the Carthaginians? I don't think so. The Bourne Stone in Massachusetts (Cape Cod) was inscribed in Punic, recording the annexation of that region by a Carthaginian

---

*Similar Canaanite inscriptions have been found on a stone in Loudon County, Tennessee.

Fig. 6.11. The 300-pound Bourne Stone was found in the seventeenth century at an Indian mission station.

Fig. 6.12. The oval face, aquiline nose, and pointed beard are not Indian traits, as found on this incense burner from Iximche, Guatemala.

governor named Hanno, who in 425 BCE had sailed down the west coast of Africa in search of gold.

> *The ruling class of these [Phoenician] people were*
> *Children of the Sun, who practiced mummification*
> *and human sacrifice. The Phoenicians were skillful*
> *metal-workers, great sailors and traders, who ransacked*
> *the countries for treasures.*
>
> WILLIAM PERRY, *CHILDREN OF THE SUN*

Other inscribed stones in the jungles of Brazil recount that the Phoenicians (who had good maps of America) and Carthaginians wandered this way, trading and hunting valuable mineral lodes. It is not really a coincidence that Minas Gerais, where the Paraiba Stone was found, contains enormous reserves of iron ore. Bolivia also has a lot of copper, silver, and tin mines; the name of its mining center, Oruru, seems to derive from the Sumerian word *urruru,* "to smelt." The Peruvian highlands are rich in mineral deposits as well; here, the oldest structures are attributed to bearded white men, called Sons of the Sea, who worked stone with iron tools.

More than twenty-five hundred years ago Phoenicians were trading in Africa (gold and silver), Cyprus (copper), Spain (iron, tin, and lead), and Sumatra (tin) (Smith 1921, 85); they did business (tin mines) in Cornwall and Australia as well, where gold and silver were also available. Tin is fairly rare but is plentiful in islands off Sumatra; Sumeria's supplies of tin were failing, "the mines gradually exhausted" (Birket-Smith 1965, 81–82). They could ill afford the loss of their bronze industry, which gave them weapons, lamps, implements, and many other useful items. Sargon himself mounted overseas expeditions to secure supplies of tin.

There was, as Ignatius Donnelly argues, no real copper or tin age in Europe, Asia, or Africa prior to the Bronze Age (bronze is made up mostly of copper); this, he thinks, is "conclusive testimony that the manufacture of bronze was an importation into those continents from some foreign country. . . . In America alone of all the world is found the Copper Age, which must necessarily have preceded the Bronze Age, teaching us to look to the westward of Europe and beyond the sea for that foreign country. We find many similarities in forms of implements between the Bronze Age of Europe and the Copper Age of America" (Donnelly 1985, 267).

Prehistoric miners, we know, extracted huge amounts of copper from the Lake Superior region of Michigan—as long ago as 16,000 BP, "[t]he Ihuans dig deep down and bring copper and silver and lead in boats to the King" (Oahspe, The Lords' Third Book 1:6).

From at least the Middle Bronze . . . the chief motive
for marine missions was . . . the securing of the minerals

> *needed by the international technologies. . . . Cuneiform*
> *literature . . . illustrates access to raw materials in many*
> *far-off areas.*
>
> CYRUS GORDON, *BEFORE COLUMBUS*

Copper and tin were just like King Oil is today. Five thousand years ago the maritime Vedics navigated around Africa and even crossed the Atlantic in search of America's copper and tin in Michigan, Colorado, Arizona, and Peru* (Lehrburger 2015, 243). The key to this claim is the discrepancy between the amount of copper mined and the actual findings of copper items in America—an unexplained gap—unless we infer a lively export trade in those ancient times. King Rameses III's expedition to America for copper in the twelfth century BCE was at "Michigan's Upper Peninsula . . . where they engaged in extensive copper mining . . . [producing] the world's highest grade copper. . . . Only from the Upper Peninsula could Rameses have obtained such large amounts of exceptional copper" (Joseph 2014c, 38).

The late Barry Fell of Harvard University virtually proved that Egyptians, Libyans, Phoenicians, and other people once settled America.† The controversial stele at Davenport, Iowa, found in a burial mound bears a trilingual inscription: in Egyptian, Punic, and Libyan. Dated around 800 BCE, corresponding to the Twenty-second Dynasty—a time of overseas exploration—the Iowa stone was probably inscribed by an astronomer-priest. Libyan explorers also left their mark in Texas, on the Rio Grande Cliffs; the inscription proclaims that they had been sent by the pharaoh Shishonq. In Cuenca, Ecuador, another ancient Libyan inscription was found, this one with the drawing of an elephant.

---

*Verses in Oahspe indicate that mining went back at least 16,000 years; for example, The Lords' Third Book 1:6 refers to the Nicaraguan "tower of Rakowana, shining with copper, silver, and gold."

†Fell also made a good case for these mariners reaching Polynesia. How else can we explain the same name Iao, used by both the Greeks and the Hawaiians to designate the planet Jupiter? Shortened to Io, the Polynesian creator god Io resonates with the Turkic and Phoenician Iao, inscribed on a 350 BCE coin, a variant of the Canaanite sun god Iao and the moon goddess Io. "Can there be any doubt that the Maori deity Io is the same as the circum-Levantine Iao?" (Anderson 1928, 351).

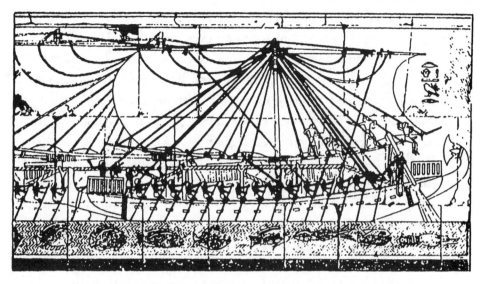

Fig. 6.13. Eighteenth Dynasty Egyptian seagoing vessel

"Megaliths *do* seem to be concentrated in places rich in metals," observed Joseph Thorndike, citing Andalusia, Cornwall, and Brittany, whose miners were "prospectors as well as missionaries. . . . Egyptian trading missionaries sallied forth to seek precious metals and to proselytize." The very paths these missionaries took can be "worked out by following the geographical distribution of tombs of the megalithic type" (1977, 44).

Phoenicians and Other Men in Black

A carved rock in Bolivia records the visit of an Egyptian priest; part of the inscription mentions silver mines near the Madeira River. It seems likely that those astronomer-priests, frequently remembered as men in black, followed after the more mercantile seamen who had paved the way in search of raw materials and foreign ores. Natives say that white men came in a boat with wings (i.e., sails). I am especially intrigued by rock pictures in the Guianas and Amazonia that show tall men in long robes with something like halos about the head. (The savior Mithra, discussed in "Sealed in Blood" later in the chapter (p. 255), was haloed, as were many of the divine Sun kings.)

From all accounts, these men in black were civilized, cultured, and kind, elevating the barbarians wherever they went. Working wonders, these teachers and priests from the east were best known as Quetzalcoatl (in Mexico), Viracocha (in the Andes), and Bochica (in Colombia)—"bearded white missionaries from the same advanced civilization" (Landsburg 1974, 50). As we will see shortly, Viracocha is described in contradictory terms in a variety of legends.

Indeed, they were the very sun gods who prefigured the Christian savior (Ryzl 2007, 26), Quetzalcoatl being "an ecclesiastic whose personality and attributes [were] . . . those of an early Christian missionary" (Daly 1889, 20, 28). His retinue, dressed in long black cassocks, landed at Panuco in Vera Cruz, then moved inland. As Harold Gladwin so bluntly describes it, "a large number of bearded white Levantines [were] hustling around looking for the best places . . . to set themselves up as gods. . . . The bearded white gods . . . arrived from various parts of India and the Near and Middle East" (Gladwin 1947, 280).

"Christian" motifs follow the old prophets and go all the way back to Zarathustra, nine thousand years ago. Therefore, although Quetzalcoatl and his fellow saviors came before Christ, we should not be surprised by "Christian" details in his story, such as the following:

> Son of a virgin
> Crosses on his robe
> Anointed with oil
> Riding an ass
> Forty days temptation and fasting
> Acts of penance
> Eucharist, small pieces of bread
> Confession and baptism
> Forgiving of sins
> Crucifixion and second coming

Quetzalcoatl and other contemporary missionaries, I believe, are one and the same as the forty-nine saviors (ca. 300 BCE) whose names and history are recounted in Oahspe's God's Book of Eskra, chapter 38. Short of listing all forty-nine names, I would like to select only a few of the most interesting and familiar. But the names themselves can be tricky; the asterisked items below indicate those who falsely *assumed* names of olden heroes or favorite names for worship. Evidently these wannabe saviors "chose any name . . . flattering to mortals" (Oahspe, God's Book of Eskra 45:11). Yohannes, for example, was based on the older name for the fish-man god Oannes, who civilized ancient Sumer (see fig. 4.4, p. 159). "What Oannes is to Mesopotamia, Quetzalcoatl is to Mesoamerica" (Gordon 1973, 78). Following are a few* of the forty-nine saviors' names.

Egypt: Thules and Gibbor
Persia: Mithra,* Bali, Belus
India: Sakai, Chrisna,* Indra* (Indra, a war god, was king of the Hindu deities)
Europe: Prometheus,* Quirnus, Osseo, Yohannas*
America:† Quexalcote,* Itura, Manito*

Bali and Belus of Persia are akin to Baal of Lebanon and Norway and to the Celtic god Bel/Baal, the main god of the Druids, god of the sun. Why then does the name pop up in Brazil, where Beli-kevem is the name of a monument bearing a drawing of a caravan—visitors? Most familiar is the Levantine Baal to whom the temple near Baalbek is dedicated. He was god-the-creator, god-the-sun of the Phoenicians, Assyrians, and Babylonians, his name readily evoking images of ancient idolatry, star worship, child sacrifice, and corrupt priestcraft. This Baal goes back to the time of Moses.

---

*The asterisked items indicate those who falsely *assumed* names of olden heroes or favorite names for worship.

†Both the Algonquins and Iroquois had traditions of fair-complected benevolent visitors. Indians of British Columbia spoke of men who worked miracles, headed by "Quaglgal." Cyrus Gordon mentions another leader from abroad named "Qoacutes" (1973, 156).

In all cycles [there were] four chief-enforced religions. . . . In the
Mosaic cycle, they were Osiris, Baal, Dagon and Ashtaroth.
In the . . . Abrahamic cycle, they were Yima, Mithra,* N'yot and
Habbaak.

OAHSPE, BOOK OF SAPHAH, FOOTNOTE TO VERSE 62

Curiously, the number forty-nine turns up at Tiahuanaco—known
as "the Baalbek of the New World." On the Gate of the Sun one sees a
flying god surrounded by forty-eight figures. Hmm. We note also that
the fish scales of the Savior Oannes/Yohannes appear on Tiahuanaco's
great sun idol, the Kalassasaya (Mesopotamian images of Oannes are
always of fish-garbed or scaled men). "The fish gods of Tiahuanaco
seem to be identical with the gods of Mesopotamia who were revered
there from the *fifth to the third* century B.C.[†] . . . and the gates of
Tiahuanaco are exactly like those of Persepolis in Ancient Persia"
(Kolosimo 1975, 210; emphasis added).

I have made one more curious observation concerning the number
forty-nine. Could it be that after their deaths these forty-nine mortal
saviors fell under the power of a strong spirit calling himself Imperator?
At least that is the impression I got from reading about the controls of
Stainton Moses, a late-nineteenth-century psychic medium who channeled scripts from Beyond. His communicators used illustrious biblical
names; their leader, Imperator, was in charge of an organized band of
forty-nine spirits. Imperator signed his name with a cross and claimed
to have influenced Stainton's entire life. Imperator himself claimed to
be under someone called Preceptor, who in turn communed with Jesus.

---

*Mithra can be a confusing figure for students of ancient history. How easy it is to
confound Mithra the First (about 4,000 years ago) with Mithra the Second (about
2,000 years ago). Spreading from India to Persia to Asia Minor and finally to the Roman
Empire (where Mithraism became the greatest rival to Christianity), the Mithraic religion has many faces. In parts of Persia, Mithra was a man, a mortal (born of a virgin on
December 25), whereas in the Mediterranean and Chaldea he was nothing less than a
god—the sun god Deus Sol. Finally, Mithra is reckoned among the chief false gods of
lower heaven, who replaced the Creator with *himself*.

†The time frame is significant and will be discussed below. We might also note the
49 million angels mentioned in the Kabbalah.

Plan Hatched by the Forty-Nine Saviors

Who are Saviors?—Familiar spirits who have kingdoms in . . .
the lower heaven. Saviors are tyrants who make slaves of other
spirits who believe in them. Their slaves are sent back to mortals
as guardian angels or familiars, in order to make captives of mortals
after death, to augment the Savior's kingdoms in atmospherea.

OAHSPE, BOOK OF SAPHAH: M'HAK 38–39

The story of the forty-nine saviors seems to have begun in the heavens
of the Earth with the formation of the Holy Confederacy: Kabalactes (a
god over India) said to his confederates, the doctrine of the Trinity* is
being entirely destroyed by the Sakaya'yan (Buddhan Faithist) doctrines.
Our heavenly kingdoms will lose their base of supplies for subjects.

Ennochissa [over China] then replied to his confederate, "Let
us seek out a number of mortals, and through them, establish our
doctrines." Whereon Looeamong, the third triune god, responded,
saying, "A most wise suggestion." So a coalition was entered
into by the triunes to give mortals forty-nine Saviors, in order
to establish the Trinity. And it was stipulated, that all forty-nine
Saviors should be put to death ignominiously in order to win mortal
sympathy.

OAHSPE, GOD'S BOOK OF ESKRA 38:17

To accomplish which, the Holy Confederacy provided that each
kingdom would supply one million angels for the army of inspiration
. . . [who] were sent down to the earth . . . to raise up among mortals
the required Saviors . . . [and to] possess the temples of spirit
communion and the oracle houses. . . .

There were thus given to the earth forty-nine Saviors . . . and

---

*These triune gods preached the doctrine of the Father, Son, and Holy Ghost—as seen
in Brahma-Vishnu-Shiva; some Hindu idols even have a triple head. Baal Shalisha was
another god of triplicity, three principles combined in one. The Babylonian trinity was
Baal-Ashtaroth-Tammuz; the Egyptian one was Osiris-Isis-Horus.

by the same army of angels that inspired these priests and magicians to miracles and the preaching of the Triune doctrines, so were they also betrayed, suffering death by enemies who were inspired by the same angel hosts to that end. . . .

Now the Triune doctrine . . . related chiefly to war. . . . Looeamong said: Behold, I went with my legions down to the earth, to war [and] . . . I have driven the worshippers of Jehovih [the faithists] to death. . . . War for righteousness' sake is just. We go to the earth to put swords and spears in the hands of the innocent and upright, saying to them: Defend yourselves! Establish yourselves! There is no Ever-Present Person. All things were created out of the Holy Ghost . . . Rise up and be men, mighty to do the will of the Son, the Father and the Holy Ghost!

OAHSPE, GOD'S BOOK OF ESKRA 38:8–32

The name Kabalactes reminds me of Kabala, Kaaba stone, the word *cabal,* and even the city Kabul. "Buddhist monks from Kabul in Afghanistan reached America at some time . . . [while] Buddhist missionary enterprise was in its heyday. . . . Now Quetzalcoatl is decidedly Buddhistic in his aspect and insignia, as well as in the traditions which relate to him. His was a religion of pious contemplation and penance. . . . They drew blood from their ears, noses, and thighs by means of thorns . . ." (Spence 1933, 187). But these pious men were not as peaceful as supposed. "To establish Buddha on earth, more than a hundred millions have been slain in war!" (Oahspe, Book of Saphah: M'Hak, 76). "So far," as these little-known chronicles go on, "Kabalactes had destroyed nine million men, women and children in the wars. He had also destroyed four thousand heathen temples, and more than three hundred cities. And he suppressed over two hundred languages" (Oahspe, God's Book of Eskra 22:44). And so it was that

when God, Son of Jehovih, saw the work of the Triunes, he bewailed the ways of heaven. Jehovih said to him: Do not bewail, My Son . . . but make a record of their works; for mortals will preserve a history of this period, which shall be called, the Era of

Saviors. And it shall stand as the darkest era in the cycle of Bon [Mosaic time]. But it shall come to pass . . . that the Triunes will become divided in their heavenly kingdoms. So God bewailed no more, but prepared a new army of a billion angels, to go down to the earth, to provide for receiving the spirits of those who were sure to be slain in wars. . . . Nor did they reach the earth any too soon, for war soon encircled the whole earth, and every nation, tribe, and people were immured in bloody carnage.

OAHSPE, GOD'S BOOK OF ESKRA 39:1–7*

Why do we fight? Why do we destroy? It was a wicked God! He called himself the Savior—the wicked monster.

OAHSPE, FIRST BOOK OF GOD 27:33

Sealed in Blood

And the angels inspired their [saviors'] enemies to put them to death, so that their doctrines would be sealed in blood. And this was done.

OAHSPE, GOD'S BOOK OF ESKRA 38:24

Just so in Mexico, the conqueror Huemac (the Great Hand) was the force inspired against Quetzalcoatl and his host. Carvings at Chichén Itzá show white men sacrificed on the victor's altars. A marble cross seen at Vera Cruz in the sixteenth century was interpreted by natives: "One more glorious than the sun had died upon a cross" (Daly 1889, 24).

In Ugaritic mythology, the beloved of the gods, Mot, "was put to death by . . . burning in fire . . . before he was resurrected, like Hunahpu and Xbalanque" (Gordon 1973, 156). Quetzalcoatl's South American counterparts are also a pair: two white men who landed on the Brazilian shore, pushing inland and preaching to the natives "after the manner of Christian apostles." Moving to the shores of Lake Titicaca, "one of them suffered death at the hands of the natives." Likewise from Peru come stories

---

*The Eskra account continues in chapter 7, p. 274 of this book, under the question of diffusion.

Fig. 6.14. Quetzalcoatl depicted crucified in Codex Borgianus, which account also relates his resurrection on the third day. Is a similar scenario remembered in the myth of two beloved gods, destined for resurrection— Hunahpu and Xbalanque—who were put to death in a bonfire?

of Viracocha, again moving westward from Lake Titicaca. On his travels he was brutally assailed by men. Other legends have him dressed as an old man, wandering over the Andes, but given "a poor reception" (Bandelier 1905, 756). Colombia's savior, Bochica (a.k.a. Zuhe) met a similar fate; the people "discharged their arrows at him" (Heyerdahl 1953, 283).

At many points does ancient history reveal that the doctrines of crucifixion, atonement, and resurrection *preceded* the Christian era and that such doctrines were in fact taught in most of the Mystery schools before the Common Era. Bali, for example, was the second member of a trinity ("Lord Second") and the *crucified* god of Orissa, India, in the eighth millennium BCE. Indra of Tibet was said to have been nailed to the cross also in the eighth millennium BCE. Some have gone so far as to say that "Quetzalcoatl . . . is Indra, whom we found crucified in Nepaul" (Higgins 1991, 1:230). Australian researcher Paul Perov has observed that "most of the crucified gods occupied that position in a trinity of gods, the Son, in all cases, being the atoning offering" (www.angelfire.com/planet/pp0/zara.html [accesssed 6-27-2016]). Thus was Quetzalcoatl the son whose "father had created the world" (Wilkins 2000, 105). In the Babylonian trinity it was Ea, the Father, Bel, the Son, and Anu, the Holy Ghost. The ancient name of Nippur was Tell Anu.*

According to Perov (who gives examples of more than a dozen crucified saviors of the ancient world), the savior-king Thulis of Egypt (1700 BCE; Thules is one of the forty-nine saviors) espoused the Trinity and died the death of the cross. Indeed, the crucifixion of Persia's prophet Zarathustra/Zoroaster nine thousand years ago was known throughout the ancient world as far east as India and China. Here in Asia, the man called Mithra was crucified in 600 BCE. Persian equinoctial ceremonies dedicated to Mithras involved crucifixion *on a tree.*

> Mithra, Bali, [and] Belus were also put to death in order to seal their words in blood. Some of them were boiled in oil, some given to the lions in the dens, and some nailed on the ugsa [wheel] and left to perish.
>
> OAHSPE, GOD'S BOOK OF ESKRA 38:25

In southern India, historians say the god-man Wittoba† was crucified in 552 BCE; he is depicted with nail holes in his hands and feet. Ancient temples in India also have a crucified Krishna, dated 1200 BCE (Childress 1988, 152).

---

*It is interesting that Anu, a Babylonian god of air and heaven, is answered by the Marquesan word for "space," *Anu.* Indeed, some have written that the Annu-naki were space aliens.

†The saviors of India included "Indra . . . Sakai, *Withoban* . . . Chrisna. . . . And these performed the same kind of miracles, and preached the Father, Son and Holy Ghost. And they likewise suffered ignominious deaths, through the inspiration of the angel hosts" (Oahspe, God's Book of Eskra 38:26; emphasis added).

Fig. 6.15. Image of ugsa (fete) in Oahspe, Book of God's Word

The Virgin Birth and the Resurrection were not confined to Christianity but were common to most of the religions of Antiquity. . . . The Crucifixion of Christ represented the murder of Tammuz. . . .

RAYMOND DRAKE,
GODS AND SPACEMEN IN THE ANCIENT EAST

Thus was Tammuz of the Mesopotamian Trinity sacrificed, apparently 1170 BCE, as an offering for our sins; suspended on a tree, he was crucified and buried, but he rose again. Atys in Phrygia repeated the drama; while in the Caucasus it was Prometheus, chained to a pillar near the Caspian Sea and afterward resurrected (at least 800 years *before* Christ). "Prometheus, Quirnus, Iyo, Osseo and Yohannas . . . were killed on the fete . . . so that their teachings would be sealed in blood" (Oahspe, God's Book of Eskra 38:28). Finally, the Celtic Druids portray their own god and savior Esus [Osseo] of Gaul as crucified (834 BCE), while the Greek Orpheus suffered the same fate.*

---

*I want to express my gratitude to my friend and colleague Paul Perov (www.angelfire .com/planet/pp0/zara.html) for his excellent research and the above information on pre-Christian saviors and crucifixion. Thanks, Paul!

Fig. 6.16. Stone amulet showing Orpheus cruci-fied, apparently on an anchor

Saviors unnumbered have died for the sins of man and by the hands of man. . . . Connected with a crucifixion are Prometheus, Adonis,* Apollo, Atys, Bacchus, Christna, Horus, Indra, Mithras, Osiris, Pythagoras, Quetzalcoatl. . . .

MANLY P. HALL,

THE SECRET TEACHINGS OF ALL AGES

When Did All This Happen?

We will perceive, in several parts of the world, the undeniable presence of oceangoing mariners around 300 BCE: Phoenicians, Carthaginians and Greeks, Cretans and Phrygians, Libyans and Egyptians. Concerning those Phrygians and Phoenicians who held supremacy at sea, Professor Barry Fell, Harvard marine biologist, comparative zoologist, pale-ontologist, and epigrapher, in his acclaimed but controversial book *America B.C.,* persuasively demonstrated that Libyan navigators (kin to the Phrygians) crossed even the Pacific Ocean; in this regard, he found convincing links between the Libyan and Polynesian languages, as well

---

*Adonis is the Hellenic Tammuz; memorials of his death sometimes involved a fresh human sacrifice (as a substitute), which was then followed by resurrection. "By sacrificing himself, the god becomes the savior of the entire race" (Birket-Smith 1965, 379).

as Oceanic links to the Anatolian (Phrygian) sea peoples. Libyan influence seems to have spread far and wide in the Indo-Pacific region; some of them settling the islands. How else to explain why so many characters of Polynesian inscriptions are essentially Libyan? Why are there so many other Anatolian elements in Polynesia?*

Now, as Perov has pointed out, it was no more than two hundred years after the time of Confucius and Buddha that "the Triunes gave mortals forty-nine Saviors . . . Mithra's ascension to heaven was said to have occurred in 208 BC. Hence, these saviors must have existed about 400 to 200 BC" (www.angelfire.com/planet/ppolzara.html). This works for Phoenicians in America in 290 BCE (Wilkins 2000, 108) and for the Anubis Cave inscriptions in Oklahoma, also about 2,300 years ago, which celebrate "the Old World god Bel [aka] Belus, Baal," while the complex itself "was dedicated to Mithra" (Lehrburger 2015, 140–45).

Also suggesting the third century BCE is the curious House of Tcuhu in Arizona's Gila Valley. This design, seen by eighteenth-century Spaniards, was etched in the sand by the Pima Indians. The puzzle or game, called House of Tcuhu, was recognized as the same diagram on Cretan coins of Knossus; it represented the acclaimed Minoan Labyrinth. The coin was in circulation from 267 to 200 BCE. The same time frame holds in Mexico, where Quetzalcoatl's nemesis, Huemac of the Iron Hand, was dominant around 220 BCE. The famous Mayan Stela 5 at Izapa in southern Mexico is also dated to 300 BCE and shows Turkish-looking men with pointy hats and beards (see fig. 6.19, p. 263).

Nevertheless, exactly *when* Quetzalcoatl trotted over to Mexico and became their savior is still a matter of considerable debate. We have authors dating him to 3000 BCE (Charroux 1972, 81); to 1000 BCE (Berlitz 1972, 135); to 400 CE or even 1050 CE (Daly 1889, 29). Within the pages of Harold T. Wilkins's informative but occasionally fanciful work, *Mysteries of Ancient South America,* we are told that Quetzalcoatl appeared between twenty thousand and thirty thousand years ago— but also that these men in black vanished around 11,000 BCE. Wilkins

---

*See, for example, the wrapped-arm statues in chapter 1, p. 46; or the Phoenician harbors (at Carthage), which "were just like those of Ponape . . . [linking] the Phoenicians still closer to the communities of the archaic civilization in Polynesia" (Perry 1968, 501).

Mazes

Other mazes in North America include the Hemet Maze, inscribed on a rock in California, and the Mohave Maze, cut in the trench of a dry lake; the Mohave Indians said their own ancestors did not cut the design. Labyrinths have also been found in Egyptian tombs. Visiting Egypt in the fifth century BCE, Herodotus saw an immense labyrinth

Fig. 6.17. Three mazes: a) a Greek period coin from Crete, b) a Cretan maze, and c) the Pima Indian House of Tcuhu at Casa Grande, "identical in every respect" (Colton 1917, 667–68). See the "Greeks" section on p. 262.

Fig. 6.18. The Hopi of Arizona drew a squarish maze (left), which looks rather like a labyrinthine design used in prehistoric Ecuador (right). Some Gnossus coins appear also in the square form.

with a total of three thousand rooms. Strabo saw it in 25 BCE, commenting that no stranger could possibly find his way without the aid of expert guides.

And we find labyrinth designs in the Pacific as well, at Malekula, where their representation of the journey made by the "immortal dead" parallels Egyptian devices. This globe-trotting culture planted elaborate mazes throughout the Mediterranean, including the maze at Clusium (the Etruscan city Chiusi), which served as the tomb of King Porscha, apparently one of the immortal dead. This cult extends all the way up to the British Isles, where the spiral maze at Glastonbury Tor and the rustic mazes in Wales and County Wicklow resemble Etruscan designs. Some mysterious labyrinths, like the Mig-Maze in Dorset, seem to incorporate astronomical information. What's more, there is a close connection between the mazelike entrances of Maiden Castle, Dorset, and those found in Ohio at Butler County's Hill Fort.

Greeks

The coasts of Brazil were lit by pharos or lighthouses for mariners; "their ruins bear many letters identical with those of the Phoenician and Greek alphabet." In Minas Geras, twenty out of forty-one characters found and documented in the eighteenth century were from the Greek alphabet (Wilkins 2000, 24, 47). Greek inscriptions have been noted in South America, in southeast Venezuela.

In Central America some of the earliest conversations between the Conquistadors and the Mexican tribes were conducted in Greek, which the Maya seemed to understand. The Aztec word for "god" was *teo* (*theos* in Greek) while their *teocalli* (house of god) reflects the Greek word *kalia* (house). Tlaloc, the Mexican water god, reminds us of *thalassa*, Greek for "sea." In North America, the Potomac River got its name from *potomos*, Greek for "river." According to Carl Lehrburger, "trade was carried out between North America and the Mediterranean for copper and furs at least six hundred years before Christ" (2015, 319–20); Barry Fell in *America B.C.* found "more than fifty words with Greek roots in the native Indian dialects of Nova Scotia and Maine.

. . . One of the Red Bird River petroglyphs in Manchester, Kentucky, has a Greek inscription."

Greek cognates in the Pacific might suggest unknown voyages to the ends of the Earth.

Hawaiian	Meaning	Greek	Meaning
aeto	eagle	aetos	eagle
noo-noo	thought	nous	intelligence
manao	think	manthano	learn
mele	sing	melodhia	melody
lahut	people	laos	people

The panpipes of Greece are almost identical to those in the Solomon Islands, while an early stone carving at Easter Island depicts an ancient ship with three masts that is much larger than those used by natives today.

Fig. 6.19. Detail from Izapa Stela 5

goes on to complain that "Lewis Spence and others" have confused Quetzalcoatl with Votan (see "Viracocha, Savior in the Andes," below, who hailed from the Mediterranean. "Quetzalcoatl," he argues, "lived long before . . . Votan," whom he dates to 290 BCE and identifies with "men of a Phoenician, Canaanite or Carthaginian race" (Wilkins 2000, 104–6, 123). But this is just the race—and the time—of our forty-nine saviors, among whom Mexico's Quetzalcoatl is perhaps the best known. I'll throw in with Lewis Spence, who, having examined that new wave of art and architecture on American soil, says their introduction must be dated "some time shortly before the beginning of our present chronological era" (Spence 1933, 187). This is close enough to the time frame of the settlement of Mayapan—the Mayan "equivalent of Quetzalcoatl and Viracocha [was] a gentle king-god named Kukulkan . . . [who] built a great city, Mayapan . . . then went away" (Landsburg 1974, 50).

Viracocha, Savior in the Andes

The Inca rulers traced their lineage back to Viracocha; yet Peruvians also say Viracocha was the Creator himself! They believed in one Supreme Being, called Viracocha or Pachacamac, and it was he who made men and animals out of clay figures at Tiahuanaco and breathed life into them. At Tiahuanaco is a statue of a tall, bearded man presumed to be Viracocha, Son of the Sun. In Quechua, *Vira* means "sun" (rather like the Brahmin sun god, Vira-dj).

When Viracocha is portrayed as a man, he is the culture hero of the Andes who brought all the blessings of civilization including architecture and engineering. But, wondrously, he is also reckoned as the rain god who sent mighty storms, even cataclysms, upon mankind for their sins—destroying everyone (save a single couple) in an immense deluge. This happened because the giants whom he had created out of stone displeased him, and so he sank them in a deep flood. Other versions, though, have him arriving in Peru *after* the flood, indeed a kind of Noah who is said to have entered Tiahuanaco when it was *already a dead ruin*!

Obviously, the name and figure of Viracocha have been made to serve multiple purposes among Peru's storytellers and opinion shapers, and there is no reconciling these contradictory histories. As a Noah type, he sent his brood to different continents; but in a trice he is a god again, appointing his subgods to oversee the works of his brood in those different lands! We must conclude then that the sacrosanct name of Viracocha is capable of turning up in legends of vastly different time periods.

Pac as in Pachacamac

The actual dispersal of Noah and his sons from a common homeland comes into focus with Viracocha's alternate name: *Pac*hacamac or Tua*paca*. This *Pac* is also seen in Pac-hamama, Peru's Mother Earth. (Pac-ha, according to Aflredo Gamarra, also indicates "a world age.") I submit that *Pac* (var. *Pak*) originally meant "pure, clean, white." In Peru, for example, tu-pac meant "bright, shiny." This resonates with Pak-in (in the far-off Caroline Islands) and with New Zealand's Pak-eha ("white man"), representative of their tradition of Pak-ehakeha, a white race who "live in the sea." Meanwhile, North America's Pah-ana (like the Maori Pakeha) means "white person" in Hopi, just as South America's Pak-oyoc designates the white ruling class of the Incas. In southern Hawaiian dialects Pak-ao is a priestly name, and Pak-aalana was the temple (*heiau*) whose taboos were the most sacred on Hawaii. The religious value of Pak names appears again in Peru's Pac-hacamac, ancient oracle and mecca for pilgrims throughout the Incan empire. The remarkable resemblance of Japan's underwater structures off Okinawa to Peru's ancient city of Pachacamac (as discussed in chapter 11, "Yonaguni," p. 461) gives us all the more reason to suspect that the Pac name is both universal and prediluvial. After all, Pac turns up again in Unu Pac-hacuti, which means the deluge after which Peru was populated. A flood figure, Manco Ca-pac, was Peru's ancestor of the Emergence.

Manco Ca*pac* is Cuzco's heavenly founder who arrived in Peru after a great flood; as leader of the Emergence, he is a Noah who instructed the indigenous people in all the arts of civilized life. Pac-ari Cave is known as Lodging of the Dawn, out of which the first people emerged. Probably related is U-pac-a, a five-thousand-year-old archae-ological site in Peru, while Pac-cai-casa is the name of that country's earliest tool site. I was struck by William Ellis's mention of a Manco Capac in the mythology of the *Polynesians*(!), quoted as he who sired "the father and mother of mankind" (1931, 112).

Manco Capac is said to have come to Peru from Old Mexico, and here Zi-pac-na is a hero in the Popol Vuh, while Pac-al ("shield") was the royal ruler entombed at Palenque. In southeastern Mexico is the famous archaeological site at Bonam-pak, while Xtam-pak is a major site in the Mayan lowlands. There is also Mexico's Oxtotic-pak.

Western Asia is also in the mix; the Brahmans called their predeces-sors Pak-handi. It is also interesting that Pak-istan is named after Pak, in this case meaning "pure, clean." Is Ca-pak-cur, the Kurdish place of healing waters, related to this idea of purity? Also in the Mideast, Shuri-pak on the Euphrates is part of the Babylonian flood story, for it was from there that their own Noah was saved. Also, Ar-pac-hiyah, north of Nineveh, is a very old and sacred (i.e., pure) spot (as seen in chapter 8, p. 348, under "Tholoi"; also see Ar-pak-sad of Shem, in Genesis 11:12).

Pacha means "sacred vessel" in both Sumerian and Quechua. In Viracocha's (a.k.a. Pac-hacamac's) territory, Cuzco's sacrificial ceremony to the sun god is called Ca-pac Hucha. Huayna Ca-pac, a more recent conqueror of Quito, also took the name, as did Inca Tu-pac Amaru. Other Incan kings took the name Pac-hacuti. Curious that the sarcopha-gus in which the Incan Prince Ca-pac reposes in Lima is of Egyptian type.

It seems that a "missioner" named Manco Ca*pac,* at least according to Wilkins (2000, 16), was also an historical man in black who came to Peru. Perhaps the most interesting avatar of Viracocha finds him also as a man in black. Like Colombia's Bochica and Mexico's Quetzalcoatl, he was a wise man with a bushy black beard, clad in austere black robes. Advancing from the shores of Lake Titicaca, Viracocha converted the natives and built the monuments. And he performed miracles. Bochica, Colombia's and Venezuela's man in black, also came from the east, taught the worship of the sun, wore long garments, was tall and white, and had a bushy beard, introduced government and laws, clothing and town building, and performed miracles, just as Quetzalcoatl "was considered the god of magic" (Heinberg 1989, 125). Nevertheless, the Motilone Indians say that this man Bochica was a false prophet who led them astray.

Viracocha, august of countenance, a worker of miracles and healing, could call down the fire of heaven. Every one of the forty-nine saviors "performed miracles, such as healing the sick, giving sight to the blind, and hearing to the deaf, and raising spirits of the dead to life" (Oahspe, God's Book of Eskra 38.24). Upon his departure, Viracocha simply spread his cloak on the sea and magically sailed away, vowing, messiah-like, to come back from the land to which he sailed. What land was that? Gladwin (having noted that ancient Peru and Troy exhibit the same polygonal masonry) was convinced that Viracocha came from Asia Minor (see chapters 1 and 2, discussing extensive parallels between South America and Asia Minor/ Turkey). Viracocha's very beard and aquiline nose are characteristic of the ancient peoples of Asia Minor. Language comparisons are also noteworthy: linguists have found a correspondence between Incan words and the Turkic dialect of Chuwashen, the latter actually containing the name Viracocha, meaning "the good spirit from space" (Von Daniken 1974, 208). The Quechua's worship of Viracocha also links South America to Mesopotamian origins,* for Sargon, priest of Kish (var. Quiché) had another name: Viru-kasha (kocha = holy). He was part of the priesthood of Zaques, and in fact this was the exact name of the high priest of the *Bochica*!

Quetzalcoatl

An almost accurate description of Quetzalcoatl is "an early Christian missionary" as the Spaniards thought (Daly 1889, 20). But the fact is,

---

*See chapter 5, "Sumerian–South American Comparisons," p. 210, on correspondences between the Sumerian and Peruvian vocabularies.

Fig. 6.20. Sculpture of Quetzalcoatl, the Lord of Life

we can hardly credit everything that is said about Quetzalcoatl, for he is variously and conflictingly drawn as

- Noah, in at least one Mayan version
- The fifth king (or high priest) of the Toltecs; or name of the (hereditary) priesthood itself
- The Creator himself
- A deity: Ehecatl, god of the wind, son of the sky god and earth goddess
- The American Atlas, whose function was to hold up the sky
- A mortal: black haired (and black faced in Aztec manuscripts) vs. blond haired in legends
- Wore a black robe vs. wore a white robe
- Going barefoot vs. wore sandals
- Arriving from the southeast vs. arriving from the northwest
- Descending from a hole in the sky; arriving from Venus in flying machines; an astronaut from a distant world (Kolosimo 1975, 164); an extraterrestrial initiator* (Charroux 1972, 120)

---

*A savior-*initiator* circa 250 BCE could not have been the *first* civilizer in Mesoamerica; rather, he appeared at a time when the *olden civilization* was on its last legs and ripe for renewal.

- Saint Brendan, Saint Thomas, or Christ himself (according to Lord Kingsborough)
- A Norseman who wandered south from Vinland, blown off course to Mexico
- A teacher who admonished men to live peaceably, to kill not even animals, but live on vegetable food vs. clad in buskins of tiger skin; a warrior, a military conqueror, whom the Maya regarded as a foreign oppressor, a wicked man who led an army
- A very merciful and humane man, a prophet who taught, "bear injuries with humility and leave vengeance to God" (Daly 1889, 25) vs. a rejected prophet who promised to return and *avenge* his wrongs

One version of Quetzalcoatl's "ignominious death" comes from the Mexican tradition that has a demon capturing the royal sage and making him perform "all sorts of ignoble acts. Overcome with shame, Quetzalcoatl burnt himself to death" (Kolosimo 1975, 163). Other accounts say he was exiled, or his end came through the "enmity of a rival deity" (Daly 1889, 18); or he was taken to the Morning Star (Venus) in a spaceship, or his ashes rose up and turned into the Morning Star.

The Era of Saviors

Our struggle is not against flesh and blood, but against . . . the powers . . . the spiritual forces of wickedness in the heavenly places.

HOLY BIBLE, EPHESIANS 6:12

We have already touched on Persia's renowned savior Mithra, who proclaimed himself the chief and highest of all personages; prophet of war, he commanded, "Invoke Me with sword uplifted" (Oahspe, Book of Saphah: Basis of Vede 36 and Ho'ed). One way or the other, human sacrifice, slavery, and war are the inevitable inheritance of the false angels and their saviors. Viracocha/Pachacamac, Supreme Armor-clad

Ruler, brought war; his Temple of the Sun was actually a fortress. And what did the ancient Muiscas of Colombia do in memory of Bochica the Savior, their "gentle and humane" civilizer? They chose a victim every twenty years, whose death at age fifteen presumably assured a new cycle of life. This victim, "as at Stonehenge, was a boy . . . taken to the eastern slopes which had seen Bochica, the white savior, enter the Muisca land. . . . Then he was led in procession to . . . the priests [who] wore masks . . . and they killed him as a sacrifice . . . a cloud of arrows shot at him, his heart torn out and offered to Bochica" (Wilkins 2000, 115–16).

In Polynesia peace or war was decided only by a few individuals, usually the king, priest, or main chiefs. As William Ellis explains:

> I never had an opportunity of attending one of their national councils when the question of war was debated, under the imposing influence imparted by their mythology, whereby they imagined the contention between the gods of the rivals was as great as that sustained by the parties themselves. (1931, 278)

Though Ellis, who was a missionary, has the islanders *imagining* "contention between the gods," something more than mythological imagination informed these people. Indeed, their conception of things was on a par with the Maya, whose universe was thought to be "the scene of a constant struggle between antagonistic cosmic powers" (Birket-Smith 1965, 474).

We learn in fact that the wars, which developed between the four false Gods (Looeamong, Thoth, Ennochissa, and Kabalactes), lasted for another five hundred years.

> And then they came to terms, and ratified a division of the earth and her heavens into four great parts, with fixed boundaries. And they stipulated that the spirits of all mortals, at time of death, should go to that heaven which reigned over the portion of the earth where they had lived. . . . And [these gods] now fell to work in earnest to adorn and glorify their heavenly kingdoms, cities, palaces, and

thrones. And each of them exalted their great war captains who had fought so long for them.

OAHSPE, GOD'S BOOK OF ESKRA 51:1–4

These prolonged internecine battles of the false gods are part of the mythology of many races, based—as this interlude has tried to show—on realities, not imagination. Perhaps the truest remembrance of Quetzalcoatl's *finale* is the one that retires him amid a war between the Powers.

If there is a lesson to be learned from all this, I am afraid it is that we must take a certain portion of so-called ancient wisdom with a grain of salt. Quite a bit of it may in fact be nothing more than olden propaganda.

ACROSS THE POND

Bonfires and Secret Voyages

*[Thor] Heyerdahl believed that the world's oceans were
not barriers, but highways for the great seafaring empires
of antiquity, and that Sumerians, Egyptians, Phoenicians,
Hittites, and Harappans were traveling all over in their
distinctive reed boats, which were easy to build and highly
seaworthy.*

MARK WILLIAMS, *IN SEARCH OF LEMURIA*

The totora reeds that David H. Childress saw at Rano Raraku on Easter
Island were the same as the reeds at Lake Titicaca in the Andes. This
made him think of Thor Heyerdahl's hypothesis that reed boatsmen
once ranged the entire world. Heyerdahl cites "such reed boat centers as
Tiahuanaco and Chan Chan in South America, Easter Island, Lothal
and the coastal cities of the Indus Valley Civilization, Mesopotamia,
Egypt and Morocco—centers for this world-wide trading culture"
(Childress 1988, 315).

As we saw in chapter 6 in the case of the forty-nine saviors, ambitious leaders were never above arrogating the names of olden heroes. Too
often have we been fooled or misled by the eternal conceit of taking the

*Fig. 7.1. Egyptian reed boats, as pictured on a New Kingdom
tomb, which are similar to those in South America*

name and luster of bygone saints and idols—thus crippling our ability,
as historians, to judge the time frame correctly. The biggest confusion
arises from such anachronisms, meaning where influence shapers have
cunningly adopted elements from *earlier* times (to achieve the heroic
aura). A great deal of historical distortion has arisen from such men as
have arrogantly exploited an ancient name or symbol for their own ends.

Another serious handicap to the interpretation of the past is that
records of certain early voyages and enterprises were systematically
destroyed. The Phoenicians notoriously kept secret their trade routes,
"destroying all sources of knowledge having to do with the sea and
navigation in the West . . . so that their rivals should not acquire any
knowledge of the sea lanes" (Homet 1963, 174). Yet, the point of this
chapter (and this book) is that the Phoenicians (a generic term, really,
which might cover mariners of Egypt, Arabia, Crete, Aegean, and western Asia) were merely the tailenders. We know that they were preceded
by the oceangoing Minoans, Cabiri, Sydyk ("Just Men"), and Phrygians
who were among the nations that held in succession the supremacy at
sea. My point is that the Phoenicians were heirs to some great civilization of the more remote past. Indeed, "the very period which we
select as the beginning of real seamanship, the Phoenician, is shown

as having been . . . at the bottom of a curve," wrote Charles Hapgood (1996, 241), so affectingly exposing the lamentable misteaching of history, whose tight orthodoxy will brook no savants earlier than the second millennium BCE navigators of the Mediterranean world.

Four Possibilities Exist

Now when we find strong similarities in far-distant cultures, there are at least four possible explanations:

1. Common origin in the motherland of man, similarities like mortarless joins may have been taught by prediluvial mentors with their origin on Pan. Factors that help me identify such common origin include: a) when the culture has an authentic, detailed flood story; and b) when they have names like *Pan, Ku, Mu, Mai, Sam, Hin,* and other Panic words in the vocabulary. In such cases I am more inclined to take their myths of survival from a lost land at face value.

2. Diffusion: We well know that common points shared by distant cultures might, alternatively, be due to later (postdiluvial) contacts, resulting from voyages, migrations, colonization, and so forth. This is the reason we are so interested in the travels of the Phoenicians and their predecessors. "Classical civilization did indeed sail all over the world, up and down the Americas, across the Indian Ocean . . . and across the Pacific. . . . Polynesians almost certainly did cross the Pacific to the Americas—constantly!"* (Childress 1988, 341).

---

*"Traces of Polynesian influence are to be found on the coasts of America; these, I hold, are due to expeditions that have sailed from Polynesia to the east. . . . There was a navigator in ancient times named Maui, who visited some country toward the sunrise named Uperu (Peru)" (Smith 1921, 36, 39). It is also a curious fact that Polynesia and California share the same creation myths and mother-of-pearl fishhooks, while Tahiti's legend of binding the sun with a rope made of his sister's hair is repeated in North America (Henry 1928, 466). Whichever way the influence flowed, the northwest coast Indians of America and the Polynesians look like kissing cousins, not only in stature, blood types, craniometrics, and complexion but also in the near identity of their double canoes.

3. Similarities observed in countries far removed from one another could simply be due to coincidence. Generally called independent invention, it is also known as "convergence" among academics. For example, Colin Renfrew makes metallurgy a "chance discovery" by different peoples (Renfrew 1973, 190); Renfrew also suggests that the Neolithic chambered tombs found from Ireland to Malta "developed independently . . . by local evolution" (Renfrew 1973, 124–25) (but see my view in chapter 8, p. 348, "Tholoi"). Brian Fagan opts for the independent invention of agriculture; in which case we might as well assign today's soccer craze among, say, Turks and Brazilians to "independent invention" (Fagan 1999, 148). I believe we can distinguish diffusion (contact) from independent invention when a *complex* of traits are shared by two different cultures; in such cases independent invention is not likely. Cyrus Gordon, professor of Mediterranean studies and ancient Semitic languages, put it this way: "The evidence for diffusion grows when an intricate complex, with numerous interlocking details, is involved . . . [then] it becomes harder to attribute the host of close similarities to the supposed universal oneness of the human mind" (Gordon 1973, 145).

4. Finally, we may have to deal with otherworldly influences as in the case of hosts of angels who taught *the same things* everywhere, just as they sang to mortals the song of the flood. This was possible because "the Lord provided the inhabitants of the earth with oracle houses; in which, the Lord could speak face to face with mortals, through his angels, chosen for this purpose. In this manner the Lord taught mortals" (Oahspe, The Lords' Fifth Book 6.3). In chapter 4 we saw an example of instruction from the angel world where Noah was "spiritually" warned of the Flood. In another example, India, as seen in chapter 5, was entrusted, in the same manner, with heavenly names. We will probe this question in more detail in the next chapter where spirits huts (tholoi) are considered.

The Ihins prepared a stone . . . and the Lord came down in the night and engraved it. And through his angels he taught the Ihins the meaning of the characters engraved on it. And the Lord said: Go into all cities in *all the countries of the world,* and provide copies of the tablet I have given. So it came to pass that... the first language of the earth (Panic) could be preserved to the races of men. And it was so.

OAHSPE, FIRST BOOK OF THE FIRST LORDS 4:3–4 (EMPHASIS ADDED)

In this way the same angel lessons reached Faithists and initiates in different parts of the world. To illustrate this process, an editorial comment (on the Book of Saphah: Fonece, The Seventh Degree in the Order of Israel) notes that the inscriptions of Fonece (proto-Phoenician) are in part found in China, India, Persia, Arabia, as well as with the mound-builders of America. These Phoenician rites were common to China and America at the same period of time.

Fig. 7.2. Tablet of Fonece, in Book of Saphah

A further example pertains to the time when

Anubi sent tens of thousands of angels into *all the regions of the earth.* By inspiration and otherwise, these angels established the rites of Anubi.... And by the same means the Maichung, of Jaffeth [China], were made into Faithists; and by the same rites the Effins of Vind'yu [India], were converted into Faithists, adopting all the [same] rites and ceremonies.

OAHSPE, BOOK OF WARS 7:2–4 (EMPHASIS ADDED)

Therefore we are not surprised by Oklahoma's Anubis Cave inscriptions—the name appearing also in Egyptian religion.

Around 400 CE the Egyptian monk Panodorus would write that the angels (Egregori) descended to Earth and held congress with men, teaching them about the stars (astronomy). In the same vein, as told in the Book of Aph (13:10–12), the Tetracts were given as everlasting names, *alike* to the Faithists of Guatama, Jaffeth, Shem, and Ham. And these bywords were most vigorously observed for thousands of years by the Hebraic, Vedic, and Algonquin peoples. Thus have writers found so many parallels between Amerind, Hebrew, and Hindu motifs.*

The American moundbuilders were not Hebrews or Hindus, but *all* of these people were Faithists, under a common inspiration. It is then only natural that many of the shared words and symbols pertain to holy days and ceremonial life. William Penn, for example, had noted that the Indians and Jews not only agree in rites but also reckon by the moon, offer the first fruits, have a kind of feast of the Tabernacles, lay their altars upon twelve stones, and keep a mourning period of one year.

As for the Vedics and Algonquins, in western Tennessee, a quart-size vessel of excellent workmanship was dug up, an effigy jar displaying the same topknot as worn by the Florida mummies and the Indic Buddha as well as the Japanese and the Polynesians. The Tennessee vessel was in three colors—red, black, and yellow—the same as found

---

*Thus did Churchward identify American and East Indian tablets as having come "originally from the same source—the Sacred Inspired Writings of Mu" (1970, 18).

on India's ceramics. The archaeologist also expressed surprise at "the identity of religion professed by the Hindus and the aborigines of Tennessee . . . [in addition to] the striking similarity in the paints and modes of applying them" (Dewhurst 2014, 340). As we will soon see, the *same* teaching tablet was given to the Algonquins, Trojans, Persians, Arabians, and Greeks 5,400 years ago, indicating that each of these cultures kept a holy sanctuary with common teachings. Marcel Homet even found "pure Trojan" motifs in the northern Amazon; both people "engraved all the same drawings and patterns" (Homet 1963, 168, 172). Trojan spindle whorls also make an exact match with Toltec ones. (The ancients of Turkey and the Americas, as we saw in chapter 1, show a host of parallels.)

On the High Heogula Ophat (Tennessee) . . . was situated the school and college of great learning . . . where tens of thousands of students were taught.

OAHSPE, FIRST BOOK OF GOD 25:6
(REFERRING TO THAT TIME OF UNIVERSAL
TEACHING 5,400 YEARS AGO)

Fig. 7.3. Tennessee pot from grave mounds with central design of ball-and-cross, as also found in India and at Troy. Again linking Troy and Tennessee, both peoples were moundbuilders, and both produced exquisite pottery. In fact, the finest ceramics in North America, with very unusual sculptural decoration, were in those Tennessee mounds.

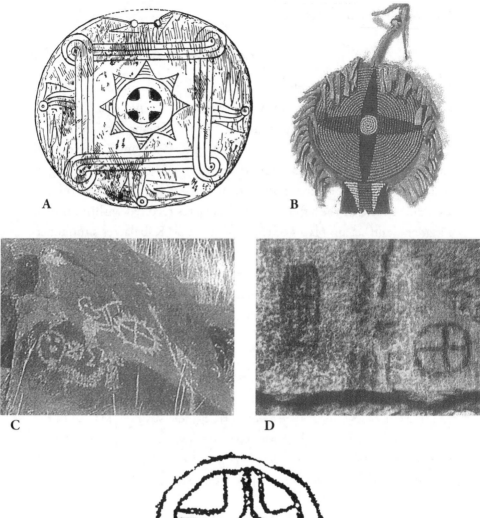

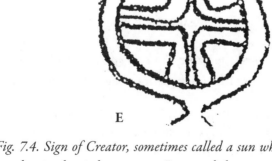

*Fig. 7.4. Sign of Creator, sometimes called a sun wheel or Celtic cross,
wherein the circle represents Love and the cross represents Light:
a) engraved shell from Tennessee burial; b) the encircled cross also
appears among the Flathead Indians and the Crow; c) petroglyphs in
New Mexico; d) at Pedra Pintada; e) a stylized design from Turkey's
Hittite civilization (similar to the wheel cross at Turkey's Çatalhüyük).*

There Is Yet Another Possibility

Warring gods (through their earthside proxies) managed to import their doctrines and dogmas into new regions. Turning back to the Era of Saviors, with its Triunes and subgods, we find the prediction that "in time to come, man of the earth will look abroad . . . and say: How did the Vind'yu [Indian] Gods come to be in Roma?" Now the war begun by the triune gods "extended into their own kingdoms [in heaven]. . . . In Vind'yu, five of the sub-Gods of Kabalactes revolted within his own kingdom, and set up places of their own. . . . So Kabalactes summoned his remaining chief officers . . . and he said to them: 'Pursue these rebellious captains . . . and despoil them utterly. . . . For this purpose, I appoint Yima* as my Holy Ambassador and Earth Warrior. And I give to him two billion [angel-]warriors, so that he may make quick work of my rebellious chiefs. . . .'"

> Yima† and his hosts did as commanded, but not suddenly; for an angel war ensued and it lasted forty-six years before the five rebellious sub-Gods were beaten from their strongholds . . . but they escaped, taking half a million angel warriors with them, and they emigrated to Uropa, *to the city of Roma* [Rome], where they established themselves. . . . Thus the deposed Vind'yu Gods became Gods of Roma.
>
> OAHSPE, GOD'S BOOK OF ESKRA 39, 40

But see, Yima assumed the name of *a true god* who had been known four thousand years before his time(!)—in the age of Zarathustra.

---

*On the war between Mithra and Yima, see Oahspe, Book of Saphah: Basis of Vede, 36.
†The name Yima entails a careful study. In the present context he is certainly a false Lord: "Yima, a Savior; self-assumed Lord of the earth . . . with many provinces in atmospherea. He sent emissaries [spirits] to the temples and oracles of India, for over a thousand years, and thus compelled mortals to worship him. . . . In atmospherea [lower heaven] he had four hundred million slaves" (Oahspe, Book of Saphah: Basis of Vede 6). It was this same Yima the False who claimed to be "the only begotten Son [of the Creator] . . . [and] inspired mortals to construct the written doctrines of the Vedas as they now are."

Yima, Jehovih's Son, [reigned] during this dawn . . . when mortals
learn[ed] to know the Lords and Gods who rule over them.

OAHSPE, BOOK OF FRAGAPATTI 34:14

Hero of Iran and the first man, Yima was regarded as the father of
the human race, a Noah, ordered by Ahura-Mazda, the Great God, to
build the ark. And in the next cycle three thousand years later, the good
god Yima inspired Po, the great prophet of China.

Who Were the Ancient Sea Kings?

But I digress. We are still wondering about those ancient mariners who
crisscrossed the globe, long before the textbook dawn of civilization.

> *The evidence . . . points to the existence in very ancient
> times of a worldwide civilization . . . with a uniform
> general level of technology. . . . It looks as if this people
> had visited most of the earth.*
>
> CHARLES HAPGOOD,
MAPS OF THE ANCIENT SEA KINGS

As Hapgood, professor of the history of science, discovered, there
are accurate Turkish maps of the *Western* Hemisphere that are more
than 10,000 years old. Even 12,000 years ago, in the Age of Osiris,
man "excelled in all manner of inventions . . . in mathematics . . . in
navigation . . . in making magnetic needles and telescopes" (Oahspe,
The Lords' Fifth Book 7:2). Yet this was only a renaissance, for
18,000 years ago in the Middle Kingdom of Guatama, "they built
great boats with crossbeams and sails of cloth" (Oahspe, The Lords'
Third Book 1:6). But even this is topped by the 24,000-year-old
"ships [that] sailed abroad on the seas" (Oahspe, The Lords' First
Book 2:20).

> *At one time the whole planet was accurately mapped . . .
> [by] a civilization whose members were aware of . . . the*

distribution of the masses of land and sea . . . in the same
way as the average educated man today.
RICHARD E. MOONEY, *GODS OF AIR AND DARKNESS*

The legendary Mu folk of Hawaii, say their chroniclers, were renowned shipbuilders and navigators who took their ships all over the world. These prediluvial sailors of the Pacific enjoyed a thriving trade with Asia and America, according to the Rosicrucians. Their best cities, as Churchward describes them, were "built at or near the mouths of great rivers, these being the seats of trade and commerce, from which ships passed to and from all parts of the world" (2011, 26). In fact, he was told by Caroline Islanders that "the people who occupied these islands when the islands were not islands but a great land, had very large boats in which they sailed all over the world and were sometimes gone for more than a year" (1931a, 101).

There is no shortage of navigational lore in the great traditions of the Pacific Islands. In Mangaia the hero Tangaroa, represented as fair haired, is dubbed Controller of Migrations, while in New Zealand, says Percy Smith in his informative book *Hawaiki,* whites should not be regarded as an oddity, nor made into fairies or spirits. They were a maritime race, though largely lost to history. Indeed, writer Mark Williams went to the trouble of tracking down "obscure books written . . . about 1900 . . . [suggesting] that a unified culture existed throughout the Pacific very early in pre-history . . . and that it spread to China, Japan, Mexico, and Alaska . . . creating a 'Pacific School of Art' with distinct artistic motifs and styles" (2001, 143).

In this connection, we certainly are struck by the high incidence of boat drawings in Neolithic and earlier art. Cave paintings in the Kimberly region of western Australia, judged to be at least seventeen thousand years old, display perhaps the oldest drawing of a boat anywhere in the world. Notable is the high prow, which would be unnecessary in inland waters; the drawing suggests the open ocean. Sizable boats with raised prows are also to be seen in the Magdalenian cave art of Mesolithic Europe.

In the Americas too are carved representations of an ancient ship in

Massachusetts at Lake Assawompset; out west, in the Cimarron region between Colorado and Oklahoma, is the carving of an ancient ship—not far from a Phoenician inscription that pays homage to the wife of Baal (Noorbergen 1982, 105). Pictures of Cretan-type vessels at Isle Royal in northern Michigan go back at least 8,000 years (Dewhurst 2014, 203), while 4,000-year-old Cretan anchor stones (as well as pendants and tablets) have been found in other parts of North America. Cretan and American ceramics picture ships of quite similar appearance. Artists in both Amazonia and Crete modeled depictions of a four-masted barque at least 5,000 years ago. "These ships in full scale were capable of taking aboard some eight hundred passengers. . . . Their Cretan name is . . . Cara-Mequera." Yet the Tupi-Guarani of Brazil use exactly the same name, Cara-Mequera, according to Marcel Homet (1963, 170), who goes on to inform us that the Amazonian people living near Pedra Pintada do indeed have legends of Europoid giants in their midst.

"Was the New World discovered by the Phoenicians? Some would put them in Brazil . . ." (Longman 1978, 53). That huge stone monument of Pedra Pintada ("Painted Rock") stands 95 feet high and 300 feet long; its inscriptions and painted dolmens have a North African look.* Carthaginians? Phoenicians? Egyptians? All the figures at Pedra Pintada are in profile just like ancient Egyptian paintings. Many of the natives here were large and light haired, their skulls also different from most Indians.

Arabinya Visits Uropa: Egyptians/Cushites in the British Isles

The civilization of modern Europe has grown out of that of the Saracens to a much greater extent than is generally recognized.

JOHN D. BALDWIN, *PRE-HISTORIC NATIONS*

---

*Harold T. Wilkins illustrates matching ideograms from North Africa and Bolivia in his *Mysteries of South America* (p. 122). Indeed, the bulge of North Africa is much closer to the bulge of northeast Brazil than Europe is to North America.

The first settlements of Arabians in Spain, according to the erudite John Baldwin, were no later than seven thousand years ago. The migration actually represents one of history's most extraordinary cases of diffusion, entailing a massive northwesterly foray into Europe some eight thousand years ago—ultimately linking Egyptian and British culture. This is why "the British," according to Tom Valentine "used the inch as their unit of measure. So did the builders of the Great Pyramid. In fact, the British apparently inherited all their units of measure from [Egyptian] peoples" (Valentine 1975, 59). The Egyptians and the builders of England's Stonehenge used six as a basic number. The sarsens at Stonehenge are a copy of the obelisks in Egypt. To archaeologist Elliot Smith, the designers of Stonehenge must have been either Egyptians or Phoenicians. Arabia too "still has the ruins of ancient structures precisely like Stonehenge," says Baldwin, adding that "the Arabians or their representatives in Spain and North Africa went northward and began the Age of Bronze" (Baldwin 1869, 367). Likewise does Cyrus Gordon see an unmistakable "relationship between megalithic structures from Malta to Stonehenge, especially in their common horseshoe formations, trilithons, pottery and tools" (Gordon 1973, 80).

The Arabo-Egyptian influence in the British Isles is a long-standing puzzle to prehistorians. How and when did it happen? As far as local legend goes, the Scots and Irish "wee bodies," the Picts, are said to have arrived from Hamitic North Africa via Malta and Spain. The Euguvine Tablets mention "night-sailing to Ireland from Iberia" (Baldwin 1869, 374). Along the way, these small Iberians* left an alphabet not unlike that of the British Druids, using the ancient Arabian device of naming letters after trees. This is also how Egyptian faience beads ended up in Britain; they are found all along the Iberian shore and then in the graves of Wessex not far from Stonehenge. Even Egyptian-style mummies have been found in the British Isles.

This singular migration eight thousand years ago is recounted in Oahspe's Book of Fragapatti wherein the god Fragapatti† and his hosts

---

*Note that the name Iberia (covering Spain and Portugal) is repeated in the olden name of Ireland: Hiber-nia.

†This god was remembered in India as Prajapati, Lord of Creatures.

wenttothekingdomsof Uropa,firstGoddessof a barbarian division of the earth. . . . There were few corporeans [mortal inhabitants] in her division. . . . Nevertheless, Jehovih said to Uropa: You shall found here a kingdom . . . and it shall become mighty in heaven and earth. . . . The corporeans [use] neither copper nor iron, but use stone. Therefore send five hundred of your ashars [angels], who are well skilled in the art of inspiring mortals, to Arabin'ya [North Africa plus Arabia]; and you shall cause fifty men to migrate into your lands, men skilled in mining and working copper and iron.

And your ashars shall inspire them to go to the mountains and find the ore, and then to work it, making tools, and implements for hunting and fishing. So Uropa sent angels to Arabin'ya, and they inspired fifty men to go to Uropa. . . . And in four years, behold, not less than twenty thousand men had migrated from Arabin'ya. And the ashars inspired them to marry with the druks and half-breed Ihuans. And in this way a new people of higher light was born into Uropa's division.

OAHSPE, BOOK OF FRAGAPATTI 40:1–4

The ninth-century Irish manuscript "Lebor Gabala Erenn" traces the voyages of early people from Egypt to Spain and on to Ireland. "In

Fig. 7.5. Oahspe map showing "Arabin'ya" and other old names of lands. (In the time of Abraham, Egypt was called South Arabinya.)

his fascinating book *Gold,* C. H. V. Sutherland maps out an identical course via crude mining remains left by these explorers . . . whose search for precious metal led them to the rich deposits in County Wicklow, Ireland" (Cohane 1969, 34). And as Ignatius Donnelly has it, "the oldest people mentioned in Ireland, the Formorians, came from Africa . . . in powerful fleets . . . beginning the Bronze Age in these countries" (i.e., Gaul and Britain). These Formorians were "a sept descended from Cham [Ham] . . . a civilized race . . . called F'omoraig Afraic . . . that possessed ships . . . [and were] led into the country by the Lady Banbha or . . . Berba [Berber?]" (Donnelly 1985, 408). Indeed, Baldwin found an ancient relationship between the North African Berbers and the Skots (or Scots), both of whom have the syllable *Mac* meaning son (Baldwin 1869, 240, 327). And the missing link connecting these two distant lands is Spain, whose Basque people do physically resemble the Berber; Basque blood type also matches that found in Egyptian mummies (Chatelain 1980, 198).

> *Both English and Celtic share a common substratum*
> *that is closely related to the Hamitic-Semitic languages*
> *including the Berber dialects and Egyptian.*
> JOHN P. COHANE, *THE KEY*

The Europeans' curly hair and Rh blood type are also part of that North African legacy. British author and esotericist B. L. Trench somehow reconstructed this "strange and significant journey made . . . between Egypt and England, seven or eight millennia ago. . . . There are records which show North African priest-initiates journeying in a northwesterly direction via the Straits of Gibraltar, then through southern Gaul; continuing north, they reached Carnac* in Brittany. They then turned west, up to the British Isles" (1974, 109–10). Trench does not think they were simply missionaries; rather, these "initiates" were men of learning and science.

---

*Brittany's Carnac looks like an incarnation of Egypt's Karnac.

Fig. 7.6. Carnac menhirs in Brittany

Celts are Aryan Egyptians.

JOHN PILKEY, *THE ORIGIN OF THE NATIONS*

As a result of this long-ago migration, the Welsh language is strangely similar to the ancient tongue of the Nile. And for the same reason, the dolmens are called ker-ham in Brittany, the *ham* standing for these migrating Hamites who civilized significant portions of western Europe. "Persons who have inhabited Brittany," remarks Donnelly, "and then go to Algeria, are struck with the resemblance between the ancient . . . Bretons and the Cabyles of Algiers. In fact, the moral and physical character is identical. . . . Listen to a Cabyle speaking his native tongue, and you will think you hear a Breton talking Celtic" (1985, 389).

Thanks to that same ancient migration, the Basque and Irish show several curious parallels: same music, bagpipes, flutes, tambourines, head cap (*boina*), and elements of vocabulary, for example, the word for "stone," *aitz.*

Solutrean and Suddenlies

There are so many countries in the world where the elements of culture seem to have appeared suddenly, including the Fertile Crescent (the supposed Garden of Eden), where astronomy, mathematics, and writing manifested too abruptly to have "evolved." Well, Hindu records do speak of a migration to Babylonia (Fertile Crescent) out of India perhaps fifteen thousand years ago (discussed, if you recall, under "Shem" in chapter 5, p. 180). But when the dates are older than this it probably indicates culture bearers from the motherland itself, in which case it is the sudden injection of culture and inventions from Pan that would account for similarities in widely separated lands. The motherland interpretation is only valid when the dates are in the vicinity of twenty thousand to twenty-four thousand years ago (see "The Land of Pan Went Down Twenty-Four Thousand Years Ago" in chapter 9, p. 378).

There is indeed a general sense among protohistorians that the "suddenlies" are really *carryovers* from somewhere else: "The sudden appearance of Cro-Magnon man . . . [furnishes] concrete indications of former advanced civilizations" (Berlitz 1972, 160). Why, for example, are twenty-two-thousand-year-old engravings of animals in *Mexico* so much like the twenty-two-thousand-year-old Cro-Magnon art in *France*? And why are Mexican ball games so similar to those of the French Basque? Well, the Basques are descendants of the Cro-Magnons; their ancestors were probably the earliest postdiluvial Europeans. Curiously, they also possess numerous traits in common with Arawaks and Caribs, who show Polynesian beginnings. Therefore we are encouraged to view their kinship with the Basque as arising from diaspora, meaning common origin from the same place, the motherland of man—Pan.

Which makes us wonder, Why do we always hear about Cro-Magnons *in Europe* but never about Cro-Magnons in the Americas? After all, Cro-Magnon's Solutrean culture circa twenty-two thousand years ago has been discovered at the Great Lakes, in Colorado, Washington, and Arizona; this is much earlier than the twelve-thousand-year-old date of the standard model. Europe's Solutrean spearheads are almost identical to the Clovis points in the American Southwest, and they are nothing

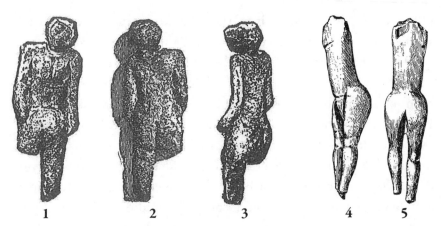

Fig. 7.7. Nampa Venus (left) found in Idaho (figs. 1-3) resembles Cro-Magnon figurines (right) found in France (figs. 4-5).

Fig. 7.8. Cro-Magnon cave drawing of some kind of vessel

like Siberian ones (which would be expected if Native Americans really entered this country across the Bering Straits* from Siberia). Andrew Collins suggests "that the Solutreans took to the high seas† and ended up in North America . . . some twenty thousand years ago. . . . The Solutrean hunters became the forerunners of the Clovis culture . . ."

---

*"Let us have done with those uncertain, unsatisfactory and futile attempts to people America by Behring's Straits, and let us follow on the right way . . . by the Isles of the Southern Pacific Ocean" (Lang 1877).

†Some date this "mass migration during the Stone Age [to] nineteen thousand years ago—the Solutrean epoch" (Chouinard 2012, 162), but as I see it, 19,000 is a date that more strongly suggests cousins dispersed from Pan.

(2014, 180). The reference is to those Solutreans who produced the spectacular cave art of France some twenty thousand years ago.

The *burin,* Europe's Upper Paleolithic engraving tool with chisel-like edges, was used in America as well; indeed, Solutrean artifacts have been found in Chile, Peru, Venezuela, South Carolina, and so forth. Brazil's harpoon heads are Cro-Magnon in type; Marcel Homet notes the same kind of dances in prehistoric France and the Amazon, particularly the famous Dance of the Magician featuring adornment with deer antlers. In northernmost Brazil the Homet expedition came upon a hollowed-out tree trunk used to bury the dead; likewise, in certain Celtic cultures, "which is to say the pure Cromagnons, the dead are usually . . . laid in the hollowed-out trunk of an oak tree." Such a practice, Homet concludes, "can belong only to a culture that possesses a common point of origin" (1963, 90), and it is, I think, significant that examples of the hollowed-out trunk *are still current in Oceania"* (68–69; emphasis added).

Across the Pond

There is an abundance of legends and traditions
concerning the passage of the Irish into America, and their
habitual communication with that continent.

JOHN D. BALDWIN,
PRE-HISTORIC NATIONS

Speaking of burials, why do genetic tests link western Europeans to eight-thousand-year-old Florida burials? Why are buttons, rings, and spearheads in the American mounds so similar to those of Bronze Age Europe? But long before those Bronze Age cultural exchanges took place, a notable similarity was evident among the *earliest* settlers of America and the British Isles. "The Old Irish, nearest the Celtic root stock, maintained a very early connection with a civilized race across the western Ocean. . . . In the Argentine, today, there is actually an Indian tribe speaking *Erse* [Gaelic]!" (Wilkins 2000, 24, 80). Some of those same Indians possess blue eyes and reddish hair.

I was struck by the Erse word for "rock" (or place of strength or fort), *dun,* probably a forerunner of the word *dungeon.* The duns in the Aran Islands were built of massive walls, some 12 feet thick. The Mayan word for "rock" is similar, *tun,* showing up in places like Naach-tun; Chac-tun, with the ruins of fifteen-step pyramids and inscribed *stone* slabs; Nix-tun-Chi'ich (Guatemala); Uaxac-tun, or "Eight Stones" (it is Guatemala's oldest city, an important astronomical center with an elaborately decorated pyramid); Dzibilchal-tun (Yucatán); Pu-tun (Gulf coast); Chakanpu-tun; Xul-tun and Xaman-tun, ancient sites; Chanpu-tun (Mayan lowlands); and Lubaan-tun, where the world-famous crystal skull was found.

Tun is also seen in words like Ka-tun, the calendar *stone* of the Maya, and in the extraordinary Lol-tun caverns with its man-made corridors and chambers built into bedrock and called chul-tun. Rock is again the key element at Colombia's Tun-ja, with its standing stones, and at Peru's Ha-tun-colla, with its stone pillars.

In far-off Japan too, *tun-tu* is the Ainu word for building support, while in Siberia, Tun-guska translates as Stony River. In western China as well, Tun-huang, situated along the Silk Road in the Tarim Basin, is famous for its artificial caverns enclosing corridors and large rooms, in particular the Cave of the Thousand Buddhas with temples and shrines hewn into the rock. Its stairways are linked in legend to the tun-nels of Shambhala. No, I would not be surprised if the English words *tun-nel* and *ton* (tonne) had this common root. I might even reconstruct the English word *stone* as (s-tun). Indeed, all these congeners suggest a Panic origin: the Polynesian word for "crust" or "shell" is *tunu,* and for "stone" is *wha-tu; tu* means "stability" in the Society Islands, ke'e-tu means "volcanic stone," and tu'u means "ceremonial stone platform" (in the Marquesas). Mala-tun-iun, a lost race of Melanesia, was famous for its remarkable work in stone (Perry 1968, 28).

Nevertheless, the Celtic strain in Brazil could have been introduced at a later date, like the dolmen of Serra do Joelho in the Amazon Basin, which is inscribed in "the aspect of a true Celtic monument . . . [as] found in Brittany, Scandinavia, and England" (Homet 1963, 38–39). Similar comparisons include the following:

- the identity of the snake formation near Stonehenge and its duplicate near Peebles, Ohio
- the Celtic appearance of the Kensington Rune Stone
- the Celtic-style Round Tower of Newport, which also compares with ancient towers in Colorado and New Mexico
- megalithic Vermont sites with orientations similar to Ballinaby, Scotland (Mavor 1991, 31)
- Celtic-looking rocking stones in Orange County, New York, in Massachusetts at Ashburnham, and in New Hampshire at Andover and Durham—all of which smack of a Bronze Age provenance

Fig. 7.9. Peekskill, New York, rocking stone, so much like those of Europe including a 20-ton rocking stone at Dunkeld, Scotland, where cairns and ancient rites use "certain stones of the place" (Mavor 1991, 235).

Fig. 7.10. "Compare this picture of a copper ax from a mound near Laporte, Indiana (left) with this representation (right) of a copper ax of the Bronze Age, found near Waterford, Ireland . . . almost identical" (Donnelly 1985, 266).

Barry Fell thought Mystery Hill, with its Ogham inscriptions, was a Celtic monument; the stones line up to mark the major Celtic festivals. Construction style at New Hampshire's four-thousand-year-old megalithic Mystery Hill is reminiscent of Skara Brae in the Scottish Orkneys; the site has Phoenician inscriptions and stalls similar to the chambered tombs of the Orkneys, whose cairns also parallel America's Stonehenge, as does its top slanted monolith and its Sunrise Stone.

British grave cists, archaeologists cannot deny, are uncannily like American ones. Best known is the elaborate passage grave and ceremonial center at Newgrange in eastern Ireland (fig. 7.11, p. 294), brought to mind in 1981 when the Murray Farm Tunnel Chamber in Holmes County, Ohio, was discovered. The Ohio complex was found to be identical in various features to Ireland's narrow passage graves. About six thousand years old, the Ohio chamber was cut from solid rock and is nearly 60 feet long, just like its counterpart in Ireland. Not only did the Murray Farm Tunnel remind experts of Ireland's famed underworld, but the *orientation* of the Ohio chamber was found to be identical to ancient ruins at Uxmal, Yucatán. All these analogies stand as clues to a worldwide civilization even prior to the Bronze Age.

Notwithstanding Celtic cairns and inscriptions of a *later* date found all across North America—from Maine to Arkansas—that do indicate extensive Bronze Age expeditions, there is yet a much more archaic connection between these sons of Guatama and their Old World cousins in Ireland. We are talking about two layers—one from the diluvial age (more than 20,000 BP) and the other in the later Neolithic or Mesolithic period. Probably belonging to the later layer is Mexico's Day of the Dead festival, almost the same as the Celtic celebration; even Mexico's culture hero Kukulkan sounds a bit like Ireland's counterpart Cu Chulainn. "The Aborigines of America," thought one nineteenth-century scholar, "were of Celtic origin; their monuments . . . are as old as any in Europe, and derived from the same common ancestor" (Finch 1824, 149–61). Gaelic migrants called Papas may have populated Iceland as well as Central America (Charroux 1972, 75). However, Papa ancestry may actually originate in the motherland, Papa and Tangaroa being the names of the original parents in Tahiti, the name Papa representing Mother Earth in much of Polynesia.

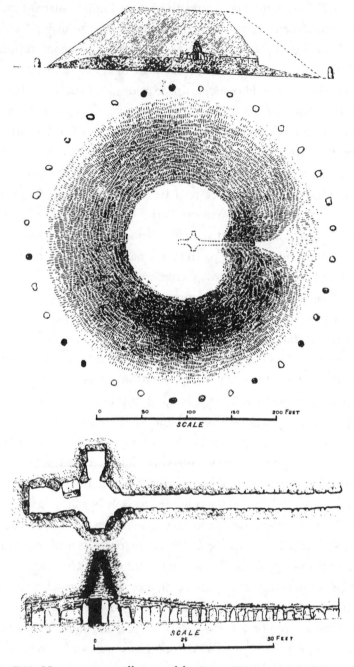

Fig. 7.11. Newgrange, as illustrated by James Fergusson in 1872, is one of the most notable passage graves in Ireland. Joseph Mavor compares it to ancient structures at Upton, Massachusetts (Mavor 1991, 238).

Mighty Navigators

People have always gone forth in boats to explore, trade, and find new places to live. It is fundamental to human nature.

PATRICK CHOUINARD, *FORGOTTEN WORLDS*

The Maori's earliest-known voyager, Tama-rereti, "explored a large part of the world" (Smith 1921, 115–16). At Easter Island, a very old stone carving shows a ship with three masts, a great deal larger than those used by the natives at the time of contact. Similarly, archaeologists in the Indus Valley have found a terra-cotta seal at the site of Mohenjo-Daro showing a large high-prowed ship with a spacious on-deck cabin, surely a sign of "an ancient science of cartography and navigation that explored the world and charted it accurately" (Hancock 2002, 126, 669). Indeed, Valmiki's Ramayana describes the early people of India as fully literate "navigators whose ships traveled from the Western to the Eastern oceans, and from the Southern to the Northern seas, in ages so remote that the sun had not yet risen above the horizon" (Lehrburger 2015, 239–40). Their 120-foot long ships, capable of carrying seven hundred people, were planked, had compasses, and "used the Pacific Equatorial Counter Current . . . to visit the North and South American continents" (Lehrburger 2015, 239–40). In Churchwardian terms, these mighty navigators were the Muvian "Cara Mayas" who had settled both the Old World (India) and the New World (Mexico). Churchward, we know, collaborated with the geologist William Niven, who had excavated a great number of inscribed tablets in Mexico that the colonel thought were written in the same script he had seen on ancient tablets in India.

Compelling parallels between the Indus Valley civilization and southeastern tribes in North America, as Americanist Joseph Mahan sees it, speak for "an ancient culture of truly worldwide influence"* (1983, 155).

---

*Or simply under common inspiration?—as we saw above where the Vedics, Algonquins, and Hebrews all received the same sacred teachings.

"the prophets come again under the light of dan "

DAN Time of Light

Fig. 7.12. Found near Mexico City, Niven's tablet #0294 (left) compares to a glyph called Dan or Dang (right) from the Panic Tablet of Semoin. Dan illustrates the Earth riding through the roadway of the stars, passing through regions of light and darkness. Because Se'moin (see below) is antediluvian, Niven's tablets may also be of great age.

Early in the twentieth century explorer Ruth Verrill found a five-thousand-year-old Vedic inscription in Bolivia signed by people from the Land of Twilight (i.e., the Valley of the Indus). This would be layer number two (as discussed above). Similarly, Wilkins remarks upon "the queerly Sancritian sound about words in some of the South American Indians' tongues . . . [and] links between the strange letters of old Brazil and characters found in Sanscrit" (Wilkins 2000, 186, 118). Sanskrit, thought to be a maritime language, also relates in certain ways to Polynesian tongues, as we saw in common names in chapter 5: Manu, Puna, Hirto. But before we decide *which way* the influence flowed—and when—let us not forget that those who once inhabited Easter Island were *also* great navigators, as were the pre-Hawaiians, whose Mu people were acclaimed shipbuilders and mariners. Natives of Kusai Island say that "the people who once lived here . . . had large vessels in which they made voyages far distant . . . taking many moons to complete" (Churchward 2011, 74). Ru, a deified ancestor in Polynesia, circumnavigated the Earth (Henry 1928, 459). Steering double canoes 150 feet long that could carry four hundred men, the Polynesians were "bold navigators long before the Phoenicians ventured out of the Mediterranean" (Anderson 1928, 5).

> In those days, there were great cities of hundreds of thousands of inhabitants, and thousands and thousands of such cities in all the five great divisions of the earth. And man built ships and sailed over the ocean in all directions, around the whole world.
>
> OAHSPE, SYNOPSIS OF SIXTEEN CYCLES 1:21

Rongorongo

Rongorongo, it seems, was brought to Easter Island in the twelfth century by Hotu Matua, leader of the Long Ears, the aristocracatic Children of the Sun, comprised of the reddish-haired Anua Motua, who subjugated the Short Ears, the common folk of the island. They had arrived from the east after their islands sank in the sea. And when they took power, they saw the (preexisting) statues, the stone gods called moai, and decided to imitate them by lengthening their ears, at least according to Jean-Michel Schwartz (1973, 124–25). But the Short Ears rebelled and overthrew them. Then they too lengthened their ears!

Lengthened earlobes was a mark of aristocracy among the reddish-haired Incan Orejones ("big ears"). Some speculate that the Orejones are the ones who brought script (rongorongo) to Easter Island from South America. Others say it was the other way around, that the Peruvians knew "of the arrival in their country of foreigners who came by sea and landed on the western coast" (Baldwin 1869, 265). It is further suggested that these invaders, these Sons of the Sun, "made the ancestors pile up stones for a great temple, whereon these great lords might take refuge" (Wilkins 2000, 16).

Either way, in common with the Pacific Islands are Peru's step structures and terraces, petroglyphs and geoglyphs, tools and customs and works of art, all of which have led historians like Homet, Heyerdahl, and Brown to reason that it must have been the pre-Incas who influenced the Pacific cultures. The standard model, however, insists that any similarities are "completely accidental. . . . All scientific evidence ruled

Fig. 7.13. Inscribed on wooden boards, rongorongo, the undeciphered
"singing tablets" of Easter Island, apparently contain the keys to prayers,
hymns, songs, genealogies, and so forth. Rongorongo similars have been
noted as far away as China, Pakistan, Egypt, and Colombia, in the latter
case among people who painted these glyphs on wooden sticks. The Motilone
of Venezuela used that script up to the twentieth century, as did the Cuna
of Panama and the ancients at Tiahuanaco (Joseph 2006, 75).

Fig. 7.14. Comparing the glyphs
of Easter Island, India/Pakistan,
and China. Rongo, incidentally,
means "sacred."

out consideration of South America as the home of the Polynesians"
(Suggs 1962, 233, 88). If Suggs is right, why do plants like cotton, coco
palms, peanuts, sweet potato, and gourds seem to have been imported

Fig. 7.15. An Easter Islander: long ears, which are also seen on statues at Raivavai south of the Society Islands and in the Maldives, appear on living people as well, in the Marquesas and also on classical images of Buddha.

Fig. 7.16. Incan long ears. It was the Incan nobles' custom to deform their earlobes; the costly ornaments that weighed them down drew attention to their wealth.

from the Americas to Polynesia? According to Heyerdahl and Jean-Michel Schwartz the originators of the Easter Island statues came from South America. "The inspiration of the Ahu Vinapu could only have come from South America" (Schwartz 1973, 175). After all, the need to erect gigantic statues, like those in South America, is not found in the rest of Polynesia—only on Easter Island, closest to South America.

Nevertheless, no Peruvian tools or pottery have turned up in the Polynesian isles. Opinions differ sharply. "No American tribe ever migrated into the Pacific" (Lissner 1962, 312). Colin Renfrew also asserts rather dogmatically that rongorongo was independently created (Renfrew 1973, fig. 40). End of story. Contacts, it seems, are virtually taboo. But for all we know, cultural influences may have been in *both* directions—and at different times. It would not be hard for a large catamaran to cross the ocean to the coast of South America. "It is useless," argued Percy Smith, "for some writers to insist that the prevalence of the S.E. trade winds would form a bar to voyages from Central Polynesia to the American Coast" (Smith 1921, 37), especially if they followed the countercurrents that blow from the northwest Pacific to the east. It was in fact Lewis Spence's opinion that "American civilization owed its inception to Polynesian immigration" (Spence 1933, 189). It certainly is curious that a god named Kon Tiki is an important part of both the Peruvian and Polynesian pantheon!

Complicating this already difficult issue, Schwartz points out similarities between rongorongo and archaic Chinese writing (whose word ku-wan means "ancient pictures"). He thinks China is the source of the rongo script and that the missing geographical link is lost Mu, which "disappeared as the result of a cataclysm" (Schwartz 1973, 124). Besides China, India, as we've seen, is also in the mix, for numerous glyphs from Bronze Age Mohenjo Daro match up with Easter Island's rongorongo. As Joseph sees it, "both cultures received the originally Lemurian script independently from their Pacific Motherland, where the first written word was inscribed" (Joseph 2006, 68). This may be so, although Indic forays across the Pacific Ocean may actually be of a much more recent date. For example, American plantations with Indic strains of cotton and jute can be no earlier than the third or fourth millennium BCE (Chatelain 1980, 116, 194). It was also in the fourth millennium that miners from the Indus Valley left their traces in Michigan, Colorado, and Peru (Lehrburger 2015, 244).

AMERIND/CHINESE COGNATES

Meaning	Amerind: Location	Chinese Cognate
Weave*	teteka: Mexico	tek
To rob, take^	nameya: Mexico	niam
Flag*	pantli: Mexico	fan
Sun	tona: Antilles	tun
To break or burst^	pakiy: Peru	p'ek
Eagle	vanac: Peru	feng (phoenix)
Sheep	wanaco: Peru	yang
Toad	poko: Chile	pok
Chief	hvinca: Chile	huang
Earth	tue: Chile	thu
Whisper^	nhim: Brazil	nym
Mankind	mena: Brazil	min
Stupid, thoughtless^	telp-ochtli: Mexico	tulb-a
Algonquian	**Chinese**	**Translation**
mai'ah	ma	expression (the term is mai in Panic)
peboa^	m'boa	winter; destroyer (winter is p'boa in Panic)
hagni^	ah'gni	fire; to burn (same in Sanskrit)
go'ongwe*	oe'gwong	love-offering
ni'oh'ghoo	ni'ghoo	prayer
shu	su	enlightened; prophetic
yope'ang	yoke'eng	sacred star
haw'git	git'haw	sun, the all-heat (same in Arabic)
hogawatha^	hogawata	mastodon

* = could be loaned words (i.e., introduced)
^ = not likely to be borrowed words

Mysterious Scripts

Writing in India, thought Churchward, was perfectly developed fifteen thousand years ago; some trace it back to "Rutas," a lost civilization and continent, which, according Ceylonese chronicles, had a

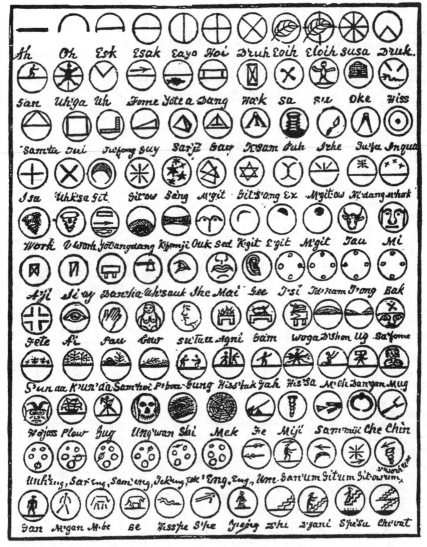

Fig. 7.17. Se'moin Tablet with 121 symbols. Plate 62 from Oahspe. Some sort of script called tuhituhi was used in Irihia (see chapter 2, p. 73, "Irin and Irihia," the lost lands), the hero Tamatea writing in a cave to preserve it.

hundred thousand towns along the coast. Writing may indeed be much older than we have supposed. "And the Lord spoke to the Ihin, saying: Go provide me a stone and I will engrave it with my own hand, and it shall be called Se'moin . . . a testimony to all nations . . . of the first written language in all the world" (Oahspe, First Book of the First Lords 4:2; relating to a time about 70,000 years ago).

Besides resembling Easter Island's rongorongo, Hindu writing is also similar to the syllabic script of the Caroline Islands, at Oleai, which is no less than 8,000 miles from Easter Island. The Oleai script has sixty characters (syllabic?); though no longer understood, it is

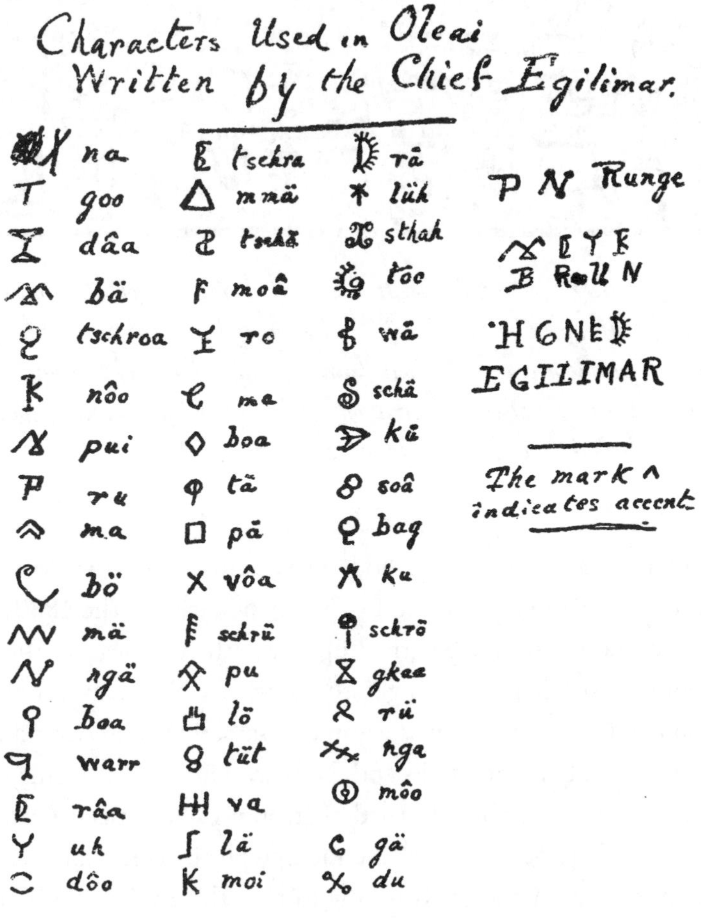

Fig. 7.18. Oleai, as Professor Brown saw it, was once the written language of an archipelagic empire.

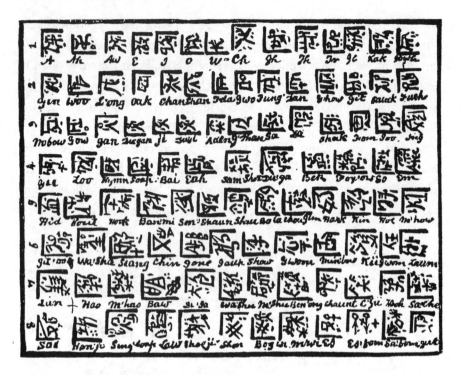

Fig. 7.19. Plate 71 from Oahspe. It is also cited in the Book of Saphah. "Kii [indicates] truth, a tribe called Kii, a religious tribe on the continent of Pan. An abused people are also Kii. Kii, learning, one who tried to understand." We find the name also in Churchward who lists Ki as meaning "people, inhabitants" in the Akkadian language (1931, 234).

said to have been left by "the gods of yesterday." Also in Micronesia were the Panape tablets, burned by the missionaries in the 1880s.

Mysterious scripts have turned up in South America, on the opposite shore of sunken Pan; huge stones in the Surinam jungle bear undeciphered inscriptions, just as unknown scripts were found at San Agustin, Colombia, and at Ilo and Sahpuayaku in Peru. In his travels, Alexander Von Humboldt learned that books had indeed been made in Peru in earlier ages. Some of the hieroglyphs in Peru—and China—read from top to bottom; this is how to read the Tablet of Kii and the Se'moin tablet from Pan. "Initiate here reads from top of first row of tablet downward —Ed." (Oahspe, Book of Saphah: Fonece).

Fig. 7.20. Photo of Colonel Fawcett taken one year before his disappearance. More than half the (alphabetic) characters that Fawcett found in Brazil were identical to those he had discovered in the jungles of Ceylon more than thirty years earlier.

To date, four hundred signs or elements of a pre-Incan writing system have been identified. Another written script in this region, with fifty-six different characters, appears on metal plaques and stelae (Von Daniken 1974, 35, 54). Other unidentified writing systems in South America include the little-known alphabetic script in Matto Grosso, Brazil,* associated with the high Tupi culture and, significantly, thought to originate in the Pacific; after all, the Tupis have a prominent flood myth.

The golden-haired Tapuyo "Indians" in eastern Brazil are considered refugees of a lost civilization. As we saw earlier, Colonel Fawcett described the Tapuyos as "fair as the English." On a mission, England's intrepid Percy H. Fawcett penetrated the interior of Brazil in the early twentieth century in search of this lost civilization of the Tapuyos' ancestors, a people who once dwelled in stone palaces and cultivated the high arts. The part of Brazil that Fawcett explored, Matto Grosso, is full of such legends, as well as intriguing ancient scripts, both ideographic and alphabetical.

As for the ancient Mexicans, Niven's findings suggested a *precursor* to Mayan hieroglyphs dating more than twelve thousand years old. The Maya themselves once made books of long strips of native paper folded zigzag (like early Chinese manuscripts) and bound between a pair of wooden covers; all were destroyed, after which, knowledge of writing was

---

*Wilkins illustrates a strange but elegant series of characters engraved on great stones in the wilds of Brazil, showing affinities with Greek, Arabic, and Phoenician (2000, 45–47).

apparently lost. The Maya said that Itzamna, the "god" of medicine (really, the high priest), had invented writing; this god or priest is a Noachic figure; that is, portrayed on icons as short, white, and with a prominent nose, rather like the *antediluvian* patriarchs. T-*enoch*-titlan includes the name Enoch, the patriarch whose name literally means "Initiator."

If script was *given* to the Maya (by god, angel, priest, or new settler), it would then explain why their writing seems to emerge full-blown, as far as archaeology can tell, just as their mathematics and astronomy have no known precedents—except for the Olmecs, who are considered the earliest civilizers in Mesoamerica. But where did *they* learn it? Well, Peter Kolosimo identifies Mexican inscriptions as "of the same type as found on Easter Island" (Kolosimo 1975, 53); while the written tablets in Niven's hoard, according to Churchward, are in "the Uighur-Maya hieratic alphabet" that came directly out of the motherland of man (Churchward 2011, 220).

In 1833 soldiers in California discovered boulders covered in writing at Lampock Rancho that were similar to a find made near Los Angeles on the island of Santa Maria. In Oregon, rocks at Klamath Falls are inscribed with characters, some of which are similar to Sanskrit, Greek, and Latin; a sprinkling of Greek and Latin words are even found in the local dialect. The Modoc Indians call the place Valley of Knowledge.

Carved Histories

Was the original Valley of Knowledge in Pan? Why was the legendary and utopian archipelago in the Arabian Sea called *Pan*chaia? Its temple had golden columns on which were engraved all the histories of the gods and records of the human race. In Polynesia too, "at a very remote period, the national marae of Havai'i [was] named Fruitful-myriads-who-*engraved*-the-rocks-of-Feoro"; it is even thought that their practice of tattooing is a "recollection of the ancient hieroglyphic system" (Henry 1928, 287, 120). Can we then conclude that writing was in fact prediluvial? According to Oahspe, twenty-four thousand years ago "the rabbah made records in writing on stone; the which they taught to their successors" (The Lords' First Book 2:16).

Along the Fertile Crescent, it was the epic hero Gilgamesh who engraved in stone the story of the flood; Chaldean tradition has the king ordering the history of all things to be committed to writing *in advance* of the deluge. Indeed, one Sumerian tablet at Nineveh records the words of King Ashurbanipal, who declared he could read the stone carvings of the days *before the flood.*

Other Mediterranean traditions hold that the chosen people called "Sethites" had escaped the submersion of Pan and preserved the original inventions, histories, religion, and ethics on monuments of stone; thus is the Sethite Enoch (great-grandfather of Noah), in the Scottish Rite of Freemasonry, named as the builder of a granite column and a brass column, each engraved with knowledge of the arts and sciences intended to survive the coming flood. Andrew Collins wonders if "the original books of Seth [could] have been carved stone pillars, like those uncovered today at nearby Göbekli Tepe" (2014, 339).

Stone tablets of knowledge are certainly recurrent themes in the great traditions of diluvial man. "Hunters find stone tablets under a tree" came an 1892 report from Illinois describing two sandstone tablets with strange inscriptions. Meanwhile, in Arizona the Hopi Indians speak of True White Brother, who prepared holy records into which the Great Spirit breathed all teachings and prophecies. These tablets were then given to each of the four races, after which the chief led the faithful into their new lands. The Hopi story of teaching tablets resonates not only with our account of the Ihin diaspora but also with Josephus's history of the antediluvians who inscribed all wisdom on two pillars, which Hermes then discovered after the flood. In ancient Egypt, Manetho, the high priest of Heliopolis, also said that in the days before the flood Thoth (Greece's Hermes Trismegistus) inscribed on stelea the essence of all knowledge.

Hallowed Records

Although the standard model of ancient history assumes that writing began with Bronze Age city-states essentially for the purposes of the power elite, it must have begun much earlier—with *sacred,* not secular, records. Engraved stelea and pillars figure extensively in the legends of the preflood patriarchs (the "True White Brothers"). Most notably, in the story of Lamech (son of Methuselah and father of Noah), this great patriarch impresses the knowledge of his forefathers onto two mighty pillars.

In the scheme of things, pillars are interchangeable with tablets; Minorca's monoliths in Catalan are called *taulas* (tables). There in Spain, Heracles, tradition says, stopped at Tartessos where he erected two pillars at Gades' (Cadiz) Temple of Heracles. Related tradition has Moses's words of law written upon two tablets of stone; similar narratives explain that the holy descendants of Seth (who was Adam's third son) and of the patriarch Enoch were tasked with preserving the original religion, science, and arts of peace, and to transmit them to future generations on monuments of *stone,* that they might not be lost.

An African rendition has tablets kept at the foot of Mount Kenya by the Kukuyu (note the *Ku*) tribe. In Asia as well, thin gold tablets found in the Gobi Desert "relate the history of mankind . . . before the cataclysm" (Charroux 1967, 195). In the farthest East too, symbols on Yonaguni tablets off Japan seem to connote "a vast Pacific motherland" (Chouinard 2012, 40). Even in Australia, huge limestone pillars near Roper River are said to have been the work of a white race—a memorial of the flood?

Finally, off Callao, Peru (significantly, in the direction of Tahiti), findings mentioned in chapter 1, pp. 22–23, include unknown hieroglyphics inscribed on a stone column—which reminds us of hieroglyphics inscribed on sunken columns *east* of Tahiti. There are also undeciphered inscriptions on Fijian monuments, on the island of Manua Levu: here, a 40-ton monolith bears a script that no one has been able to decipher (Kolosimo 1973, 150). Peru's Ica Stones (see fig. 3.12b, p. 130) may shed some light. Engraved with great precision, they have been interpreted as containing records of Mu, its astronomy, its arts of surgery, its fauna, and so forth. Some of these engravings depict submersion of lands. Called "talking stones," their nickname reminds us of the "talking boards"—the rongorongo tablets. At one time there must have been hundreds of these boards recording the history and religion of Easter Island and Hiva, its lost motherland. Functionally, the rongorongo talking boards were their own version of the inscribed pillars that told the history of the flood. As we saw in chapter 1, Panama's majestic columns at Cocle are covered with inscriptions in an unknown language; while today, the picture writing of the Kunas, inscribed on wooden tables, resembles rongorongo.

The Basque Connection

Comparable words (cognates) stand out as our keenest clues to a mutual Panic origin. "The five peoples who were saved from Pan [were] commanded to preserve Panic words in their respective countries, which they did, many of which exist to this day" (Oahspe, The Lords' Fifth Book 5:1). Thanks to the mother tongue, deep-lying resemblances exist between seemingly unrelated language groups. This is particularly notable in the agglutinative type (where radicals can be compounded in a single word and the same root can be a verb or a noun). Polynesian languages of today are famous for their compound words; for example, *Te-atua-nui-e-maru-i-te-ra'i* (great-god-who-overshadows-the-sky).

Out of Pan, three of the five fleets—Jaffeth, Yista, and Guatama—retained elements of agglutinative grammar. This is still seen in the Basque tongue (a Jaffetic branch), which is "as typically agglutinative as any Asiatic or American tongue. . . . The verb habitually includes all pronouns, adverbs and other allied parts of speech." As an example, the single Basque word for "the lower field of the high hill of Azzpicuelta" runs: *Azpilcuelagarayeosaroyarenberecolarrea.* "No wonder the French peasants state that the devil studied the Basque language for seven years and learned only two words" (H[addon], 1911).

As a Jaffetic offshoot, the Basque language has some common traits with the Altai family. But the Basque people and tongue antedate the rest of Europe; Basque-type bones have been found in Europe's megalithic tombs (Wernick 1978, 66), ranking them as pre-Celtic and pre-Indo-European. In other words, we can tentatively identify the Basque as the earliest *postdiluvial* people in Europe. The fact that a tongue similar to the Basque is found in the Caucasus points us to Turkic and ultimately Asian beginnings. Yet Marcel Homet discovered that "the ancient Caucasian language shows many similarities with the old

Brazilian* dialect of Tupi-Guarani" (Homet 1963, 83). And the Tupi, as we have elsewhere noted, are, like the Basque, among the first postdiluvial settlers of their region. Remote cousinship explains these otherwise inexplicable ties. According to Santillana, "Finland, Esthonia and Lapland are . . . ethnically related to the Hungarians and to other faraway Asia peoples [like the] Votyaks, Voguls, Ostyaks. They speak languages which belong to the Ugro-Finnish family, as totally unrelated to German as Basque would be" (Santillana 1969, 26). Rather,

Fig. 7.21. Map of Jaffetic language influence in Europe, extending to the Basque in the Pyrennes, Etruscans in Italy, Finno-Ugric in Scandinavia, and Gaelic in Ireland; "The Irish and Armenians are racial cousins" (Churchward 1931a, 123). No surprise then that the world's longest town name is in Wales: Llanfairpwilgwyngyligogerychwymdrobwillantysiliogogogoch. All seem to trace back to a Turkic root in the Caucasus.

---

*It seems that sixteenth-century Basque speakers were able to make themselves understood among the natives of Amazonia, conversing with these Indians, each side using his own language. Apparently a similar kinship exists between the (Bolivian) Araucanians and the Basques of Spain and France.

Finno-Ugric is similar to Sumerian. "These languages are described as agglutinative . . . as found in Turkish" (Pilkey 1984, 29).

Churchward liked to indulge in a favorite anecdote in which an Irishman and some Basque meet up (in Cuba, of all places) whereon Pat exclaims, "These people and I spake the same languidge, Gaelic" (see p. 36; the Basque also love bagpipes). Underscoring the Eastern (Jaffetic) root stock of Gaelic, Churchward recounts a similar tale, this one of an Irish soldier in Nepal/Tibet, who declared, "Begorrah! These little divils are talking in me own languidge!" (Churchward 1931b, 123).

Many wild theories have been promulgated as to the origin of the Basques, several scholars affiliate them with Lapps, Etruscans and Picts. The hazel eyes, broad head, and short stature of the Basque indicate Finnish (Ugrian) descent, and, like the Finns, the Basque race . . . wandered from Asia into Europe.

Professional skeptics like Sprague De Camp sniff at "fantastic linguistics that classify languages into nonsensical groups like 'Uralo-basque,' which included such unrelated tongues as Dakota, Chinese . . . Sumerian . . . Otomi . . . the Mayas and Kiches of Central America . . . the Aztecs and the peoples of the Caucasus" (De Camp 1975, 88). Yet they are all agglutinative languages, and Basque does indeed show affinity with Algonquin-Lenape and other Amerind languages. Na-Dene (Navajo) shows some relationship to the language of the Sumerians, which in turn has links to Japanese. In fact, "Basque and Japanese both . . . resemble Quechua and . . . Basque words [are] mixed in with the native languages in Central America and Peru. . . . The word garua ('drizzle') was the same in Quechua and Basque" (Berlitz 1972, 186). Although ancient Chinese and American writing systems arose independently of Sumerian, all of them are agglutinative languages; single words can be as long and descriptive as sentences. Even today, the Chinese syllabary uses signs similar to the pictographs of ancient Sumeria.

China and the Americas

Favorable winds could have helped men reach California from China. Traveling the North Pacific, crews could have been swept along by the

Kuroshio, the strong, warm current flowing eastward from Japan. The very old Chinese work, dated 2250 BCE, *Shan Hai King,* the "Classic of Mountains and Seas," accurately describes numerous geographical features of North America.

The ancient Chinese, noted John Baldwin, "were acquainted with the American continent. . . . Their ships visited it" (Baldwin 1869, 401). The peanut is not native to China, but peanut plantations sprang up there as much as five thousand years ago. Source? Some scholars think it was America. Conversely, Erich Von Daniken thought "the fantastic five-strand necklace of green jade in the burial pyramid of Tikal in Guatemala . . . comes from China" (Von Daniken 1970, 93), just as Churchward thought the jade talisman of Maya's Queen Moo must have been Chinese. Monuments in the Amazon jungle are made of jadeite, which is not otherwise known or mined in South America. But "the supply of Tarim Basin [western China] jade from ancient times is well established. . . . [It is] yet another mineral and item on the ever-growing list of materials that were traded thousands of years ago, across . . . the entire world" (Coppens 2012, 244). The ever-growing list of Chinese motifs in America includes the following:

- Hieroglyphics in the American Southwest (Dewhurst 2014, 198).
- Chinese frieze motifs and statuettes at Mexican sites as well as along the Pacific Northwest (including Ipiutak area), with all the appearance of Shang Dynasty iconography.
- Feline figures, which appear as a major theme in both Shang and Olmec art.
- Shang Dynasty bronze vessels' geometric figures and spirals seen on Nazca (Paracas) pottery in Peru.
- Dragon influence in Paracas art as well as in British Columbia and Mexican.
- Jade statuette at Tuxla, Mexico, with symbols similar to those of China's Zhou Dynasty (Lehrburger 2015, 312).
- Identical ancient dance costumes among the Peruvian Aymaras and the Chinese.
- Buddhist figures that sit on tigers at Mayan centers.
- Buddhist priests are called lamas while Mexican priests are

Fig. 7.22. Olmec head of jade, found at Tenango, with Asian features

called tlamas; the vocabulary of a tribe in Sierra Madre Mountains includes Chinese words (Churchward 2014, 10).

- Tajen (Tajin) styles of vessels and round mirrors are almost indistinguishable from China's fifth-century Chou style.
- The Maya are the most Chinese-looking of all Amerinds; "blue spots" are known to appear on the lower backs of both Chinese and Native American babies (Lehrburger 2015, 311).
- Both societies used the large and small month count for their calendars; the same methods to predict eclipses were used by the Maya and China's Han Dynasty, 2000 BP (see "Amerind/Chinese Cognates," p. 301).

Canals, Qanats, and Canoes

In olden times serious travel was more by waterways than over land. In America, about six thousand years ago,

> Oyoyughstuhaipawehaha built the canal (oseowa) of Papaeunugheutowa, which extended from the sea of Hoola'hoola'pan (Lake Superior) to the plains of Aigonquehanelachahoba (Texas). . . . Thusaiganganenosatamakka built the great east canal, the Oseowagallaxacola, in the rich valley of Tiedaswonoghassie, and through the land of Seganeogalgalyaluciahomaahomhom [most likely Louisiana and Mississippi]. . . . Between the great kings and their great capitals were a thousand canals, crossing the country in

every direction, from east to west and from north to south, so that the seas of the north were connected with the seas of the south.

OAHSPE, FIRST BOOK OF GOD 25:1, 4, 9

The people traveled in kanoos [canoes], and carried the products of the land to all directions. . . . In those days the kings and learned men set their hearts on building canals. . . . The great glory and honor of man at that time lay in this achievement. For God [Gitchee], perceiving the virtue and wisdom of men, had sent his angels to teach man the mystery of canal-making; to teach him to compound clay with lime and sand, to hold water . . . how to soften copper like dough; how to harden copper like flint rock, for axes and mattocks for building canals.

To the south of Onewagga lay the kingdom of Himallawowoag-anapapa, rich in legends of the people who lived here before the flood; a kingdom of seventy cities and six great canals coursing east and west, and north and south, from the Ghiee Mountain, in the east, to the west mountain, the Yublahahcolaesavaganawakka, the place of the king of bears, the Eeughohabakax [grizzly].

OAHSPE, FIRST BOOK OF GOD 25:11–13, 18

These chronicles of the ancients are matched by recent discoveries. "One finds a regular system of dams extending from Lake Superior . . . to the Gulf of Mexico" (Dewhurst 2014, 167). In a remote age there were sophisticated civilizations with canal systems in Florida, Louisiana, and Texas. Ancient canals on the southwest coast of Florida are known to have been 12 feet deep and 55 feet wide, 1½ miles long, reaching to the sea. Another canal, though, was more than 5 miles long; both were explored in the 1880s by Andrew E. Douglass (Corliss 1976, 45–51).

And in the Southwest the ancestors of the Pueblo Indians built canals (Perry 1968, 350). Although "encroachments have destroyed all trace of most prehistoric canals" in Arizona, careful excavation revealed one of the canals to be 9 miles in extent. These are the Hohokan canals; I think it is relevant that the Hohokan dialects trace back to languages spoken in the Pacific. The amount of earth moved in these enterprises was stupendous, as was "the

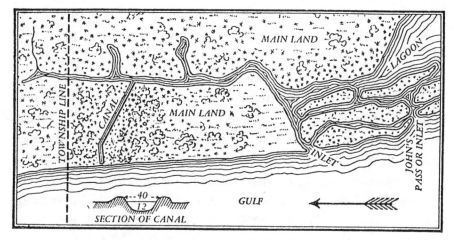

Fig. 7.23. A canal showing tool marks on the reef is still traceable in the waters off Key Largo.

engineering know-how displayed in the design of . . . Arizona's canal system" (Corliss 1976, 38–45). These farmers near the Gila River had trade relations as far off as Mexico; their heirs were the Pima and Papago Indians.

To the south we find six major canals at Teotihuacan, some still in use; in those places, the best way of getting about was by canoe. "Radar looks into the past, finds Mayan canals," reports the Associated Press, (*Kansas City Star,* October 21, 1981): the aerial survey penetrated tropical vegetation, revealing prehistoric canals. Beamed also over Belize and Tikal, the survey shows huge tracts of swampland drained by the ancient engineers. NASA radar imagery over the Guatemalan jungle has shown canals, while in Yucatán, aerial photographs reveal that canals once cut through the swamps, some more than 7 miles long. Aerial inspection of canals at Quintana Roo were confirmed by ground inspection (Adams 1991, 124, 129, 146).

Farther south, Bolivia's ancient Tiahuanaco boasts the remains of very wide, stone-lined canals that once connected the Pacific Ocean and the Amazonian Sea.

There were also canals at Marcahuasi in the Peruvian Andes, in the Chacha region, and high in the Bolivian Andes at Puma Punku near Tiahuanaco, evincing "Lemurian construction style" (Childress 1988, 220). In southern Peru the Nazca people once patterned irrigation canals and large stone reservoirs. Nazca, Mochica, and Chimu were all once in this region. Mochica canals were 70 miles long, some still in use. Here too the Chimu capital, Chan-Chan, was a very large city with aqueducts more than 100 miles long, starting from the Pacific. Did canal building originate on Pan? *Arawa,* in the Pacific, means "canoe," and the Arawak tribes of early Colombia* and Amazonia, with their "numerous impressive earthworks in the form of drainage canals . . . derived their cultural superiority from their original native land. . . . The Cassiquiare, [connecting] the Orinoco and Rio Negro, is partly the result of Arawak canal works" (Birket-Smith 1965, 479).

Tiahuanaco, we might add, is built along the same lines as Metalanim on Micronesia's Panape which is also intersected by canals. Panape, "untold millennia ago" (Von Daniken 1974, 122), was crisscrossed with stone-lined canals 27 to 100 feet wide and capable of passing a modern battleship. "The Venice of the Pacific," Panape is thought to have had at least 50 miles of canals. Kusai, with ruins similar to Panape, also had stone-lined canals, crossing each other at right angles. In New Zealand too the Maori say that early whites, the Moriori, built the irrigation terraces and canals. The Moriori, as we have elsewhere noted, take us back to the earliest possible horizon, and as we will see in chapter 11, p. 438, their DNA turns up in ancient western America. Were Pacific Islanders the first on Earth to construct canals? We have only begun to find these old but sturdy works.

OCEANIC ISLAND CANALS

Where	What
Kosrae	90 canals, some 5 miles long
Tonga	huge, 35-feet-deep, immense canal encircling Mua (pyramids also in the district)
Melanesia	irrigation canals (Perry 1968, 29)
New Guinea	large irrigation canals, dated 10,000 BP, still visible today
Hawaii	irrigation canals built by the Menehune on Kaua'i
Easter Island	passages linked with the sea were once canals (Kolosimo 1973, 143)

*"A highly civilized race" that once lived in the highlands of Colombia constructed systems of irrigation canals. Those people who once inhabited the jungles of San Agustin "built irrigation canals and erected colossal statues" (Wilkins 2000, 184).

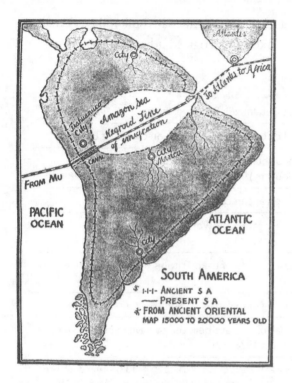

Fig. 7.24. Canals in South America, illustrated by James Churchward (1931a, 23, 86), who claims they are 18,000 years old. This is corroborated in Oahspe: "And to the north land of Uphsic and E'chaung, the still river (canal) Eph'su begins, running to the wide oceans" (The Lords' Third Book 6:1; in the time of Apollo, about 18,000 years ago).

Are prehistoric canal works in the Old World the offspring of the diaspora from Pan? In Central Asia canals were called "karez," east of the Caspian. Churchward discusses dried up canal beds in the Gobi Desert (1931a, 216). And archaeologists have found old canals in the Gobi—were they Uighur works? In India too ingenious canals were built by the Mohenjo governors; according to Valmiki, these people were mighty canal makers, architects, and navigators of large ships.

> Great was the peace, beauty, and glory of Vind'yu in that day. Her rivers and canals coursed the country over, and her industrious sons and daughters, two hundred million, were . . . the pride and glory of the earth. [But wars laid low] all kingdoms, cities, places of sacrifice, and places of learning. And in one hundred years the mighty people of Vind'yu were reduced to beggary and scattered tribes of wanderers. The great canals were destroyed, and the upper and lower country became places of famine and barrenness.
>
> OAHSPE, BOOK OF WARS 25:3, 46:20

In Mesopotamia six thousand years ago, Sumerians built military canals; under Ur-Nammu, waterways linked and irrigated urban settlements.

Where	What
Turkey (Asia Minor)	Canals at Çatalhüyük 9,000 years ago
Arabia	"qanats," or underground irrigation canals, at Bahrain
Egypt	King Necos built wide canals extending to the Arab gulf (4 days journey)*
Greek island of Elba	huge subterranean canals
North Africa & Canary Islands	extensive irrigation network
Tunisia	the ancient people of Lake Tritonis built canals (De Camp 1975, 191)
Italy	Etruscan irrigation canals
Britain	Stonehenge blocks are believed to have been moved by canal (Corliss 1976, 52)

*Even before the time of Menes, Egypt was building canals (Wilkins 2000, 138)—later discovered by airborne infrared sensors. One First Dynasty canal was 375 miles long, running from Abydos to Fayyum; the time frame confirmed in Book of Wars 19:2, which speaks of these "canals, filled with boats carrying produce, fruit and cloth . . ."

These are my chosen, that live in mounds. . . . They are the people of learning. They survey the way for the canals. . . . These are a great people.

OAHSPE, THE LORDS' THIRD BOOK 1:14–15

A French trapper of colonial times who spoke the Indian tongue heard about these long-ago people who built the mounds and canals. "They were teachers, but very, very tiny."

Gus Cahill has written that "the art of building these canals . . . was derived, like architecture and other arts involving the use of mathematics, originally from the Ihin tribes. . . . In the valleys of the Ohio and the Mississippi . . . they have left their traces for us to puzzle over still—the vanished race known to us as the Mound-builders" (1965, 151). So let us move on and find out, once and for all, who the "mysterious moundbuilders" really were.

HUDDLED HOUSES,
HEAVENLY HILLS,
AND HOLY HUTS

I have set aside this chapter to probe arrangements for living—and for communing—among the ancients, which clearly point to a common origin of the holy tribes, as opposed to the many examples of diffusion and other later developments that were explored in the preceding chapter. For it is said that after the Flood,

> in the lands where I will take My people, let them build mounds and walled cities with ladders to enter, after the manner of the ancients. *In all the divisions of the earth,* alike and like shall they build walls ... that beasts and serpents may not enter.
>
> OAHSPE, THE LORDS' FIRST BOOK 2:10 (EMPHASIS ADDED)

In southern Brazil, for example, a dead city found in the wilds was large and regularly laid out, with a walled suburb (Wilkins 2000, 47). In North America, Zuni *walled* towns seemed unusual for Native Americans, although we do find walls also in Georgia, near Macon, the walls encircling sixty acres of Brown's Mount. To the first

Fig. 8.1. Top: Hopi Old Oraibi village in the 1920s, kivas in foreground, clustered dwellings in background. Bottom: A postcard from Hopiland of Walpi Indian village.

Spanish explorers the Zuni village looked as if it had been "crumpled all up together." Similar clustered compounds were found among the Mandans—"like hives clustered together" (Dewhurst 2014, 301). In Mexico's Teotihuacan Valley at the Zacatenco village called Cuanalan, houses from a very early period are found *in clusters* inside walls. Tulum (Mayan) is also a walled city, of sixteen acres, the doorways seemingly built for miniature beings; these "dollhouses" *clustered* together to form a town. In chapter 1 we also found the little people of San Blas, Panama, in the habit of clustering their dwellings, their houses found

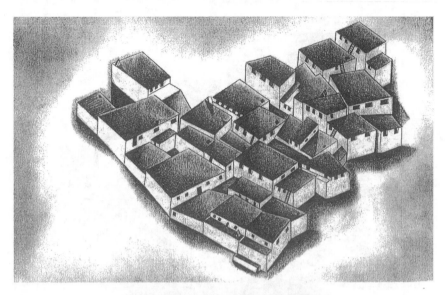

Fig. 8.2. Two figures of Turkish "clustered" town without streets at Çatalhüyük on Konya Plain. Top: With the buildings hard against one another, villagers had to walk across their neighbors' roofs to reach their own quarters. They too had outside defense walls of solid mud-brick and short crawl-through-type doors. Bottom: Flat roof and wooden ladder was the only means of access. (Drawings by Jose Bouvier.)

Fig. 8.3. Some villages were clustered in North Africa. Top: Abandoned Libyan village at Tripolitania. Isn't it interesting that Barry Fell found affinities also between the Zuni and ancient Libyan languages? And as the Libyans are forefathers of the Berbers and Tuaregs, we find the same sort of clustered housing in Morocco. Bottom: Moroccan adobe (attobi) Berber village, almost identical to the pueblos of the American Southwest. (Drawings by Jose Bouvier.)

densely packed together, as in Mexico (at Casas Grande) and Argentina, but also in Scotland on Skara Brae and in Ireland on Skellig Michael.

Çatalhüyük's continuous perimeter wall (no entrance) actually consisted of abutting buildings that clung together. The site on the Anatolian Plateau with an estimated population of five thousand is considered one of the oldest cities in the world, at 8500 BP. Turkey's Nevali Cori, even older at 10,000 BP, was also clustered, as was Hattusa. In fact, the predecessors of the Sumerians, as seen in the Mesopotamian ruins at Choga Manis, also built houses abutted one against the other. We can trace this arrangement all the way back to Gujerat, India—at Dwarka, the ancient houses are clustered tightly, as though seeking protection.

Yet we also find this in Greece; cluster houses and their surrounding walls were called "sacred enclosures" at Zagros, dated to the eighth century BCE. On Cyprus as well, Khirokitia's circular stone houses were "tightly squashed together" (Mithen 2003, 104), not unlike the close-packed houses in the Valley of Djowf in Shomer, Arabia.

Both Philostratus the Elder and Herodotus, the "father of history," wrote of extremely short people in Libya, whose Maxye people claimed to descend from the men of Troy in western Turkey. And, yes, Libya's cluster houses look a great deal like Turkish (Hittite) ones. For more than eighteen thousand years survivors of the flood—whether in Africa, Arabia, Europe, India, Turkey, the Near East, or the Americas—retained the ancient way of protecting their towns.

Fig. 8.4. Left: Libyan "cluster" people put a wheel cross on their pottery. Right: Wheel cross is also seen on Cocle pottery, produced by the ancestors of the clustered San Blas people.

Apartment Houses Five Thousand Years Ago

Many of the same people, as you can see from the foregoing illustrations, tiered their dwellings. In New Mexico and Arizona, some homes ran up to five stories high. The "apartment house" culture of these Pueblos is believed to be as old as five thousand years. Oraibi at Third Mesa (see fig. 8.1a, p. 320) with "its Berber-like houses . . . piled up without mortar" is the traditional place where the Hopi migration ended (Williams 2001, 222). Here, in the heart of Hopiland, the Faithist wheel cross, sign of Creator, is again noted among their ancient petroglyphs.

That migration was from Mexico, so we are not surprised to find similar tiers in places like Guerrero, Mexico, with its three-story adobe buildings, not unlike those of the Incas. In the Yucatán, Puuc-style architecture at Campeche includes some four-story apartments. Again we have similars in far-distant Anatolia, at Derinkuyu, where underground cities entail several-storied houses and rooms that could hold thousands of people. Here in Asia Minor, the Hittites built their towns

Fig. 8.5. Hittites portrayed as very short people: a Hattini depiction of a Hittite king-priest (left), and a Hittite plate (right) in the Swiss Truniger Collection.

on the plan of the sacred tribes—layered dwellings—so much like the Pueblos. And, like the Hopi, the original Hittites were short of stature and pious, descendants of the Good Little People.

Early theorists viewed the Pueblos and their predecessors, the Cliff Dwellers, with their many-storied adobe towns, as descended from the original moundbuilders, a peaceful and industrious people, as are, famously, the Hopi and Zuni. Never on the offensive but systematically defensive, the Pueblos arranged their villages—with six or more tiers— in such a way that doorless houses are stacked one over the other in protective clusters, each tier being set back of the one below, so that the roof of a house below forms the dooryard of the one above it.

Ladders and Walls: Keep Out!

I left the ruins of my cities, which had no gates of entrance, and houses without doors of entrance, that ye might have testimony of this race of [holy people].

OAHSPE, THE LORDS' FIFTH BOOK 4:20

In Turkey the foremost tribes built under the same inspiration—at Göbekli Tepe the enclosures are almost abutting each other and seem also to have been entered from above, an opening set in the roof. The setup is similar at Çatalhüyük, where one entered through the roof by climbing a wooden ladder. For the archaeologist to pass through one interior room to the next, he must crawl through a small doorway. Little people? They also had the wheel cross, giving us one more reason to suspect they shared a mutual heritage with the Pueblos and mound-builders of America.

Not far from Turkey, near Nineveh, at Assyria's Tepe Gawra, settlements of the "Halafian" type were distinctively lacking in streets, and their living quarters were clustered, meaning they were crammed into a beehive complex of rooms—many windowless—with an opening in the roof to permit entrance by ladders. As long ago as 12,000 BP, Mesopotamians at Qermez Dere used ladders to access their subterranean dwellings, something like the Pueblo kivas (Mithen 2003, 425).

Yet the same motifs pop up in the Scottish Shetlands, where the earliest archaeological levels sport strange windowless stone buildings, like a huddle of Inuit igloos, as well as "roundhouses" that left an open space in the roof. At Skara Brae in the Orkneys, north of the Scottish mainland, stands a remarkable Neolithic site of stone houses connected by slab-roofed lanes that are *only 4 feet high.* Doorways here are about 3 feet high ("a mere hatch"). The whole village, apparently occupied by small-statured people, had a low sort of midden mound built up around it, making it a quasi-underground affair. Of unknown origin, this village plan was all fitted together into one compacted mass of houses and passages. Each house had a large central smoke hole in the roof, again reminding us of their Pueblo cousins. The Hopi Indians lived on high mounds (mesas) and built ladders to enter their dwellings through roof holes (rolling back the *nuta,* the straw thatch opening). Entrance through the skylight was reached by ladders, which were pulled up at night or when dangerous animals or an enemy appeared, thus transforming the village into a fairly impregnable fortress. They also provided a roof hole in the *kivas** (semi-underground spirit chambers), where the opening did double duty as roof hatch and smoke hole.

> The skyhole served at once as doorway, chimney, and window.
>
> BRIAN FAGAN, *WORLD PREHISTORY*

Branches off the same trunk, the primitive little people of southern Africa, the Bushmen, built in a like manner, constructing round, windowless walls of stone on the hills near their permanent waters. The structure was roofless; at night they merely climbed over the wall. How like the setup at Peru's Pachacamac and Grand Chimu, north of Trujillo, where the huts could be entered only from the roof.

---

*Khiva is also the name of an ancient city-state in Uzbekistan, inhabited for 10,000 years, and named after its "sun-baked pit-houses where ladders were used to enter from the roof. This is precisely what kivas look like in the Hopi world" (Lehrburger 2015, 251–52).

In all the divisions of the earth . . . My angels shall teach you how to build ladders and how to use them. And . . . at night ye shall take the ladder in after you. . . . And man provided the cities with ladders and he provided the mounds with ladders also.

OAHSPE, FIRST BOOK OF THE FIRST LORDS 3:7 (EMPHASIS ADDED)

In the Mandan origin myth, ascent and descent from the *inner Earth* home was by means of a "grapevine"—was this a rope ladder? "Inner Earth" may simply reflect their living in the "hollow hills" (i.e., *in* the mounds), as in Turkey, where structures were sunk into the hilltop, creating "cellars in the Earth."

The Mysterious Moundbuilders

Honest-to-goodness mounds—"those great piles of earth" heaped up by men and women in the deep past—often translate as "mountains" in the legends of the world's people. For example, when tradition states that the children of Adam and Eve dwelled on the "*mountain* of God" prior to the time of the flood, this is metaphorical of the Ihins, the sacred people, the moundbuilders (Oahspe, The Lords' Fourth Book 3.16). Some of the western tribes regarded them as people from another world who dwelled on Earth for a long season to teach them of the Great Spirit. For thousands of years these holy tribes with a spark of the divine maintained their separateness by living high up on the mounds. In fact, it was once thought that all the pyramids and tumuli of the world were imitations of "the holy mountain" in Eden.

But most of these Edenic mountains were actually the *mounds* of the little people on Pan; the first Garden, after all, was said to be situated on an eminence. Isn't this also why Oceanic tradition says the lost land was hilly—a "land of clay *hills*" (see chapter 11, p. 422, discussing Og)? In Mexico's Codex Cortesianus, Mu is called "the land of earth hills"; the temple site Aka-Pan-a at Tiahuanaco means "hill" in the Aymara language.

Robert Charroux, discussing mounds by the hundreds in the American countryside, wonders "if the real *Land of the Hills* of our Celtic ancestors was perhaps in North America" (Charroux 1972, 90). But the Americans (Guatamans) only *continued* the mound-building tradition of their ancestors ("Adam and Eve") from Pan, just as J. M. Brown deduced that the white inhabitants of Polynesia brought the mound culture to America. In the Marquesas, to build a ceremonial plaza, they cut away the entire side of a knoll to obtain the earth needed. The practice harks back to their ancestors who built their mounds out of earth (and wood). Melanesia's earthen mounds, thought ethnologist W. H. R. Rivers, were raised by a people lost in antiquity. At other "unexplained" mounds in the motherland there still dwell some rather light-brown and even blond natives. New Caledonia, for example, shows signs of a very ancient culture, with its mounds, pillars, canals, and terraces; some of its people are brachycephalic, with light-brown or even blond hair.

Bone fragments taken from huge tumuli in Wisconsin, Illinois, Ohio, and Mississippi show that the builders of these artificial hills were a Europoid type (Kolosimo 1973, 91)—but a vanished race, the extinct Ihins. And if the fourteen-thousand-year-old pottery at Wisconsin's Ross Lake mounds resembles that of Japan's Caucasoid Jomon people, the missing link, the common source, might well be the motherland. Consider only the mounds at Samoa—here, the Pulemalei Mound (among other *flat-topped,* 40-feet-high "star mounds") contains *no burials.* This, we will soon see, signals the *earliest* builders.* On New Caledonia's Isles of Pines, artificial hillocks could be more than thirteen thousand years old. Also with a claim to deep antiquity is the artificial hill in Tonga near Hoteva at the mouth of the Mua Lagoon, with similars in different parts of the island group.

North America

"We are not the first civilized inhabitants of North America," commented John Baldwin under discussion of the ancient moundbuilders in the Ohio and Mississippi Valleys (1869, 54). These early moundbuilders were "white people of great intelligence and skill," offered Josiah Priest in his 1833

---

*Samoa, in other parts of this book, is suggestive of the oldest horizon in Oceania.

Fig. 8.6. Plate 81, Port Pan: Tablet of the Mound Builders, from Oahspe

book *American Antiquities and Discoveries in the West.* This is why some of the most advanced groups, like the Shawnee, came out of Ohio.

The Choctaw Indians, so rich in little people lore, held that a race of diminutive folk, teachers, lived on Earth before them. And who were those little people? They were none other than the mysterious mound-builders who left their own tiny bones and diminutive sarcophagi in Ohio, Tennessee, and Kentucky. Such skeletons, deposited in coffins not more than 4 feet long, were found near Cochocton, Ohio, in an ancient cemetery. They are very numerous, said the earliest report, apparently tenants of a considerable city. Lexington, Kentucky, thought

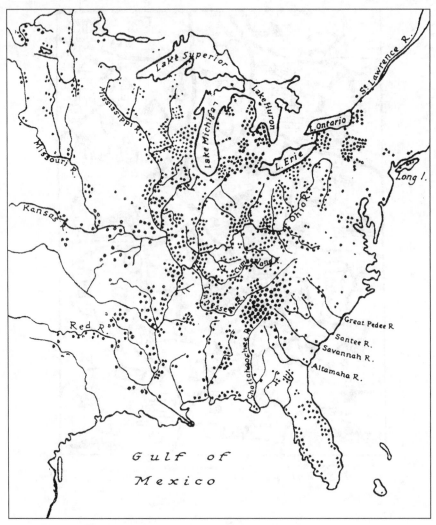

Fig. 8.7. North American mounds, after Cyrus Thomas

historian George W. Ranck, was built on the metropolis of a *lost race* that flourished centuries before the Indians who are themselves a tall people; the early moundbuilders were a short people, rarely over 5 feet tall. In Ohio alone were more than ten thousand man-made hills that were flat topped; platform mounds at Marietta seem to have been built for protection: 30 feet high, their nearly 700-foot-long passage to the river was flanked by 8-foot-tall embankments.

My righteous shall live in mounds of earth, stone, and wood, where the Ugha (serpent, tiger, and all other evil, devouring-beasts) cannot come upon them.

OAHSPE, BOOK OF SAPHAH: AGOQUIM 8

Just as protection is a key to the clustered, walled cities that we examined above, protection was the key to the mounds. Thus we observe that none of the *original* mounds were less than 18 or 20 feet high, for they were meant to be inaccessible. As people of peace, the sacred tribes, wherever they lived, were sworn against war and killing and could defend themselves only by making their homes unreachable against potential invaders or predators. As for large beasts, the reader might recall Minnesota's effigy mound, in the shape of an elephant, or the elephant effigy sculptures found in the mounds at Davenport, Iowa. Now, given that elephants died out in the Western Hemisphere ages ago, this proves not only the great antiquity of the moundbuilders but also the existence of mighty beasts that the little people were up against some twenty thousand years ago. Workers in Ohio and elsewhere have uncovered the remains of elephants, saber-toothed tigers, mastodons, and so forth. Horse bones (at that time long extinct in America) have been found near "artificial hills" in Illinois. Reptiles too appear to have been enormous in the late Paleolithic.

Cruvara, serpent with four legs. This was the lizard species, and in the time of Yi-ha they were large enough to eat twelve full-grown men at a meal. They were of a dark green color, and fifty paces in length.

OAHSPE, BOOK OF SAPHAH: BASIS OF VEDE 50

In the South the Creek Indians said the oldest mounds were built many ages *prior* to their arrival; indeed, most tribes said the moundbuilders were of a different race, the "Little Ones" often remembered as the teachers of their tribal elders. The original moundbuilders—who simply *lived* on the (flat-topped, not conical) mounds—were eventually replaced by others; it was these successors who began to use the mounds

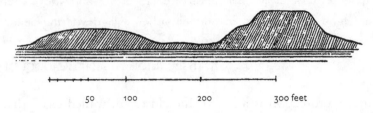

50   100   200   300 feet

*Fig. 8.8. A 37-foot-high Georgia mound. The older mounds were
flat topped, mostly earthen, and better built than later ones.*

as mortuary structures. In the first case, the mounds were simply their homes, not their graves! The later cult of building temples on artificial mounds was based on reverence for the original sacred people—the moundbuilders. So, be it noted that rich burial goods and sepulchral decorations, death masks, and elaborate sarcophagi—none of these extravagances ever pertained to the founders of mound culture, the little people. Indeed, the race that built sepulchral mounds were not little but often tall, like the 7-foot giants who, according to the Lenni Lenape Indians, built mounds, fortifications, and burial places for their warriors. Whereas the Ihin mounds were always high and steep, the giants' mounds, like those near the Missouri River, were often less than 10 feet high and filled with bones. A mound in Ohio that *gently sloped down the hill* contained a "male skeleton nine feet in length" (Dewhurst 2014, 246).

The earlier American mounds were comparable to the Egyptian pyramids to this extent: "no *original* burials were found in the principal chambers of any of the large pyramids" (Zink 1979, 57; emphasis added). But in America, after the disappearance of the Ihins (ca. 5000 BP), the craze for monumental burial structures, usually for chiefs, took hold, big time, with the result that today all the best-known mounds are of this type: Adena, Hopewell, Etowah, Cahokia, Moundsville, and so forth.

In fact, the later moundbuilders have very little in common with the first builders of mounds, the little people. The skeleton of a giant was found near Tennessee's Cumberland River in association with a stone hunting horn and "bloody axes" (Haywood 1923). Obviously, some of the later moundbuilders sacrificed humans, like the bloodthirsty Aztec

A

B

C

Fig. 8.9. a) The conical Miamisburg, Ohio, mound. b) Nineteenth-century painting of a conical mound at Marietta, Ohio. The conical mound, whose peak is obviously unsuitable for living, is of relatively recent date. c) Grave Creek Mound, at Moundsville, West Virginia, is conical, with tombs inside. Dated to about 200 BCE, it would belong to the late Adena Period, which culture some say was founded by tall, white Celts. Though the sandstone tablet found inside the mound is said to be in the Celtic language, other characters match up to Etruscan, Egyptian, Aegean, Scandinavian, Phoenician, Greek, and Tunisian!

sacrificers or the Caddo Indians of yore, who flourished in Texas and built burial mounds for their chiefs, "some of whom appear to have been accompanied by sacrifices" (Grunberg 2014, 10).

In the Southeast the little folk of Cherokee memory were reclusive in their mounds. These tiny Nunnehi/Yunwi Tsunsdi lived throughout the southern ranges and were especially associated with the town of Franklin, North Carolina, which was built on the site of the Cherokee city of Nikwasi, where one can visit the noted "Indian Mound" that once supported the Cherokee sacred council house. The Cherokee did not construct the mounds, however; they had merely found them in place upon migrating to the region. The little people had built a large townhouse *under* (read: *inside*) the Nikwasi mound, and it was claimed that a perpetual flame burned within it. Yes, living was under the earth, to the extent that the Ihins lived on *and in* the mounds, just as the holy little people of Ireland's sidhe mounds lived "underground" in their raths and souterrains.

> *At one time a specific, now vanished, race of "Mound Builders" was supposed to have existed. Today we know that this is wrong. All these mounds . . . scattered across the country were constructed by the ancestors of the Indians.*
>
> Kaj Birket-Smith, *The Paths of Culture*

> *We know nothing about them. They were here before the red man.*
>
> A Missouri Indian, when asked about ancient mounds and graveyards (quoted in Corliss 1978)

It has become increasingly clear that we will never solve the "problem of the moundbuilders" if we persist blindly in the "Red Man" theory. The oldest mounds in Fulton, Ohio, belonged to a "race [that was] not nomadic, as were the Red Indians" (Wilkins 2000, 133). And as William Perry saw it, "although the culture of the mound-builders shows manifest signs of continuity with that of the Indians," some of the arts are strikingly different, such as "dolmen-like burial chambers made of large slabs . . . carved stone images . . . pottery heads and death masks . . . all of which are unknown among the Indians" (Perry 1968, 14).

A regional chronicler here in my own part of northeastern Georgia wrote:

> Scientists say that the Indians must have been the mound builders.
> . . . However, the Mound Builders were a prehistoric race that lived
> here before the Indians. In my childhood I used to hear of a legend,
> told by the Indians to the first white settlers—namely, that a race of
> people lived in the valleys of the Tennessee River before them called
> the "Little Men," and that they were the mound builders." (Ritchie
> 1948, 5)

Those little men of course were the Ihins. Note the *hin* in Olig-hin, which was the name of the river central to the first moundbuilder civilization.

Mounds South of the Border

"The practice of building [North American] mounds came from Mexico" (Perry 1968, 13). Mayan mounds, called kus (note the *ku*), are found in abundance not only all over the jungles but also at many well-known sites such as Teotihuacan, Chichén Itzá, and Palenque and also the "artificial plateau" at San Lorenzo in Olmec country and the huge oval mound at Cuicuilco near Tlal-pan (note the *pan*) in southern Mexico, "erected by an unknown prehistoric people" (Cohane 1969, 170). In Guatemala "it is hardly possible to walk a hundred yards without finding tree-covered mounds" (Charroux 1972, 80). Large mounds, up to 50 feet high are also found at Tikal and in Honduras as well.

Our moundbuilders, significantly enough, seem to have first appeared along the *west* coast of Chiapas—people who cultivated the earth and made sophisticated pottery, just as archaeologists have found "magnificent ceramics" at Mitla, Mexico, in Mound A, some 40 feet high, clearly a "man-made elevation" (Adams 1991, 334). "Hundreds of thousands of earthen tumuli covered the Mexican countryside . . . the Mexicans [later] transformed the most notable tumuli into pedestals for their temples" (Charroux 1972, 67).

Moundbuilders in northern Brazil at Marajo Island also produced exceptional ceramics. Arawak centers along the Amazon and Bolivian lowlands show artificial mounds. Mounds in Arica, Chile (with the telltale *Ari*), can run as high as 120 feet. Tiahuanaco's chain of artificial hills are very flat on top; buildings, thinks Erich Von Daniken, are probably concealed beneath them (1970, 23). Peru's mound-studded site at Caral has been called "the oldest town in the New World" (Coppens 2012, 132); flat topped and at least 17 feet high, these are "not natural hills." The flat summit is to be found in the motherland, at Tonga, where "nothing is known" about the history of its artificial hill (made of lumps of coral) that rises 15 feet (Perry 1968, 24).

Mounds Everywhere

Dispersed from Pan, the mound-building culture was everywhere of a like nature. "The mounds of Europe and Asia . . . [and] America . . . were made in the same way" (Donnelly 1985, 136). Studying Ohio's mounds, local sage Caleb Atwater also came away with a sense of the underlying unity of mankind. All human cultures, he cognized in *Description of the Antiquities Discovered in the State of Ohio and Other Western States,* vol. 1, seem to have radiated from a single point. They came to Asia, they came to Africa, they came to Russia, they came to America, they came to Egypt, and their "similarity of works almost all over the world indicates that [they] sprang from one common origin." Indeed, it was their arrival, their very presence that insured the progress of humanity "in the first ages, after the Dispersion, rising wherever the posterity of Noah came."

Be it a mound in America, a tumulus in Scandinavia, a barrow in England, a sidhe in Ireland, a tepe in Greece, a tell in western Asia, or a kurgan in Russia, these structures were of the same stamp. William Pidgeon, in his *Traditions of Deecoodah and Antiquarian Researches,*

1852, concluded that Noah and his sons must have built mounds on every continent. (Deecoodah was Pidgeon's Winnebago informant.)

Today's academic scholars sniff at such conclusions, happy in most instances to chalk up similarities to coincidence. But the question remains: Why were these mounds everywhere held sacred—like Ireland's sacred Hill of Tara and Hill of Ward? Irish annals speak of the Eire, the Firbolg little people living on their unapproachable "mountain" (i.e., mounds), the Great Refuge of the Righteous. The Daoine Sidhe, the wee bodies, were hailed as the oldest and finest families of "perfected men." The Irish peasantry held a deep and abiding tradition of these "fairy mounds," the green sidhe (raths and souterrains) built by the "People of the Hills," the little Picts and Danes and Tuatha De Danaan—the immortals. What's more, to the Hibernian or Caledonian eye, the American mounds were a carbon copy of the countless "hollow hills"* dotting the Irish and Scottish landscape, once inhabited by the dignified leprechauns.

Out in the Orkneys, a genteel race of wee bodies inhabited these "Islands of Wisdom." Maes Howe in the Orkneys has a 36-foot-high earthen mound covering a passage grave, which is the same height as Newgrange's mound, the latter, it is thought, belonging to the legendary Tuatha De Danaan. Newgrange (see fig. 7.11, p. 294), 30 miles north of Dublin on the River Boinne, is built on a 45-foot-high mound. The largest and greatest of Ireland's sidhes, it is flat topped, the ground plan forming the shape of a Celtic cross, the wheel cross—the most distinctive signature of the lost race. The site, unsurprisingly, is devoted to the "Son of the Good God," the complex said to belong to the fairy folk, meaning the distinguished Tuatha De Danaan.

There is hardly a place on Earth *without* mounds; the ancient Redin people in the Maldives, a tall, white-skinned folk with blue eyes and hooked noses were moundbuilders who erected temples and cities. They were among the early seafaring stonemasons, *not of European origin,* their forerunners found in Easter Island (Childress 1988, 81). The early

---

*The Picts' houses, so common in the north of Scotland, were sunk beneath the surface. On digging into the green mound, a series of large chambers open up.

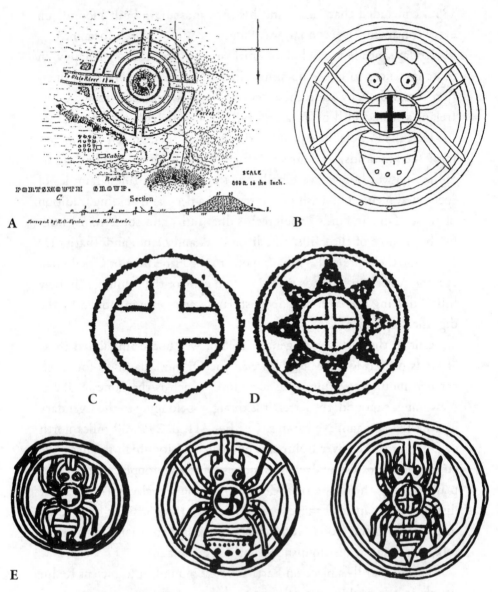

Fig. 8.10. a) Ohio ground plan in shape of wheel cross. b) Ohio scarab with wheel cross at center. c) Design from Spiro Mounds, Oklahoma. d) Symbol of Mu. The Celtic Cross (a.k.a. wheel cross, ball cross, sun wheel, etc.) is one of the most ancient signs of Creator—not merely a glyph of the four quarters of the compass, nor of the four seasons, nor of the sun: the emblem was sacred long before the advent of sun worship. e) Three images found on pottery in the American mounds.

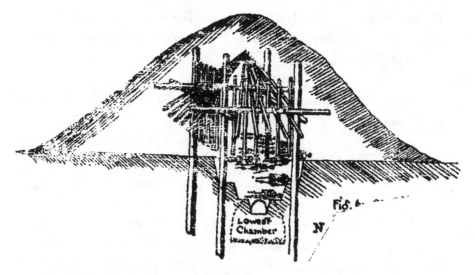

Fig. 8.11. The kurgans of Siberia are only about 8 feet high, though some Scythian burial mounds in Russia and eastern Europe are very large. This one is in the Kuban region, at Kostromskaya; in the lowest chamber lay the chief, above him were more than a dozen people who accompanied him into death.

Jomon of Japan also built huge mounds; we find similars in Central Europe* and many parts of Russia and Scandinavia, the mound folk of the latter area said to be 4 feet tall with pale, translucent skin. In fact, geologist Robert Schoch has recently written about a huge "ancient artificial earthen mound," 34 feet in height, "the largest human-made mound in Western Norway. . . . It has never been excavated" (2014, 38). The oldest legends of Norway speak of the mound folk as elves of great skill; they are the master smiths and shape-shifters of the Eddas.

We should also include the dwellings of the white and brown dwarfs in the Nine Hills of Rugen, which are all small mounds; nor should we forget the tumuli of Africa or the ancient mound fields of Bahrain on the Persian Gulf where archaeologists unearthed sites "associated in local legend with Noah" (Cohane 1969, 115), also thought to be

---

*The Greek and Turkish tepe mounds contain *sanctuaries,* not burials (see "Tepes," p. 344), just as the mounds recently discovered by satellite imagery in Kazakhstan are quite empty.

"Dilmun," western Asia's Garden of Eden. Today ancient mound works are also known in Egypt, Jordan, and the Levant, where Tell Ashareh still stands 70 feet high.

> *All the sacred history of Egypt is based on a primitive mound.*
>
> ANTOINE GIGAL,
> "SECRETS OF THE SERAPEUM AT SAQQARA"
> (KREISBERG 2012, 232)

There are countless round mounds in Iran and Iraq, otherwise known as the "leveled mountains" or "artificial hills" of the Sumerians. These "startling prominences" on the plain between the Tigris and Euphrates were flat topped with steep sides. In the nineteenth century French consul in Mosul Paul E. Botta had a chance to ride out to the round mounds surrounding the city and could not resist the urge to dig. This was the first excavation of Kuyunjik and first discovery of cuneiform tablets. Then in 1842, Botta met British diplomat Austen Henry Layard and told him of his finds. Layard, traveling out to the desert from his own government post in Mosul, marveled at the line of lofty Assyrian mounds, which he judged to be the first great settlement of the region. Indeed, the Sumerians called them Du-ku ("holy mounds," note the telltale *ku*) and regarded them as the birthplace of the gods. In northeast Syria some mounds tower nearly 90 feet above the plain; Tell Mozan is only one of numerous artificial hills in the area.

Similarities among Moundbuilders Worldwide

"The strong resemblance," mused an early American investigator, Ohio's Caleb Atwater, "between the works in Scotland and ours, I think no man will deny" (Silverberg 1968, 69). In fact the mounds and "clusters" and outer walls and roof holes appear in many other parts of the world—Old and New—each adapting the protective design in its own way. Nevertheless, the measurements of the mounds were almost identical in Mesopotamia and Ohio/Tennessee, their flat-topped mounds built to the cardinal points. Likewise were Babylonian/Assyrian examples of cloth also "almost identical" to pieces found in the Ohio mounds (Dewhurst 2014, 243–45, 326).

A similar result was obtained from craniometric comparisons. Barry Fell was able to match skulls of Tennessee's ancient moundbuilders with look-alikes in the Philippines—all were *Homo sapien pygmaeus*. Yet decades before Fell published his finds, it had been noted that "the dwarfishness [of the world's little people] . . . who have retained so many traits in common . . . suggests that all of these far-flung groups may be linked in a common ancestry" (Gladwin 1947, 44). Indeed, other workers have connected these prehistoric Tennessee, Ohio, and Kentucky moundbuilders to populations in Malaysia, Fiji, and the Sandwich Islands, their common artifacts "clearly of a Polynesian character . . . the North Americans, Polynesians, and Malays were formerly the same people or had one common origin" (Ellis 1969, 122). Most recently, Steven Sora has noted "the great similarity between the mound building of the Midwest and that of the northern isles of Japan" (Sora 2014, 26, 61–62).

In fact, the common stock goes back to diluvial times. After the Flood of Waters, there appeared mound-building people all over the world, survivors from the lost lands of the Pacific. Writers have remarked the sameness of the tumuli seen everywhere from the lakes of Canada to Mexico to "the icy promontories of Kamschatcka [*sic*] through the barren steppes of Tartary, the level plains of Russia, and all the northern regions of Europe" (Corliss 1976, 86). In the same way have the tells of Mohenjo Daro been linked to the American mounds, which in turn bear resemblance to work of the Celts, Danes, Scythians, Cretans, Chinese, Berbers, and Hebrew.

Not only was the Star of David found among the American mounds, but, like the Hebrews, the earliest Americans had first fruit ceremonies, circumcision, and rites of purification, as well as similar holy days and commandments. As mentioned, Hebrews and Algonquins were Faithists circa 11,000 BP—they shared similar words, for example, king (*melek* and *malku*) and priest (*bileam* and *balaam*) and praise (*allelujah* and *halulaez*). Early European observers noticed that the Cherokee people tended to speak without hardly moving the mouth. "Preserve ye the sounds that man maketh in the throat and without the tongue and lips" (Oahspe, Arc of Noe, The Lord's First Book 1:57). The root of the tongue is more active in these languages; it is easier to pronounce Hebrew and Algonquin allowing the sound to escape with the mouth nearly closed.

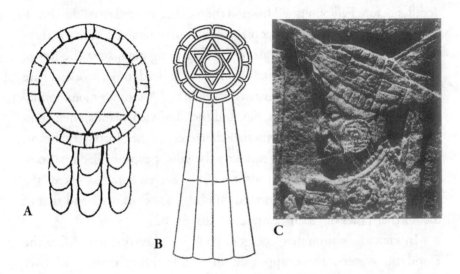

Fig. 8.12. a) Native American mukagawin (note the Mu, which syllable, as seen in chapter 9, so often indicates spiritual authority): "the prophet shall have a Mukagawin, the true sign of poverty. . . . For whom I have made to live in poverty in this world, I will exalt in heaven. I have made only the poor to be My prophets" (Oahspe, Book of Saphah: Agoquim 11). b) Look-alike cosmogonic diagram of the land of Mu, which Churchward says can be traced back 35,000 years. c) At Mayan Campeche, the stela shows their flood hero wearing a boat-shaped hat, while his earplug shows the Star of David, which is normally associated with King Solomon; nevertheless it also appears on the Stone of Uxmal. Cyrus Gordon speculates that King Solomon's fleets, which the Bible tells us went off to a distant gold-bearing land, may have gone to the Rocky Mountains during the early Iron Age,* corresponding to Solomon's time (1973, 146–47).

---

*Prehistoric iron making in Ohio was discovered at Spruce Hill in Ross County, with traces of copper smelting and casting.

Advanced Cultures Living on Mounds

Although living in the so-called Stone Age, the moundbuilders possessed a culture quite alien to most who dwelled in that archaic period; the moundbuilders were, for one thing, sufficiently advanced to maintain contact with distant countries. For another, tablet drawings found in the Ohio Valley indicate knowledge of fetal development and surgery (Dewhurst 2014, 245). Because the *earliest* moundbuilders are a lost but advanced race, we can better understand why, at Ross Lake, Wisconsin, extremely ancient pottery of superior workmanship is found *under* layers of much cruder pottery. Churchward, in a statement that always struck me as amusing but spot-on, declared that "North Americans were highly civilized and were experts in the arts and sciences, tens of thousands of years before these idiots and degenerates of Europe existed" (Churchward 2011, 172). Which is to say, whereas Guatama was settled immediately after the Flood (i.e., 24,000 BP), Europe remained a barbaric region, even fifteen thousand years after the Flood.

The signature of all ancient high culture was agriculture; right in the area of those Midwestern mounds archaeology has located the earliest American cultigens such as squash and sunflower. Indeed, all the oldest mounds are located in alluvial regions, which afforded ample scope of horticulture, capable of supporting a large permanent population. Yes, the earliest horizon in North America boasted cities and urban centers. "Most of the major moundbuilder sites had roads, gates, and walls surrounding them . . . [as well as] sewage systems and canals. . . . In some cases the towns were also manufacturing centers and show signs of high trade and commerce of great sophistication" (Dewhurst 2014, 168).

One passionate Americanist wrote, knowingly, that "the mound builders were *distinct from any of the other North American tribes.* . . . Their pearl-encrusted garments, their finely woven textiles . . . prove that they were . . . far in advance of the Indian tribes" (Verrill 1927, 21; emphasis added). Distinctly un-Indian were mound artifacts such as inscribed tablets, hieroglyphic writing, telescopic tubes, the science of surveying, astronomical calendars, glass beads, and batik weaving, along with the remains of metallurgy, architecture, and temple pyramids.

No Amerind tribe built such immense, carefully designed mounds or possessed such high-quality utensils and ornaments. Written tablets of unknown origin have been unearthed in North America suggesting great age; in the nineteenth century an inscribed slate wall was uncovered during coal operations in Ohio. These undeciphered hieroglyphics had lain 100 feet below the surface (Steiger 1974, 51). That's deep (i.e., old).

And why are historians apparently oblivious to mound-building cultures *in the Old World*? America, as we know it, is a young country; so her mounds were still in place when Europeans came to these shores a mere five hundred years ago. The Old World, on the other hand, *is* old, much of her landscape greatly modified over the millennia. Also, large portions of Asia have never seen the archaeologist's spade. A 20-foot-high mound excavated in Thailand is a single example, out of three hundred other *uncovered* mounds in Thailand; near Ban Chiang, this mound has the world's oldest bronze artifacts and fabulous ceramics. I do not think it coincidental that twelve-thousand-year-old skeletons in Thailand "resemble those of Polynesians" (Joseph 2006, 231). This is but one of many missed clues that would lead us back to the motherland of man.

The sacred heights initiated by the moundbuilders have another aspect, and these are the tepes—exalted *in both hemispheres*.

Tepes

Isn't it interesting that places called "tepe" in both the Old and New Worlds were also situated on eminences and occupied by a priestly caste? In Troy and Sumeria, *tepe* translated as "hill"; Cayonu Tepe-si (in Turkey) is a mound. Meanwhile, across the pond, in the Quechua language of Mexico, *tepeu* means "lord of sacred heights" (Tepeu is also a Mayan name for the Creator). A hint of the deep antiquity of tepe comes from Mexico's Cerro de Tepecalte, which is considered the oldest monument in the Americas. In the Pacific itself, Tepeu is the name of one of the oldest ceremonial platforms on Easter Island. In the Marquesan archipelago we find the name of various rises beginning with *tep*, like Tepakeho Tohua; in northern Tahiti, Tepo-rionu'a. Even in North America, *tepe* means "tower" (in the Cheyenne language).

Some of us have heard of a few of Mexico's tepes: Popoca-tepe-l (volcanic), Chapul-tepe-c ("grasshopper hill"), Tutu-tepec ("Hill of the Bird," a Mixtec center), Tzaltzitepec ("Hill of Shouting"), Tlahchival-tepe-tl ("Artificial Hill" at Cholula), Tehuan-tepe-c, Tepexpan, Tepe-xi, Xilo-tepe-c, Ix-tepe-te, Citla-tepec, Coa-tepec, Huas-tepec, Tepeji del Rio, Tepeaca, and Tepexijeno. In Nicaragua we have Ome-tepe Island and the town of Jino-tepe; in El Salvador is the Llama-tepec volcano. In Amazonia, Tepe Quem is another (extinct) volcano, and Wei-Tepu means "sun-mountain."

In the Old (Turkic) and New (Nahuatl) Worlds, we can see that tepe has the same meaning—hill or high place—often designating a mountain enclave, a sanctuary. The "Land of the Hills of our Celtic ancestors," thought Robert Charroux, "may well be in Mexico where barrows and tumuli are numbered in tens of thousands." These he relates to the legendary Sidhe "people of the hills" in Greater Ireland, "where every virtue [was] practiced . . . everyone happy there" (1972, 71, 93). But judging from the spread of this word *tepe,* isn't it more likely that a shared root, a mother language, is at play, rather than an influence going from America to Europe or vice versa? After all, even in Malaysia tebe-w is the sacred hut erected by the Batek for ritual singing; in this connection, Frank Joseph has found Argentine pottery adorned with line drawings that duplicate Malay themes. To complete the circuit, Joseph also connects Argentina's standing stones to the twelve-thousand-year-old pillars at Göbekli Tepe—by virtue of their corresponding designs and geometric patterns. These South American menhirs show affinity not only with Göbekli (Anatolia's "Navel Hill") but also with Polynesia's "Navel of the World." In which case Polynesia's Ahu *Tepeu* may indeed be the alpha dog.

It seems to me that the sacred tepe moved westward through the Orient under the influence of the Sons of Jaffeth. Earlier writers spoke of important ruins near the eastern shore of the Caspian Sea at a place called Gomush-*tepe.* Here were seen the remains of a great wall and aqueduct, ruins that extended even into China. Not too far from China is the monastery of Adzhina Tepe (in the Vaksha Valley of Tajikistan). In what looks like a westward-moving swath, the next landmark is

Fig. 8.13. A Sialk-style bowl (left) painted with the ancient sign of Creator, the ball cross; note the similarity to the Mexican wheel cross (right), this one from the Xochicalo Pyramid, which Churchward calls the "Tian Chihans," symbol of the Four Great Primary Forces of the Infinite. It is no coincidence that most of the Western Hemisphere's tepes are in Mexico (see "The Hub: Central America," p. 204).

Balalik Tepe in southeast Uzbekistan. Next is Tillya Tepe ("Golden Hill") in northwest Afghanistan, thought to be an ancient fire temple. Persia follows in the westward march with its many Tepe-named monastic sites. Pottery associated with Tepe Sialk, near Tehran, shows a familiar motif of the sacred tribes—the wheel cross. These wheels can still be seen by the roadsides in parts of China and India.

> As this wheel is without beginning or end, so is the Creator. . . . Thus spake Zarathustra: Let the wheel of My name be by the roadside, that he who passeth, may turn it, in remembrance of the I AM. This shall be a prayer . . . and I will hear them.
>
> OAHSPE, BOOK OF SAPHAH: INTERPRETATION 9

Mesopotamia and adjacent regions are loaded with archaeological tepes, including Assyrian ones (Tepe Yorgan, Tepe Gawra, Sultan Tepe) and Sumerian ones (Geoy Tepe, Tepe Asiab). The abundance of tepes ends in Asia Minor* (Turkey) with its Kuz Tepe, Kul Tepe,

---

*In Europe there is also the Albanian Tepe-lene and the Greek tepes, though these were usually singled out for kingly burials.

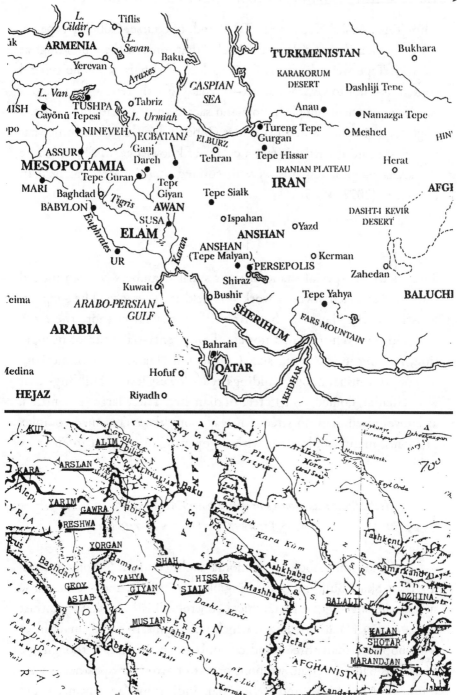

Fig. 8.14. Numerous tepe sites seen in two maps of Central Asia; some of these mounds have been excavated.

Alim Tepe, Arslan Tepe, Kara Tepe, and, of course, Göbekli Tepe.

"It is likely," muses Robert Schoch, "that some of these buildings at Göbekli Tepe were the locus for a variety of rituals. . . . The general consensus—not to say it is correct—is that Göbekli Tepe was a religious site, a very ancient temple, a holy and sacred spot, a series of shrines, a pilgrimage site. . . . When I consider Göbekli Tepe, the first thing that comes to mind is that this was a center of knowledge. . . . Even before the archaeological remains were discovered . . . the area was held in reverence" (2012, 45–51).

Tholoi

Thanks to the special shape of their spirit chambers, we can indeed trace those ancients whose work was held in reverence. The shape in question is the "beehive" hut. Assyria's Tepe Gawra (note the *tepe*), near old Nineveh, revealed no less than twenty-six strata of occupation, making it a very old site. Considered "Halaf" (pre-Sumerian), it sported unusual adobe buildings at its lowest level—buildings that were circular, domed, and 15 feet in diameter. These large settlements, as above noted, had no streets; it was more like a crammed complex of rooms, many windowless, with an opening in the roof to enter by ladders.

> *Tell Halaf was Noah's original postdiluvian camp.*
> JOHN PILKEY, *THE ORIGIN OF THE NATIONS*

In Turkey the elaborate ceremonial architecture at Cayonu, including their Skull Building (indicating blood sacrifice), and the immense size of the site suggest hierarchical control. This is in sharp contrast to the earlier Halafian villages, which were egalitarian and small, most with no more than three hundred souls—Faithist size. Although the Halafians had copper, no weapons of war or arrows or spearheads were found at Arpachiyah and Tell Halaf, indicating "an advanced and peaceful people," as Mary Settegast put it in *When Zarathustra Spoke*. They sought, as followers of the prophet Zarathustra, to promote and nurture the religion. . . . Excavators have found the Halaf culture to have been characterized by a great many small and highly autonomous communities. . . . Zarathustra's followers had no distinction of occupation or class—an egalitarian arrangement . . . [also involving] more private ritual activity. . . . The Zoroastrian religion is known for a scarcity of sacred architecture . . . [exhibiting] the virtual absence of recognizable religious structures . . . or ceremonial architecture. (2005, 72–73)

Ah, but their fine domed huts *were* their religious structures and ceremonial architecture! Settegast goes on to mention the Halafian founders of Umm Qseir in northeast Syria: here, around Aleppo, one can still see beehive-shaped houses, and they are rather like others in the ancient Near East, such as the earliest houses in Jordan, which were dome shaped (10,000 BP). In Iraq too, nine-thousand-year-old Yarim Tepe (note the *tepe*) was a town with active obsidian traders, copper, impressive pottery, farming—and a few small and round domed buildings. Such tholoi, as they are called, were also discovered at Babylonia's Uruk III. Perhaps the best known of these ancient domes are those at Arpachiyah

Fig. 8.15. Halafian painted pottery from Arpachiyah in northern Iraq

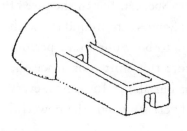

Fig. 8.16. A tholos at Tell Arpachiyah, near Mosul; the 7,000-year-old site was considered an elite ritual center.

on the Turko-Syrian frontier; true to form, they are windowless.

"Arpachiyah" actually may be a biblical name. Abraham was Noah's descendant through *Arpachshad*. The holy lineage, telescoped, was from Noah to Shem to Arpachshad to Eber to Nahor to Abraham. Now the tholoi at Arpachiyah, which was a well-organized settlement with cobbled streets, were impressive, up to 32 feet across—yet windowless and completely empty. That emptiness is significant; as we will see, it was nothing more than a gathering place.

The town itself contained the pottery and distinctive amulets and figurines of the Halafian people; especially notable are their obsidian carvings. Perhaps the Halafians were one and the same as the gentle shepherd kings who "lived in peace, wandering about, making trinkets, which they oft exchanged with the inhabitants of cities" (Oahspe, Book of Wars 21:4). Their ancestors in Persia had once been the principal seers of their day, "And nowhere in all the world did man prosper so greatly in the Osirian philosophy as he did in Par'si'e . . . most of all among the Shepherd Kings" (Oahspe, The Lords' Fifth Book 6:35). What we want to explore is the relationship between that prosperity and their humble domed buildings.

Turkish tholoi, at the eight-thousand-year-old Hittite settlement of Hattusa, were also windowless, as they were at Çatalhüyük, the latter a well-known Anatolian site as old as Neolithic Jericho. Here were uncovered the world's earliest landscape paintings, along with the oldest pieces of finely woven cloth. Çatalhüyük had as many as sixty-three windowless cult buildings—but only 103 dwellings—suggesting a center of worship.

But by the time the tholoi cult spread from western Asia to Oman, Libya, Egypt, Crete, Cyprus, and Greece their purpose changes radically; no longer a holy gathering place, the beehive huts are now converted into *tombs*. Temples are derived from tombs, declared the great English sociologist and Darwinist Herbert Spencer. But in the case of the tholoi, I think it was just the opposite! Somewhere around the sixth or seventh millennium it became popular to bury important persons under mounds and even megaliths. Before this shift took place the pyramids in Polynesia "were not used for burial. . . . In Samoa, every householder was a priest. . . . The priestly class was not the powerful

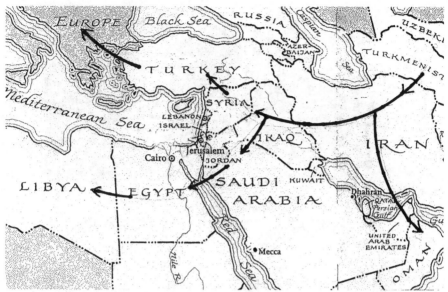

Fig. 8.17. Map of tholoi swath across the Near East, from Turkmenistan to Turkey. Note that the tholoi swath closely matches the tepe sweep, as seen in fig. 8.14, p. 347.

body it was in other groups" (Anderson 1928, 458)—these other groups being the builders of the *langi,* the royal tombs. But the Samoan temples, *fale-aitu,* were not used for burial in earlier times (see the discussion in chapter 11, p. 426, where Samoa is likewise drawn as the oldest of Polynesian societies). Empty domes have also been found at Panape in Micronesia.

Just like the mounds, the tholoi were turned in to tombs—in Bulgaria, Croatia, Italy, Spain, Portugal, and Brittany, as well as Laos and China.* But when excavators find the supposed "tombs" empty (i.e., no bones), they conclude that they must be of the older type, which is to say, the old windowless oracle chambers built solely for the gathering of the faithful. Such were the first tholoi.

---

*Mound graves became all the rage in China, Korea, and Japan, with their grand imperial tombs. The custom of erecting a mound of earth above the illustrious grave straddled the Stone and Bronze Ages in Europe, Russia, and Central Asia, as well as in the eastern woodlands of North America.

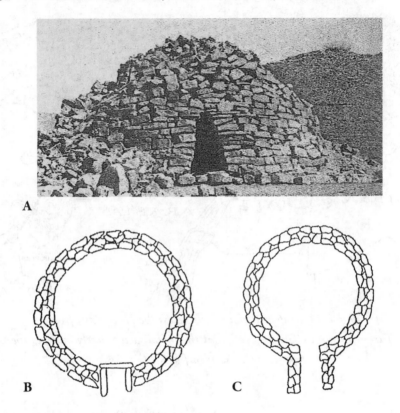

Fig. 8.18. a) Third millennium BCE beehive tomb in Oman. b) Libyan tomb from Cyrene. c) Cretan tholos-tomb. All the passage graves of southeast Europe appear to be derived from the Cretan round tombs. The Egyptian versions were oven-shaped tombs with vaulted roofs.

In dark chambers the angels of heaven [came]. . . . And these angels taught mortals . . . the mysteries of spirit communion; how to sit in circles and in crescents . . . how to attract righteous spirits.

OAHSPE, BOOK OF WARS 7:6

When archaeologists found tholoi that were completely empty, they drew a blank. "Their origin and significance cannot be explained. . . . It is very difficult to imagine what their exact function was" (Silverberg 1968, 69). And so the guessing began. Were they granaries or store-houses, like the *serdab* chambers found in many Egyptian pyramids?

Although it was known that the serdab was built for the soul, or Ka, many Egyptologists still viewed them as storage places, like the underground storehouses in royal tombs. In America the tholoi found in Upton, Massachusetts, were dubbed "colonial root cellars" by archaeologists. But why do these humble "root cellars" follow the stately keyhole plan, whereby the chambers were approached through rectangular corridors, called dromos, as seen in the Arpachiyah structure? Because they were consecrated chambers; entrance was guarded.

This "keyhole" arrangement is found also among America's Southeastern tribes, where, for example, the entrance to the Cherokee council house (a rotunda) was at the end of a 6-foot-long hallway. The same plan, called *yacatas,* was used in Mexico at Michoacan and Monte Alban. But here they were *tombs,* the kings buried with considerable pomp, reflecting the ineluctable shift from the gentle, egalitarian chamber of worship to bloated sepulchres for a pampered elite. Quite a change.

In the northern parts of the British Isles we can deduce the original purpose of these beehive domes. In Ireland, next to Newgrange's "fairy mounds" and 4300-year-old beehive graves, we find genuine tholoi, identified as the *oracular* shrines of the Dagda (Tuatha De Danaan). In the same vein, anchorites are the presumed builders of the beehive houses common at other Irish and Scottish megalithic sites. Indeed, all the way from the Orkneys to Spain we find passage graves with corbeled roofs. The Spanish dromos can be up to or even slightly exceed 30 yards long.

Before Thy sacred altar will I come, knowing Thy angels will come also. Yea, they shall teach me Thy decrees.

OAHSPE, BOOK OF SAPHAH: ARABINIA RITES AND CEREMONIES 15

We must conclude that the ancient tholoi found empty, with neither bones nor weapons nor articles of any kind, were built to the specifications of spirit communion. Windowless, they were intentionally dark. "The ancient prophet caused the worshippers to sit in the dark" (Oahspe, Book of Cosmogony and Prophecy 11:13). Significantly, the *earliest* American mounds contained no weapons; the altar-containing mounds on the Ohio River were destitute of remains. The same can

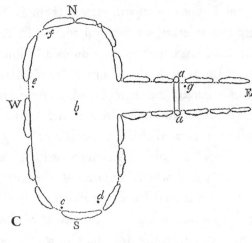

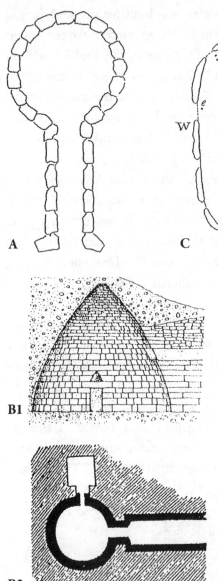

Fig. 8.19. Imitators kept the sacred keyhole design used by the ancients. a) The 14-foot-long entryway to the Upton, Massachusetts, tholos was built of megalithic stones; other beehive structures in New England were found in northeast Connecticut and at New Hampshire's Mystery Hill. b) Greece's Treasury of Atreus shows (1) the beehive, and (2) the keyhole plan; near Pylos one again finds tholoi used as tombs, probably of the same age, 1500 BCE, as the great Mycenaean tombs. c) Chambers with dromos in Danish Bronze Age tumulus.

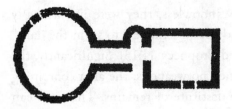

Fig. 8.20. Plan of secluded chambers at Pygmie Isle, Scotland, where one chamber is circular (tholos) and the other oblong (dromos).

be said of the windowless domes that Colonel P. H. Fawcett found in Brazil—completely empty, their interior free from the grime associated with all cooking or illuminating agencies. And this tells us they were not ordinary dwellings; they had a different purpose, an otherworldly purpose—to link up with the immortals, just as the "dark circles" of nineteenth-century Spiritualism entailed sitting *en rond,* forming a kind of etheric battery.

No Window on the World, but on the Otherworld

"Oracle structures [were] made without windows, so Jehovih's angels could come in sar'gis [apparition] and teach His Holy Doctrines" (Oahspe, Book of Wars 21:4). This sacred structure was known as the "well-covered house," designed for the rites of communion practiced by the moundbuilders, in which space the angels could come and teach.

The Egyptian [temple] had a Dark Room, so also the Maya.
JAMES CHURCHWARD, *THE LOST CONTINENT OF MU*

The key to this unique architecture is the exclusion of light. Utter darkness. These stark, windowless domes, whether made of earth, stone, or wood, are actually found all across the globe. Ancient Celtic temples had

Fig. 8.21. Sar'ji/sarguz from Oahspe's Tablet of Semoin and plate 83: Temple of Darkness. Sar'ji refers to a materialized angel, or to a mortal capable of seeing such. Its cognate sarguz refers to a pyramid, a building with chambers for sprit communion.

no windows. In Africa, tholoslike structures are called *masobo,* meaning "ghost house," indicating communion with spirits. "By inspiration, the Lords established spirit chambers . . . where the prophets sat to learn the decrees of the Lord" (Oahspe, Book of Apollo 14:10; indicating a period of time at least 16,000 years ago).

We realize that almost all of the domelike buildings of the ancient day, imitating the humble ghost houses of their forebears, were dedicated to otherworldly matters. Such were the onion-domed temples, mosques, tombs, mausoleums, observatories, ceremonial chambers, spirit huts, and council rooms—like Lebanon's Domes of the Prophets or Sumeria's Sacred Hut or the *iwans* of Persia or the vaulted roof of Ctesiphon or Egypt's serdab. Several millennia ago in Egypt, to attain the degrees of Anubi, rites and ceremonies were held in *dark* chambers.

Let man build consecrated chambers in My temples so that My spirits may come and explain [the heavens].

OAHSPE, BOOK OF SAPHAH: OSIRIS 56

Indeed, the Pyramid Age itself may have been inaugurated through God Osiris, who spoke directly to King Thothma (pharaoh) saying:

Provide thou a dark chamber and I will come and teach thee. Thothma provided a dark chamber and then Osiris . . . came to him, saying . . . In the form of a pyramid shalt thou build a Temple of Astronomy . . . measure for measure, will I show thee every part . . . with chambers within . . . suitable for thyself and [other] . . . adepts.

OAHSPE, BOOK OF WARS 48:26–27

In Peru the Castle of Chavin de Huantar has "three floors, each of which has its own system of ventilation [but] neither doors nor windows. This suggests it represents a space-ship" (Kolosimo 1973, fig. 30). However, the absence of doors and windows, rather than indicating a spaceship, more likely signals the ancient temples of darkness. A dark chamber has been noted also at Panape (in Micronesia) and at the summit of pyramids in Mayan cities, structures that "had no doors, no

Fig. 8.22. Navajo hogan

windows . . . so the priests must have performed their rites . . . in complete gloom" (Lissner 1962, 318).

In North America the dark room was called *hoogadoah.*

> For the light of My angels to come and abide with My people, you shall provide the hoogadoah, the well-covered house . . . when My chosen are within, all shall be dark, so that My angels may teach them.
>
> OAHSPE, BOOK OF SAPHAH: AGOQUIM 9

The Navajo call their sacred round huts "hogan," which may be a shortening of hoogadoah.

Indeed, the Navajos say they received the design of the hogan from their tutelary spirits. "The circular Hogan . . . is constructed to encourage harmony, just as the spiritual beings first instructed," recounts Charlie Cambridge, a Navajo himself with credentials in both anthropology and archaeology. Cambridge adds, "the circular hogan possesses spiritual power"; legend claims the first hogan was "connected to heaven." Today the traditional hogan is still used for ceremonies and "to keep themselves in balance."

Similar traditions were kept by the Mandans, who had beehive huts

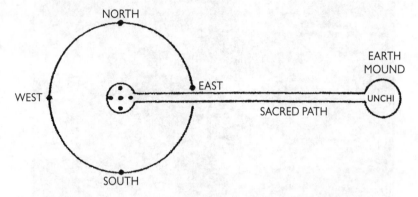

Fig. 8.23. Native sweat lodge in keyhole configuration.
Some medicine wheels are also of this shape.

made of earth and by the Lakota Indians when they perform the *yuwipi* ceremony. "Yuwipi has to be performed in complete darkness. . . . If there's a mirror, they'll cover it. . . . They make sure that not a speck of light can enter . . . [then] the singing and drumming starts. . . . The spirits enter. . . . They'll sing and talk with us" (Brave Bird 2009, 105).

The great and immortal Lame Deer also helped explain the setting for yuwipi: "One must cover all windows and doors with blankets. Not the smallest flicker of light is allowed . . . even the faint glow of the Moon would spoil the . . . blackness. A soul . . . starts talking to you . . . 'I have come to help you. So listen carefully'" (Lame Deer and Erdoes, 1994, 177).

While yuwipi is a "finding-out" ritual, *inipi* is the Lakota purification rite, the sweat lodge; the configuration of the lodge bears the same keyhole shape as the tholoi of western Asia, with its armlike path extending outward from the hut.

Another member of this family is the subterranean *kiva* of the Pueblos, round, dark, and sacred, some with the familiar keyhole-shaped entry, like those discovered at Mesa Verde. Canadian Indians also had circular pits whose "purpose was baffling," though probably used for "vision seeking" (Mavor 1991, 145). Halfway around the world Malaysia's séance huts are on the same plan. Here the "merry and cheerful little people" say that their ancestress Tangoi built the first *panoh*, the spirit hut (a similar word, *o-pan-i,* designates a special hall at one end of the Polynesian marae/temple). Pan-oh is where the Negrito shaman goes into trance. It is not unusual to find other *Pan* words associated with "the spirits" (i.e., the ancestors). In Melanesia, for example, Pan-oi is shade, the netherworld of spirits. In Korea pan-su is "spirit-expeller"; likewise among the black Caribs, pan-tu means "ghost."

Pan words also came to signal special ceremonies, such as Choe-pan, the original name of Native American rites. Among the Acagchemen (a California tribe), their annual festival was called *Panes*—a rite of renewal. In the Old World, the Pan-nychic rites featured the Mysteries of Demeter. In France, fadas (house spirits) were once classed together with Sylvans and Pans. The Sanskrit word *pundit* appeared in Vedic spelling as pandit. Other *Pan* names of sacred significance include the following:

Pan-ku, creator god in Chinese legend
Pango, god in Central Africa, among the Loango people
Topan, heaven in Aztec
Teopan, temple court in Mexico
Panche, a temple in Colombia
Pandimandalam, holy district in India
Panopolis, sacred city in Egypt

From the millions who went under in the Deluge comes the words *pan*ic and *pan*demonium. Let us move on for a close look at the greatest catastrophe ever experienced on Planet Earth—the sinking of the continent of Pan.

HOW CAN A WHOLE
CONTINENT DISAPPEAR?

Garden of Eden?

*Man's first home on earth . . . now forms the bottom of
the Pacific Ocean.*
JAMES CHURCHWARD, *THE LOST CONTINENT OF MU*

Every schoolchild is taught that civilization started in Mesopotamia,
the Fertile Crescent, the supposed cradle of human culture, eventually
spreading far and wide over the face of the Earth. This is actually biblical orthodoxy. Not science. "Eden," says Dame History, "was located in
the lower Tigris-Euphrates Valley. Archaeologists and historians have
confirmed that" (Balsiger and Sellier 1976, 8).

Nevertheless, the Sumerians themselves said that civilization was
brought to them by godlike beings from the sea who gave them laws,
cities, agriculture, and science. Indeed, Berossus, Babylonia's acclaimed
priest-historian, recorded that some race of supreme intelligence had
brought knowledge to the ancient peoples of Sumeria who, until then,
lived as savages. Further, Sumerian tradition reveals that they learned
astronomy, medicine, and mathematics from "strange outsiders"; one

Babylonian legend has their forefathers arriving in Mesopotamia after a long sea journey from a destroyed homeland.

Flood in the Fertile Crescent

At the time of the Flood, Noah and family are said to have lived in the Fertile Crescent, at least according to Genesis 6 and 9. Well, a real flood did submerge the Euphrates Valley some 5,000 years ago. Though extensive, it was still local; such flooding was common in the region. The myth of Noah then has his descendants migrating to all parts of the Middle East, eventually peopling the entire Earth—China, Africa, Europe, America, Polynesia.

But how could this be if the megaliths of France, Spain, and England are much older than the ziggurats of Mesopotamia, or if the high point of Tiahuanaco culture in South America was 15,000 years ago?—antedating Mesopotamian culture by almost 10,000 years. And why is it that medicinal plants were used in Chile 13,000 years ago? We get the same time frame, 13,000 BP, from radiocarbon dates for those mysterious cement pillars on the Isle of Pines in the Pacific Ocean. Isn't it absurd to identify the "Great Flood" as some local inundation in the Fertile Crescent when living traditions—Egyptian, Indian, Teutonic, Greek, Mayan, and so forth—name the flood survivors as their own ancestors?

"Mesopotamia cannot be the oldest . . . geologically speaking, it is a very young formation. . . . Therefore we must look to the north . . ." (Birket-Smith 1965, 427). Ah, the north. Sumerian roots do seem to go back to the north in the region of Turkey, some say to Dera Sor, in eastern Turkey, others say to Göbekli Tepe. "In the popular media Göbekli Tepe has been hailed as the world's first temple . . . and the original Garden of Eden" (Schoch 2012, 44). But such conceptions are merely a measure of our current progress in archaeology, not a measure of historicity. The root is still hidden.

As far as the Egyptians knew, the first humans came from a land called Punt; as a source of silver and gold, Zimbabwe was a candidate

Fig. 9.1. The destruction of Mu, as illustrated by James Churchward in 1925

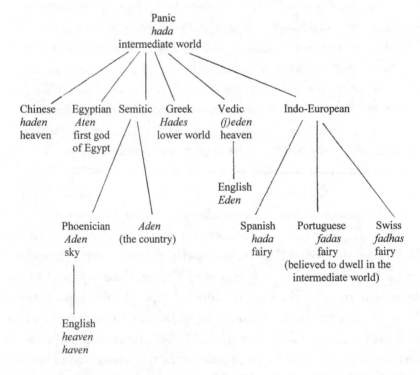

Fig. 9.2. Chart showing Panic words hada *and* eden. *Note that aden, cognate with Aten, meant "sky" in Panic; in the Midrash, Gan 'Eden meant "the world beyond death."*

for the mysterious whereabouts of Punt, which, in addition, was described as an enormous island from which the Teachers came long ago. Barry Fell thought Punt was Sumatra; other candidates include Atlantis, Somalia, and Australia. The Egyptian concept of Eden, however, is more generally based on the Garden of "Aten" (or Eten), a kind of paradise, dedicated to their god Aten.

"Atlantis Was No Myth, but the Cradle of Civilization, Declares Hedges" was the headline of a 1935 *New York American* article. Hedges was F. A. Mitchell-Hedges, who had found an extraordinary crystal skull in Lubaantun and championed the engulfment of Atlantis as the cause of the Flood, "a cataclysm that wiped out millions. Here upon Atlantis was the cradle of civilization." Hedges, of course, was following in the footsteps of Ignatius Donnelly, who pegged Atlantis as the true antediluvian world, the place where man first rose from a state of barbarism—going even beyond Plato, who never claimed that Atlantis was the source of all civilization.

There are many other opinions of Eden: Rene-Maurice Gattesfosse thought that civilization was born on an Arctic continent—Hyperborea. The Flem-Aths had it at the other pole. Leon Mayou thought the Sahara Desert, once so fertile, was the biblical Eden, which agrees somewhat with the current fad in paleoanthropology, which makes Africa the cradle of all the human races. Quixe Cardinali placed his Eden near the Gulf of Aden. John Calvin fancied it was in Iraq, near Basrah; other theologians said Jerusalem. Andrew Collins, more recently, suggests the Armenian highlands (2014, 225, 232, 237). Muslim tradition, on the other hand, looks to Ceylon's Adam's Peak as their jumpstreet—which would accord with the long-held belief that Asia must have been the Garden of Eden.

It was even fashionable at one time to locate man's beginning in America. Early in the 1900s it was proposed that Ohio had been the site of the biblical Garden, and that the *Serpent* Mound in *Adams* County were obvious clues! Mexico's Valsequillo was also dubbed a Garden of Eden, after fancy spearheads and fine stone stools were excavated there and dated anywhere from 35,000 to 250,000 BP! Then again, it could have been South America. The Andean Altiplano, a few theorists argued, was the point of exit of the human race—possibly along the shores of Lake Titicaca. "The world was born at Ica [Peru]" (Charroux 1974, 60). Another Andean possibility was Caral (Coppens 2012, 134). Or was it Brazil? "Ancient South America [at Brazil] was probably the cradle of the world's earliest civilization" (Wilkins 2000, 125).

In *The History of Creation,* Ernst Haeckel, Germany's foremost evolutionist of the nineteenth century, wrote that the Garden could be found in a sunken South Indian continent called Lemuria: "Most circumstances indicate Southern Asia as the locality in question." This would have been in the Indian Ocean, which held "a continent extending from the Sunda Islands . . . to the east coast of Africa. This large continent Lemuria . . . is of great importance [as] the probable cradle of the human race" (1876, 2:325–56).

Pan-anu* te tai (Sea Flows to Land)

Oai tuto e tomi 'ia papanui Tinaku, ma he tai-toko e hetu?
(Who would have thought to bury the great Earth in a
roaring flood?)
TAHITIAN CHANT OF THE DELUGE (TE TAI TOKO)

Scientists say a great landmass (dubbed "Pacifica") must have broken down very gradually, representing a long-term subsidence over millions of years, leaving only a few islands. But tradition says the opposite—that it happened quite *suddenly.*

And the rich valleys of *Mai* with her thousand cities shall be rent with the madness of men and women fleeing before the waters of the ocean.

OAHSPE, SYNOPSIS OF SIXTEEN CYCLES 3:27;
REFERRING TO THE LAND OF PAN (EMPHASIS ADDED)

---

*Note that pan = land

And they all perished. Thus is *i-mai* the Aneiteum Islander's word for the future state, where the ancestors dwell, just as *mai-aurli* signifies the spirit beings of the first Polynesian ancestors. Perhaps this is related to *Mai*ndi, the Basque fairy kingdom, or to *mai*tu, the word for spirit in the Paumotu Islands; which is to say, the Great Submergence is often associated (even confused) with spirits of the dead. Some of the islands are still "terribly haunted by ghosts" (Fornander 1969, 2:82).

The overwhelming madness of those victims is underscored in the Lhasa Record—"Agonizing cries of the multitude filled the air"—just as the Quiché Popol Vuh states that "men ran here and there in despair and madness." Did the Valley of Mai also give us the word *may*hem, just as Pan itself gave us *pan*ic?

A Panic name, Mai is found embedded in one of the Hawaiian terms for the lost lands: Hoahoa-Mai-tu, remembered also in the Society Islands as Mai-aoiti (at Sanders Island) as well as in Tahiti at Mai-ripehe, and in the island simply named Mai in New Hebrides, whose tutelary god is Mai-siki, similar perhaps to the Mai royal lineage on Bora Bora and Laa-mai-kahiki, the fourteenth-century leader of Hawaii. Include also Mai-den and Mai-ao Islands, near Tahiti; Mairassi, New Guinea (where the cult founder of the Koita people is Kiri-mai-kulu); Mai-ana Island in the Kiribatis (the region where Amelia Earhart disappeared). Mai is also embedded in whare-mai-re, the Polynesian college of the priesthood; in the Samoan word ata-mai, meaning "wisdom or skill or cleverness"; and perhaps also in Hawaiian *maitai,* meaning "good, beautiful, excellent, proper" (in Tahiti, maitai means "to be well, good or holy"); Marquesan *mainai* means "handsome," similar to Old Irish *maini,* meaning "precious."

One staple food in Polynesia is the indigenous banana, maika (var. maia), a very old word in Easter Island and Tahiti. Polynesians tended to name foods and plants after the land in which they grew (Smith 1921, 63). Hence also mai-le, a Hawaiian vine, and mai-re, a sacred fern in the Society Islands. The various names for sweet potato include mai-ri and rau-mai-re; Nuna-mai-u was a sacred plant in the Andes; mai-eque was a field hand in the Aztec language. Was *mai* generic for staple foods?

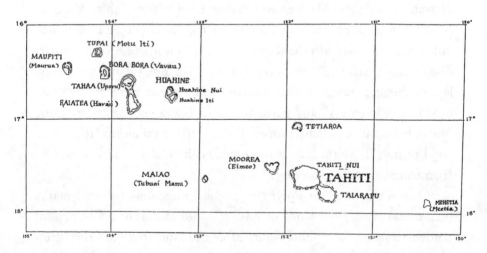

Fig. 9.3. Top: This Easter Island ahu is called Mai-taki-te-Moa, which may be related to Tutu-mai-ao, the name of a people who migrated to New Zealand in early times. The Maori of New Zealand elevated Ronga-Mai to the status of a sky god. Most significantly, Mai-tai is a Maori term for white people. Bottom: Map of Society Islands showing the island of Mai-ao.

Mai-se, Irish for food
Maz, Old High German for meat
Mai-ze, English for corn
Mai-z, Spanish for corn
May-se, Livonia for bread

I wonder if Pan's valleys of Mai were so rich because of volcanic effluvia? Along the Pacific Rim numerous volcanoes have taken this name Mai, perhaps in remembrance of lost Havaiki, a land of volcanoes. In Mangareva it is said that the land of Havaiki, once so large and high, was carried off by Pere (Pele, god of volcano), leaving them "only this low island" (Williamson 1933, 2:215). Accounts of the flood speak of widespread volcanic activity; some believe Mu itself was sundered by volcanoes. "Nowhere upon the face of the earth are to be found evidences of volcanic outbursts equal to those found in Polynesia" (Kolosimo 1975, 150). Mai-named volcanoes along the Pacific Rim include the following:

Asa-mai-ama, Japan; it blew in 1793
May-uyama, lava dome on Kyushu Island
Maion, Philippines
Guaca-mayo, at Cocle, Panama
Maipo, Chile
Sierra Mai-gualida, in Venezuela, near two volcanoes
Mount Kat-mai and **Hi-mai-n,** volcanoes in Alaska
Nune-maya, in the Pacific
Mount Mai'ao, extinct volcanic crater in the Society Islands

Churchward asserts that "all who left the Motherland in any direction were called Mayas" (1931a, 20). Indeed, Mayab means "land of the chosen ones" among the Maya of Mesoamerica, whose tribal name is actually the same as Valmiki's Maya—of India, the first colonizers of the Deccan—a white race (Churchward 2011, 83). Prince Maya was India's earliest architect and astronomer, living more than twenty thousand years ago, according to Churchward, who also called the settlers in Burma "Naga-Maya." Did May-myo, in Burma, also take the ancient name? And what about Chiang Mai in Thailand, the largest city in the north? We might also include India's Mai-tri Upanishad, as well as India's settlement in Egypt called Mai-oo. Egypt's own Mai-dun also comes to mind as does Mai-wand, Afghanistan, and Is-mai-labad near the Caspian in Iran, with the wheel-cross sign of Creator. Of interest too is a place called Mai-kap along the Black Sea, with an inscribed stone telling the history of a great sea journey.

In some places Mai may be seen to recall the actual race that survived the flood—the little people, *Homo sapien pygmaeus*. In New Zealand, for example, the Nuku-Mai-Tore were the little and kindly folk whose home was in the trees (Anderson 1928, 116)—perhaps reminiscent of the tree temples built and used by the Ihins. In Shem, Negritos in ancient India were called pyg-mai-oi. In Guatama, the little people known to the Ojibway were called Mai-mai-gwaaysiwuk; they might be seen paddling their "stone canoes." In Ham, Africa* has its Mai Mai pygmies as well as the Tenda Maie people and the Mai-thoahiana of Kenya, earth gnomes skilled in the arts of metallurgy. In Jaffeth are the Mai-chung people; in Yista, Mai-opira on Hokkaido is the place where the Ainu god came down—the Ainu are a short-statured people.

By the time the Greeks and Romans got ahold of Mai, it was fully mythologized, as we see in the following list.

> **Maia,** the wife of Pan
> **Maya,** the seventh daughter of Atlas
> **Maia,** the mother of Mercury and goddess of Earth
> **Maira,** the mother of Adonis

As a mother figure, Maya was also Buddha's mother; mayi = mother in Sanskrit, while mai-ka means "mother" in Bulgarian. Mai-e means "midwife" in Tahiti and Greece! Indeed, the words *maid* and *maiden* probably have the same root.

---

*Mai places in Africa include Gal Maia, in the Sahara; Maiduguri, Nigeria; Mayotte, East Africa; Maiko River, Zaire; Mainyu River, Cameroon; Maitengwe, Botswana; and Mayumba, Gabon.

While maya took on the meaning of "magic power" in Hindi, the Andaman Islanders, south of India, merely used the term maia to indicate chief or elder or ancestor. In the Hervey Islands, May-akitanga served as a symbol of the chiefly lineage; she was a sacred maid blanched to become most fair. The chiefly connotation also appears in New Zealand where mai-i-rangi was a Maori chiefly term. We find this also in the English word *mayor,* while the Spanish word *mayor* indicates elder, bigger, greater. Mai actually means "foremost" in the Mayan language; as an example, Ah Kin Mai = chief sun priest.

In the Americas, the venerated Mai appears mostly in the naming of lands and tribes.

Mayaguez, Puerto Rico
Mayari and *Mayaguara* Island, Cuba
Jamaica
Mayda, an erstwhile island between Bermuda and Bahamas
Maiquetia, Venezuela
Maicao, Colombia
Maicuru, Brazil
Maiongong, natives of Brazil's Rio Branco region
Umaita Cataract, Brazil
Pacasmayo, seat of the Mochica civilization in Peru; Lake **Umayo**
   also in Peru
Vilcamayu, in Peru
Mayapi, an equatorial tribe
Mayoruna, a tribe known for their telepathic "Amazon beaming"
Samaipata, lost city in Bolivian jungle
Mayo **Indians,** of the North American Southwest
Maimi, Southwest Pueblo site
Maidu **Indians,** of California (in their flood legend only two people survived)
Mayo, Yukon

Even in Europe we have Ireland's County Mayo; England's Maida Vale; Mainake, Spain; Maia, Portugal; Maiche, France; Kala-mai, Greece; and

Maycarne, Crete. A northern European tradition of sky falling may be a recollection of the destruction of Mai, for here the Scandinavian world pillar called May-lmen Stytto was legendarily erected so that "the world would not fall down" (Collins 2014, 210).

Panic

In the Mexican version of the great catastrophe the people were torn to pieces, buried in the sands and in the sea. Men were seen running, filled with despair as their houses tumbled down. Thus do the words *panic* and *pandemonium* owe their existence to the unspeakable cataclysm that obliterated a continent and its millions of inhabitants. Greek mythology could never explain why the sylvan god *Pan* had the power to inspire abrupt and inexplicable horror—panic. His unseen presence aroused feelings of panic in men passing through his lonely places in the wild. We also note with interest that the Spanish word for frighten is es*pan*tar.

Nor is it surprising that numerous Pan words relate to water.

Panthalassa: old term for Pacific Ocean itself
Sociapan: name of the ancient sea in Texas
Hoolahoola-pan: first name of Lake Superior
Tapan: word for ark in Armenian
Panticapes: a river in ancient Scythia

Fig. 9.4. The god Pan

Panaro: mouth of the Po River in Italy

Apan: word for lake in Mexico, as in Metzli-apan (Moon Lake), plus Lake Zum-pan-go

Panuco, Zahapan, Mopan, Xamilpan, Actopan, Papaloapan: rivers in Mexico

Panajachel: on Lake Atitlan, Guatemala; also Pantaleon on the Pacific coast

Lake Pipanaco: in Argentina and Chile

The name Mu, a synonym of Pan, also occurs in many water-related words, such as port cities (landing places) like Muza (Arabia), Mu (Crete), and Mukawa (Japan).

Word	Meaning	Where
mu	wet	Quiché Maya
mulua	water	Lowland Maya
muyal	rain clouds	Maya
muluc	flood	Maya
Chac Mul	rain god	Mexico
mu	water	Pima and in Arabic and Akkadian as well
Mu or Limu	submerged land	Chumash, near Channel Islands, California
Mugu	beach	
mugeres	island	Mexico
mu-olok-wit-uppu	island	Kuna, Panama
limu	seaweed; goddess hair (submerged)	Hawaii
limua	long rain	Hawaii
mumuku	squall at sea	Polynesia
timu	rain	Samoa (in the Maldives it means "island")
mutunui	islet	Southeast Pacific

Word	Meaning	Where
mutu	island	Tahiti
DuMu	only survivor of flood	the aboriginal Lolo of China
Hmu	ancestors of the Hmong who survived a terrible deluge	Thailand
Mount A-mu-yao	a landing spot from Deluge	Philippines
Mulu	river	Borneo
Mujaji	goddess of tempests	South Africa
Munume	god invoked during drought or flood	Uganda
Te-mu	earliest god of creation, an underwater deity	Egypt
Muallakah	village where Ark was built	Syria
Patkinya-Mu	water clan that commemorates the flood	Hopi, Muia was the name of the Hopi homeland in the Pacific (Heinberg 1989, 78)

The long-extinct Mu folk of Kauai, like their cousins the Menehune, are little legendary forest people of Hawaii's uplands and deep valleys. Bearing a similar name is the ancient city of Mu'a on Tonga; mua means "foremost" in Tahiti and "first" in other parts of Polynesia; mumuki means "the first man" on Rarotonga.

Other Mu names in Oceania include:

Mu'nu, meaning "ancient cities" in Tonga
No-mu-ka Island, also in the Tonga group
Munawata Island, Trobriands
Murupi, New Guinea
Murrian, an Australian light-skinned race

Mu words in the Islands—and elsewhere—tend to crop up in terms for VIPs.

*Fig. 9.5. One of Churchward's maps of Mu, the Motherland of Man.
(Mu = mother, in Chinese.) See also map of Pan, fig. 4.2, p. 142,
showing a valley (at center) named Mu. Muriwaioata is one Polynesian
name for the kingdom lost in the Pacific.*

Word	Meaning	Where
Mulon	title of chief	Malekula
Lono-Mu-ku	goddess	Hawaii
Mu Re	earliest ancestor	Hawaii
Ha Mu-ka	god of the Mu people	Hawaii
Umu	high priest	Tahiti
muhu	candidate for the priesthood	Society Islands

MU NAMES CARRIED BY SHEM

Word	Meaning	Where
Mula & Mulai	progenitors of Korku people	India
Muria	a Gonds people	India
muni	sage	India (in Sanskrit)

MU NAMES CARRIED BY SHEM (cont.)

Word	Meaning	Where
Mu	a Dravidian god	South India
Mukeyyer	oldest name of Ur	Mesopotamia
Murad Su	the eastern Euphrates River	Mesopotamia
Memuneh	headman	Israel (in Hebrew)

MU NAMES CARRIED BY HAM

Word	Meaning	Where
muato	king	Congo Basin
Mu-karib	priest-kings of Sabea	Arabia
Mursid	spiritual guide	Arabia
Mutawan	religious enforcers	Arabia
Muqarribua	ghost-priest	Arabian peninsula
Mu'allakah	Noah's ark said to be built here	village in Syria
Biah-mu and Mukna	temple ruins	Egypt
Nah-mu	name of yellow race	ancient Egypt
Mulumga	a people	Africa
Mutua	pygmy group	Uganda

MU NAMES CARRIED BY JAFFETH

Word	Meaning	Where
Tien-Mu	a fabled land across the Pacific	China
mu	ancient word for governor	China
Mu Kung	king of the gods	Chinese legend
Mupsh	name of king	hittite

MU NAMES CARRIED BY JAFFETH (*cont.*)

Word	Meaning	Where
Murias	a city from which the founding Irish migrated	Scythia
Mu	settlement	Crete

MU NAMES CARRIED BY YISTA

Word	Meaning	Where
Mu-nakata Nokami	first inhabitants after the flood	Japan
Mim-mu	first emperor, "son of Mu"	Japan
Mukawa	Ainu place	Japan
Mount Muroba	a sweet juice	Japan

MU NAMES CARRIED BY GUATAMA

Word	Meaning	Where
Muyok	lost city of Chachapoyas	Peru, region full of ruins
Muyu	a pampa	Peru
Muyna	town near Cuzco	Peru; also the Chi-mu Empire
Muribeca	place with lost cities of gold	Brazil
Muaco	16,000-year-old artifacts	Venezuela
Muzo	a tribe	Colombia
Muysca	culture with flood legends and white gods	Colombia
Muna	Mayan site near Uxmal	Mexico
Pimu	former name of Catalina Island	California
Hav-Mu-suv	superior civilization of old, say Paiutes	California
Point Mugu	archaeological site	California

Many Mu names have a sacred meaning.

Word	Meaning	Where
muhibbin	devotees	Arabia
Muharram	a Shia festival and sacred month	Islamic countries
Lukh-mu	first god	Chaldea
Mu-lil	ruler of Earth & Hades	Chaldea
Mu	magical aircraft	Sumeria
Mu Kung	king of gods	China
His Wang Mu	goddess	China
Mukasa	supreme deity	Uganda
Mulungu	a god	Tanzania
Mulugu	Supreme Being	Gyrianmas people, East Africa
Muso Kovoni	Mother of Life	West Africa
Mut	Father of All Things	Tiahuanaco, Bolivia
Muluc	one of the four Bacabs	Mexico
Mutul	a lord	Mexico
Chac-Mul	rain god (Chac-Mool)	Mexico
Muramura	spirits of the constellations	Australia
Mukagawin	emblem of the prophet	North America

Time of the Flood

Legends of a great flood are nearly universal. From Samothrace to Samoa, from Kashmir to Lithuania, from Mexico to India, from Tibet to Polynesia, the legend lives on in story and song, in clay, stone, papyrus, and parchment, in drawings and pictographs carved on rock walls, on cliffs and boulders, on tombs and temple walls. According to Graham Hancock more than five hundred deluge legends are known from around the world.

Fig. 9.6. Edouard Riou's engraving of the "Great Asian Flood"

But *when* did this great inundation take place? Timing is everything . . .

Although there are traditions of a flood in the Near East that occurred about 5000 BP, which is a geological fact, it was not *the* flood. In fact, the Chaldean sages established a time lapse of almost *forty* thousand years between the Great Deluge and the first dynasty. Clearly this conflicts with "young Earth" biblicists who contend that the Deluge occurred only five thousand or six thousand years ago, some say in 3446 BCE or 2341 BCE. The latter date is somewhat consistent with Frank Joseph's date of 2193 BCE, which he says was followed by the final Muvian catastrophe in 1628 BCE (2006, 241). Others would place the event 2,250 years prior to Plato's time, circa 4650 BP (Deal 1984, 61).

Such recent dates, though, sharply conflict not only with the Chaldean one but also with the Rosicrucian date of 80,000 BP or 100,000 BP, the latter date given by other occultists (Charroux 1971, 100; Wilkins 2000, 187). Multiplying that figure is the grandiose Brahmanic date—"before the Himalayas existed," meaning hundreds of thousands of years ago—in a class with Madame Blavatsky's Lemuria, which supposedly went down about eight hundred thousand years ago.

But even this estimate is conservative compared to standard geology, which dates the existence of Pacifica to eons long, long gone.

- **30 mya (million years ago):** Some scientists think that the margins of the Pacific continent persisted until Oligocene or Miocene times. A. R. Wallace and others favored a Miocene date.
- **60 mya:** Final disappearance of Pacifica was at the beginning of the Tertiary Period (Kolosimo 1975, 48).
- **75 mya:** Others put it in the Mesozoic; some say the Pacific landmass lasted until the end of the Cretaceous Period.

Notwithstanding all this difference of opinion, recent scholarship of the alternative bent, the New Orthodoxy, tends to put the destruction of Mu and the Deluge at 12,000 BP. Churchward inferred a like figure from Mexico's "Troano Manuscript." A universal deluge twelve thousand years ago, some claim, explains the disappearance of Cro-Magnon's Lascaux culture.* In a similar vein it is said that the Old Stone Age came to an abrupt end 12,000 BP, "just when Mu was . . . overwhelmed . . . at the close of the last ice age" (Joseph 2006, 224). But it is still an open question whether the high sea levels twelve thousand years ago were occasioned by Noah's flood or by the melting glaciers that marked the end of the so-called ice age.

The Land of Pan Went Down
Twenty-Four Thousand Years Ago

Nevertheless, D. H. Childress has Lemuria sinking about twenty-four thousand years ago, based on one of his favorite sources, the Lemurian Fellowship (Childress 1988, 75). A similar date, 22,000 BP, is cited as a time when ocean levels dropped, water supposedly having rushed away to fill the basin created by the sinking of Mu (Williams 2001, 110). This period is called the Mankato by geologists, being the time of the last glaciation.

---

*His "disappearance" was actually due to the back-breeding Cro-Magnon man, the scenario discussed in my book *The Mysterious Origins of Hybrid Man.*

The Deluge, as I see it, divides the Upper from the Lower Paleolithic, occurring in the period of cosmic time called the arc of Noe, twenty-four thousand years ago. Noah's ark? Or arc of Noe? On ancient medals the Deluge is depicted with *Noe* lettered on the front of the ark. Noe in Japan means "Lord" (see chapter 4 where *Noe* is discussed on p. 138).

THE CYCLES IN *OAHSPE*

	Years Duration	Under Etherean	|ARC|
1st ERA	3,000	Sethantes	
	3,000	Ah'shong	
		Hoo Le	
		C'pe Aban	
2nd ERA " RES "		Pathodices	
		Goemagak	
	3,200	Goepens	
	3,000	Hycis	
3rd ERA " SCYIY"	2,700	See'itcicius	
	2,900	Miscelitivi	
	3,000	Gobath	
	3,100	F'aiyis	
4th ERA "HRISTA"	3,070	Zineathaes	
	2,600	Tothsentaga	
	3,400	Nimeas	
		Neph	
5th ERA "CAYAY"	3,600	APH	Arc of Noe
	3,200	SUE	Arc of IZARACHA
	2,800	APOLLO	Arc of RUPTA
	3,200	THOR	Arc of MOS
6th ERA "HEM"	3,000	OSIRIS	Arc of DAE
	3,100	Fragapatti	Arc of LOO
	3,400	Cpenta-armij	Arc of SPETA & LOO
	3,400	Lika	Arc of BON
KOSMON 7th ERA "HYRIM"		**OURANOTHEN**	
8th ERA "AH"			

Fig. 9.7. Chart showing cycles and arcs; note the arc of Noe in the fifth era

There were made images of stone and copper and engravings thereon of the children of Noe, and of the flood.

OAHSPE, THE LORDS' FOURTH BOOK 2:20

Linguists say that if the two thousand indigenous languages of the sixteenth-century Americas came from a common source, it would have taken about twenty-five thousand years for them to diverge into their present form. Indeed, 24,000 BP is the time that the first Paleo-Caucasoids turn up both in the Americas and China; cousins, they were children of Mu—China's Choukoutien Man and America's Plains Indians resembled each other morphologically, both carrying the genes of Panic people. Danish geneticists, in addition, have now found twenty-four-thousand-year-old Siberian DNA that is "closely related to that of modern Native Americans. . . . The genetics tell us about homelands" (Swaminathan 2014, 13).

Stephen Oppenheimer, an expert on "Edens," has people entering the New World twenty-two thousand to twenty-five thousand years ago—and yes, they are Caucasian, as seen in California's Los Angeles Man, dated 24,000 BP. Charcoal campfires in Nevada have been dated to 23,800 BP (Irwin 1963, 29), while artifacts made of bone in the Yukon also yield that date, as do the fine engravings and anatomically modern human skulls found at Flagstaff, Arizona, and the skilled basket makers, in their small-size burial vaults uncovered in southwestern Pennsylvania.

Such engravers and artisans were also in early Peru—made famous by the Ica Stones, some of which depict the submerged lands from which their forefathers had been saved (see chapter 7, p. 307, "Hallowed Records"). Conservative dating of the populating of the Americas explodes with a raft of new (and old, suppressed) evidence in the Western Hemisphere. For example, it is known that "Peruvian prehistory began over 22,000 years ago at Ayacucho" (Zink 1979, 111); in those highlands the "earliest complex in the central Andes dates to about 22,000 BC" (Adams 1991, 25–26). Exactly the same date, according to Tony Earll in *Mu Revealed,* is noted in Mexico's scrolls for the sinking of Pan. Valsequillo (Mexico) artifacts of modern type are also of that date. In the Bahamas too the

Bimini Road "is professionally dated at 23,000 BP" (Imhotep 2014, 7).

In the Old World records kept by the Babylonian priesthood give a similar result, tracing the first dynasty after the flood to the year 24,500 BP. Java's Gunung Padang also goes back twenty-four thousand years, according to Robert Schoch. Meanwhile, Africa's earliest rock art falls into the same time frame, as does France's cave drawing. And that (Aurignacian) culture sprang up "suddenly, almost fully developed, about twenty-three thousand years before the beginning of the Christian era" (Spence 1933, 222). Is it for the same reason that the earliest artists in the region of Siberia's Lake Baikal are dated 23,000 BP? A human leg bone recently found near Lake Baikal was "dated to about 24,000 BP. . . . The individual was closely related both to Europeans and to Amerindians" (Stoecker 2014, 27). Chances are the Baikal finds are also related to a twenty-four-thousand-year-old Sunghir burial (near Moscow) containing thousands of ivory beads—one of the earliest examples of jewelry. Most intriguing is the tradition in Vladimir, Russia, that holds that their village is twenty-four thousand years old. Indeed, prehistorians think moderns first spread through central Siberia and Russia around that time. The earliest Venus figurines are also part of the mix, dated in Russia to 24,000 BP.

J. M. Brown thought European languages diverged from Polynesian some twenty thousand to twenty-five thousand years ago. It has also been theorized that the hexagrams making up the I Ching "originally came from Mu 24,000 or so years ago," perhaps explaining why "some prehistoric Mexican hieroglyphs are strikingly similar to . . . the so-called trigrams of the legendary Chinese emperor Fo-Hi. . . . The I Ching may have been originally used by a now-vanished culture that once existed in the Pacific" (Childress 1988, 95).

Are Destructions Cyclical?

You shall also remember that many great inventions are forgotten. The world has been peopled over many times, and many times laid desolate.

OAHSPE, BOOK OF APOLLO 2:8

Some scholars toy with the idea that world destructions obey cyclical laws. Robert Charroux suggested that "our little planet [may] be subject to periodic deluges and upheavals, related to cosmic fluctuations"; a great flood, he thinks, occurs every twenty-one thousand years. Therefore "we may assume that there will be another Universal Deluge in the year 11,748" (Charroux 1967, 53–54; 1974, 26). Other European occultists have come up with similar formulations. "Who the biblical Noah really was no one knows; there must have been many previous civilizations with Noahs of their own" (Drake 1974, 150). From the science side, a few astronomers believe that a comet or asteroid big enough to cause global devastation smashes into our planet once every hundred million years.

Well, yes, the idea of periodic catastrophe was entertained by the ancient Mexicans, Chinese, Hebrews, Babylonians, Arabs, Persians, and Indians. Such calamities, it was generally believed, effaced all on Earth but were followed by renewal. Yet these accounts do not usually agree in their particulars—when and how often. The Hindu Grand Cycle, Maya-Pralaya, for one, is known as the Day and Night of Brahma. In the sacred book of Manusmitri, a cycle called the "Day of Brahma" lasts 4.32 billion years, which is about the age of Earth itself, as modern science reckons. However, the "Day" will come and go; we are now allegedly in the seventh of fourteen Brahma Days. One world ends and another begins. Mexican cosmogony entails several cycles, or "Suns," each of which ends in a catastrophe. The Mexicans also had an obsession about disaster striking every fifty-two years. Venus, they said, caused death to the world, being one of several constellations that fell from the sky at the time of the Great Deluge.

Another school of thought focuses on regular calamitous pole shifts (a subject explored in my previous book *Delusions in Science and Spirituality*). "Perhaps the last pole shift was the cause of the submergence of Hiva. . . . The Pacific continent may have been alternately above and below water . . . over the past 400 million years" (Childress 1988, 241, 292).

Periodic conflagration was also a part of Greek thinking, various schemes of *kataklymos* offered by Aristotle, Plato, Anaximenes, Anaximander, Heraclitus, Aristarchus, Hesiod, and the Stoics. "The ancient Greeks said that at the end of every 12,000 years, the beds of the oceans are displaced, and a semi-universal deluge takes place" (Wilkins 2000, 32).

Warrior Waves and Other Disasters

Twelve thousand years ago, at the end of the ice age,* sea levels supposedly rose when the ice sheet started its retreat; presumably, huge amounts of water melted and the ocean rose hundreds of feet, inundating islands and coastal regions. Wouldn't this explain the flood? Was the South Pacific overwhelmed with a sudden jump of sea level, at the Boelling Interstadial? Some scientists, however, say that increase was not sudden at all but took place over thousands of years. Yet others say that flooding twelve thousand years ago had nothing to do with ice but that some heavenly body collided with Earth and burst through its crust, resulting in "rains and floods [that] constituted the deluge about which we read in Scripture" (Kolosimo 1975, 16–17).

Hawaiian legend says that the flood came as a "warrior wave," perhaps 100 feet high. In Mexico a flood of appalling destruction is blamed for the burial of an ancient metropolis near Mexico City: 7,000 feet high and inland, the region, now covered with boulders, gravel, and sand, is thought to have been an ancient ocean port. It is adduced that only a tidal wave of colossal proportion could have done the deed. But tidal waves, say critics, could not have produced the biblical flood that remained on the land fully 150 days.

Even diluvial *rains* have been called into question. Some Polynesian flood legends do not mention rain at all. The waters, they say, came from the other direction, from the "fountains of the abyss." Other versions explicitly blame waters from above *and* below. In the Zuni record, for example, the reservoirs of both above and below were opened, unplugged. In Jewish legend the land was inundated by male waters from the sky and female waters from the ground.

---

*The ice age theory is another *idée fixe* debunked in my previous book, *Delusions of Science and Spirituality,* chapter 3.

. . . the gates of *heaven and earth* were opened. And the earth rocked to and fro, like a ship at sea; and the rains fell in torrents; and loud thunderings came up from beneath the floor of the world. And the sea came up on the land . . . and the land was swallowed up . . . and all the living on Whaga perished, except the Jhins, who floated off in the ships.

OAHSPE, THE LORDS' FIRST BOOK 1:41–43 (EMPHASIS ADDED)

Genesis 7:11 tells us that "the fountains of the great deep burst forth." Does this mean earthquakes opened the abyss? Le Plongeon's translation of the Troano Codex has the country twice upheaved by earthquakes. Some take this to mean that a radical pole shift was followed by a crustal slip and tectonic collisions, destroying the continent of Mu. "A series of major earthquakes," as Churchward has it, was unleashed by "unstable gas belts" inside the Earth.

Though all this seems to come under the heading of "natural disaster," there are theorists who blame a man-made cause such as the etheric technology of the ancients. The Hindus, for instance, apparently wrote of an "atomic war that must have annihilated Mu" (Charroux 1967, 70; this is discussed in chapter 3, p. 102).

Or was it a "plasma event . . . [that] could vaporize large amounts of water from lakes and oceans [and] in turn rain down continuously and cause widespread flooding" (Schoch 2012, 181–82)? Robert Schoch thinks so, citing "the long-distant memory of a major solar outburst, a major plasma event, and the subsequent geological disturbances. . . . According to some Hopi elders, their ancestors emerged from below the ground. Could these ancestors have been survivors of a plasma event who had sought refuge from the surface onslaught?" (2012, 181–82).

Others blame the moon, which, it is postulated, careened to the Earth, crashing in to it, and maybe even shifting the poles. The Hans Hoerbiger theory, for one, supposed that 250,000 years ago the Cenozoic moon approached and submerged most of the lands. Later the "planet Luna" was somehow captured, and this event submerged both Atlantis and Lemuria. Otherwise put, "12,000 years ago our present Moon wandered into the earth's gravitational field and was made captive" (Wilkins 2000, 29). Great guesswork. Yet others speculate that the constellations changed places. Perhaps it was "the pole star Vega and its counterpart in the South, Canopus [that] started moving away from their allotted positions," causing the seas on Earth to rise (Kreisberg 2012, 129). Or did a star called Bal fall "where today there is only sea" (Lhasa Tablet)—in other words, causing the sinking of a continent?

Other flyby theories would blame a direct asteroid or meteorite impact. "The force of the collision activated earthquakes and volcanic explosions* throughout the world and caused huge tidal waves to break over the land" (Berlitz 1984, 204). It is reasoned that if a meteorite 30 miles in diameter struck the ocean, it would cause a tidal wave capable of submerging coastal areas; if it fell on land, it could supposedly cause a pole shift. All spectacular speculation.

Still others suggest a supernova event—star shrapnel devastating Earth, disrupting its axial tilt. Maybe the planet between Mars and Jupiter was destroyed, upsetting the gravitational balance of the solar system and the position of the Earth's axis and resulting "in tremendous inundations" (Von Daniken 1974, 213). It could have been a "tremendous comet . . . [whose] terrible impact caused the Earth . . . to lurch and tilt violently at the axis. . . . When our Earth was hit by a wandering comet . . . a terrific force . . . tore it from its old orbit . . . and drove it outward into space! The whole Earth tilted violently" (Wilkins 2000, 20, 30). But Earth shifting on its axis has also been blamed for ice ages, and ice ages supposedly *lower*—not raise—sea levels.

Whatever the cause, there must have been a horrible holocaust of fire, judging from surviving records.

- Hawaii: flames 3 miles high shot from the Earth.
- Egypt: the land sank into a fiery abyss.
- Maya: everything vanished in a vortex of fire and water.
- Peru: the people were killed by a fire that fell from the sky; then came the deluge.
- California (Washo): the mountains caught fire.

---

*One legend of Hawaiki has it destroyed by a huge volcanic outburst.

- Northwest coast Indian: a "fire-drill" set the world aflame; rocks were burning, everything was burning. And then the water rushed in.

And the Heavens Dropped

Earth and wide Heaven above came together . . . all the land seethed.

HESIOD, *THEOGONY*

The earth trembled and the heavens dropped.

FROM THE SONG OF DEBORAH IN JUDGES 5:4

There is always a grain of truth in the great traditions—and even in childish fairy tales like Chicken Lickin—which tell us that the sky once fell. The Icelandic Eddas recount a time when "heaven was cloven," whereupon stars fell, the sun darkened, and water engulfed. The Finnish *Kalevala* also reports that the sky collapsed. Mexican codices, in like manner, say that "the earth shook to its foundation . . . the sky sank lower . . . the waters uprushed with violence . . ." just as the Cashinaua of western Brazil say the heavens burst, fell, and killed everyone.

Australian Aborigines remember an event wherein MuMuNa (a fiery serpent) fell from heaven causing a devastating flood. In China too it is said that when the Emperor of Heaven tried to obliterate mankind, the sky was caused to become low and the earth sank (told in the Shan Hai Ching). "The pillars of heaven were broken," says the Chinese deluge story, "and the earth fell to pieces." But their creator god Panku (note the *Pan* and the *ku*) saved the day and kept the sky from falling entirely. In Europe it was said that the ancient Celti feared no one, but only that the sky might collapse. And this is why they need to hold up the sky. Thus do we see the four dwarfs Austri, Vestri, Sudri, and Nordri supporting the sky, the Norse gods having placed a dwarf at each of the four points of heaven to hold it high above the Earth.

Though this is a legend of the far North, we find its exact counterpart in Mexico, whose sacred book, Chilam Balam, recounts that

Fig. 9.8. A green enameled statuette shows Mesopotamian god Shu uplifting the sky; his priesthood bridged heaven and earth.

subterranean fires burst forth, bringing a rain of fire and ashes. Then the heavens were seized and split asunder. This was the downfall of the epoch called the Third Sun, after which the four Bacabs, sons of the supreme god, were appointed to support the four corners of the Earth. These skybearer dwarfs were called "Sustainers."

Muisca natives of South America say that after a wicked goddess caused the world to flood, Huitaca was appointed to hold up the sky forever—much as Atlas was made to support the heavens in Greek mythology or Tarhuhyiawahku in Iroquois legend, or Ru (Sky Raiser) in Polynesia.

> *Tawhaki caused a deluge by stamping on the floor of heaven.*
>
> POLYNESIAN MYTH

Other Oceanic legends tell a similar tale.

- Tekaofo Islanders: the sky was low
- Caroline Islanders: stars were falling
- Micronesians: falling stars were followed by earthquakes
- Tongans, Tahitians, and Samoans: the heavens fell down

The Mexicans said that no sooner did the sky approach the Earth than, in the space of a single day, all was drowned; their Popol Vuh mentions that a resinous thickness descended from heaven. "I wonder," wrote Robert Schoch, "if the 'rain of resin' falling from the sky might reference powerful auroral displays and plasma phenomena . . . [or] extraterrestrial dust . . . jettisoned from the *collapsing magnetosphere*" (2012, 207; emphasis added). Now we're getting somewhere; we will have to look at how the vortexian walls of the magnetosphere were crushed. The African tribes of Wanyoro, Kanga, and Loanga have a tradition of the collapsing sky that annihilated a great portion of the human race. "The god Kagra *threw the firmament* upon the earth to destroy mankind" (Velikovsky 1965, 90). Indeed, the firmament was thrown. . . . But how?

How the Gods
Broke Pan Asunder

The God who creates also destroys.

JOHN PILKEY, *THE ORIGIN OF THE NATIONS*

Jehovih hath decreed a pruning-knife to a traveling world. . . . Aph crushed in her walls and pruned her to the quick . . . cleaned up the whole earth and her heavens, as one might sweep the floor of a house.

OAHSPE, BOOK OF FRAGAPATTI 1:5 AND

BOOK OF APH 2:7, 8:3

As these extraordinary accounts in Oahspe have it, the land was sunk using the force rays of thousands of starships, thus breaking the foundations of the continent. From the biographies of the great Sir Arthur Conan Doyle we learn that after the death of Lady Doyle's dear brother Malcolm, she became more psychic; on one occasion, her spirit guide Pheneas explained how even earthquakes and tidal waves can be caused by teams of spiritual scientists at work connecting "vibratory lines of seismic power."

It seemed as if Titans in the skies were bombarding the Earth.
HAROLD T. WILKINS,
MYSTERIES OF ANCIENT SOUTH AMERICA

The god of the storm smashed the land like a cup.
EPIC OF GILGAMESH

Lo, My etherean hosts come unarmed and by a breath, blow away their [earthlings'] mighty kingdoms!

OAHSPE, BOOK OF OSIRIS 3:8

Earth science as such does not hold the key to the disappearance of the great Pacific continent; we search in vain for a terrestrial mechanism, a convulsion of nature. "Continents cannot sink" (Nunn 2009, 17). Natural forces were not at play. There is nothing in geological time to compare to the vanishment of an entire continent. Therefore I am tempted to declare that there is more truth in that Wanyoro legend—that God threw down the firmament—than in all the wild guesswork turned out by today's secular theorists who, by and large, being atheists or agnostics or even Christian Scientists, cannot conceive of the creative or *destructive* powers of the gods.

The following excerpts are drawn from Oahspe's Book of Aph, which describes the event in its fascinating particulars.

Man shall be taught to know My power; and after that, My wisdom. . . . I know what is for their own good; and My decree has gone forth. . . . The too prolific earth contributes more to the corporeal than to the spiritual man. . . . Now a wave of My breath speeds forth in the broad firmament. The red star [Earth] flyeth toward the point of My sharpened sword. . . .

I will scoop her up like a toy, and her vortex shall close about like a serpent hungry for its prey. . . .

By the power and wisdom of Jehovih, the continent of Whaga is to be cut loose and submerged, and her [festering] heavens carried away. . . .

My etherean ships of fire shall surround Wagga on every side. And I will cut loose the foundations of the earth, at the borders of the oceans and the mountains of Gau. . . .

When His voice called the legions in high heaven, myriads of shapely stars moved in from every side, even from below and above the earth; and these were ships of fire coursing the firmament, in which rode the Gods and Goddesses, called by Jehovih to the labor of earth and hada.

Closing in on every side they came, nearer and more compact, and brighter, with sparkling pillars of fire . . . till all the space surrounding the earth was hedged in with this army of Jehovih's etherean ships of fire. . . .

Quickly, now, the ships of fire formed in line, extending . . . down to hada [the lowest heaven above Earth]. . . . And in the line of the etherean ships, the plateaus of rank were stationed; and the hosts of Gods and Goddesses took their places, according to the rank of wisdom, power, and love manifested in the etherean departments from which they came. . . .

And I [Aph] divided the line into sections, each with two hundred and fifty ships, and there were one thousand sections. And every ship was contracted ten thousand fold, which was the force required to break the crust of the earth and sink a continent. . . . For every ten sections I appointed one hundred marshals and one God, and for every ten Gods one Chief . . . according to their rank in the heavens. . . .

And I said: In Your Strength and Wisdom, O Jehovih, join the heavens above with the earth below! And the end of the etherean column that extended down to the earth was made secure around the borders of Whaga, by the sea and the high mountains to the north. Again I said: O Jehovih, deliver the earth from evil!

And the vortex of the earth closed in from the rim, and lo, the earth was broken! A mighty continent was cut loose from its fastenings, and the fires of the earth came forth in flames and clouds, with loud roaring. And the land rocked. . . . And again the vortex of the earth closed in on all sides, and by the pressure, the land sank beneath the water, to rise no more. And the corporeans went down to death; and the fetals and familiars [earthbound spirits] gave up the battle; neither did they have anywhere to stand, nor did they know how to go to any place in all the heavens.

OAHSPE, BOOK OF APH 1:28–30, 2:10, 3:4–20, 6:1–8

Circum-Pacific Tip-Offs

There is a Japanese tradition that says the islands of the Pacific appeared after the waters of a great deluge had receded. In the American Southeast the Yuchi Indians have a similar story—the sky gods fished up the first land from the waters. Samoan legend too has the archipelago "fished up" from the ocean after the flood. And this is about the same as the Hawaiian and New Zealand story of a demigod fishing up their land from the sea. In the Tahitian version, when Havaiki went down, the gods pushed up Tahiti and the Tuamotu islands. Other foundation myths of the world repeat the theme that the rise of one country was caused by the sinking of another. Is this why Native American flood legends and those of the South Pacific are called "Emergence" myths? In Peru there is an ancient legend of a cataclysmic event, some terrible shock to the Earth in which the sea broke out of bounds and "the mountain of Ancasmarca rose, like a ship on the waves" (Velikovsky 1965, 61).

Did the sinking of Pan indeed cause other lands to rise? Did the continental plates collide, thus uplifting the land that we call the Andes? Although mountain building is still a debated question and no doubt a gradual process in certain instances, there is reason to believe that the South American Cordilleras went up suddenly and violently. Few elevations in the world are so precipitous—from coast to dazzling heights. What if the sundering of the Earth brought so much pressure against the Nazca Plate (in the eastern Pacific), thrusting the Andes, almost instantaneously, miles up into the air?

Did the continental plates lock together, pitching forward and throwing the mountains up? Violent movement in one direction could have set off violent countermovement in another direction. This point/counterpoint model is part of J. M. Brown's argument. "The rise of the two cordilleras of the Andes . . . must have had full compensation in subsidence; and this is apparent in the long stretch of the Paumotus and the almost islandless seas to the south of them. . . . There is no such landless area on the face of the earth than this southeastern region of the Pacific Ocean. The voyage from New Zealand to Easter Island is drearier and more eventless than any other in the world" (1924, 50).

In fact, the Andes chain is the most *recent* of the world's great mountains, the western portion thought to be no more than twenty-five thousand or thirty thousand years old. Generations of writers have pointed out features of the Andean landscape that indicate a former *coastal* position of these mountains. Such markers include the following:

- Fossil bones of mastodon, whose habitat was actually marshy, low-lying areas.
- Images of sea horses on these high mountain monuments.
- Calcified remains of marine flora at 11,000 feet elevation; Lake Titicaca, high in salinity, has chalky remains of ancient seaweeds.
- Tiahuanaco gives all the appearance of a harbor town suddenly uplifted; the region today is a virtually uninhabitable wasteland.
- Tilted angle of deposits that must have been originally level.

> *The cataclysmic rise of lands produced by the sinking of others recurs throughout circum-Pacific folk traditions.*
> FRANK JOSEPH, *THE LOST CIVILIZATION OF LEMURIA*

Similar elevation is equally evident along the Asiatic side of the Pacific Ocean, like the wide mountain ranges in Kamchatka, Japan. Magnetic anomalies—ghost lights (as on Panape and in the Andes), compass aberrations, mysterious fires, not to mention frequent earthquakes*—are all concentrated along the Pacific Rim, hinting at a long-standing after-effect of enormous seismic pressure. Although conventional geology is

---

*Blue flames are associated with earthquakes in both Japan and San Francisco.

loath to admit it, there is something frightfully unique about this part of the world—the great horseshoe surrounding the Pacific Ocean.

> *The Pacific Ocean has always been a problem for*
> *geologists. Why is there no large land mass over such*
> *an enormous area—some twelve thousand miles from*
> *Singapore to Panama? Why is most of earth's land found*
> *on just one side of the globe?*
> MARK WILLIAMS, *IN SEARCH OF LEMURIA*

Why, indeed.

In the standard model the Pacific has long been empty; in this view, it is simply a "long-lived fallacy that there had to be a land mass in the southern hemisphere to counterbalance the land mass . . . in the north" (Cameron 1987, 125). But is it not curious that the Pacific is more than three times wider than the Atlantic Ocean? More than three-quarters of the world's islands lie in the Pacific Ocean. Let us move on then to that very special part of our mysterious planet, known as—the Ring of Fire.

RING OF FIRE

In a mutual fit of hyperbole, many of the world's peoples have described the flood as a *universal* event. Physical evidence of flooding, though certainly found all over the world, does not indicate or vindicate the "Universal Deluge" of biblical fame but merely represents regional inundations occurring at different times. Nevertheless, numerous traditions have boldly dramatized the event, relating the following:

> a flood engulfed most of the Earth
> disaster struck the whole planet
> the globe was a teeming chaos
> the deluge was worldwide
> giant waves circled the globe
> all of humanity returned to mud
> there was no continent left on any point of the horizon
> all races perished, except for a few people
> the lake of waves drowned all mankind, save one couple

Genesis 6:11 recounts that God told Noah that he had determined to make an end of all flesh. Hebrew tales, contributing to the biblical myth, had the waters covering the Earth, even the high mountains, whereon every living creature perished. Marine fossils and high water

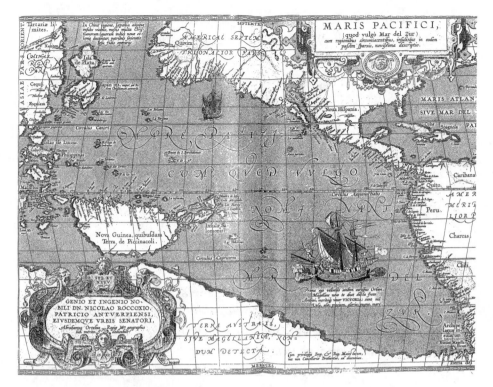

Fig. 10.1. Sixteenth-century map of the Pacific Ocean

marks on mountains throughout the world are often cited as proof of the biblical account. But there could be other explanations for this—those mountains might have been underwater in the deep past, millions of years before man walked the Earth. In some instances it could be a matter of lowered sea level. "The past few million years have been a time of steadily decreasing ocean volume" (Macdougall 1996, 216). As an example, on Greenland, which was once three islands, some beaches have been "raised" 1,700 feet. Consider also the high-water marks on plateaus as well as raised beaches at places like Valparaiso, Chile, and Paracas, Peru, where former shorelines have been greatly elevated.

The work of Sir Leonard Woolley along the Tigris-Euphrates seemed at first to corroborate the biblical story; he found 11 feet of silt covering a large area of Mesopotamia; this indicated a flood perhaps

25 feet deep. However, the final analysis revealed it was no more than a local flood. While Woolley was excavating the famous site of Ur, Stephen Langdon made a similar discovery at Kish, a few hundred miles north. Yet the flood deposits at the two sites were *not contemporary*, nor did Langdon's flood cover the whole city. Finally, the Ur site showed no interruption of human occupation, which would clearly be expected if the catastrophe had been a major one.

No, the flood—wherever it was—was not worldwide; even Charles Darwin, along with Charles Lyell, the father of modern geology, maintained the Deluge was not a universal event. So where *was* it?

Archipelagoes

> *The South Sea at one time formed a large Pacific*
> *Continent, and the numerous little islands, which now*
> *lie scattered in it, were simply the highest peaks of the*
> *mountains covering that continent.*
> ERNST HAECKEL, *THE HISTORY OF CREATION*

J. Macmillan Brown was one of the strongest voices arguing that there was at one time a continent if not a densely populated archipelago (inhabited by white men) in the South Pacific. The fact is that all across

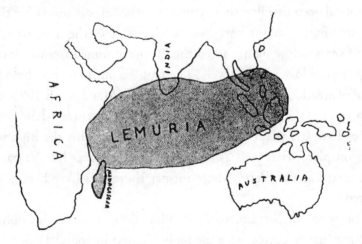

Fig. 10.2. Haeckel's map of Lemuria

the Pacific whole archipelagoes have risen and fallen.* Davis Land is one familiar example—just southeast of the Tuamotu group, and not far from Easter Island, that island was discovered in the 1750s, but could no longer be found in the following century. Other Pacific islands that have vanished in the past few hundred years include Royal Company, Emerald, Dougherty, and the Nimrod Archipelago.

Oceania is vast. It includes some twenty-five thousand islands scattered over about three million square miles. Over the years many have emerged and others sunk into the depths. Easter Island, it is known, lies on an unstable base, between three fracture zones. Traditions on Sala-y-Gomez, which lies a few hundred miles away, say the two islands were formerly connected. Easter Island "is merely the remnant of an archipelago . . . the submergence of which was the primary reason for . . . migrating overseas to America" (Verrill 1943, 12). Indeed, legends of Easter Island (Rapa Nui) say that it was once the center of a large archipelago called Marae Ronga. In *Mysteries of Easter Island,* Francis Maziere proposed a continent, or at best, an archipelago, connecting Easter to the Galapagos Islands (off Ecuador). Consider, in this regard, those underwater pillars found in this region (off Callao, see chapter 1, pp. 22–23); oceanographic maps indicate that the (offshore) Nazca Ridge was once a land bridge connecting Peru to a (now sunken) archipelago.

This geographic continuity is corroborated by cultural continuity, such as the many customs and artifacts shared by Pacific Islanders and South Americans, including owl-eyed figures, blow guns, plank canoes, lime-chewing, head-hunting, men's house, and masked dances. The Mapuche people of Chile make polished stone axes of the same type made in New Zealand.

The belief that chains of archipelagoes formerly helped link parts of Pan to America is particularly compelling in the case of the northwest coast Haida. The northwest coast Indian custom of chewing tobacco mixed with lime is echoed all the way across the Pacific in Japan's and East Asia's custom of chewing betel with lime. All along the Pacific

---

*Patrick Nunn's book, *Vanished Islands and Hidden Continents of the Pacific,* covers the subject in depth.

*Fig. 10.3. Pot with
incised design from the
Jomon period of Japan*

Rim are cultures with carved masks, sea dragons, and totem poles (Williams 2001, 143). It is not unusual to find cultural cousins in far-distant circum-Pacific lands.

PACIFIC RIM AFFINITIES

Regions	Subject of Comparison
Japan and Ecuador	Jomon and Valdivia pottery, respectively
Jomon (and southeast insular Asia) and Native America	dental morphology: sundadonts
Sundaland and America	language: both use numerical classifiers, put verb first in sentence, have pronouns beginning with *m* and *n*
East Asia and the Andes	metal types, techniques, and decorations
Indochina, Ecuador, and Peru	identical balsa rafts (De Bisschop 1959, 47)
East Asia and Mexico	arts, symbols, calendar
Tikal and Anghor Wat	steepness of pyramids
Central America and Cambodia	architecture and customs (Spence 1933, 188), agriculture and handicraft
Chichén Itzá and Cambodia	style of monuments
Mayan Puuc and Cambodia	half-columns, facades, doors, and windows
Mexican Tajin (Totonac) and Burma	niche pyramids (pagoda)

Fenua Nui

In the Pacific Islands, Hawaiki is one of the most common terms for the lost land, "the ancient Father-land," about which Percy Smith comments "that a continent rather than an island is referred to, and this is the description given to me of Hawaiki-hui by . . . a very learned member of the Ngai-Tahu tribe of the [Maori] South Island: 'Hawaiki-nui was a mainland (*tua-whenua*) with vast plains . . . and a high range of snowy mountains; through this country ran the river Tohinga'" (1921, 44–45). Tohinga includes the telltale *hin,* signifying the original white race of Oceania.

> *Hiva is a land that is gone. Now it is below the Pacific Ocean.*
> MARCOS, AN EASTER ISLANDER

Why do Malekulans say there was originally no sea, only land? All the islands, according to Tahitian tradition, were once united in Fenua Nui, one large continent, of which Tahiti is but a fragment. Tua-whenua is another name for the vast mainland from which the Polynesians say they came. On Panape, legend again speaks of a bygone continent, here called Kalu'a, "Our motherland rests at the bottom of the ocean." Indeed, Panape's mountains have no shells, suggesting the true mountains of Pan, even though the standard model says that all Pacific Islands are either volcanic or coral. What then of the islands that more resemble mountain peaks?

> *These islands are the remains of a series of mountain chains.*
> LEWIS SPENCE, *THE PROBLEM OF LEMURIA*

Did great mountain ranges once cross the Pacific continent? Today the islands of the Carolines, Tahiti, Marquesas, and Hawaii are mountainous, some peaks in Hawaii higher than 12,000 feet. Ocean-floor maps of the Pacific outline mountain ranges; in the 1950s great elevations were found in the southern part of the East Pacific Rise. By 1977 an erstwhile country was identified based on submerged plateaus (the Manihiki and Ong-Java) in the ocean near Australia. An international

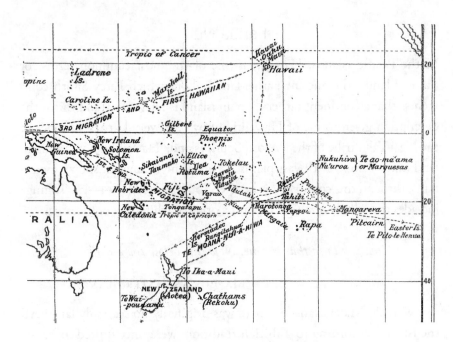

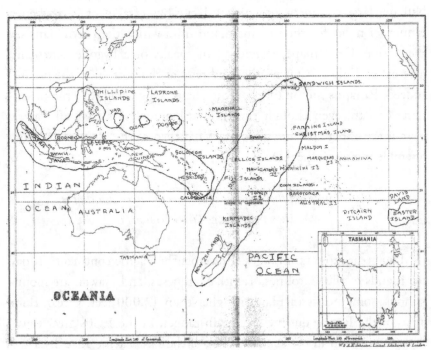

Fig. 10.4. Two maps of Pacific Ocean from
Lewis Spence and Percy Smith

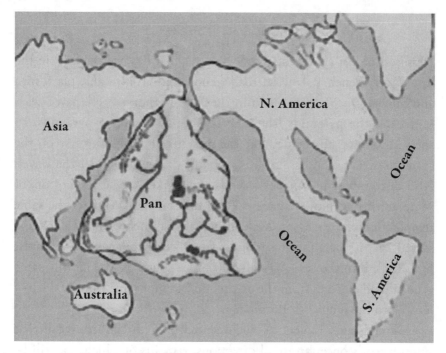

Fig. 10.5. Map showing rivers and mountains of Pan

team of geophysicists, calling it the eighth continent, named it "Pacifica."[*]

Fifty years before that, soundings had revealed river courses *east* of Japan. But even before that, the map of Pan published in Oahspe in *1882* showed two long rivers, which appear to flow from *highlands*. According to the current editors of Oahspe, Ruth and Vernon Wobschall,[†] there were no mountains in Churchward's version of Mu. Yet "Oahspe was clear about the mountains of Pan, particularly those in the north where Japan, the northern remnant, remained above the ocean." It was fifty years after the publication of Oahspe that United States Navy soundings in the 1930s discovered those mountains east of Japan.

---

[*]Nevertheless, the guardians of the standard model find a way to impugn the lost land. "Today most geologists regard the Manihiki Plateau not as a fragment of Pacifica but as a Large Igneous Province formed 120 million years ago at a junction between three plates" (Nunn 2009, 66).

[†]See, http://oahspestandardedition.com/OSAC/PanSubmergedContinent.html (accessed 5-22-2016).

Roads to the Sea

Despisers of lost continents simply ignore what has been sighted in the waters off French Polynesia: roads, enormous stone walls, platforms, and pillars. On Malden Island in the Line Islands as well, paved ways lead from the pyramids (the deserted island has forty pyramids) to the sea, looking all the day like the remains of a highway system; the road, constructed of basalt blocks, simply disappears under the waves. Also discounted are Panape's legends of a sunken city at the bottom of Metalanim Bay. Now Panape—3,400 miles distant—boasts the same temple architecture as on Malden, which, say historians, was once a sacred isle; its neighboring islands, from which pilgrims came, must have sunk into the sea. A full 1,500 miles south of Malden the same type of road emerges from the ocean—in a straight line from Malden—leading to the jungles of Rarotonga.

Easter Island Tablets, as documented by Churchward, recall that smooth roads once ran in all directions, remains of which can still be seen (2011, 66, 24). Yap in the Carolines also whispers of an ancient, vanished civilization, judging from remains of solid roads neatly paved with regular stone blocks. A United Nations research mission in 1972 found evidence of a submerged city between Maui and Oahu. But United States Naval Intelligence corked it: Top Secret. Nevertheless, diplomat Farida Iskoviet, sent by United Nations president Adam Malik found the ruins of a lost land in Hawaiian waters to be genuine.

> E fenua tu tahi, o Havai'i-nui. (All was one land, Great Havai'i.)
>
> TAHITIAN LEGEND

The vast Pacific Ocean covers more than one-third of the Earth's surface; a triangle with points at Japan, Jakarta, and Pitcairn Island, it covers 60 degrees of latitude and 120 degrees of longitude. To give you some idea of the great distances between Pacific islands see the list on page 403.

Easter Island to Tahiti = 2,300 miles
Easter Island to Hawaii = 4,000 miles
Easter Island to Fiji = 4,200 miles
Easter Island to New Hebrides = 5,000 miles
Tahiti to Fiji = 2,670 miles
Hawaii to Tahiti = 2,000 miles
Hawaii to the Marshall Islands = 2,360 miles
Hawaii to New Zealand = 3,200 miles

Flora and Fauna

Despite the great distances between islands, there is a close resemblance of the flora and fauna of Hawaii and Southwest Polynesia; "the affinity of the land shells* is even more convincing" (Brown 1924, 48). The same birds inhabit the Ladrones in the west and the Marquesas in the east—separated by 5,000 miles, indicating, at least to the great naturalist Alfred R. Wallace, that these islands "are but the relics of a more extensive land" (quoted in Spence 1933, 172).

I find it curious that Polynesia has no reptiles bigger than a lizard, yet their mythology is full of monster snakes (the deadly *mo'o*), once the terror of the inhabitants. Were these great serpents extinguished when the continent of Pan went down? *Mo'o* meant "alligator or crocodile" in the legends of the distant past, none of which exist today in Tahiti.

D. H. Childress brings to our attention a species of sacred flower, the *tiare apetahi,* which grows on the volcanic slopes of Raiatea, though also seen 500 miles away at Rapa Iti and the Marquesas; he wonders if this data pertains to "a lost continent in the Pacific" (1988, 268–69).

Fiji and Samoa have species of iguanas that are descended from those in the Galapagos Islands; many others, which could not swim

---

*Joseph Christy-Vitaly in his book *Watermark* informs us that land shells from the mollusk family, spread all across the Pacific, "have a natural aversion to salt water . . . their distribution and close relationship has convinced a number of botanists that a large, continental land-mass once existed in this vast oceanic region. . . . The evidence creates the impression all these animals were stranded by some sudden and dramatic event in the recent geologic past" (2004).

great distances, are still found at far-removed locations. The supposed explanation is that they arrived on natural rafts, like pumice mats. Patrick Nunn likewise attempts to explain away the same butterfly species in the Marquesas and Pitcairn Island—thousands of kilometers apart—as merely the result of a favorable "equatorial ocean current." He also invokes that old standby "parallel evolution" to explain the same biota on far distant Pacific islands. He also argues, ineffectively I think, that plate tectonics (another standby) can explain all this, and therefore we no longer need land bridges to account for the spread of biota; further, "biotic colonizations of the Pitcairn Group from eastern French Polynesia . . . was facilitated by the exposure during the ice ages of now-submerged islands" (2009, 52, 58, 68).

Further Signs of Boluto

Closely related Negrito groups of Oceania are also widely dispersed, yet they are not mariners; so how can we explain their occupation of far-distant islands? Abraham Fornander, one of the first great authorities of Polynesian life and history, remarked "the singular spectacle of a people so widely scattered, yet so homogeneous in its physical characteristics, language, and customs. Marquesan and Hawaiian cosmogenesis," he also notes, "is almost identical, though 3,000 miles of ocean separate them" (1969, 1:1, 82–85). The cosmogonic myths of the Marquesas are also strikingly analogous to extremely distant New Zealand's. And though more than 2,000 miles of ocean separate the Marquesas from Easter Island, their languages and artifacts (fishhooks, adzes, etc.) are remarkably similar. Indeed, the same "rotating" fish hook is used from Polynesia to Melanesia. The paring tool of the Marquesas is "identical with shell peelers found in Melanesia thousands of miles to the west" (Suggs 1962, 106).

Just as tattooing is practiced all across Polynesia, "the appearance and language of these islanders are essentially the same over thousands of miles" (Kolosimo 1975, 56). They not only speak languages derived from the same stock but also share customs, sagas, and religious beliefs. Their lost homeland is called Burotu on Fiji and Boluto on distant Samoa.

Fig. 10.6. Marquesan rotating hook, also common on Easter Island and Hawaii

The people inhabiting nearly all the islands from New Zealand to the Sandwich Islands . . . all have certain rites and customs which, like their related dialects, indicate a common origin.

JOHN D. BALDWIN, *PRE-HISTORIC NATIONS*

The greater gods of Polynesia "are practically the same over the whole oceanic area" (Spence 1933, 72). Though Hawaii and New Zealand are thousands of miles apart, they have the same legend of a demigod named Maui fishing up the land from the sea. This tale is told in all parts of the Pacific. Hawaii's "bird men" glyphs, moreover, are identical to those at Easter Island, 4,000 miles away to the south. But most of all is the eternal puzzle of the rongorongo boards. Most scholars have had no choice but to agree* that Easter Island's rongo-rongo script could have served no purpose on such a tiny island (64 square miles); it must have been part of a much wider civilization. "It is absurd to think that it could have originated in a small island" (Spence 1933, 208). Script also appears in the Carolines, at Oleai, about which

---

*Most, not all! The straight-laced historian will argue, for example, that "the Easter Island tablets show us how a system of signs . . . could develop in a relatively small society" (Renfrew 1973, 186). The statement blithely ignores rongorongo cognates found in the Carolines and even in China, India, and Panama.

the same could be said. Some of the hundreds of Easter Island's rongo-rongo glyphs are found in the far-off Caroline Islands; while numerous elements of Easter vocabulary match up with words on Rarotonga, Hawaii, and Formosa. Even across a stretch of 6,000 miles there are close linguistic ties; the syntax and lexicon of Tonga, Samoa, Hawaii, and New Zealand are so intimately related that we must hypothesize the former existence of a shared mother country. "There is no difference in quoting a dialect of a single Pacific Island . . . for there is relationship between almost all these vernaculars, and we can draw the same conclusions from tongues of any of the Pacific tribes" (Wadler 1948, 169).

Easter Island's megaliths, moreover, are of the same stamp as those in the Marquesas, while the ruins at Mangaia, near Cook Island, though far distant from Easter Island, resemble them. Although more than 700 miles separate Tahiti from Rarotonga, both islands belonged to a common megalithic culture. Tahiti, with her stone temples (marae), is situated many thousands of miles from the Marianas, yet their immense stone structures seem to be the work of a single people; the Marianas' lattes "bear a general resemblance to the colossi of Easter Island, despite the 7,750 miles separating them" (Joseph 2006, 109).

When we consider the buildings used for men's societies throughout Oceania, we again find them of a common type across the board. Fiji's secret stone enclosures (and name of the cult) are called *nanga,* and they resemble the marae of Polynesia. Though more than 4,000 miles of ocean separate the Marianas from Tahiti, the Marianas' men's societies form an intermediate between the areois of Tahiti and the clubhouse of Melanesia, while similar associations flourished in the Carolines. Marquesan and Tahiti areoi platforms are similar, as are those of Pitcairn and many other islands, enough "to suggest a common origin" (Childress 1988, 266–67).

Miracle of the Pacific

Panape legend says that the ruins on Nan Madol were built by two brothers, Olochipa and Olochopa; Tahitians also say that the areois began with two brothers—Orotetefa and Urutetefa, after their splendid kingdom was destroyed by a cataclysm. These two pairs of names are variants of one original, though found as much as 4,000 miles apart. Samoan legend also records that only two men survived the flood, just as two brothers are said to be the founders of Marquesan society. (In Central America the Sumu people say that two brothers created the world—the older one named Pa-*Pan*!)

Though Panape's artificial islets make up a Venice-like city of gigantic blocks, the rock itself is unfamiliar, possibly hewn from lands now submerged. Indeed, Nan Madol's type of basalt is not found anywhere on the island; no one knows where all that stone came from. Ditto the basalt ruins on Kosrae. "We may not be wrong in concluding that the great stones erected at Pohnpei [Panape] and Kosrae were brought from Mu." Despite that enormous distance, Kosrae is a "mirror image of Nan Madol" (Joseph 2006, 28, 48, 39). Separated by 450 miles, the columns off Nan Madol and the latte pillars of Guam are nonetheless similar. Nor is there any platinum in the Carolines to account for Panape's platinum-made "coffin receptacles." Was that platinum mined in a country that disappeared into the deep blue sea?

Panape's small population today could never have built her vast, gargantuan edifices. Like Easter Island, it is a remote speck of an island with relatively few inhabitants who possess no clue as to its former manpower and technical know-how. To those who have seen and studied it firsthand, Panape's great cyclopean ruins imply a lost empire.

> There are 11 square miles of huge public buildings. . . . Rafting over the reef . . . and hauling up these immense blocks . . . to such a height . . . must have meant tens of thousands of [laborers who] had to be housed and clothed and fed. Yet within a radius of 1,500 miles . . . there are no more than 50,000 people today. It is one of the miracles of the Pacific unless we assume a subsidence of twenty times as much land as now exists. (Brown 1924, 52)

On Tonga (which name appears to come from the Panic word *T'ong,* meaning "south," see Book of Saphah: Osiris 65) the tons of coral limestone used in their famous monumental arch must have been ferried

Fig. 10.7. Tongatapu acclaimed trilithon, Ha'amonga arch
drawn by Churchward in 1876

in by survivors from Buroto; holes in the reef at Uea may still be seen. Similarly, the stone statues on Micronesia's Palau, at Babeldaob, were sculpted from andesite, which is not native to the island. Babeldaob is rich in stone statues, some quite similar to the moai of Easter Island, an immense distance away.

Joseph also brings into the discussion the uncommonly large food-producing terraces on Palau, the scope of this agricultural project "so vast that its yields could have provided for hundreds of thousands of people, far more than have ever inhabited Palau." For Joseph, the same interpretation would hold for works in the Marianas where the latte "required techniques for their construction far beyond those found among the resources of these obscure islands . . . [implying] an impact made on the Marianas in the remote past by an advanced population" (2006, 111).

Lemuria

To the occultist, Lemuria may be best known as the home of Madame Blavatsky's "third root race." This hypothetical land got its name from the lemurs that inhabit Madagascar, India, Africa, and Malaysia; the

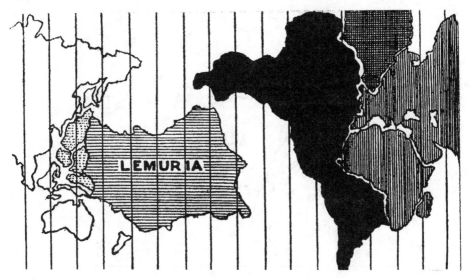

Fig. 10.8. Rosicrucian map of Lemuria

fabled land of Lemuria was introduced to explain the spread and distribution of these animals across a supposed land bridge that once connected southern Africa and Asia. There were also similar sediments in those lands, as well as comparable flora and fauna, all of which led to the theory that India, eastern Australia, and New Zealand once formed a single biological region covering much of the Indian and Pacific Oceans, extending even to the Antarctic and, as some suppose, to the Himalayas.

One stream of thought surmised that, eons ago, before the submergence of this great southern continent, California was the center of a civilization dominating a mountainous country with fertile valleys—before the sea rolled over the remainder of the United States. So it was believed, at least according to a league called the Stelle Group, that Lemuria was a continent embracing all of present-day Philippines, Australia, New Zealand, Oceania, western America, and everything in between!

At this point though, Lemuria can get confused with "Gondwana," the hypothetical supercontinent of the Southern Hemisphere dated to the Paleozoic era. The idea of Gondwana came into being with the

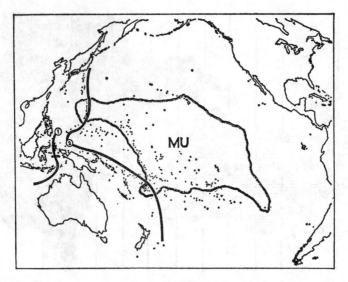

*Fig. 10.9. Wallace's Line. A. R. Wallace, Charles Darwin's cofounder
of evolution, spoke of the breakup of landmasses into islands but
couldn't explain the upheaval responsible for it.*

observation of striking resemblances between Permian fossils and rock
formations of South Africa on the one hand and those found in the
part of central India called Gondwana. These were schist and sandstone formations that occur also in Madagascar, Australia, and South
America. It was thought that all these places had been united in a single
landmass during the Mesozoic Age, or about 150 million years ago.*

To add to the marvelous confusion regarding the shape of Old
Mother Earth, there was also a continent called "Rutas" in Sanskrit
tradition, located in the Indian Ocean. The Frenchman Louis Jacolliot
studied these records and came away with the impression that Rutas
actually meant a continent stretching from Ceylon to Sumatra to
the Pacific Ocean—but many hundreds of thousands of years ago.
Blavatsky, though, thought Rutas lay in the North Pacific, while she
called the Indian Ocean landmass "Daitya."

---

*The interested reader can consult D. H. Childress on why and how the Gondwana
theory was disproved (1988, 35, 156).

Pretty confusing, eh? Nevertheless there was no doubt that a line of separation divides the region of continental/insular Asia from the outlying islands to the east; Wallace's Line defined a sharp division of Eastern faunal types from Australian ones, which were further linked to the Marquesas and the Hawaiian Islands. Malaysia is full of monkeys, cats, and elephants—a sharp contrast to the kangaroos and marsupials in Australia.

Although Bali and Lombock in the Malayan Archipelago are less than two hours apart, their animal life differs greatly, as does the fauna from Java to Celebes. Ernst Haeckel (a German evolutionist) interpreted Wallace's Line as indicating that Malaysia was formerly attached to the Asian continent, while the Celebes, Moluccas, New Guinea, Solomon Islands, and such were formerly connected with Australia.

Boomerangs

But what theory can account for the similar mammalian faunas in Australia and *South America*? If a Pacific continent once connected them, this would explain why early Australians, according to DNA studies, shared similar genes with Tierra del Fuegans, ancient Brazilians, and Californians. BBC News Sci/Tech announced on August 26, 1999, that "First Americans Were Australian."* The first Californians were not Mongoloid in type (as the stubborn Bering Strait hypothesis demands) but Australoid; the throwing stick (for hunting small prey) of the Diegeno California tribe looks a lot like an Australian boomerang,† other crossovers including tool-making techniques and male initiation rites. California and Australia also admit matching soils and trees—the oldest in the world; eucalyptus and acacia are native only to those two lands, which also share identical lizards and tree frogs.

America's opossum is the only marsupial in the world outside of Australia. Marsupials in Patagonia "show an Australian stamp . . . [suggesting] some sort of land-connection between South America and

---

*http://news.bbc.co.uk/2/hi/sci/tech/430944.stm (accessed 5-1-2016).
†A boomerang was also used in India and Africa.

Australia" (Spence 1933, 178–79). Likewise are there mutual resemblances among the birds, amphibians, and fish found exclusively in these two regions.

"North American terrains share . . . faunas and floras with New Zealand, [New] Caledonia, the Antarctica peninsula, and Chile. . . . The existence of Pacifica may . . . provide the continental connection . . . needed to explain the evolutionary history of flora such as the angiosperms, and fauna such as various fusilinids and mammals around the Pacific" (Childress 1988, 239).

Bottle gourds of Peru are identical to those of Polynesia, as are amaranth, peanut, jackbean, lima bean, and jicama; the two locations also show the same type of oven, fishhook, and fish poison. Cassava and yams grow in South America and Micronesia; plants native to Polynesia like the banana are found in Peruvian graves. Of course, the standard model deplores such link-ups; Patrick Nunn accounts for the identity of Colombian and Melanesian coconuts by invoking "ocean currents [which] could have carried coconuts throughout the tropical Pacific" (2009, 110).

The sweet potato may indicate Polynesian influence on the Pacific coast of South America—although the jury is out on that one, because sweet potatoes were all over Central America *and* Polynesia—where "the kumara grew wild in the open places." Later it was planted the same way, in small mounds, at Tahiti and the Antilles. But Polynesians claim that they have always had kumara—from time immemorial, having brought them from Hawaiki. Sweet potato was apparently native to Wha-ga (Pan); "the kumara appears to have been in charge of Wha-nui [var. Whaga?] . . . quite possibly a territorial designation. It is said that the root was stolen by Rongo-maui from Whanui." A Maori chant, *Ko Hawaiki te whenua, e tupu noa mai te kumara,* translates as "Hawaiki is the land where the kumara grows spontaneously." Interestingly, we find the name Pan embedded in the Maori story explaining the origin of kumara: "It is the offspring of *Pani*-tinaku, a woman who is said to have been the wife of Rongo-maui. . . . Pani is the person who gave the food to Hawaiki" (Smith 1921, 143, 149, 37–8). Hence, pan is "bread" in Spanish.

The Outsized Ocean

The Pacific contains the only tectonic plate without a
continent on it.
        TJEERD VAN ANDEL, *NEW VIEWS ON AN OLD PLANET*

We can see that the Earth's crust is still wounded along the edges of
the Pacific plate. What trauma does it bespeak? It is my impression
that geologists outside the Anglo sphere have been a bit more forth-
right about these "anomalies" of the Pacific. The Russian scientist
V. V. Belousov, for example, has written in *The Geological Structure of the
Oceans* that the Pacific Ocean grew considerably at the expense of great
chunks of continents that, together with their young ranges of mountains, were inundated by it. Yes, inundated.

So why do theorists try to explain the enormous extent of the
Pacific Ocean with theories that sound even more far-fetched than
the idea of a lost continent? The first imagined culprit is a large satellite that carried away a section of our crust, leaving a scar in the deep
basin of the Pacific. The next likely guess is that in some long-ago eon a
rogue protoplanet slammed into Earth, broke up the Pacific lands, and
blasted a huge amount of debris into space. Some of the debris clumped
together to form the moon.

Back in the late nineteenth century it was Osmond Fisher and
George Darwin (Charles's son) who proposed that the moon had been
a piece of the Earth's crust thrown off in an earlier age when the Earth
was spinning much faster. The moon's mass, however, is too large for
the purpose and also has a different specific gravity than the Earth's
crust. Furthermore, why would crust, torn from the Earth, go into orbit
rather than simply fall back into the ocean?*

But theorists undaunted by the failings of the Fisher-Darwin
hypothesis are drawn, maybe for the wrong reasons, to explanations of

---

*More likely the moon's genesis goes something like this: In the early days of the vortex
of the Earth, so swiftly flew the outer rim that border eddies ensued, from which nebula
congregated until the Earth had a nebulous belt around it. This belt in time, losing pace
with the Earth's vortex, condensed, and made the moon.

violence, such as the notion of an immense explosion caused by "the collision with a planetesimal or a satellite . . . [thus] excavating a large crater of several thousand kilometers in radius. . . . The great masses of material that were swept back and dropped at the rim of the crater formed discontinuities of crustal structure . . . responsible for the peripheral features of the Pacific Basin" (Corliss 1983, 345). The features of that crust have been a point of contention for many years. The trained geologist, for some reason, is deeply offended by the lost continent idea, and just to prove his point, has authoritatively declared that not a single piece of continental rock (i.e., granite) has ever been found on any of the Pacific Islands; they are strictly basaltic. Supposedly. But dredging data has provided evidence for continental crust under the deep abyssal plains of the northwest Pacific as well as for "paleolands in the southwest Pacific" (Jones 2008, 245). Science nonetheless insists that "continental-type rocks are not found in the Pacific, and theories as to magnificent causeways and sunken continents have been disproved" (Wilson 1975, 39).

Land areas, we do understand, are mostly "sialic" (i.e., composed of light rocklike granite), while the sea bottoms are most "sima," heavy rocklike basalt. Lava is basaltic; islands like Samoa are made up of volcanic rock. Geologists therefore do not believe such islands are the remains of any continent, but merely the outgrowth of volcanic eruptions. East of the andesite line, declares De Camp, "not one pebble of continental-type rock has ever been found" (1975, 158). Therefore we can forget any romantic ideas of lost continents . . .

However, volcanoes near the Pacific trenches pour out andesite lavas, which are "intermediate in composition between oceanic and continental rocks, rather than the basalt typical of the mid-ocean ridge" (Van Andel 1985, 94). Scientist George Gamow, reverting to the moon-grabbing theory, explains the basalt as follows:

Fig. 10.10. Apolima Island, Samoa

It is quite likely that the area now occupied by the Pacific is the very place where the huge bulk of matter now forming the Moon was torn away from the Earth. . . . There is hardly any doubt that the floor of the Pacific is formed exclusively of basaltic rocks as if some cosmic hand had removed the entire granite layer from all this vast area. (1948, 56–57)

Only in the Pacific is granite so wanting. Gamow goes on to explain that

the upper crust of the Earth is a layer of granite from 50 to 100 kilometres thick resting on a much thicker layer of heavier basalt. This is true of all the continents and also of parts of the Earth's crust that are submerged beneath the waters of the Atlantic, Indian, and Arctic oceans. . . . However, the granite layer is considerably thinner. But the vast expanse of the Pacific is a striking exception. (1948, 56–57)

Explanation? Maybe Gamow is right that "some cosmic hand"—like the legions of Aph, as described in the previous chapter—made quick work of the granite layer.

Nevertheless, "the islands of Melanesia . . . are basically continental" (Cameron 1987, 22). Continental trees like *Podocarpus foliolatus* as well as other continental flora grow on Fiji and Tonga. And why have archaeologists found tools in Polynesia that are made from continental rocks like chert? Actually, there are parts of the Earth's crust that are neither strictly sialic nor simatic, as found in the Philippines, New Guinea, Japan, and Fiji. Chert is found in the Pacific Islands; quartz implements, granite mortars, schist, diorite, and jade are found in New Guinea (Perry 1968, 29), while nephrite is the New Zealand material out of which the Maoris fashioned their tikis.

Garnets have been found on Rurutu, feldspar on Huahine. In Bora-Bora there are masses of rock containing feldspar and quartz; in Maupiti "a species of granite is found in considerable abundance" (Ellis 1931, 12). When Robert Suggs explored Nahotoa Cave in the Marquesas (between Taipi and Taihae), he found it "surrounded by granite cliffs" (Suggs 1962, 163). We also learn that the island of Partida, lying in the Pacific off the

Mexican coast, is formed of granite; in fact, from Partida an underwater plateau extends all the way to the Galapagos Islands off Ecuador. Here, dredging has brought up branches, wood, logs, and decayed vegetable matter. Off Guatemala too are heavy beds of conglomerate—which is sialic. Apparently "not a single station between Acapulco . . . and the Galapagos Islands could be characterized as strictly oceanic" (Spence 1933, 133). Such facts tally with Francis Maziere's belief that an archipelago once linked the Galapagos with Easter Island and the Marquesas, while Churchward himself was "under the impression that originally the Galapagos Belt and the Japanese-Ladrone Belt were one. Subsequently a cave-in took place . . ." (Churchward 1935, 184).

Sediments

We should also ask why Atlantic sediments, on average, are twice as thick as Pacific ones. Is it because the Pacific has been the scene of large-scale geologic disruption in relatively recent time? One type of sediment in particular has caught the eye of Panologists: clean white ash on the eastern Pacific floor, laid down quickly and recently, appears to be of terrestrial, not volcanic, origin.

Lack of calcareous mud is another mystery; deep sediments in the Pacific (from the equator northward) are unlike those on the rest of the world's oceans. The Pacific does not contain calcareous mud from the shells of crustaceans, creatures that settled cumulatively to the bottom over long ages. Isn't it possible that some titanic force obliterated that layer or that Pan, not long since, was above sea level? While the mid-ocean ridge of the Atlantic is buried under a thick blanket of continental sediment, the Pacific's ridge is naked, unburied. Why? There is also something called cold residue that formed below the mid-Pacific ridge when the ridge was displaced by an unknown upheaval of the Pacific mantle. Whatever the impact was, it was sufficiently great to produce an enormous plume of lower-mantle material that pushed up beneath places like Tahiti.

And then there is the coal. Too bad Churchward was no longer around when coal, which is a product of continental land, was discovered on Rapa Iti (south of Tahiti, near Mangareva), silencing the detractors of his beloved Mu and proving the Pacific Basin to have once been high and dry. The colonel would have also enjoyed the discovery of "super-swell" across the Central Pacific, the term indicating a vast region of shallow sea—and things called "seamounts."

Seamounts

These submarine mountains called seamounts may be key. Actually, Churchward was still alive when the first of these underwater mesas was found off the coast of California in 1933. But it wasn't until 1956 that sediments retrieved from the summits of *mid-Pacific* seamounts made a clear statement about their past history: they contained fossils of shallow-water species—although now found at depths of up to 2½ miles! How could such displacement have occurred?

Quite tall, many standing 10,000 feet above the ocean floor, the tops of these mounts, which are also called guyots or abyssal hills, seem to have once gazed down on dry land. How so? The ripple marks seen on guyots only form by wave action (i.e., at the surface). Rings of fossil corals on guyots in the South Seas, now at a depth of 800 feet, cannot have formed in water deeper than a hundred feet or so. What's more, the astonishingly flat tops of these gigantic guyots or "tablemounts"— most more than 5 miles in diameter—could only have formed above water by subaerial weathering.

Furthermore, researchers have noted a striking but puzzling uniformity in the *height* of North Pacific seamounts. "It would appear they *together* experienced a process or event responsible for their inundation. . . . Are these guyots . . . the former lands of Mu? Buildings and pillars found off Peru at the same depth imply as much" (Joseph 2006, 294–95; emphasis added). The reference is to Callao, Peru (see chapter 1, pp. 22–23); note that the Callao tsunami of 1746, which was 80 feet high, sank nineteen ships anchored in its path (De Camp 1975, 176).

It came as a surprise to academic archaeologists (but not to Panologists) when the Cobb Seamount, part of a chain of sunken mountains reaching as far as the Gulf of Alaska, gave up man-made artifacts including eighteen-thousand-year-old pottery. Finally, the most striking

418   ᴄᴏ RING OF FIRE

feature of the Pacific Ocean's hundreds of seamounts is their posture; some found at the edges of oceanic trenches are tilted, although they of course were formed in an upright position. What unthinkable impact could have tilted them?

Black Hole in the Pacific

Speaking of trenches, the Tonga Trench has been described as an "incredible gash"—7 miles deep; meanwhile, on the other side of the Pacific, "abysmal submarine trenches are eating up land like the black holes of outer space. And like black holes, gravity measurements near the trenches show marked departures from expected values. . . . If a submerged continent really does exist in the Pacific, this deep trough marks its western border" (Williams 2001, 75). Along that border, at Panape, someone once ran a little experiment, placing a pocket compass against the basalt blocks; it spun around and around, the magnetism showing a corkscrew pattern rather than the expected vertical one. Also, a strangely weak gravity above Pacific Rim trenches has been noted but never explained.

Some of Oceania's trenches lie farther below sea level than Mount Everest rises above it—Everest rises 29,000 feet in the air while the Mariana Trench is the lowest point on Earth at 36,000 feet below sea level. Another record holder, the Ring of Fire that surrounds the Pacific tectonic plate contains most of the world's active volcanoes. The Mariana Trench, at the plate's western edge, methodically swallows the westward-moving crust, this area experiencing some of the worst volcanic eruptions. Cosmologist and researcher M. H. Jones asks, "If trenches mark where sea floor, moving away from a central ridge, descends beneath the continents, where are the trenches on either side of the Atlantic?* If the trenches on the rim of the northwest Pacific are swallowing sea floor manufactured along a midocean ridge, where is that ridge? What forces could have caused such large-scale distortions of the sea floor?" (2008, 249–50). Like the matching heights of the seamounts, the Pacific's most prominent trenches lie at the *same depth*

---

*The only trench in the Atlantic is the one in the Caribbean.

below sea level, "suggesting they were all products of a similar process" (249–50). What's more, materials expected only in shallow water are found on the floor of some of these trenches.

> Deep trenches almost follow the same outline of the ancient continent. . . . The Tonga/Kermadec trench begins a series of Fracture Zones . . . that stripe the South Eastern and North Eastern Pacific in a wide arc. This arc follows the Eastern contour of the outline of Pan, as shown in Oahspe, and ends in the Aleutian Trench in the far North. . . . Maps of these details were not available at the time of Oahspe's publication [1882].
>
> HTTP://OAHSPESTANDARDEDITION.COM/OSAC
> /PANSUBMERGEDCONTINENT.HTML (ACCESSED 5-23-2016)

Submarine volcanoes are particularly active in the region of the Kermadec and Tonga Islands. Rapid subduction of the Pacific plate fuels the intense volcanism that has made the Ring of Fire so famous. Volcanoes typify the Pacific Basin, just as most tsunamis originate in the Pacific. The most devastating tsunamis of centuries past have occurred along that rim.

> Lima, Peru, 1724: waves 80 feet high
> Kamchatka, Russia, 1737: waves 210 feet high
> Arica, Peru, 1868: waves 52 feet high
> Iquique, Chile, 1877: waves 80 feet high
> Krakatoa, 1883: waves up to 100 feet high
> Sanriku, Japan, 1896: waves up to 100 feet high

Secret of the Wet Zone

With the recent unexpected discovery of a vast quantity of underground water along the Pacific Rim (enough to fill an ocean), oceanographic scientists are dumbfounded. The cause remains unknown, except to surmise that some extraordinary event caused an enormous amount of water to find its way beneath the land surrounding the Pacific.

Announced in 2007, this anomalous body of water, the size of the Arctic Ocean, lies beneath eastern Asia at a depth of 400–800 miles, this "wet zone" running from Indonesia to northernmost Russia. It is suggested that the water got there when the ocean bottom was pulled beneath the continental plates all around the Pacific Rim. Predictably, scientists attribute all this to a cataclysm that occurred tens of millions of years ago. It is the kind of scientific guesswork that intentionally precludes the lost continent interpretation. Removing Pan/Pacifica to the remotest eons is simply scientific strategy—even policy—bent on effacing all evidence of Pleistocene civilization in the Pacific, the motherland of man. If the extraordinary wet zone threatens to confer a breakthrough for Panology, clever geologists would nip it in the bud, quash it, with polysyllabic mumbo jumbo blaming everything on the supposedly dependable science of subduction and plate tectonics.

But can plate tectonics explain everything? Cosmologist Ruth Wobschall does not think this slippage of immense amounts of water beneath the Earth's crust can be explained by natural geological process. "Unless theorists consider the forceful sinking of a continent in the Pacific Ocean (outside of geological cause and effect), they will continue to tail-chase without any realistic solutions. . . . [Science] claims that the cause was water seeping, after degassing of the Earth's mantle . . . and that water is required for lubrication and stability of land masses! However, these theories explain nothing, especially why this phenomenon is seen only in the area where the continent of Pan was sunk. . . ."*

Ring of Fire

Unlike all the oceans of the Earth, the Pacific is surrounded by a ring of fold mountains—in the Andes, Antarctica, Japan, Kamchatka, southern China, Australia, New Guinea, New Zealand—with intense volcanic and seismic activity. The mountainous western coast of North and South America and the eastern coast of Asia see the greatest earthquake activity, accounting for 80 percent of Earth's seismicity. Elsewhere on our planet, quakes and volcanism are not specifically located at the

---

*Personal communication.

boundaries of continents and oceans; nor are mountain ranges typical of coasts but more likely to be in the interior. It is also curious that only in one part of the world is the expected mid-ocean ridge actually at the *edge* of the ocean; the South Pacific ridge, running northward to become the North Pacific ridge, reaches right up to the West Coast of North America—defining the San Andreas Fault.

Horseshoe shaped in overview, the Pacific Ring of Fire is marked by a nearly continuous chain of oceanic trenches, volcanic arcs (over 450 volcanoes) and plate movements; most of the world's serious earthquakes occur along the Ring of Fire. The largest ones (at the two sides of the fault) have occurred in Japan (1891), Alaska (1899), and San Francisco (1906). Says Nunn, "The Pacific Ring of Fire is the band of active volcanoes that runs along the borders of the Pacific Ocean. Its existence has often been used to justify the impression of the Pacific as a primeval place, the site of some great global cataclysm. This is incorrect. The Ring of Fire traces the places in the Pacific Basin where crustal plates are being destroyed along convergent plate boundaries" (Nunn 2009, fig. 2.3). Though standard scientific patter attributes the Ring of Fire to the ordinary workings of plate tectonics and subduction, there is nothing ordinary about it. Another way of viewing the phenomena is offered by Childress who has astutely pointed out that the submerged platforms in the southwest Pacific "show typical crustal structures . . . [and] may thus be fragments of Pacifica" (Childress 1988, 240).

The seismic passivity of the *mid-ocean* region is in direct contrast with the relentless tectonic activity in the region *surrounding* it, where we find not only dissimilar crustal structures in close contact but also coastal landmasses that are folded as if by thrust against the denser and stronger mass of the Pacific Basin. Though quakes are still common in the New Hebrides volcanic islands, it has been observed that the period of Oceania's greatest seismic activity has passed—there is "a diminution in the old-time severity of earthquakes" (Williamson 1933, 2:211). As Lewis Spence put it, "no continents have since been submerged . . . and it remains as a logical consequence that the numerous [legends] of continents formerly existing must be a legacy from an older race—the fair-haired native race of Oceania" (Spence 1933, 72).

THE LAND
OF CLAY HILLS

Og [on Wagga], with her thousand cities . . . shall sink to rise
no more.

OAHSPE, SYNOPSIS OF SIXTEEN CYCLES 3:28

New Zealanders say that their ancestral home was a hilly land. Hawaiians too recall that their founder, Lono, came from a sunken country called "the hilly land of Tau." Even in Mexico's Troano Codex, Mu is dubbed "the land of clay hills," where Homen, by his strong will, had caused the earth to tremble; overnight, "the country of the hills of mud was submerged."

In North America, Og-allah was a term used to describe their ancestral records and achievements (Cohane 1969, 138). Probing this curious name, Og, and those muddy hills of clay, we find that among the Bay of Bengal Andamanese *og* is the word for common clay, similar perhaps to Og-wila, an English term for volcanic ash, or to Egypt's legendary Og-doad, who first appeared on the "mound of creation," producing man from clay. In other parts of the Mediterranean world the word *Og* was associated with a race of primeval giants. Og in Hebrew means "gigantic": King Og of Bashan, a remnant of the giants, was so

large that he was buried in a 14-foot sarcophagus in Jordan (an exagger-
ation, for he was only 9 feet tall—Deuteronomy 3:3–7). Let's remember
too the Welsh giant Ough. In fact, the classic *og*re of European fairy
lore probably has the same root.

At one time in the Levant, Og signified the great god of the ocean,
and he (being a giant) walked by the side of the ark during the Flood,
the water reaching only up to his knees (according to rabbinic tradition). Another version (in the Aggadah) has Og sitting on top of the
ark, riding out the Flood. It seems that "Ogygios and Noah were
often confused," the former name "intimately connected with floods."
Indeed, Og was "the only survivor of the Great Deluge" (Cohane 1969,
107–10). A related idea is expressed in the Sanskrit term og-haja which
meant "deluge-born." In Tibet, Og-min is the Bon name of their culture founder, who came among them from a lost continent.

In Europe, *Ogyges* was also a founder—in this case of Boaetia—being
the Greek king at the time of the flood. In fact, the Greek word *ogygios*
means "primal," "with the connotation of antediluvian" (Santillana 1969,
209). Just so, the names of certain primal groups may be part of the mix:
Ag-og-we, G-og-o, and Tagal-og (whose ancestor is thought to have come
from Melanesia). Finally, Og-ir is the Norse god of the sea and death.
Do all these "ogs" go back to the sunken land of clay hills? Og, in many
languages, shows a connection to rivers and islands.

- Ogy River, Belgium
- Ognon River, France
- Oglio River, Italy
- Og River, England
- Oghil in Aran Islands (off Galway), which also have the Ogwen
  River
- Ogygia, an island in the sea, legendary home of the sea nymph
  Calypso, according to Homer
- Oglus Island, near Crete
- Ogyrus Island, off Arabia
- Ogasawara Jima, Japanese name for the Bonin Islands in
  the Pacific

Tir Nan *Og,* to the Irish, is the legendary lost island across the sea, while *Og*ham is the Celtic "tree-language" (alphabet), which is evidently related to *Og*mios or *Og*ma, the god whom the Irish credit with the invention of writing-stones at Munster. In Irish mythology Ogma reigned over the Tuatha De Danaan, the founders of Ireland.

Historians Stubbornly Discount Indigenous Culture in the Pacific

The ancestors of the Polynesians, according to textbook scruples, came *from Asia* around 1500 BCE; and when it comes to placing the *fair-skinned* people* of Polynesia, they must have hailed from some land beyond its boundaries, perhaps through Singapore. But Polynesians are not Asian in type; and whence the "white strain in the Polynesians?" asked Harold Gladwin, reviewing the theories, most of which favor "Europoid" or "Caspian" origins or perhaps the genetic contribution of Indic seafarers or voyagers from Mesopotamia, Persia, or Baluchistan. "These straws are all blowing eastward" (1947, 234). *How far east?*

> *Traditional anthropologists typically ignored the [Easter Island] natives' own legends, and said that they came by way of Tahiti . . . a few hundred years before Europeans first visited them. Such mysteries as Rongo Rongo writing and the incredible stone platform at Vinapu are ignored.*
>
> DAVID H. CHILDRESS, *LOST CITIES OF ANCIENT LEMURIA AND THE PACIFIC*

One example of those "traditional anthropologists," Kaj Birket-Smith, sees "no reason for going into the more or less fantastic theories . . . regarding Polynesian origins. The idea of a submerged continent in the Pacific Ocean . . . can unhesitatingly be relegated to the world of fantasy" (1965, 460). Why are academics so bitterly opposed to the rediscovery of Pan? This attitude parallels their equally flawed out-

---

*See "Pacific (Rim) Whites" in chapter 2 on indigenous whites of Oceania, p. 75.

look on America: it *must* have been empty, uninhabited, until relatively recent time; the Indians are not truly indigenous, as only migrations (across Beringia) can explain their settlement of the Americas.

Only a gutsy few, like historian W. Colenso or the late nineteenth century's A. Lesson thought the Pacific Islanders were autochthonous. In the standard model, however, ancestors of the Polynesians and Maoris (just like those of the Amerinds) are made to come from Asia. According to this view, less than four thousand years ago migrants from Java or Singapore or Indonesia went to Australia, New Guinea, and later to Melanesia and Micronesia, and lastly into western Polynesia (1150 BCE at Tonga).

But, "the Polynesians could not have been in long or close contact with the Indonesians without becoming acquainted with the art of pottery and carrying it with them into the Pacific" (Anderson 1928, 22). Nor did these so-called migrants bring with them to Polynesia the Indonesian loom, glass beads, wooden nails, coconut-based alcohol, or matriarchy (Polynesians are patriarchal). Heyerdahl, in addition, notes that the Indonesian or Malayan nose and head form "is the antithesis of the Polynesian" and that Malayan B blood is absent in Polynesia (1953, 23).

The same dogma has these migrants reaching the Society Islands and the Marquesas by about 300 CE and finally Hawaii around 650 CE. "The evidence upon which this pattern is based, however, is so slender that the sequence will doubtless be revised again and again" (Zink 1979, 151). Besides, Fijians and Marquesans say that they have always dwelled there (Williamson 1933, 1:300). "Radio-carbon [results] . . . were astonishing to us, demonstrating an age for Marquesan culture far greater than had previously been supposed" (Suggs 1962, 229). In fact, there are still traces of the *Homo erectus* gene pool in the Melanesian (and Australian) population.

> *The Melanesians have no traditions of migration into*
> *their region; they claim to have been created on the spot.*
> WILLIAM PERRY, *THE CHILDREN OF THE SUN*

It is really outdated (Darwinian) monogenism (represented today by the absurd Out of Africa hypothesis) that insists that the Pacific

Islanders had to have come from somewhere else. Samoans say that they have always been there; they do not have migration legends. In fact, "Samoa was a great hiving-off centre" (Perry 1968, 78). "The Samoan group was the mother group"; as regards language changes, "a sibilant has been preserved in Samoan which has become a simple aspirate elsewhere" (Fornander 1969, 2:3, 3:9)—meaning, the *original S* changed to *H*. Professor A. H. Sayce showed how the change of the Samoan *S* to *H* in Tahitian, Hawaiian, and Tongan indicates that the Samoan is the older. The Samoans also have an authentic flood legend: "The sea arose, and in a stupendous catastrophe of nature, the land sank to the sea. . . . The new earth, the Samoan Islands, arose out of the womb of the last earth" (Williamson 1933, 1:37).

Nevertheless the Polynesian forebears, it is taught today, must have lived somewhere else—perhaps in Indochina—the argument being that when the ambitious Chinese empire in the second millennium BCE rose to power, it touched off a movement of people outward. But if the movement was from China in the Bronze Age, why are there no Chinese artifacts in Polynesia?

Lapita Shards

Lapita, New Caledonia, gave its name to the distinctive pottery style that came out of Southeast Asia around 1500 BCE. Lapita ware is used by archaeologists to trace the supposedly earliest migrations into the Pacific via the Bismarck Archipelago, reaching Polynesia by 1000 BCE. It was the Lapita culture of pottery makers, say most historians, that settled Fiji, Tonga, and Samoa and finally eastern Polynesia less than three thousand years ago.

In the words of traveler-explorer Mark Williams, these Lapita folk supposedly "hunkered down [at Tonga and Samoa] for several centuries and developed their culture before moving on through the rest of Polynesia. . . . Evidence of fishing gear is rare—curious if these [Lapita] sites belong to Polynesians, the world's greatest seafarers. . . . The Lapita hypothesis sounds convincing until I discover that pottery-making was unknown in ancient Polynesia . . . Polynesians used shells and gourds

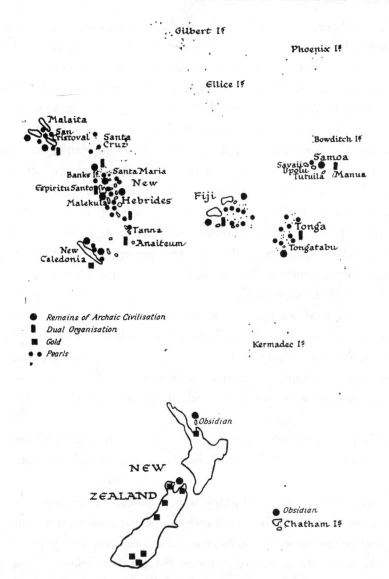

Fig. 11.1. New Caledonia, at left, seen in relation to the Polynesian islands.

as containers." Noting the contradiction, Williams concludes sardonically, "So pottery is used by scholars to document the history of a people without pottery. . . . Archaeologists might have thrown logic out the window. Perhaps the pottery . . . came from an older culture . . ." (2001, 78). (See below for more on pottery of that older culture.)

Lewis Spence was another who bucked these pseudo-migrations: "I cannot subscribe to the theory . . . that the Polynesians arrived from Northeastern Asia . . . and I fail to understand how to reconcile it with the belief that they formerly inhabited a continent now submerged" (Spence 1933, 76). It may actually be the other way around, meaning, significant movements of people from Pan to Southeast Asia. This is how De Bisschop sees the dispersion of the double canoe; he points out that "the east-to-west direction of the Polynesian migrations [is seen in] the word heke . . . meaning 'travel with the sun,' and so to 'go westward'" (De Bisschop 1959, 24, 40).

One Malaysian legend recounts that the sinking of their ancestors' ancient homeland actually raised the archipelago in which they sought refuge, settled, and now live. Both Malaysians and Samoans say their land arose when Mu went down.

But the beat goes on. Academia rules. The problem, basically, is how to account for white people in the middle of the South Seas. Some academics will go to any extreme to make the problem disappear. Extremely repugnant, for example, is Professor Patrick Nunn's attempt to make us (Mu writers) out as a pack of racists.

> The fixation of such writers . . . seems to stem from the naïve perception that they [Polynesians] are a fairer-skinned race than other Pacific Island peoples and therefore have to be the descendants of the root race of the advanced people who supposedly inhabited ancient Mu or Lemuria. Such rubbish may appear palatable, even implicit, because most new-age and many pseudoscience writers are probably writing for a fairer-skinned audience. Its racist implications . . . have no scientific evidence in their support and appear abhorrent to right-thinking people in the twenty-first century. (2009, 85)

What is racist about white indigenes in Polynesia, Mr. Nunn? I watch with chagrin as generations of scholars attempt to trace Polynesian whiteness to *anywhere* but Polynesia itself! The Maoris, as some historians classify them, were of Alpine-Caucasoid stock, originating in the Atlas Mountains of North Africa! Others propose that

Fig. 11.2. Tahitian ladies at a festival. There is nothing "naïve" about the perception that these people are quite European in appearance. What's more, the contents of chapter 2 make it likely that a civilized white race came out of Mu/Pan at the time of the flood.

the Middle East or Central Asia was their point of departure. But clearly neither the Maoris nor Polynesians are Mongoloid in type. "No Easter Islanders had Mongoloid features. No statue on the island has slanted eyes" (Schwartz 1973, 155). Neither is there any "trace of the Mongoloid hair or cheek bones in any of the natives of the central or eastern Pacific" (Brown 1924, 262). "Polynesians are not of the Far East" (Anderson 1928, 5).

And what a marvel—how an Asian/Mongoloid race could have penetrated Melanesia without leaving any genetic impact on its native black-skinned people! Williams again notes the irony. "By the time these Asiatic pre-Polynesians crossed the Andesite Line they had miraculously transformed from a small yellow race into a large brown one. Physically, a southeast Asian and a Samoan couldn't be less similar" (Williams 2001, 78). It is also contradictory that the lightest-colored Oceanic people are most *easterly* in location, with traces of native fairness growing fainter in western Oceania, thus disposing of the theory that the fair

*Fig. 11.3. a) A dark Melanesian and b) Solomon Islander in
contrast with c) and d), the Europoid appearance of Polynesians*

peoples of the Pacific came from eastward-moving Indians, Egyptians,
Persians, Alpinos, or Fulanos.

Historians bend over backward to portray the Pacific Islanders
as migrants and relative newcomers—anything but indigenous. (Of
course, migrations from India to Polynesia—especially those said to

have occurred around 450 BCE—may simply represent *later* contacts and voyages; see preceding chapters on ancient mariners.) Polynesians, according to different theories, came from India, the southeast coast of Arabia, Central Asia, Indonesia, Java, Malaysia, Korea, South America, the lost tribes of Israel—anywhere but their own homeland!

Historians also tell us that Malaysian Negritos (who had supposedly come from the mainland of Southeast Asia) made their way out to Melanesia, and that they had "traveled to SE Asia from Africa along the coastline of Southern Asia, starting 100,000 years ago" ("Early Human Migration" www.nok-benin.co.uk/religion/pottery.htm [accessed 6-27-2016). This certainly queers the peopling of Melanesia (according to Euro-American historians) as a "late diffusion" probably from China.

And by the same token, scholars insist on deriving Oceanic Negritos from elsewhere, even though there *are* aboriginal people in Melanesia— of whom practically nothing is known. The small people of Melanesia represent an older population than their tall neighbors. On Malekula (New Hebrides), the pygmies in the mountainous interior are "the last remnants of an earlier racial stock, similar to that found in the interior of the larger land-masses in the western Pacific" (Anderson 1928, 34). True blacks live in the uplands of the Sandwich Islands, just as Easter Island, Melanesia, and Fiji all have their indigenous browns and blacks with woolly hair and broad noses. Some of today's Afrocentrists have early Africans* reaching Amazonia in South America, and then, under their "adventurous spirit," continuing on out to the Pacific *with the wind behind them,* finally reaching Melanesia.

Clearly wars, drought, famine, pilgrimages, voyages of discovery— even voyages in search of the cherished red feathers—have seen Pacific

---

*According to Stephen Oppenheimer's work, variability is actually the *least* in Africa, from the point of view of tribal legends. Tracing origin myths to their geographical root, Oppenheimer found they spread *from* Oceania across the Indian Ocean *to* Africa. "In looking for a homeland . . . look for the region with the deepest and greatest diversity of story-types. . . . Africa clearly has the least diversity, Australasia . . . has the most" (1998, 398). Even geneticists have gotten a similar result, in connection with the path of disease-related molecules—the greatest diversity in the frequency of gene variants lay outside Africa. Oceania had much more variation.

Islanders on the move for a long time. But Thor Heyerdahl, for one, roundly challenged the idea that the *original* Polynesians came from Asia, island-hopping east across the Pacific. Even though "most anthropologists now believe that Polynesia was settled from the west . . . the markedly hierarchical social structure and the major monuments seen on some of the Polynesian islands are not evident to the west, in Melanesia or Micronesia" (Renfrew 1973, 160). So where is the expected continuity?

Exceptionally Long Isolation

Pan said: I am beneath the water. On the continent of Pan were words first used by man.

OAHSPE, BOOK OF SAPHAH: PAN 1:1

If Oceania truly owes its history to migrants from Africa or China or Singapore or Southeast Asia, why are there no antecedents to Austronesian languages on the mainland? If the islanders are merely a bunch of migrants, as opposed to the *original inhabitants* of Pacifica, why are their languages distinct from those of the people they supposedly came from? It also seems a miracle that thousands of Oceanic languages and cultures have "evolved" in such a short span of time. When Europeans arrived in New Caledonia, the sixty thousand islanders were speaking thirty-seven different languages! You need a lot of time to develop "the infinity of languages in western Polynesia, all remarkably different form each other" (Lang 1877, 2).

The same experts who move Polynesians out of Asia less than four thousand years ago have not only ignored "the high antiquity of Polynesian culture" (Rivers 1914, 2:475) but also the "extreme antiquity of the Polynesian language" (Fornander 1969, 1:vi). Its system of sounds is archaic. The Polynesian language type "stands by itself as the most primitive in phonology. . . . It has only twelve or fourteen sounds, when all those to the west of it . . . have from twenty to forty sounds. This is a mark of . . . exceptionally long isolation. . . . Polynesia had perfect quarantine for thousands of years" (Brown 1924, 271).

Rather than a latecomer to history, Oceania stands as the fountain-

Fig. 11.4. "Giant Birds of Fiji"—islanders have legends of megafauna that lived in the Paleolithic.

head of Austronesian language/culture, going back tens of thousands of years. The people did not come from Taiwan, as some argue, but on the contrary spread from the Pacific outward. Indeed, the native Taiwanese have stories of their origin—coming from the tropical Pacific. Maori legend refers to their fatherland (*Te Paparoa-i-Hawaiki*) as a large continent, which saw the growth and origin of man, and from here they spread to other islands in the great ocean.

Built before the Flood

"Authority has laid it down that the Polynesian immigrants did not enter the area until some time about the beginning of the Christian era.* This is in direct opposition to . . . Macmillan Brown, who thinks

---

*Since the time of Spence's writing (1930s), they have gradually but cautiously increased the time depth of human habitation in the South Seas, just as they have been forced to do with Amerinds in the New World.

that the race has been settled in its present position for a space of almost one hundred thousand years" (Spence 1933, 73).

Well, we can easily get dates earlier than the Christian era with five-thousand-year-old carbon dating for human activity in the Marianas. We might even push that back another eight thousand years or more to the era of giants (Ihuans and Ghans). The Mexicans hold that the Earth was inhabited by giants *before* the flood. As we saw in chapter 2, p. 80, the Kai people of New Guinea say the megaliths were built before the flood by white giants—exactly the same history maintained by the Aborigines of Queensland, Australia, where "enormous [human] tracks" and "enormous stone implements" put meat on the bones of the myth (Childress 1988, 98). At that time the Ihuans were the tallest, mightiest men on Earth; the Polynesians are their last-remaining descendants. Polynesians are generally considered the tallest race in the world. How could they have descended from the relatively short races of the Far East? The tallness of the Samoans and Tongans* argues for their long, very long, isolation, for it is an Ihuan trait that has long since been amalgamated with other races in every other part of the world.

Dutch explorers in the seventeenth century, arriving at Tonga, saw "uncommonly big women, among them two fearful giantesses" (Cameron 1987, 107)—almost pure Ihuans, as were the 7-foot-tall men of Panape† and the builders of the sun kingdoms, the same disbelieving giants we saw so much of in chapter 4. pp. 144–146, and the same Ghan/Khan/Can dynasties discussed in chapter 5, p. 213, under "Chan Chan." Explorers have found human bones on Panape that are twice as big as a normal man's. Paumotu tradition recalls an early race of giants (Williamson 1933, 1:15).

---

*William Howells suggested that large-bodied, big-headed people in the western Pacific must be "the result of a little natural selection . . . [given] the constant cooling breezes that blew from the open Pacific over the islands of Polynesia . . . [whereby] loss of body heat could be a serious matter. Large bodies have a relatively smaller surface-to-bulk ratio, so that heat preservation . . . is better" (1993, 201). But their large bodies are genetic and not effected by "cooling breezes."

†Also suggestive of prediluvial times are the *Nani* (little people) of Panape, said to have inhabited the islands before the Submergence.

OCEANIC LEGENDS OF GIANTS WHO
RULED IN REMOTEST ANTIQUITY

Name of Giant	Where	Details
Hono'ura	Tuamotu	his enormous footprint still seen on a rock at Takume
Pai	Tuatira	a man of great size and magnificent appearance
Raamauriri's son	Raiatea	first builder of ships, 8 feet tall
Tafa'i	Tahiti	giant blond son of a mortal and a goddess, valiant navigator and astronomer
Kur'	New Zealand	legendary giant, 10 feet tall
King Rata	Samoa, Tahiti, Fiji, New Zealand	chief builder of the Arawa canoes, taken on important expeditions

If migrations were so recent, how come we find fossil men in Oceania with archaic characteristics, even *Homo erectus* types who normally go back tens of thousands of years? Sexual dimorphism (the men much larger than the women), known to have been present in some of the *earliest* races, was found in the Melville Islands and in the Micronesian island of Palau. Excavated by a National Geographic team in July 2006, these Palauan specimens had large teeth, a wide gap between their eyes, reduced chin, and vertical depth of jaw. Scientists actually thought of these traits as prehuman! Even today some natives of New Caledonia show erectoid traits, especially in teeth, brow ridge, and sloping forehead. In the Marquesas fossil men "with very heavy, thick bones" also point to early hominids (Suggs 1962, 96). Human skulls of great age also have been found underwater at Honolulu and Molakai. A word to the wise, "datable objects found on these [Panape] islets . . . are actually the tail end of any occupation, rather than the beginning" (Childress 1988, 341).

I think it is particularly significant that Churchward saw Panape, Easter Island, Marianas, and Tonga as *prediluvial* cultures. On Panape, off Nan Madol, stone pillars are buried deep enough to suggest an age of at least twelve thousand years. And again, on Easter Island, the depth to which some of the moai are buried indicates an age of many thousands of years. Wrote Robert Schoch, "Studying the varying levels of weathering and erosion and the degree of sediment built up around the moai (some buried in up to six meters of sediment), I quickly became convinced [of] . . . a much greater age than a mere 1,500 years" (2012, 4). Slow-growing lichen on the exterior surfaces of the moai, agrees Joseph, brand them "far older than conventional archaeologists believe." Although Easter Island has been inhabited by its *present* occupants for only several centuries, these recent migrants (latecomers) merely *found* the colossi "that had been abandoned thousands of years before by an entirely different and unrelated people" (Joseph 2013, 116). On the cliffs of Easter Island are frescoes that represent a humanoid with rounded back and long skinny arms. This prehistoric creature looks rather like the antediluvian Yak, a sort of erectus hybrid.

Then too there is the oft-cited mystery of New Caledonia's Isle of Pines, with its 9-foot-high cement pillars dated 13,000 BP. They might actually be much older than that. The place even has the old Panic name Ku—Kunie is the name of the spot with those pillars, and it is near the Isthmus of Ku-to . . . echoes of lost Pan with its Temples of Khu.

Another telltale site is Samoa's Pulemelei mound, a very large pyramidal platform in Savai'i. "The jungle growth that almost entirely conceals it implies the ceremonial precinct's profound antiquity," according to Joseph, who goes on to quote local myths describing survivors of Mu who took refuge here. Joseph then reminds us that the Atahura Temple on Tahiti "was dismantled . . . [by] missionaries, because their native parishioners supposedly undermined biblical authority by claiming that 'the *marae* was built before the Flood'" (2006, 114). Thus does the old guard—not only of academia but also of clergy—resent and suppress the marvelous antiquity of Oceanic culture.

Caucasian Genes in All the "Wrong" Places

While textbook historians only allow population movements out *to* the Pacific Islands, Stephen Oppenheimer in *Eden of the East* actually traced Central European and Mesopotamian DNA to the ocean beyond Southeast Asia. Isn't this why Easter Island genes make a close match to the Basque? This makes sense since the Basque are the oldest, most insulated people in Europe, the earliest type—unchanged almost since Cro-Magnon times. Their rare blood type, Rh negative, appears in the New World (Maya), hinting at a shared gene pool before the diaspora. The Basque language falls outside the Indo-European family and is unclassifiable. Other unclassifiable and probably preflood languages include Vietnamese and a Kasmiri tongue of the Burushaski. DNA research shows that these disparate people and the Basque may have once shared the same home. Researchers like Paul von Ward think that home was Mu.

In chapter 7 we found another kind of link, that between the language of the Basque (in Europe), the Quechuas (in the Andes), the Maori (in New Zealand)—and the Lapps! Other studies relate northern Europe's small, white Lapps to their long-lost Amerind kin—blood type A, common in the Lapps, also shows up in Algonquin groups in North America. There are also similar tribal names; while the Lapps call themselves Sam-en, the Andean Aymara at Titicaca are called Sam-paya (Samé is also the name of the Brazilian culture founder, famous for his white beard). Perhaps originating in Oceania (in Sam-oa?), the *Sam* appellation is most prevalent in the Jaffetic branch and is generally indicative of sacred white founders (recall the list in chapter 2, p. 52).

The name Lapp itself has another Andean connection: Chinchi Lap-i and Kue-Lap in Peru—the latter with its high walls—perhaps related to the Hawaiian word *lapa,* which indicates a ridge, rising, or standing out. Also in Peru, King Naym-Lap was the white founder of the Chavin/Chimu* civilization. Did he or his ancestor come from Pan—with its god Anu Lap, in the Carolines, and names like Ronga-lap and Maloe-lap (in the Marshall Islands), Sara-lap (Panape), Lap-aha

---

*The Chimu people came from Pan via Mexico, where the *lap* name persists in T-lap-alan, the original homeland in Mexican legend. Toltec chronicles say that their ancestors arrived at T-lap-alan 520 years after the flood. Indeed, T-lap-acoya in the Valley of Mexico is dated just around that time (i.e., 25,000 BP). Other place-names in Mexico that seem to have taken the old name include Ti-lapa River in the Tehuacán Valley, Cuilapa, Jalapa, and so on.

(archaeological site in Tongatapu), Lapakahi (Hawaii), and Lapita (New Caledonia)? The authentic flood story told by the Lapps (as well as their very old DNA) lends credence to Panic origins: their legend says that when the wickedness of men increased, the world was overwhelmed by hurricane and sea; it was then that Jubmel set a storm wind blowing, raging, foaming, dashing, rising sky high, and crushing all things.

All these roads lead out to sea—the motherland of man. Short and pale, the Lapps and Ainu (Japan) share an unusual pearllike excrescence in their molar teeth formation with the Alaskans. This brings us to other genetic traits linking the ancient Japanese to Alaska and northwest coast Indians across the pond. The ongoing puzzle here is the presence of Caucasian genes in both these groups (Chouinard 2012, 247). DNA shows America inhabited by Caucasians more than twenty thousand years ago. Tribes of the northwest coast, Alaska, Canada, Massachusetts, and so forth stem from the same "Caucasian branch that produced the Jomon, the earliest culture creators in Japan . . . more than 15,000 years ago," just as skull types of Amerinds, including Iroquois, Michigan, Florida, Massachusetts, and Canadian groups, tally with those of the ancient Jomon and Polynesians (Joseph 2006, 149 and 2014, 166). Tribal DNA in Minnesota and Michigan shares Haplogroup D1 with the Ainu of Hokkaido, who descend from the Jomon people; in addition, the only two places in the world with the HTLV-1 virus (linked to T-cell leukemia) are Japan and Ecuador (which are also linked by Valdivia pottery).

In Washington State, controversial Kennewick Man's DNA is also linked to the Ainu. Is this because "there was a previously unrecorded population . . . nineteen thousand years ago . . . of which both the Ainu and Kennewick Man were a part?" (Chouinard 2012, 162). Bearded and narrow of nose, Kennewick Man had non-native morphology (smaller face, stockier build), the skull resembling both the Ainu and Polynesian type—not the Siberian type. Under DNA analysis, he was found to most resemble the Moriori people of New Zealand (see fig. 2.16, p. 81) and the Easter Islanders. Also similar to Kennewick Man is Spirit Cave Man in Nevada, with Europoid traits (reddish hair and Caucasian DNA), as well as the red-haired Florida bog mummies—both of whom, along with other Algonquin groups, contained Haplogroup X, typical of northern Europeans.

Most tellingly, DNA analysis has the common ancestors of Asians and Americans separating *earlier* than twenty thousand years ago. If that earlier time is twenty-four thousand years ago, it would mark the great diaspora occasioned by the sinking of Pan. Blood types indicating a strain of Polynesian DNA in American Indians should not be ignored or explained away.

> *Polynesians don't look anything like the people of*
> *Southeast Asia or black Melanesia, but they do resemble*
> *Native Americans and share their blood types. . . . Maybe*
> *there was a common source a very long time ago, a place*
> *now sitting at the bottom of the ocean.*
> MARK WILLIAMS, *IN SEARCH OF LEMURIA*

Why is there scarcely any B blood type among Amerinds while it is so common in eastern Asia whence their supposed ancestors made the trek from Siberia across a Bering Strait land bridge? Instead, genetic strains in South and Central America have been found to be closely associated with Polynesian ones and curiously absent in Siberia and Alaska. Tool types strengthen that link: the stone fishhooks of Easter Island find an exact match off Santa Barbara, California, on the Channel Islands; on the California coast itself, adzes and ax heads of Pacific origin have been found. Dennis Stanford and Bruce Bradley, in *Across Atlantic Ice,* find that spearheads and knives in parts of prehistoric America have no correlation with those found in Siberia or even Alaska. None of the Indian tribes, by the way, trace themselves back to Siberia or across the Bering Strait.

In parts of South America, mtDNA lineages match up with some Polynesian groups. At least ten thousand years ago a strain of DNA in the Amazon Basin bore a relationship to Pacific Islanders (Jones 2008, 239); see chapter 5 on multiple Brazil/Melanesian links, p. 222. Similar haplotypes of the alpha-globin gene are found among both Pacific Islanders and Brazilian Indians of the Amazonian region; it is thought that they resulted from "ancient common ancestry rather than . . . recent immigration" (Zago, et al. 1995). Whereas Asian blood type B is almost unknown in Polynesia, blood types in Easter Island are "closer to aboriginal peoples of North and South America than Southeast Asia" (Zink 1979, 168).

Genetic studies, in fact, find that the great Paleolithic migrations moved out of Sundaland (insular Southeast Asia), going north and west, to populate the Far East and beyond, *instead of the other way around*. Genomic analysis of the Onge people of the Andaman Islands (Bay of Bengal) reveals a special change in the Y chromosome, casting the insular Onge as actually *ancestral* to the populations of mainland Asia. Likewise do DNA tests confirm Caucasian genes in Thailand, among the Hmong, who say their ancestors, the Hmu (H-Mu?), escaped a terrible flood.

Finally, the DNA of those red-haired Tarim mummies discovered in western China was Europoid—"the remains older than anything the Han Chinese could point at in the archaeological record. . . . The early inhabitants of the Tarim Basin were primarily Caucasoids. . . . What brought these Europeans here?" (Coppens 2012, 242–43). But should we *assume* they came from Europe? Well, DNA says Cherchen Man of western China was a Celt; this tall red-haired mummy—with a long nose—had Celtic DNA. But more properly stated, the Celts—thanks to the westward-moving Jaffites—ended up with the same genes as Tarim Man.

"Our Home in the West Was a Pleasant Land"

It was a beautiful tropical country with vast plains . . .
covered with rich grazing grasses and tilled fields.
JAMES CHURCHWARD, *THE LOST CONTINENT OF MU*

"To those who [argue] that the islands of the Pacific were not populated until late, it must be said that the plant evidence is against them . . . very early peopling of the islands is indicated" (Corliss 1978, 736–37). The oldest Maui in Bulotu, says Tongan oral history, cultivated the ground; in the Maui Cycle (the earliest sagas), Maui's mother cooked bananas. The great number of varieties of banana grown by the Polynesians argues for considerable age in its cultivation. Donnelly infers that bananas were cultivated there "as early as the Diluvial Period . . . that nation retaining a peaceful, continuous, agricultural civilization during all that time" (1985, 58). Mai-ka, a Polynesian word for banana, seems to recollect the original land in which it was grown—"the rich valleys of *Mai*." One legend speaks of the Kena-Mu people, who were known as "banana eaters"—is their name linked to the lost continent of Mu?

Sweet potato, cotton, and corn have been under cultivation for many thousands of years in Oceania. Hawaiki, say the legends, was inhabited by a fair people "who were great cultivators—a peaceful people with straight hair," according to Percy Smith, who says this is a great puzzle (1921, 93). A puzzle, because (1) straight-haired blonds are not supposed to be native to Oceania, and (2) according to the standard model, ten thousand years ago the entire world was the domain of hunter-gatherers . . . not farmers. Yet the Hopi say their ancestors domesticated corn in the *First* World.

Fig. 11.5. Inside a Hopi house, which kept a separate area for grinding corn

According to Ireland's *The Secret Commonwealth,* a race of little people (Ihins?) had their own agriculture long before the flood. New Zealand holds "traces of a former and large agricultural population . . . a vanished people" (Perry 1923, 25). The same is reported in Oahspe.

They tilled the soil . . . [but all was] dissipated by the dread hand of war . . . their cities are destroyed.

OAHSPE, SYNOPSIS OF SIXTEEN CYCLES 3:9

In those days the [hins . . . dwell[ed] in cities and villages, and they were clothed. They tilled the ground and brought forth grains and seeds good to eat; and flax* and hemp, from which to make cloth.

OAHSPE, THE LORDS' FIRST BOOK 2:13–14;

INDICATING A TIME MORE THAN 25,000 YEARS AGO

Fig. 11.6. New Zealand cloaks of flax

---

*Polynesians still make string, fishing line, and nets out of flax, *romaha;* flax is called *harakeke* in the Maori language of New Zealand.

The vast mound works of ancient North America, as Sir John Lubbock saw it, betray "a population both large and stationary . . . which must have derived its support . . . from agriculture" (1982, 281). Historians have aptly noted that the megalithic age of cyclopean monuments implies a setting in which agriculture *must* have flourished in order to feed such a large number of workers. Shards of pottery (an index of settled, agricultural people) have been found on Panape— where 16-foot-long basalt "logs" were their building blocks; today it is a lost art.

Pacific Island Pottery

Pottery making, native to Pan, was forgotten—just as agriculture itself may be a lost art in certain lands—the "wild ancestral form" being what remains of a once-cultivated species. Robert Suggs, digging in the Marquesas, was surprised when he began to find pottery shards: "This could not be. Pottery had never been known in eastern Polynesia. . . . Nevertheless what lay in the palm of my hand was an actual potsherd from the very bottom of the stratum. . . . One fact was sure: at one point in their history the Marquesans . . . had made pottery. . . . The potter's art had simply died [and] this was precisely what had happened in many other islands in the Pacific. . . . In Tonga, the earliest sites contain the best-quality pottery. . . . Even in Samoa, pottery had been found on a very early site, and the Samoans themselves were the most surprised of all, for there was no hint in their wealth of legends that pottery had even been used" (1962, 212–13). Neither is pottery made today at Fiji's Viti Levu, yet lots of intricately decorated shards are buried in her mud. Pottery or shards have also been found on Panape, Ewa, New Caledonia, New Hebrides, Banks and Easter Islands, and Malekula.

Also in Micronesia, on Palau, at Babeldaob, an ancient culture with great monoliths and well-populated cities terraformed the land into countless horticultural terraces, yielding vast amounts of food. These

444 ～ THE LAND OF CLAY HILLS

outstanding terraces were "elaborate affairs," whole hills sculpted to resemble step pyramids. In Hawaii terraced farming was a trademark of the little bearded Menehune, the original inhabitants of the islands—which is to say, an antediluvian people. That's how their movements are traced—once driven off the large islands, they withdrew to the islets of Nihoa and Necker, as evidenced by the path of their distinctive terraces and canals. These preflood people, say Hawaiians, planted taro, stands of sugar cane, and banana trees.

In the Middle Kingdom of the Americas the people of Chiapas claim to be the first arrivals in the New World, their great leader named Nima-*kiche*. One of the first *Quiché* colonies was on the river named *Pan*uco, while the city of Panuco itself, on the gulf and boasting superb temples, is where the Toltecs say they landed. Indeed, the cradle of the Aztec race,* says Quiché mythology, was a pleasant land: *Pan*-paxil-pacayala. That name *Pan* (representing the motherland to the west of Mexico, i.e., in the Pacific) again appears in legendary Teotlal*pan*, the "Land of the Gods," *which boasted agriculture.* Two hundred feet below Mexico City, drill-core extraction unearthed pollen grains of cultivated corn tens of thousands of years old; grinding tools unearthed in California are also tens of thousands of years old.

In South America we have another inkling of farming *before* the Flood; that is, before 24,000 BP, for the pre-Inca creation myth has Pachacamac planting the first corn, yucca, vegetables, and fruit *before* creating the present race. In other words, these agriculturalists belong to the Second Age, which "ended in cataclysmic deluge." All along the upper tributaries of the Amazon one hears reports of white tribes *still* inhabiting cyclopean cities. Brazil Indians say that their white-bearded semidivine teacher Samé (remember the *Sam* names, discussed earlier) taught them agriculture. Following suit are the legendary mountains of Pukato Ti, from which a white teacher came to the Brazilian Kayapo Indians, bringing them the blessing of agriculture. In South America the Polynesian-looking Arawaks "had a considerable share in the spread of

---

*The Aztec goddess of maize and patroness of agriculture, says legend, had her home in the *west*.

maize cultivation as well as of pottery making" (Birket-Smith 1965, 477). This resonates with Peru's founder, Manco Capac, a Noah type who figures as the hero of their Emergence saga, having arrived there after a great flood. He too taught the people the wonderful arts of planting.

As for the Old World, the doughty James Churchward, after identifying the Chinese "Uighur" as sons of Mu, gave them the arts of astronomy, writing, mining, textiles, architecture, medicine, mathematics, metallurgy, and agriculture more than 15,000 years ago, long before the so-called dawn of civilization and the agrarian arts in the Fertile Crescent. If the historians are right that the world's *first* farmers were in the Near East about 9,000 years ago and that *no one* was in Oceania until 4,000 years ago, how does one explain rice farming in Korea fifteen thousand years ago, and those who grew yams and sago in Melanesia 11,000 years ago? Indeed, some of these Pacific farmers go back to antediluvian days, judging from evidence of 28,000-year-old cultivated grains in the Solomon Islands (Joseph 2006, 132).

The Megalithic Obsession

The stellar alignments observed during the Megalithic Age betray a class of learned astronomers at least twelve thousand years ago. This was a global culture; there are pyramids and menhirs on almost every continent. I can't really blame the nineteenth-century clerical mind for deploring these ancient monuments as idolatrous. It was, frankly, a craze, fanatical, "a little insane" (Fisher 1985, 204). There has been endless discussion on the identity of these sophisticated engineers and the wonderful astronomical alignments of their megaliths, but scarcely a passing word about their revolting slaughter stones or the slaves and captives so frequently forced to do the heavy lifting. I am slightly amazed that modern scholarship has so blithely overlooked the tyranny of these ancient builders.

But what was their actual purpose? The catastrophists among us tend to regard the mighty megaliths as monuments built against future devastation, drawing inspiration from native mythologies, which speak of great refuge towers, built against the recurrence of cataclysm or erected as an offering of thanks for having survived one. In this interpretation, "catastrophobia" is what inspired men to supersize their cult buildings, making Göbekli Tepe, for example, a "virtual Noah's ark in stone." Fear was the motive. These men of Anatolia, says catastrophist Andrew Collins, thought to "stabilize the world pillar and counter the baleful influence of the cosmic trickster so that the sky or the world would not fall down [again]." In attempting to "understand why they might have embarked on mammoth building projects such as Göbekli Tepe," Collins adds, "it is possible they were inspired . . . by the fear of a further cataclysm. . . . The cosmic trickster . . . has the potential to quite literally bring about the death of the world through the collapse of the sky pole. . . . By synchronizing the enclosures with cosmic time cycles [i.e., astronomy] it would help provide the builders with enough information to control the influence of comets on a supernatural level" (2014, 6, 212–13, 217–18, 126).

I don't know anything about cosmic tricksters or sky poles, but, yes, *information* could be germane, and here I agree with David Zink's suggestion that "the early detection of catastrophic earth changes [like earthquakes] may have been the most important reason for the ancients' interest in the heavens" (1979, 95). Apparently, the megalithic alignments of western Europe were giant calendars, their priests announcing the coming of the (agricultural) seasons, eclipses, and other phenomena. Analysts say that Stonehenge acted as a computer to study the movements of the Earth, moon, and sun. Mexico's giants built the Cholula pyramid to reach the skies—not really to "storm heaven" (as some of these Tower of Babel myths suggest), but simply as observatories to unriddle its mysteries. And as for practical applications, the astronomers' calculations of sunset and moonrise were needed to navigate the world's oceans; for this, "they needed observatories and they built them at Stonehenge in England, at Carnac in France, and elsewhere" (Chatelain 1980, 169).

Nevertheless, the "fear" angle remains popular: given a crop failure and fear of famine, the Maya, it is supposed, tried to propitiate their gods with more ritual and more monuments. But I don't think the ancients were quite as irrational as we sometimes portray them. They were practical; for example, Alaska's menhirs, like those at Carnac, helped travelers determine their location. I appreciate the logic of Colin Renfrew's thinking, which takes the megalithic chamber tombs of western Europe as boundary markers, a means of establishing community territories, especially arable lands, at a time (ca. 7000 BP) of population expansion (1973, 142–44, 158–62). It was all about centralizing the distribution of food and mobilizing bodies of labor.

Certainly in Polynesia, where megaliths served as a meeting place of great chiefs and of priests to elect the king, the construction of ceremonial mounds required the mobilization of a work force, implemented through the chiefdoms, and making everyone dependent on the redistribution (of food) by the high-ranking men. These great feasts, at Easter Island for example, were attended annually by people from all over the region. On Easter Island each ahu was the burial place of the lineage occupying that territory and thus the equivalent of the megalithic tombs of the British Isles; the burial ceremony at Easter Island's ahus shares features with comparable sites at Scotland's Orkney Islands.

In some parts of Polynesia immense stone tikis represented the reigning dynasty, one placed upon each boundary of crown land "that no one might transgress upon such property" (Henry 1928, 209, 141). In the Society Islands the ancestral temple, *marae tupuna,* marked out hereditary family land, establishing their ownership of that land.

But in the very beginning, strong-standing monuments were built simply to record (engrave) histories of the people. Mediterranean tradition holds that the chosen people who escaped the Great Submersion took pains to preserve the original inventions, histories, religion, and ethics, transmitting them to posterity on great monuments of stone, strong enough to withstand the ravages of time. Those egalitarian societies, in other words, did not build large or ostentatious public monuments; only hierarchical societies did. Extravagant display is the very means by which we can identify the stratified, often totalitarian systems of the ancient past.

> We do not know why the pharaohs embarked on this orgy of pyramid construction. . . . Pyramid building created public works that helped define the authority of the ruler and make his subjects

> dependent upon him. . . . [It was] a practical administrative device
> designed to organize and institutionalize the state. . . . The villagers
> became dependent on the central administration for food. (Fagan
> 1999, 222–23)

In early Mexico, when certain families got control of the best lands, they became the Olmec elite that then built "awe-inspiring artificial mountains . . . giving an impression of overwhelming power." Even their rituals were designed "to confirm supreme authority," and these were the people who set up "colossal statues of themselves" (Fagan 1999, 258–59).

This then is the story of the ambitious sun kingdoms,* as seen in chapter 6, whose megaliths did little more than enshrine the exaltation of royalty and priesthood. The marae of Polynesia were built to memorialize events like a royal marriage or the consolidation of kingdoms. It was all about the ruling elite. The great Marquesan stone head weighing 3 tons represented a heroic chief laid low in a tribal war. Oceanic megaliths, in short, had mostly to do with prestige feasts and the death cult.†

Just so were America's monuments often memorials to their heroes' exploits in war or set up as altars for sacrifice to a deity or for tribal gatherings and processions, where size was indeed a measure of prestige.

The fact that these builders were sometimes outsiders, foreign conquerors, speaks of an expansionist agenda. Prehistorian Gordon Childe thought western European tombs the work of megalithic missionaries— strict agreements in every detail of funerary architecture being evidence for a megalithic religion. These missionaries preached burial in tombs and worship of the sun.

Egypt's colossi existed to record the glories and exploits of Pharaoh,

---

*"All menhirs and cromlechs were erected for more or less the same reasons. . . . Many Stone Age monuments bear . . . a common motif . . . for peoples as varied as the ancient Egyptians and the American Indians . . . [namely] a stylized picture of the sun" (Thorndike 1977, 53).

†The Iberians, according to Aristotle, set up obelisks around their tombs—one for each enemy the dead man had killed. Tribes in India still make dolmens for the dead.

trumpeting his triumphs and valor. "The Egyptian Pharaoh . . . built temples in his own honor" (Birket-Smith 1965, 283). Both Egyptian pharaohs and Mesoamerican lords made powerful architectural statements for their absolute or even divine status—the more lavish the expenditure, the greater the authority. And this is so in Polynesia as well; after all, the height and size of Marquesan house platforms indicate the prestige of the owner. They are but status symbols; only big stones were used by powerful families in Borneo's tombs. Is it any different today? What exactly was the purpose of Mount Rushmore? To impress?

Tonga chief Tuitatui had the famous Ha'amonga trilithon built as his seat in the kava-drinking ceremonies in such a way that every person was within his sight—"so that he might be out of reach of any hand that might desire to take him off" (Anderson 1928, 461). See appendix D, "Sample of Megalithic Works in the Prehistoric World," p. 476, and appendix E, "Stonehenges Everywhere," p. 479.

How Old Are the Megaliths?

Megalithic building projects in the Old World, including Egypt's pyramids and England's Stonehenge, are generally thought to have begun around five thousand or six thousand years ago. Archaeologists are loath to date *any other* colossal works earlier than that. Indeed, it is claimed that "the impressive megalithic tombs of western Europe are set earlier than any comparable monuments in the world," at least according to Colin Renfrew, who thinks Malta's Seated Woman must be "the earliest colossal statue in the world" at 5000 BP (1973, 120, 149). But Easter Island's moai show greater antiquity than that, and what about buildings that are now under the sea* or the Mexican pyramid at Cuicuilco, found under a lava field produced by a volcanic explosion that occurred eight thousand years ago? Despite all this, it is easy to find statements like, "Between A.D. 1300 and 1500, cultures

---

*See chapter 10. Ruins of a city were found 30 miles off the shore of Easter Island. Monoliths that have been found underwater in the Pacific were possibly prediluvial in age.

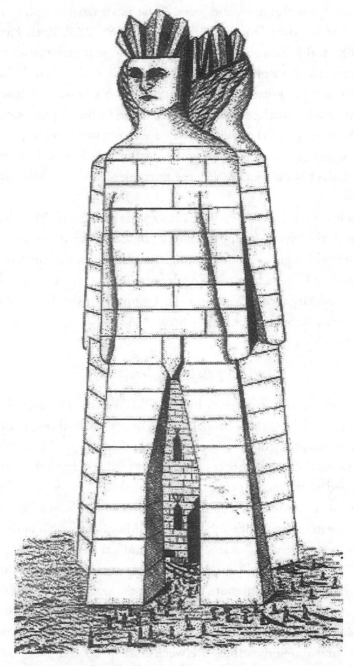

Fig. 11.7. Tower of Gall, illustrated in Oahspe, showing a three-sided colossus with the proportions and long hair of the Ghan race. This would have been in the Age of Apollo—no less than 15,000 BP.

around the Pacific *began* to build monumental structures" (Patel 2014, 23; emphasis added).

Off the coast of Florida too megaliths at the Bimini site in the Bahamas are at least ten thousand years old. In addition, the Chinese pyramids at Shensi are said to be about fourteen thousand years old. And in Turkey, Göbekli Tepe—at 12,000 BP*—is called by Collins "the oldest monumental architecture anywhere in the world" (2014, 14). Yet Hanan Pacha megaliths in Peru are thought to be preflood— at least according to Jan Peter de Jong, Cliff Dunning, and Alfredo Gamarra (www.ancient-mysteries-explained.com/archaeology-proofs .html [accessed 6-27-2016]). Meanwhile, on the north coast of Molokai is an ancient megalithic stone, about which Childress comments, "If any structures in Hawaii may be called antediluvian, this one is it" (1988, 342).

As seen above, some marae were built before the flood, the build- ers being those godless men who raised monuments to *self.* Madame Blavatsky identified these as the fourth root race, the moon-colored people who built huge self-worshipping cities and statues at places such as Easter Island and Mexico (Olmec), both of which places left sculptures of moon-eyed figures. Titanic kings were these sons of Cain, according to Hebrew legend, and they "endeavored to immortalize [their] name by means of monuments" (Ginzburg 2003, 60).

Megalithic Works in Oceania

At Malekula in New Hebrides, a 15-ton carved menhir was found in the jungle alongside other monoliths and dolmens. Natives of Malekula attribute these megaliths to five culture-bearing brothers, white men with aquiline noses (see "The Nose Knows" in chapter 2, p. 56, on those memorable noses; blond types are also found among the megalith builders in Brittany, Asia Minor, North Africa, Mexico, and Peru).

---

*In Oahspe's The Lords' Fifth Book 7:1–2, we see the dating of 12,000 BP (Age of Osiris) for the building of monuments (i.e., observatories) in the time of the sun kingdoms.

RANGE OF MEGALITHS IN THE PACIFIC

Where	What
Tahiti	pyramids, marae (stone temples)
Rarotonga, Cook Islands	monoliths, marae, basalt roads
Marquesas	cyclopean stonework at their maraes
Easter Island	great platforms (ahu), stone pyramids, colossal statues (moais), some 98 tons; monolith at Hangaroa
Hawaii	8-foot upright stones called Pohaku-a-Kane
Fiji	nangas enclosing pyramids, massive stone "tombs" on Rotuma
Gilbert Islands	pyramids
Lele Island in the Carolines	cyclopean enclosures, with very long, thick, and high (18 feet) walls
Malden Island	coral pyramids, platforms, dolmens, ruins of stone temples, exceptionally long pyramid stones
Marianas	latte, monumental blocks weighing up to 60 tons, red marble columns, pyramids
New Caledonia	stone walls and ramparts, trilithons, cement pillars
Solomon Islands	pyramids and dolmens
New Guinea	megalithic sites
New Zealand	the Kaimanawa Wall, a ceremonial platform with blocks more than 5 feet long; megalithic remains at Kerikeri and Atiamuri; stone causeways on Chatham Islands
Malekula	dolmens and other megalithic structures
Palau	monoliths, standing stones (menhirs) on Babeldaob 13 feet high
Panape, Nan Madol	blocks up to 15 tons, 16-foot-long basalt logs, cyclopean enclosures
Raiatea	step pyramids, large statues, and massive platforms
Samoa	pyramid with extremely long stone blocks
Tonga	langi (royal tombs) and dolmens, some blocks 20 feet long

A

B

C

Fig. 11.8. Examples of a) marae, b) langi, and c) Rotuma tomb

Was South American Megalithic Culture the Offspring of the Pacific?

The close similarity of the megalithic monuments of the world suggests that they belong to one people whose culture has been carried . . . widely over the earth.

W. H. R. RIVERS,
THE HISTORY OF MELANESIAN SOCIETY

There must, thought Cyrus Gordon, be "some common background" for the ancient world's monument builders (Gordon 1973, 174). In this, he was not alone. Brazil's great ruins reminded Colonel P. H. Fawcett of those found at Easter Island, Panape, Malekula, and the Marquesas. Road construction in the Cook Islands (Rarotonga) is similar to that of Peru. What was the relationship or direction of influence? Professor Brown was another who was struck by the comparable architecture in the Marquesas and Peru, remarking that "every feature of Polynesian great-stone work is repeated in . . . the Andes" (Brown 1924, 269). Many others besides—let the standard model be damned—have commented on the compelling parallels of Tiahuanaco and Panape, the former's entire complex built along the same lines as Metalanim, its acclaimed Gateway of the Sun also akin to the 109-ton trilithon on Tongatabu. Peru, Tonga, and Easter Island also share the distinctive method of tongue-and-groove stones, as discussed in chapter 3, p. 111; Easter's notched Vinapu wall is fitted with a keystone that holds the whole affair together—exactly like the keystone at Sacsayhuaman in Cuzco, whose large blocks also feature "strange knobs" and rounded corners, just like Vinapu's. In fact, the construction style at the Vinapu ruins is almost identical to that of Peru's Sacsahuaman, Machu Picchu, and Ollantaytambo.

If Pan's pyramids are older than America's we might have to rewrite history a bit. Quite possibly "the Vinapu wall went up first, which means that the cultural influence was from the Pacific toward America and not the other way around. So Heyerdahl had the whole thing backward, maybe because he totally rejected the idea of a lost Pacific continent"

A

B

C

D

*Fig. 11.9. a) Cuzco Valley Temple of Viracocha, and b) Cuzco Temple
compares to c) Vinapu, and d) Sacsahuaman fortress*

*Fig. 11.10. Stone giants, moai, of Easter Island with their unpleasantly
haughty faces. On Easter Island the stones of Ahu Vinapu are as cyclopean
and carefully tooled as those in the Temple of the Sun at Cuzco.*

(Williams 2001, 159). It seems significant that the statues from the *ear-liest* period on Easter Island bear the closest resemblance to the huge statues at San Agustin, Colombia, whose Stone Age temples and tombs also have counterparts on Easter Island. Indeed, South American ceremonial platforms are almost identical to those on Easter Island.

Let us recall that Churchward thought Easter Island and Panape were prediluvial. Panape's enormous stone ruins, built by a forgotten race, are all that remain, according to legend, of the continent of Kalu'a: "Our motherland rests at the bottom of the Ocean." Considered the oldest of the Caroline Islands, Panape, in the opinion of David Zink, was "the center of a now-sunken megalithic culture in the Pacific" (1979, 157). The stone used there is not found on the island and may have been hewn from a now submerged land. The anthropologist W. H. R. Rivers thought Panape's dynastic kings of the sun were the original builders of great megaliths, the cult spreading its pyramids, dolmens, and such, *to the rest of the world.* This of course is a jolt to the standard model, which maintains that "the practice of building megaliths . . . appeared *first* on the fringes of Europe . . . thousands of years earlier than any similar gigantic works in Tibet, Japan, Africa, or Easter Island" (Wernick 1978, 75–76; emphasis added).

Mexican architecture also aligns with that of the Pacific. Pedestals of Easter Island's moais resemble not only those at Tiahuanaco but also those of the Olmecs, who also made giant stone heads. The corbelled roofs of Easter Island's stone buildings are rather like the arches at Mayan ceremonial sites. On Hawaii too we can find such resemblances. Merrell Fankhauser has written to me that he saw on Maui "Mayan-like stone work underneath an old building, and a pyramid in Haleakala crater. Photos are in my DVD documentary *Return to Mu.*" Pillars that Merrell found on the other side of Maui lay on a "Mayan-like platform."

Although it went out of fashion in the twentieth century to marvel at such intriguing correspondences, the nineteenth-century explorer was not so diffident. For example, John Lang declared, "As to the colossal statues, consisting of immense blocks of stone and standing either singly or in groups, there is precisely the same thing to be seen in Easter Island as in Copan, Palenque, and Uxmal" (1877, 165).

Did Megalithic Culture Begin in Pan?

The style of postdiluvian architecture must have been derived from the reminiscences of the antediluvian period. . . . Perhaps the most remarkable feature of Polynesian life is the aspect . . . of an ancient but extinct civilization. . . . The monuments of that civilization are to be found all over the Pacific.

JOHN LANG, *ORIGIN AND MIGRATIONS OF THE POLYNESIAN NATION*

Archaeologists, as a rule, say they "have no idea where it all started" (Thorndike 1977, 43). Yet I think it is significant that the Mexican word for "temple-pyramid" is *pantli*—which of course includes the now familiar *Pan.* Easter Island legend speaks of a land of temples to the west that was once part of an ancient continent where cyclopean buildings were erected. Remembering also Khu and the Temples of Khu, is it not relevant that the *Ku*-Ben-Khrein people in the Amazon Basin inhabit a region where one of the most monumental megalithic temples was discovered in the twentieth century?

> *Before Noah was cold in his grave, his descendants were adepts in construction.*
>
> IGNATIUS DONNELLY, *THE ANTEDILUVIAN WORLD*

What I am suggesting is that the global megalithic culture had its first fluorescence on the continent of Pan. Sure, a Long Ear aristocracy was part of both Peruvian and Easter Island culture, but Easter Island stonework is older than its Andean counterpart. Spence, noting the identity of Cuzco and Easter Island platforms, wrote that "we cannot regard the Incan Peruvian otherwise than as the modern and late descendant of the megalithic culture of the Pacific." He goes on to propose that it was precisely a sunken landmass between the Andes and the Pacific islands that "generated a great megalithic art . . . [and] transferred it to the Tiahuanaco region. . . . A stone-building structure borrowed from the Pacific was superimposed by the Incas" (1933, 217).

Consider only the name of Ahu *Tepeu,* on Easter Island's west coast, where the people came to bury the dead and celebrate their memory, and remember their faithful offspring in the countless tepes in both Old and New Worlds, as seen in chapter 8.

In Jewish legend it was Seth's son Enosh (antediluvial) who led the first generation of idolators given to erecting huge idols. I think there is a connection here to the New Guinea Kai people, who identify their megalithic sites with white giants who lived before the deluge, a legend that is corroborated by light-skinned mummies found in that region. The Arabians also recall "men of gigantic stature . . . [who] easily moved enormous blocks of stone" (Donnelly 1985, 277). Finally, Tahitian and Samoan legend speaks of the antediluvian giants called Hiti who built the marae before the heavens fell down—and were themselves the very cause of the flood, if worldwide legends are to be believed.

Writes Charroux:

the Easter Island statues are of an antediluvian type. . . . There was a civilization [that] . . . carved upon rocks representations of animals which have long since died out [like stegosaurus]. . . . Some of the carvings [on Peru's Marcahuasi plateau], according to the angle of vision, had several faces, but you had to move into the right position to distinguish each of them." (1972, 91–92)

The play of light and shadow produced the true image only on certain days of the year (i.e., summer solstice). In Brittany also, at certain times of day, say between four and five o'clock, at Table des Marchands the same effect is seen, just as unseen markings suddenly stand forth at Stonehenge on a summer evening. This almost four-dimensional art has also been noted in the Carpathian Mountains, on the banks of the Nile, and at Avebury and Newgrange, according to the Peruvian prehistorian Daniel Ruzo. Finally, in the Pacific, Easter Island's moais, Ruzo points out, repeat these optical effects, for they apparently have no eyes, but in the play of sunlight and shade they can be clearly seen at a certain time of year. Ruzo called this global civilization "Masma." Charroux believes it was antediluvial, "In these places we have witness of a vast civilization that spread over the whole earth in the days before the Flood" (1972, 91–92).

> As the optical carving effects are widely distributed, this once again points to a world-spanning civilization at a remote period.
>
> RICHARD MOONEY, *GODS OF AIR AND DARKNESS*

The lost land called Hiva, says Polynesian legend, was full of cyclopean buildings and great gateways of stone. The last king of the sunken continent, according to Melanesian lore, led a race of fair-haired people through their land; it is they who built the megalithic structures.

It is interesting that Tongatabu is said to most resemble the megaliths of the rest of the world. Did the work begin here, then? Its trilithon arch of Ha'amonga, almost 20 feet in height, is irrepressibly akin to those of Europe. Several factors suggest great age of Tongatapu's trilithon (see fig. 10.7 of Ha'amonga arch, p. 408), for instance:

1. Ignorance on the part of local natives as to its origin (ditto on Panape, where the natives know not when these mighty works were built, it was so long ago).
2. Lime crust of surprising hardness on the monument.
3. Similar monuments on remote, uninhabited islands.
4. Survivors on Tonga must be from the age of giants: Tongans are virtual giants.
5. The arch, it is thought, must be much older than later, inferior work. (In much of the world, the more ancient the artifact, the higher its quality.)

In the most remote period, "a highly advanced building technology was at work on Tonga" (Joseph 2006, 108). The platform at the Tongatapu fortress is huge,

> built at a time of great antiquity. . . . Perhaps these stones did date
> back to an ancient Pacific empire now vanished beneath the ocean.
> . . . It may be that Tongtabu forms the intermediate link between the
> stonework of the Carolines and the megalithic monuments of other
> parts of the world. (Childress 1988, 181; quoting W. H. R. Rivers)

The Magic Circles

Ancient circles of stone seem to crop up everywhere: in Ireland at Stenness; in Wales, where they are called the Astronomer's Circle; and in Scotland, with its Ring of Brodgar in the Orkney Islands. Across the pond, at Hudson, New York, very large stones form a sacred circle. The same sort of constructions near Lake Michigan were built, say the Ojibway, by the Ancient Ones. Bighorn Medicine Wheel in Wyoming has stones arrayed in the shape of a wagon wheel. And on the banks of Canada's Winnipigon River is a circle of stones upon which the Indians, until the nineteenth century, would lay "wreaths of herbage."

Ceremonial stone circles also turn up in the archaeology of California, like the upright stone monoliths at Catalina Island, so similar to Stonehenge (see "Sun Worshippers" in chapter 6, p. 234, regarding

Catalina's sun cult, sacrifices, and 7-foot-tall man). Stone circles at "Brazil's Stonehenge," averaging 90 feet in diameter, seem to be part of a maritime archaic culture. Similar stone circles litter the jungles of Yucatán and Guatemala; those at Uxmal, say archaeologists, resemble the circles of Corsica. In Caral, Peru, as well as in Argentina and the forests of San Agustin, Colombia, comparable arrangements have been found.

Stone circles are also seen in Turkey—they are numerous at Göbekli Tepe where they can run nearly 100 feet in diameter. In Galilee the circle builders, in keeping with widespread lore of the Megalithic Age, are said to have been very tall people.

Moving east, stone circles appear in India, parts of Southeast Asia, Borneo, and the Celebes. The Mawaki Japanese circles are said to show a certain affinity with Florida's "Miami Circle" as well as with constructions found in Australia, Penrhyn Island (in the Pacific), and New Guinea, whose circle of uprights finds similars, in turn, in the Schouten group of islands, New Zealand (the Waitapu Circle), and New Ireland. India's stone circles, as at Manipur or Chota Nagpur, were originally built for seating the holy council *en rond*, exactly as is done in New Guinea. In the Marquesas, there are stone circles in "Bat Cave" on Taipi (Herman Melville's "Typee") and again in Nahotoa Cave.

No theory of "independent invention" can mask the worldwide linkage of the cromlech culture. Stone circles 60 feet in diameter discovered in the extraordinary ruins 40 miles off Okinawa, Japan, near Aka Island, remind archaeologists very much of those seen in the British Isles (Avebury), where they are called cromlechs. Maybe Japan, which was once the northwest tip of Pan, holds the answer.

Yonaguni

As this book began with Japan (Zha-Pan), so it will end.

So also, I, the Lord, will provide in the Kosmon [current] era to discover the sunken land of Whaga, so that mortals may comprehend the magnitude of the work of the Lord.

OAHSPE, THE LORDS' FIRST BOOK 2:12

Some people call it the greatest twentieth-century archaeological discovery, possibly the world's oldest building. Others say, forget it, these are *natural* formations. The area in question lies off Japan, spread over more than 300 miles of ocean floor. Here an ancient city proved to be enough of a game changer to inspire its suppression over the past few decades. Along the East China Sea, near southernmost Japan, lie the undersea remains of what appears to be a very old civilization. The ruins stretch south from the coast of Okinawa—which just happens to be the oldest seat of the ancient Jomon culture—to the island of Yonaguni, a total of eight prehistoric sites sporting the remains of grand boulevards, majestic staircases, and magnificent archways. Professor of geology and marine

In Pacific waters off the coast of Japan,
he thought he found remains of
The Lost Continent of Mu.

In Pacific waters off the coast of Japan, he
hoped to find The Lost Continent of Mu.

Fig. 11.11. Finding the lost continent: two cartoons by Marvin E. Herring

seismology at Ryukyu University, Masaaki Kimura has championed the extraordinary finds and written a book on the excavation, with chapter titles like "Discovery of a Civilization Lost in the Sea" and "A Utopia Sunk in the Pacific Ocean." It remains untranslated into English.

The Yonaguni ceremonial platform, informed observers have noted, bears an uncanny resemblance to the Hawaiian heiau, just as the stone towers of Japan might be first cousins to those at Easter Island. Yonaguni's offshore citadel resembles the langi platform at Lapaha (Tonga), especially its ceremonial staircases and solar alignments, altogether suggesting a common source.

Professor Kimura turned our attention to the symbols carved on the western part of the Yonaguni pyramid and on the surface of Japan's Ku-sabi rock. Editor and researcher Vernon Wobschall, in personal communication, wrote about this "rock specimen off Yonaguni that has carvings on it that look remarkably like those found in the Panic language tablets in [Oahspe's] Book of Saphah."

Geologists at Tokyo University believe this land was submerged at the end of the last ice age, perhaps around 10,000 BP; yet, there are Jomon works that go back at least eighteen thousand years. So the question is, did they build it? The ruins, some argue, have an Asian (i.e., mainland) originator. But the Jomon people, Japan's earliest culture bearers, bearded, fair skinned, and strong nosed, are not of East Asian descent. In fact, they were *Homo sapien pygmaeus,* little people (i.e., *tsuchigumo*), and likely the Yista branch of Pan survivors.

Fig. 11.12. Underwater structures off Yonaguni have proved to be among the most controversial archaeological finds of the twenty-first century.

Their forefathers in the Pacific were of course little people as well. The oldest of the Caroline Islands, Panape still has a tradition asserting that the land was originally inhabited by a race of little people, and their graves (if not their descendants) are still to be found here and there around the islands. At Nan Madol, lying off the eastern shore of Panape, abandoned ruins sport dwarf-size entryways where one has to crouch down to pass through. Nan Madol is as old as Yonaguni, and "these two sites are connected to each other," what with their similar ideograms, crosses, and squares—seemingly "identical petroglyphs" (Joseph 2006, 28).

Adjacent to Yonaguni's smaller stone mounds (mini-ziggurats), lying under more than 80 feet of water, came the crowning treasure: a 240-foot-long pyramidal structure whose features suggest a grand ceremonial center. Twice the age of Egypt's pyramids, the stepped structure is 600 feet wide and 90 feet tall. The steps are huge, over 3 feet high. The grand center also features broad promenades and flanking pylons, about which Joseph observes, "Some of the Monte Alban (Mexico) pyramidal structures, with their twin pylons, bear a discernibly close resemblance to the terraced formation found off . . . Yonaguni" (2006, 285).

Professor Kimura thought the ruins were the site of an ancient religious shrine dedicated to the god Nirai-Kanai, who gave happiness to the people of Okinawa. Further, this could only have been done by a people with a high degree of technology (Kimura 1997).

Opponents, however, were quick to argue that natural water erosion could account for the ruins. Kimura stands firm; it was not the work of nature. If that had been the case, we should find debris from erosion around the site, but there are no fragments of that kind.* Except for its title and contents page, which have been translated to English, the rest of Kimura's book is in Japanese. The saga of these suppressed finds badly reeks of "a conspiracy of managed information" (Joseph 1997).

Though headlined in Japan in the 1990s, the spectacular finds did not reach an American audience until 2004, the ruins hitherto coated with "a pall of silence," according to Joseph, who thinks they are noth-

---

*Other factors militate against the "natural formation" idea: the steps are of regular size; the blocks are not native to that area; and astronomical alignments are implicit in the structures.

ing less than a remnant of Mu,* with clear counterparts on the Peruvian coast; he compares Yonaguni, for example, to Pachacamac, near Lima, a religious center whose spacious plazas and sweeping staircases so closely resemble the Yonaguni structures (and as we saw above, Pachacamac was antediluvian). Tiahuanaco's perfect masonry and megalithic scale, as well as the Andes' perfectly cut and fitted stones also tally with those of the submarine structures off Japan.

Language doesn't lie. Every word and syllable must end in a vowel in Polynesia—and in Japanese—*and* in the Quechua language of the Andes. Each of these related tongues "abhors the shock of two consonants" (Brown 1924, 272). Indeed, this pattern is regarded as "original to the Arian language, consisting of open syllables of one consonant followed by one vowel. As the Arian was then, so is the Polynesian to this day" (Fornander 1969, 1:37–38). Churchward, who regards them all as cousins from Mu, comments that "a Mexican Indian and a Japanese can converse intelligibly without the aid of an interpreter" (Churchward 2011, 291).

JAPANESE WORDS WITH CORRESPONDENTS IN AMERIND LANGUAGES

Word in Japanese	Meaning	Word in Amerind	Meaning
tamoya	house	tampo/Peru	house
aru	born	ar/Brazil	born
take	bamboo	takoa/Guarani	bamboo
kumori	cloud	kamuru/Chaques	cloud
katana	sword	kotono/Mexico	to cut
ku	buy	koua/Mexico	buy

*Oahspe's map of Pan does indeed include the areas of Okinawa and Japan, though they do not appear on any of the other maps of Mu or Lemuria. "God (Neph) said: By Your light, Jehovih, I desire two ships [Yista] to go to *the north land, which was not sunk,* for they shall be a testimony in time to come. Let Your Gods, therefore, shift the winds and drive two ships aside from the rest" (Oahspe, Book of Aph 7:7; emphasis added).

JAPANESE WORDS WITH CORRESPONDENTS
IN AMERIND LANGUAGES (cont.)

Word in Japanese	Meaning	Word in Amerind	Meaning
shirap	eagle	sarpon/Mexico	eagle
kiva	place of meditation	kiva	Pueblo spirit chamber
meshi	corn porridge	maiz	corn

The paradigm-smashing Yonaguni finds have not enjoyed a warm reception in the scientific West. Detractors have been quick to neutralize interest, nip it in the bud. "We are not discussing the supposed lost continent of Mu. . . . It [Yonaguni site] is hardly the size of a continent. . . . We must be wary indeed. . . . Nature has her playful moods and has deposited simulacra everywhere, perhaps even on Mars!"* Like cures for cancer, which are promptly banned by the medical establishment, cures for our ignorance of prehistory are likewise burked, bullied, and blackballed.

But we must ask, What else besides a Pacific "middle man" could so consistently link East and West? What else could account for the fraternal twins known as Andean and Japanese culture? Ecuadorian and Japanese pottery have been declared identical twins. The solar alignment of Peru's Moche temple of the sun near Trujillo is identical to Yonaguni's orientation, and both are about 757 feet long. The iconographic and architectural details of Japan's Chikubujima (a memorial) and Peru's Chan Chan Palace drawings are almost identical.

The city of Chan Chan was divided into ten districts. According to Churchward there were ten tribes in Mu (2011, 24). Mexico's Troano text says that man on Mu had developed into ten distinct tribes and types. Huahine Island was divided into ten districts, Banks Islanders are divided into ten exogamous groups called *tagataga,* and Easter Island was peopled by ten tribes, each of which traced their descent back to a common ancestor, usually a son of the original settler of the island.

---

*Science Frontiers, online, No. 121, 1999. www.science-frontiers.com/sf121/sf121p01 .htm (accessed 5-25-2016).

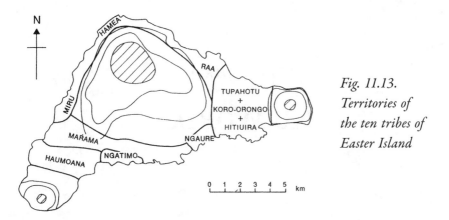

Fig. 11.13.
Territories of
the ten tribes of
Easter Island

The Troano legend of the sinking of Mu says that "the surface gave way, and then ten countries were torn asunder and scattered." And in the Popol Vuh it is said that "the lands of the Ten Regions were shaken and torn asunder and the cities with their millions of inhabitants sank beneath the sea."

The Maya had a tradition of ten kings, and in the Popol Vuh, the ten kings of Xibalba (before the time of the Quiché) reigned *in couples* under Hun-Came and Vukub-Came, and together constituted a grand council of the kingdom. The Guanches in the Canary Islands also had ten kings, and this probably relates to Egypt, which had ten nomes or provinces, their "council of ten" also reminding us of the Jewish minyan.

We have come to the endgame. We are at a point where we know there was a prior civilization—before the so-called Neolithic Revolution— many, many thousands of years before the vaunted Fertile Crescent or any other imagined cradle of man. And no wonder we are so unsure of its origin, for it was washed away with the continent of Pan. Nevertheless, it was carried over. A thousand signs point us to that lost horizon, from the mouths of tribesmen to the silent testimony of Nature—geology. Indeed, it is a lost race from a sunken land that was the teacher of humanity. But not entirely lost. Never was it entirely lost. Although they are the ancestors who were made into "gods" by the unlearned, their blood, their genes, their DNA, and their wisdom and goodness is with us still. To know the past is to master the future. Hasten the day.

APPENDIX A

KU WORDS

Leaders and even whole tribes also took on the reverential *Ku*. Beginning with the Temple of Ku in the motherland, the sacred Ku diffused to almost every part of the world. The list below, though extensive, represents but a fraction of these spin-offs.

KU WORD DERIVATIVES

Name	Where	Meaning
Kuhina	Hawaii	ministers
Ku'u-ku'u	Easter Island	a prince
Kupe	New Zealand	first king of Maori
Kura	New Zealand	Maori word for chief
Kushan	China	dynasty
Kushog	Tibet	honorable
Kumaso	Japan	aboriginal people of the islands
Kurash	Persia	first Achaemenid king (Cyrus)
Kushana	Central Asia	early rulers, "steadfast men"
Kubu	Indonesia	tribesmen
Kuchi	Afghanistan	nomads
Kurus, Kuruba	India	oldest people of the land

Name	Where	Meaning
Kurumba	India	Negritos
Kuki, Kumi, Kulu	India	hill tribes
Kuikandi	India	Dravidians
Khu'ai	Southern Africa	Bushmen
Ki-ku-yu	Kenya	tribe
Kurawi	Sudan	tribe
Kukuteni	Ukraine	a people
Kuman	Southeastern Europe	a people
Kumae	Greek	colony in southern Italy
Kulak	Slavic nations	landowner
Kuraca	Andes	Quechua chief
Kurigueres	Peru	ancient race of giants
Kuna	Panama	tribal name
Kubeo	Colombia	Indian tribe
Kuikuru	Brazil	tribe, pale-skinned
Kukurital	Brazil	tribe
Ma-ku	Brazil	tribe
Ti-kuna	Brazil	tribe
Kutenai	British Columbia	tribe
Kusseta	Oklahoma	tribe
Kuyamaca	California	Indian

KU-NAMED PLACES

Place-Name	Where	Comment
Ku-mari Nadu	Polynesia	"Land of the Sons of God"
Kue-helani	Hawaii	the floating island of the Menehune
Kukii	Hawaii	majestic ruins here

KU-NAMED PLACES (cont.)

Place-Name	Where	Comment
Kuapuiwi	Hawaii	native land
Ku emu a	Hawaii	"the earth drowned"
Sea of I-ku	Hawaii	in the deluge song
Kusai	South Seas	an island
Kunie	New Caledonia	native name of Isle of Pines
Baral-ku	Australia	sunken ancestral paradise
Kuk	Australia	swamp
Kusabi	Japan	ancient carved rock
Kumamato	Japan	on Kyushu
Toho-ku	Japan	with Jomon remains
Kuma	Japan	island off Okinawa
Kumaon, San-khu	India	
Kurukshetra	India	a large site of the Indus Valley civilization
Kanya Kumari	India	fabled continent that was submerged
Kulu	Himalayas	a valley
Khara Khutuul	Mongolia	
Ku Chi	Vietnam	
Kuching	Borneo	
Kupang	Timor	
Kuhistan, Kunar	Afghanistan	provinces, the former with 14,000-year-old cave drawings
Khujut Rabua	Iraq	ancient center of learning; batteries found here
Kuyunjik	Iraq	royal archives kept here
Khunik	Iran	cave
Kuwait, Kubra	in the Red Sea area	

KU-NAMED PLACES (*cont.*)

Place-Name	Where	Comment
Kura Valley	near the Caspian	
Kura Depression	in the Ba-ku region of the Caucasus	
Kusadasi, Kulu	Turkey	
Wadi Kubbaniya	Egypt	farming as old as 18,000 BP
El Kula	Egypt	
Kuneo Province	Italy	
Kukuyu	Kikuyu people, Kenya	
Kufra	Libya	oasis
Kumasi	Ghana	
Kumbi	Mali	
Kuru	Ethiopia	
IN THE NEW WORLD		
Kumorah	New York State	
Kuliacan	Mexico	
Kucican	Mexico	Yucatecan ruin with ancient causeways
Kuhualcan	Mexico	
Cuba	island	
Curacao	island	
Cuzco	Peru*	
Kuelap	Peru	
Cuenca	Ecuador	
Kuyuwini	British Guiana	
Kuraca	Brazil	river
Kuyaba	Brazil	

*In Peru, there is a certain tendency to suffix the *ku:* Tujamanaku, Sahpuayaku, Tiahuanaku, Guismanku, Yanacu. Apparently this was also done in Babylonia where various priestly officers—Ramaku, Nisaku, Abaraku—also suffixed the -*ku*

APPENDIX B

WORLD
COGNATES

The base word for "fire" spread from Pan to a wide range of locations:

Word	Place or Language	Meaning
ignek	Greenland	fire
ignis	Latin	fire
ignite	England	start fire
egnek	Chukchi	fire
hagni	Algonquin	burn
guni	Java	fire
ogni	Slavic	fire
ah'gni	Chinese	burn
aghri	Kurdish	fire
agni	Sanskrit	fire
agie	Sumatra	fire
agin	Bengal	fire
adgi	Tungus	god of fire
ahi	Hawaii, Tahiti	fire

The word for "house/abode" spread from Pan to the settlements of Shem, Ham, Jaffeth and Guatama:

Place or Language	Word for House/Abode
Pan	oke
Marquesas	oka ("rafter")
(Skt)(Shem)	kr-oke, or oka; Phoenician: okel
Egypt (Ham)	oke
Chinese (Jaffeth)	o-ak
Chinese	Oke'spe (spirit house)
Greek	oikos
Lithuanian	ukis ("hut")
America	hok or ok (Pawnee, Algonquin)
Guarani	Oko

As all languages descended from the original Panic, they retained words in common—here are a few examples:

Word	Meaning	Language
yuk	tie	Peruvian
yokta	tie	Korean
yugh	yoke	Persian
yuga	unite	Sanskrit
zug	join	Arabic
jugum	join	Latin
jow	yoke	Welsh
jok	join	German
juk	join	Dutch
ok	join	Swedish
yoke	join	English

WORDS THAT APPEAR
IN BOTH QUECHUA (PERU)
AND
MAORI (NEW ZEALAND)

Quechua Word	Meaning	Maori Word	Meaning
munay	love	muna	love
nucu	my	noca	I
kara	skin	kiri	skin
pura	between	pura	between
kuraca	chieftain	kura	chieftain
apay	lift	hapay	lift
awki	father	auki	old man
huaca	sacred object	waka	sacred object*
inga	prince, king	inganui	the lord
kokotuai	pigeon	koko	pigeon
kumara	sweet potato	kumara	sweet potato†
mutu	mutilated	mutu	mutilated
papaya	a fruit	payapa	a fruit

*Wakan also means "sacred, taboo" in the Sioux language.
†The word is almost identical in Sanskrit and Tahiti.

Quechua Word	Meaning	Maori Word	Meaning
pahuai	run	pahu	run, leap
para	rain	paraara	thunderstorm
unu	water	unu	drink water
naka	nearby	naka	next to
koto	small things	kotokoto	small

SAMPLE OF MEGALITHIC WORKS IN THE PREHISTORIC WORLD

NEW WORLD

Structure	Where	Details
heads	Olmec, Mexico	colossal snarling stone heads buried in the ground
cyclopean blocks	Bahamian isle of Andros	underwater, square cut
colossi	British Guiana	70-foot humanlike figures
300-ton blocks	Puma Punku, Bolivia	supermegalithic masonry
stone slabs	Tiahuanaco, Bolivia	130 tons; Gateway to the Sun hewn from a single block weighing 11 tons; 40-ton stones each step at Kalassasaya
gargantuan ruins	Sacsayhuaman, Peru	300-ton blocks
cyclopean cities	along Xingu River, Brazil	in vicinity of White Indians
incised monoliths	Orinoco headwaters of Venezuela	attributed to a white race
menhirs	Colombia	Infiernito, more than 100 menhirs in rows

NEW WORLD (*cont.*)

Structure	Where	Details
standing stones	Argentina	up to 15 feet high
step pyramids	Florida Everglades	in Seminole Indian area

OLD WORLD

Structure	Where	Details
megaliths	Turkey's Göbekli Tepe	oldest known megalithic site in Turkey
immense blocks	Baalbek, Lebanon	60-foot-long stone blocks weighing more than 1,000 tons
pyramids	Island of Marathos, off Syria	28-foot-long blocks of stone
pyramids	Egypt	
statue of Memnon	Thebes, Egypt	600 tons
monoliths	Zimbabwe, Africa	13 feet tall
menhirs, dolmens	Morocco, Senegal, Algeria	some 15 feet high
statues	Bamian, Afghanistan	one Buddha was 180 feet tall (since destroyed)
cyclopean monuments	India, in the Deccan dolmens in central India	rock-cut temples and pagodas
massive ruins	Cambodia	Angkor Wat
dolmens	Korea	mostly sepulchral monuments
pyramids	China	apparently still unexcavated
menhirs	Siberia	burial monuments
Yonaguni ruins	off Japan	underwater megaliths
Kuki monuments	Indonesia	megalithic
Gunung Padang	Java	may be 20,000 years old

OLD WORLD (*cont.*)

Structure	Where	Details
Tana Toraja	Celebes, north of Java	huge, ancient stones resemble European menhirs
walls and monuments	Nias Island, off Sumatra	megalithic
megaliths	Borneo	in remote areas
dolmens, megalithic monuments	insular Southeast Asia, as at Sumba and Roti	
11-foot blocks	New Guinea	on Mt. Kambu
8-foot-high obelisk	New Guinea	
structures	Spain	Andalusian huge stone-cut constructions
menhirs	Corsica	carved with human features, almost 10 feet high
stone sepulchres	island of Thera	colossal "giants" tombs
tomb	Malta	made of massive stone blocks
dolmens	Ireland	as well as monuments, menhirs, and stone circles, some stones 100 tons
stone heads	Fence, France	something like those found at Easter Island and Olmec
standing stones	Denmark	up to 27 feet tall; also megalithic tombs
megaliths	southern Sweden	dozens of megalithic sites

Fig. D.1. Long dolmen at Valdbygaards in Denmark

APPENDIX E

STONEHENGES EVERYWHERE

Menhirs and dolmens are legion in South America, China, India, Mongolia, Turkestan, and the Middle East as well as in Wales, Cornwall, Brittany, Switzerland, Germany, Spain, and Corsica. European megaliths have been compared to similars in almost every part of the world. Isn't it obvious that this was a worldwide culture?

Place	Details
Easter Island	arrangement of monuments recalls the circles of Stonehenge and menhir alleys of Brittany
Siberia	Corsica menhirs are of the same type
China	dolmens are similar to those in western Europe
Ceylon	18-foot-high monoliths similar to Stonehenge
Kasseem, Arabia	great ruins, uprights in circle
Florida	"Florida Stonehenge" found recently in Miami
Illinois	Cahokia alignments and measurements like Stonehenge
Ohio Valley	henges almost identical to those in Scotland; Ohio's Portsmouth Earthworks structurally similar to Stonehenge

Place	Details
New Hampshire	megalithic buildings of Mystery Hill compare to similars in Europe, the site called "America's Stonehenge"
Alaska	like Carnac menhirs, which helped travelers determine their location
Mexico	La Venta menhirs also compare to Carnac
Peru	masonry similar to Etruscan work and stone forts of Ireland (Aran Islands)
Bolivia	Tiahuanaco's dolmens and menhirs similar to those in Scandinavia and Brittany, its alignments like Stonehenge's
Amazon Basin	megalithic figures like those found in France; upright granite blocks in Amapa, Brazil, called "Brazilian Stonehenge"

BIBLIOGRAPHY

Adams, Richard E. W. 1991. *Prehistoric Mesoamerica*. Norman: University of Oklahoma Press.

Anderson, Johannes C. 1928. *Myths and Legends of the Polynesians*. London: George G. Harrap.

Asher, Maxine. 1974. *Discovering Atlantis*. Los Angeles: Ancient Mediterranean Research Association.

Atwater, Caleb. 1820. *Description of the Antiquities Discovered in the State of Ohio and Other Western States*. Vol. 1. Circleville, Ohio: American Antiquities Society.

Baldwin, John D. 1869. *Pre-Historic Nations*. New York: Harper & Brothers.

Balsiger, Dave, and Charles E. Sellier Jr. 1976. *In Search of Noah's Ark*. Los Angeles: Sun Classic Books.

Bandelier, Adolph. 1905. "Traditions of Precolumbian Landings on the Western Coast of South America." *American Anthropologist* 7: 250–70.

Berlitz, Charles. 1972. *Mysteries from Forgotten Worlds*. New York: Dell Publishing.

———. 1984. *Atlantis, the Eighth Continent*. New York: Fawcett Crest.

Birket-Smith, Kaj. 1965. *The Paths of Culture*. Madison: University of Wisconsin Press.

Brave Bird, Mary. 2009. *Ohitika Woman*. New York: Grove Press.

Brinton, Daniel G. 1976. *The Myths of the New World*. Blauvelt, N.Y.: Multimedia Publishing Corp.

Brown, Hugh A. 1967. *Cataclysms of the Earth*. New York: Twayne Publishers.

Brown, J. Macmillan. 1920. *The Languages of the Pacific*. Honolulu: Bishop Museum Press.

———. 1924. *Riddle of the Pacific*. London: T. Fisher Unwin.

Cahill, Augustine. 1965. *Darkness, Dawn and Destiny*. London: Regency Press.

Cameron, Ian. 1987. *Lost Paradise*. Topsfield, Mass.: Salem House Publishers.

Caunitz, William J. 1993. *Cleopatra Gold*. New York: Crown Publishers.

Charroux, Robert. 1967. *Masters of the World*. New York: Berkley Publishing.

———. 1971. *One Hundred Thousand Years of Man's Unknown History*. New York: Berkley Publishing.

———. 1972. *The Gods Unknown*. New York: Berkley Books.

———. 1974. *The Mysteries of the Andes*. New York: Avon Books.

Chatelain, Maurice. 1980. *Our Ancestors Came from Outer Space*. London: Arthur Barker.

Childress, David Hatcher. 1988. *Lost Cities of Ancient Lemuria and the Pacific*. Stelle, Ill.: Adventures Unlimited.

———. 1992. *Lost Cities of North and Central America*. Stelle, Ill.: Adventures Unlimited.

Chouinard, Patrick. 2012. *Forgotten Worlds*. Rochester, Vt.: Bear & Co.

Christy-Vitaly, Joseph. 2004. *Watermark*. New York: Paraview Pocket Books.

Churchward, Jack E. 2011. *Lifting the Veil on the Lost Continent of Mu*. Huntsville, Ark.: Ozark Mountain Publishing.

———. 2014. *The Stone Tablets of Mu*. Huntsville, Ark.: Ozark Mountain Publishing.

Churchward, James. 1931 (a). *The Children of Mu*. London: Neville Spearman.

———. 1931 (b). *The Lost Continent of Mu*. New York: Paperback Library.

———. 1935, 1968. *The Second Book of the Cosmic Forces of Mu*. New York: Paperback Library.

———. 1970/1934. *The Cosmic Forces of Mu*. New York: Paperback Library.

Cohane, John P. 1969. *The Key*. New York: Crown Publishers.

Collins, Andrew. 2014. *Göbekli Tepe: Genesis of the Gods*. Rochester, Vt.: Bear & Co.

Colton, Harold S. 1917. "Is the House of Tcuhu the Minoan Labyrinth?" *Science* 45, no. 1174: 667–68.

Coon, Carleton. 1965. *The Living Races of Man*. New York: Alfred Knopf.

Coppens, Philip. 2012. *The Lost Civilization Enigma*. Pompton Plains, N.J.: New Page Books.

Corliss, William. 1976. *The Unexplained*. New York: Bantam Books.

———. 1978. *Ancient Man*. Glen Arm, Md.: Sourcebook Project.

———. 1983. *Handbook of Unusual Natural Phenomena*. New York: Random House.

Daly, Dominick. 1889. "The Mexican Messiah." *American Antiquarian* 11: 17–37.

Deal, David Allen. 1984. *Discovery of Ancient America*. Irvine, Calif.: Kherem La Yah Press.

De Bisschop, Eric. 1959. *Tahiti Nui*. New York: McDowell, Obolensky.

De Camp, L. Sprague. 1975. *Lost Continents*. New York: Ballantine Books.

Deloria, Vine, Jr. 1995. *Red Earth, White Lies.* New York: Scribner.

Dewhurst, Richard. 2014. *The Ancient Giants Who Ruled America.* Rochester, Vt.: Inner Traditions.

Dixon, Roland B. 1964. *Oceanic Mythology.* New York: Cooper Square Publishers.

Donnelly, Ignatius. 1985. *The Antediluvian World.* New York: Crown Publishers.

Drake, Raymond. 1968. *Gods and Spacemen in the Ancient East.* New York: Signet Book.

——. 1974. *Gods and Spacemen of the Ancient Past.* New York: Signet Book.

Eddy, Mark. 2014. "Remembering Dorset." *Ancient American* 18, no. 104: 12–17.

Eiseley, Loren. *Darwin's Century.* Garden City, N.Y.: Anchor Books, 1961.

Ellis, William. 1831/1969. *Polynesian Researches.* London: Peter Jackson, Late Fisher, Son & Co.

Fagan, Brian M. 1999. *World Prehistory.* New York: Longman.

Fell, Barry. 1977. *America B.C.* New York: Demeter Press.

Finch, John. 1824. "On the Celtic Antiquities of America." *American Journal of Science* 7: 149–61.

Fisher, Ron. 1985. "Easter Island: Brooding Sentinels of Stone." In *Mysteries of the Ancient World.* Washington, D.C.: National Geographic Society.

Flem-Ath, Rand, and Rose Flem-Ath. 1995. *When the Sky Fell.* New York: St. Martins Press.

Fornander, Abraham. 1969. *An Account of the Polynesian Race.* Rutland, Vt.: Charles E. Tuttle.

Fraser, David. 1983. *Land and Society in Neolithic Orkney.* Vol. 1, British Archaeological Reports (BAR British Series) 117. Oxford, U.K.: Archaeopress, 140.

Gamow, George. 1948. *Biography of the Earth.* New York: Mentor Books.

Ginzburg, Louis. 2003. *Legends of the Jews.* Philadelphia: Publications Society.

Gladwin, Harold S. 1947. *Men Out of Asia.* New York: McGraw Hill.

Good, Timothy. 1994. *Alien Contact.* Fort Mill, S.C.: Quill House Publisher.

Goodman, Jeffrey. 1983. *The Genesis Mystery.* New York: Times Books.

Gordon, Cyrus. 1973. *Before Columbus.* New York: Crown Publishers.

——. 1974. *Riddles in History.* New York: Crown Publishers.

Grunberg Banyasz, Malin. 2014. "Off the Grid." *Archaeology,* May/June, 10.

H[addon], A. C. 1960. "The Language and Origin of the Basques." *Nature* 188: 1064–67. www.nature.com/nature/journal/v188/n4756/pdf (accessed 6-27-2016).

Haddon, Alfred Cort. 1911. *The Wanderings of Peoples.* London: Cambridge University Press.

Haeckel, Ernst. 1876. *The History of Creation.* New York: Appleton and Company.

Hancock, Graham. 2002. *Underworld*. New York: Crown Publishers.

Hapgood, Charles. 1996. *Maps of the Ancient Sea Kings*. Kempton, Ill.: Adventures Unlimited.

Harrison, E. R. 1960. "Origin of the Pacific Basin." *Nature* 188: 1064–67.

Hawkes, Jacquetta. 1962. *Man and the Sun*. New York: Random House.

Haywood, John. 1923. *The Natural and Aboriginal History of Tennessee*.

Heinberg, Richard. 1989. *Memories and Visions of Paradise*. Los Angeles: J. P. Tarcher.

Henry, Teuira. 1928. *Ancient Tahiti*. Honolulu: Bishop Museum, Bulletin 48.

Heyerdahl, Thor. 1953. *American Indians in the Pacific*. Chicago: Rand McNally.

Higgins, Godfrey. 1991. *Anacalypsis*. 2 vols. Chesapeake, N.Y.: ECA Associates. (First published London, 1836.)

Homet, Marcel. 1963. *Sons of the Sun*. London: Neville Spearman.

Honore, Pierre. 1964. *In Quest of the White God*. New York: G. P. Putnam & Sons.

Howells, William. 1993. *Getting Here*. Washington, D.C.: Compass Press.

Huggett, Richard. 1989. *Cataclysms and Earth History*. Oxford, U.K.: Clarendon.

Imhotep, David. 2014. "Ancient Aliens . . . Ancient Shmaliens." Reader Forum *Atlantis Rising* 107 (September/October): 7.

Irwin, Constance. 1963. *Fair Gods and Stone Faces*. New York: St. Martin's Press.

Jacolliot, Louis. 1879. *Histoire des Vierges* [in French]. Paris: Lacroix.

Jones, Martha Helene. 2013. *The Lost Data on the Chariots of the Elohim*. N.p.: Lulu.com.

Joseph, Frank. 1997. "Underwater City Found near Japan." *Ancient American* 3, no. 17: 2–6.

———. 2006. *The Lost Civilization of Lemuria*. Rochester, Vt.: Bear & Co.

———. 2013. *Before Atlantis*. Rochester, Vt.: Bear & Co.

———. 2014a. "Florida's Enigmatic Mayan Outpost." *Atlantis Rising* 104 (March/April): 46–47, 72.

———. 2014b. *The Lost Colonies of Ancient America*. Pompton Plains, N.J.: New Page Books.

———. 2014c. "Mysteries of the Land of Punt." *Atlantis Rising* 103 (January/February): 38.

Kimura, Maasaki. 1997. *A Continent Lost in the Pacific Ocean* [in Japanese]. Tokyo: Daissan-Bunmei.

Kirch, Patrick V. 1997. *On the Road of the Winds*. Honolulu: University of Hawaii Press.

Kolosimo, Peter. 1973. *Not of This World*. New York: Bantam Books.

———. 1975. *Timeless Earth*. New York: Bantam Books.

Kreisberg, Glenn. 2012. *Mysteries of the Ancient Past*. Rochester, Vt.: Bear & Co.

Kueshana, Eklal. 1970. *The Ultimate frontier.* Chicago: Stelle Group.

Lame Deer, John (Fire), and Richard Erdoes. 1994. "Yuwipi: Little Lights from Nowhere." Chap. 11 in *Seekers of Vision.* New York: Simon and Schuster.

Landsburg, Alan, and Sally Landsburg. 1974. *In Search of Ancient Mysteries.* New York: Bantam Books.

Lang, John D. 1877. *Origin and Migrations of the Polynesian Nation.* Sydney: George Robertson.

Lehrburger, Carl. 2015. *The Secrets of Ancient America.* Rochester, Vt.: Inner Traditions.

Lissner, Ivar. 1962. *The Silent Past.* New York: G. P. Putnam's Sons.

Longman, Byron. 1978. "Who Really Discovered the New World?" In *The World's Last Mysteries.* Washington, D.C.: Reader's Digest Association, 51–61.

Lothrop, Samuel Kirkland. 1937. *Cocle, an Archaeological Study of Central Panama.* Cambridge, Mass.: Memoirs of the Peabody Museum.

Lubbock, 1982. John. *Pre-historic Times.* New York: D. Appleton.

Macdougall, J. Douglas. 1996. *A Short History of Planet Earth.* New York: John Wiley and Sons.

Mahan, Joseph. 1983. *The Secret: America in World History before Columbus.* Madison, Wis.: J. B. Mahan.

Marsh, Richard Oglesby. 1934. *White Indians of Darien.* New York: G. P. Putnam's Sons.

Martinez, Susan B. 2015. *Delusions in Science and Spirituality.* Rochester, Vt.: Bear & Co.

Mavor, Joseph, and Byron Dix. 1991. *Manitou.* Rochester, Vt.: Inner Traditions.

Mithen, Steven. 2003. *After the Ice.* Cambridge, Mass.: Harvard University Press.

Mooney, Richard E. 1975. *Gods of Air and Darkness.* New York: Stein and Day.

Morley, George. 1955. "Etherean Ships." 1942 lecture reprinted by London: Kosmon Press.

National Geographic Society. 1992. *Mysteries of Mankind.* Washington, D.C.: National Geographic Society.

Noorbergen, Rene. 1982. *Treasures of the Lost Races.* New York: Bobbs-Merrill.

Norman, Eric. 1973. *Gods and Devils from Outer Space.* New York: Lancer Books.

Nunn, Patrick. 2009. *Vanished Islands and Hidden Continents of the Pacific.* Honolulu: University of Hawaii Press.

Oahspe: A New Bible in the Words of Jehovih and His Angel Embassadors; A Sacred History of the Dominions of the Higher and Lower Heavens on the Earth for the Past Twenty-four Thousand Years. 1960 . The Raymond Palmer Edition. First published New York & London: Oahspe Publishing, 1882.

Oppenheimer, Stephen. 1998. *Eden in the East.* London: Weidenfeld & Nicolson.

Patel, Samir S. 2014. "Tonga." *Archaeology,* November/December, 23.

Perry, William. 1923/1968. *The Children of the Sun*. Grosse Pointe, Mich.: Scholarly Press.

Picknett, Lynn, and Clive Prince. 2001. *The Stargate Conspiracy*. New York: Berkley Books.

Pidgeon, William. 1852. *Traditions of Deecoodah and Antiquarian Researches*. New York: Thayer.

Pilkey, John. 1984. *The Origin of the Nations*. San Diego: Master Book Publishers.

Preston, Douglas. 2014. "The 9,000-Year-Old Man Speaks." *Smithsonian*, September, 52–63.

Reader's Digest. 1978. *The World's Last Mysteries*. Pleasantville, N.Y.: Reader's Digest Association.

Renfrew, Colin. 1973. *Before Civilization*. New York: Knopf.

Ritchie, Andrew Jackson. 1948. *Sketches of Rabun County History*. Rabun County, Ga.: Rabun County Historical Society.

Rivers, William Halse. 1914/1968. *The History of Melanesian Society*. Cambridge, U.K.: Cambridge University Press.

Roberts, Scott Alan, and John Roberts Ward. 2014. *The Exodus Reality*. Pompton Plains, N.J.: New Page Books.

Roux, Georges. 1992. *Ancient Iraq*. New York: Penguin Books.

Ryzl, Milan, and Lubor Kysucan. 2007. *Ancient Oracles*. Victoria, B.C.: Trafford Publishing.

Santillana, Giorgio de, and Hertha von Dechend. 1969. *Hamlet's Mill*. Boston: Gambit.

Schoch, Robert. 2012. *Forgotten Civilization*. Rochester, Vt.: Inner Traditions.

———. 2014. "The Tankering and the Petroglyphs." *Atlantis Rising* 107 (September/October): 38.

Schwartz, Jean-Michel. 1973. *The Mysteries of Easter Island*. New York: Avon Books.

Scott-Elliot, William. 2000. *Legends of Atlantis and Lost Lemuria*. Wheaton, Ill.: Quest Books.

Settegast, Mary. 2005. *When Zarathustra Spoke*. Costa Mesa, Calif.: Mazda Publishers.

Silverberg, Robert. 1968. *Mound Builders of Ancient America*. Greenwich, Conn.: New York Graphic Society.

Smith, Percy. 1921. *Hawaiki*. London: Whitcombe & Tombs.

Sora, Steven. 2014. "Kennewick Man." *Atlantis Rising* 103 (January/February): 26, 61–62.

Spence, Lewis. 1933. *The Problem of Lemuria*. Philadelphia: David McKay.

Steiger, Brad. 1974. *Mysteries of Time and Space*. New York: Dell Books.

Stemman, Roy. 1976. *Atlantis and the Lost Lands*. Danbury, Conn.: Danbury Press.

Stewart, George R. 2008. *Names on the Land*. New York: New York Review Books.

Stoecker, William. 2014. "Ancient Wanderers." *Atlantis Rising* 106 (July/August): 25, 61.

Stuart, George. 1973. *Discovering Man's Past in the Americas*. Washington, D.C.: National Geographic Society.

Suggs, Robert. 1962. *The Hidden Worlds of Polynesia*. New York: Harcourt, Brace & World.

Swaminathan, Nikhil. 2014. "First American Family Tree." *Archaeology,* May/June, 13.

Thorndike, Joseph, Jr. 1977. *Mysteries of the Past*. New York: Scribner.

Time. 2015. "Discovered." October 26, p.17.

Tomas, Andrew. 1973. *We Are Not the First*. New York: Bantam Books.

Trench, Brinsley lePoer. 1974. *Temple of the Stars*. New York: Ballantine Books.

Valentine, Tom. 1975. *The Great Pyramid*. New York: Pinnacle Books.

Van Andel, Tjeerd. 1985. *New Views on an Old Planet*. Cambridge, U.K.: Cambridge University Press.

Velikovsky, Immanuel. 1965. *Worlds in Collision*. New York: Delta Books.

Verrill, A. Hyatt. 1927. *The American Indian*. New York: New Home Library.

———. 1943. *Old Civilizations of the New World*. New York: New Home Library.

Von Daniken, Erich. 1970. *Chariots of the Gods?* New York: Bantam Books.

———. 1974. *The Gold of the Gods*. New York: Bantam Books.

———. 1975. *In Search of Ancient Gods*. New York: Bantam Books.

Von Ward, Paul. 2011. *We've Never Been Alone*. Charlottesville, Va.: Hampton Roads Publishing.

Wadler, Arnold. 1948. *One Language*. New York: American Press for Art and Science.

Wernick, Robert. 1978. "Strange Stories of Western Europe." *The World's Last Mysteries*. New York: Reader's Digest Books.

White, John. 1980. *Pole Shift*. Garden City, N.Y.: Doubleday.

Wilkins, Harold T. 2000. *Mysteries of Ancient South America*. Kempton, Ill.: Adventures Unlimited.

Williams, Mark. 2001. *In Search of Lemuria*. St. Mateo, Calif.: Golden Era Books.

Williamson, R. W. 1933. *Religious and Cosmic Beliefs of Central Polynesia*. 2 vols. London: Cambridge University Press.

Wilson, Clifford. 1975. *The Chariots Still Crash*. New York: Signet.

Wollaston, Alexander Frederick Richmond. 1912. *Pygmies and Papuans*. New York: Sturgis and Walton.

Zago, M. A., E. J. Melo Santos, J. B. Clegg, et al. 1995. "Alpha-globin gene haplotypes in South American Indians." *Human Biology* 67, no. 4: 535–46.

Zink, David. 1979. *The Ancient Stones Speak*. New York: E. P. Dutton.

INDEX

Books of Related Interest

Delusions in Science and Spirituality
The Fall of the Standard Model and the Rise of Knowledge
from Unseen Worlds
by Susan B. Martinez, Ph.D.

The Lost History of the Little People
Their Spiritually Advanced Civilizations around the World
by Susan B. Martinez, Ph.D.

Time of the Quickening
Prophecies for the Coming Utopian Age
by Susan B. Martinez, Ph.D.

Atlantis in the Caribbean
And the Comet That Changed the World
by Andrew Collins

Before Atlantis
20 Million Years of Human and Pre-Human Cultures
by Frank Joseph

Atlantis in the Amazon
Lost Technologies and the Secrets of the Crespi Treasure
by Richard Wingate

Atlantis beneath the Ice
The Fate of the Lost Continent
by Rand Flem-Ath and Rose Flem-Ath

Forbidden History
Prehistoric Technologies, Extraterrestrial Intervention,
and the Suppressed Origins of Civilization
by J. Douglas Kenyon

INNER TRADITIONS • BEAR & COMPANY
P.O. Box 388
Rochester, VT 05767
1-800-246-8648
www.InnerTraditions.com

Or contact your local bookseller